Siegfried Kracauer's American Writings

Siegfried Kracauer on vacation, early 1950s. Courtesy of Deutsches Literaturarchiv, Marbach.

Siegfried Kracauer's American Writings
Essays on Film and Popular Culture

SIEGFRIED KRACAUER

Edited by Johannes von Moltke and Kristy Rawson
With an Afterword by Martin Jay

University of California Press
BERKELEY   LOS ANGELES   LONDON

University of California Press, one of the most distinguished
university presses in the United States, enriches lives around the world
by advancing scholarship in the humanities, social sciences, and natural
sciences. Its activities are supported by the UC Press Foundation and
by philanthropic contributions from individuals and institutions. For
more information, visit www.ucpress.edu.

University of California Press
Berkeley and Los Angeles, California

University of California Press, Ltd.
London, England

© 2012 by The Regents of the University of California

Library of Congress Cataloging-in-Publication Data

Kracauer, Siegfried, 1889–1966.
 Siegfried Kracauer's American writings : essays on film and popular
culture / Siegfried Kracauer ; edited by Johannes von Moltke and
Kristy Rawson ; with an afterword by Martin Jay.
  p. cm.—(Weimar and now: German cultural criticism ; 45)
 In English with some essays translated from German.
 Includes bibliographical references and index.
 ISBN 978-0-520-27182-1 (cloth : alk. paper)—ISBN 978-0-520-27183-8
(pbk. : alk. paper)—ISBN 978-0-520-95200-3 (ebook)
 1. Motion pictures. 2. Motion pictures—Reviews. I. Von Moltke,
Johannes, 1966– II. Rawson, Kristy, 1963– III. Title.
 PN1995.K6955 2012
 791.43—dc23   2011046517

21 20 19 18 17 16 15 14 13 12
10 9 8 7 6 5 4 3 2 1

WEIMAR AND NOW: GERMAN CULTURAL CRITICISM

Edward Dimendberg, Martin Jay, and Anton Kaes, General Editors

1. *Heritage of Our Times,* by Ernst Bloch
2. *The Nietzsche Legacy in Germany, 1890–1990,* by Steven E. Aschheim
3. *The Weimar Republic Sourcebook,* edited by Anton Kaes, Martin Jay, and Edward Dimendberg
4. *Batteries of Life: On the History of Things and Their Perception in Modernity,* by Christoph Asendorf
5. *Profane Illumination: Walter Benjamin and the Paris of Surrealist Revolution,* by Margaret Cohen
6. *Hollywood in Berlin: American Cinema and Weimar Germany,* by Thomas J. Saunders
7. *Walter Benjamin: An Aesthetic of Redemption,* by Richard Wolin
8. *The New Typography,* by Jan Tschichold, translated by Ruari McLean
9. *The Rule of Law under Siege: Selected Essays of Franz L. Neumann and Otto Kirchheimer,* edited by William E. Scheuerman
10. *The Dialectical Imagination: A History of the Frankfurt School and the Institute of Social Research, 1923–1950,* by Martin Jay
11. *Women in the Metropolis: Gender and Modernity in Weimar Culture,* edited by Katharina von Ankum
12. *Letters of Heinrich and Thomas Mann, 1900–1949,* edited by Hans Wysling, translated by Don Reneau
13. *Empire of Ecstasy: Nudity and Movement in German Body Culture, 1910–1935,* by Karl Toepfer
14. *In the Shadow of Catastrophe: German Intellectuals between Apocalypse and Enlightenment,* by Anson Rabinbach
15. *Walter Benjamin's Other History: Of Stones, Animals, Human Beings, and Angels,* by Beatrice Hanssen
16. *Exiled in Paradise: German Refugee Artists and Intellectuals in America from the 1930s to the Present,* by Anthony Heilbut
17. *Cool Conduct: The Culture of Distance in Weimar Germany,* by Helmut Lethen, translated by Don Reneau
18. *In a Cold Crater: Cultural and Intellectual Life in Berlin, 1945–1948,* by Wolfgang Schivelbusch, translated by Kelly Barry
19. *A Dubious Past: Ernst Jünger and the Politics of Literature after Nazism,* by Elliot Y. Neaman
20. *Beyond the Conceivable: Studies on Germany, Nazism, and the Holocaust,* by Dan Diner
21. *Prague Territories: National Conflict and Cultural Innovation in Franz Kafka's Fin de Siècle,* by Scott Spector
22. *Munich and Memory: Architecture, Monuments, and the Legacy of the Third Reich,* by Gavriel D. Rosenfeld

23. *The Ufa Story: A History of Germany's Greatest Film Company, 1918–1945*, by Klaus Kreimeier, translated by Robert and Rita Kimber

24. *From Monuments to Traces: Artifacts of German Memory, 1870–1990*, by Rudy Koshar

25. *We Weren't Modern Enough: Women Artists and the Limits of German Modernism*, by Marsha Meskimmon

26. *Culture and Inflation in Weimar Germany*, by Bernd Widdig

27. *Weimar Surfaces: Urban Visual Culture in 1920s Germany*, by Janet Ward

28. *Graphic Design in Germany: 1890–1945*, by Jeremy Aynsley

29. *Expressionist Utopias: Paradise, Metropolis, Architectural Fantasy*, by Timothy O. Benson, with contributions by Edward Dimendberg, David Frisby, Reinhold Heller, Anton Kaes, and Iain Boyd Whyte

30. *The Red Count: The Life and Times of Harry Kessler*, by Laird M. Easton

32. *The Dark Mirror: German Cinema between Hitler and Hollywood*, by Lutz Koepnick

33. *Rosenzweig and Heidegger: Between Judaism and German Philosophy*, by Peter Eli Gordon

34. *The Authority of Everyday Objects: A Cultural History of West German Industrial Design*, by Paul Betts

35. *The Face of East European Jewry*, by Arnold Zweig, with fifty-two drawings by Hermann Struck. Edited, translated, and with an introduction by Noah Isenberg

36. *No Place Like Home: Locations of Heimat in German Cinema*, by Johannes von Moltke

37. *Berlin Alexanderplatz: Radio, Film, and the Death of Weimar Culture*, by Peter Jelavich

38. *Berlin Electropolis: Shock, Nerves, and German Modernity*, by Andreas Killen

39. *A Concise History of the Third Reich*, by Wolfgang Benz, translated by Thomas Dunlap

40. *Germany in Transit: Nation and Migration, 1955–2005*, edited by Deniz Göktürk, David Gramling, and Anton Kaes

41. *Weimar on the Pacific: German Exile Culture in Los Angeles and the Crisis of Modernism*, by Ehrhard Bahr

42. *The 1972 Munich Olympics and the Making of Modern Germany*, by Kay Schiller and Christopher Young

43. *Berlin Psychoanalytic: Psychoanalysis and Culture in Weimar Republic Germany and Beyond*, by Veronika Fuechtner

44. *Cinema and Experience: Siegfried Kracauer, Walter Benjamin, and Theodor W. Adorno*, by Miriam Bratu Hansen

45. *Siegfried Kracauer's American Writings: Essays on Film and Popular Culture*, edited by Johannes von Moltke and Kristy Rawson

Contents

Preface: Notes on This Edition ix

Acknowledgments xi

INTRODUCTION: AFFINITIES 1

PART I. A CULTURAL CRITIC IN NEW YORK 27

1. Why France Liked Our Films (1942) 33
2. Hollywood's Terror Films (1946) 41
3. Jean Vigo (1947) 47
4. The Revolt against Rationality (1947) 51
5. On Jewish Culture (1947) 54
6. Filming the Subconscious (1948) 57
7. Psychiatry for Everything and Everybody (1948) 62
8. Those Movies with a Message (1948) 72
9. National Types as Hollywood Presents Them (1949) 81
10. The Mirror Up to Nature (1949) 105
11. Preston Sturges, or Laughter Betrayed (1950) 109
12. Art Today (1961) 115
13. About the State of the Humanities 117
14. A Statement on the Humanistic Approach 124
15. Talk with Teddie (1960) 127

PART II.	FILM REVIEWS	133
16.	An American Experiment (1941)	137
17.	*Dumbo* (1941)	139
18.	Film Notes from Hollywood (1941)	141
19.	A Few American Films (1941)	142
20.	William Wyler's New Bette Davis Film (1941)	143
21.	Flaherty: *The Land* (1942)	145
22.	*For Whom the Bell Tolls* (1943)	146
23.	*Paisan* (1948)	150
24.	The Decent German (1949)	157
25.	The Eternal Jew (1956)	162
26.	A Few Notes on *The Connection* (1961)	165
PART III.	BOOK REVIEWS	167
27.	In Eisenstein's Workshop (1943)	171
28.	The Russian Director (1949)	173
29.	The Movie Colony (1942)	176
30.	A Lady of Valor (1947)	178
31.	The Teutonic Mind (1948)	181
32.	Consciousness, Free and Spontaneous (1948)	183
33.	Indologian Holiday (1948)	185
34.	Portrait in Film (1948)	188
35.	Total Teaching (1949)	190
36.	Pictorial Deluge (1950)	192
37.	Movie Mirror (1950)	195
38.	*Réflexion faite* (1952)	197
PART IV.	TOWARD A THEORY OF FILM	199
39.	Stage vs. Screen Acting (1950)	201
40.	The Photographic Approach (1951)	204

41.	Silent Film Comedy (1951)	213
42.	The Found Story and the Episode (1956)	217
43.	Letter to the Editors of *film 56* (1956)	226

AFTERWORD: KRACAUER, THE MAGICAL NOMINALIST /
MARTIN JAY   227

    Notes   237

    Index   277

Preface
Notes on This Edition

This edition presents Kracauer's shorter writings published in English during his years in the United States, as well as a number of unpublished materials from this period.

While we erred on the side of inclusiveness, this collection does not claim to be comprehensive. Selecting the published texts, we have made three minor exceptions: First, we have generally refrained from including published essays that subsequently appeared unchanged in Kracauer's major works, *From Caligari to Hitler: A Psychological History of the German Film*, *Theory of Film: The Redemption of Physical Reality*, and the posthumous *History: Last Things Before the Last*. Because of their significance within the long gestation period of his "book on film aesthetics," as he called it, we do, however, include a condensed version of the opening section of *Theory of Film* on photography, which appeared in the *Magazine of Art* almost a decade before the book was published, as well as a précis of passages from the *Theory of Film* chapter titled "The Found Story and the Episode," which, identified as "excerpts" from the "comprehensive syllabus of his book," was published in *Film Culture* in 1956. Second, we have omitted a few brief book reviews, particularly ones that basically summarize a book's contents rather than providing an evaluation indicative of Kracauer's own convictions; we have, however, retained all reviews, however brief, that express Kracauer's personal methodological assumptions or intellectual leanings. Third, we have omitted here a series of important texts on the subject of propaganda and communications research, since these will be appearing in a separate edition prepared by Graehme Gilloch and Jaeho Kang.[1] In consultation with the editors of that volume, we have striven to ensure that, together, the two anthologies will provide a comprehensive picture of Kracauer's research and publication activities during his American years, above and beyond the better-known monographs on Weimar cinema, film theory, and historiography.

To the published body of work that (with the exception of some film notes for *Cinema 16* and a piece titled "The Mirror Up to Nature" from the British *Penguin Film Review*) appeared in American journals and newspapers between 1941 and 1958, we have made three kinds of additions: First, although Kracauer began writing exclusively in English only a few months after his arrival in the United States, he did publish three articles in the leading Swiss newspaper, *Neue Zürcher Zeitung*, in 1941. Because these reviews deal explicitly with Hollywood cinema and were written in the United States, we have translated them for inclusion in this collection. Second, we include a number of English-language typescripts from the Kracauer archive (housed in the Deutsches Literaturarchiv, Marbach). Some of these appear to have been destined for publication but ultimately were not printed; others were evidently designed as proposals for further discussion.[2] These include writings on subjects as diverse as Jewish culture in America, the state of the humanities, and the role of "art today"; reviews of individual films—notably Rossellini's *Paisan*, clearly a cinematic milestone in the eyes of Kracauer, whose review is published here for the first time in the original English; and Kracauer's notes on a "Talk with Teddie," a record of an apparently heated conversation he had with Adorno in Switzerland in 1964. The significance of this text for the relationship between Kracauer's thinking, as honed during his New York years, and the Critical Theory of Adorno (now back in Frankfurt) has been well known since the publication of Martin Jay's insightful essay on the two thinkers' "troubled friendship."[3] That significance has only increased now that the vagaries of this friendship have been fully documented with the publication of Adorno and Kracauer's lifelong correspondence.[4]

Acknowledgments

Like Siegfried Kracauer's own multidisciplinary endeavors, Kracauer scholarship has proliferated in recent years in many directions. But no matter how widely they range, all attempts to situate Kracauer as a cultural critic, a film theorist, a journalist, a novelist, an architect, and a philosopher ultimately come under the gravitational pull of what is undoubtedly the center of any work on Kracauer: the German literary archives nestled in the hills above the Neckar in Marbach. For an editorial project like ours, this gravitational pull is particularly strong, and we submitted to it more than willingly. Our first debt of gratitude, therefore, is to the Deutsches Literaturarchiv and its knowledgeable, gracious, ever helpful staff. We are likewise indebted to the other institutions at which we conducted research for this volume: the Center for Jewish History, the Schlesinger Library at Harvard University, the Sterling Memorial Library at Yale University, and the New York Public Library.

For their input, suggestions, and assistance, we would like to thank Kerstin Barndt, Nathaniel Brennan, Gerd Gemünden, Noah Isenberg, and Dana Polan. We owe a particular debt of gratitude to the late Miriam Hansen for her encouragement and endorsement of this project at a critical juncture. Kracauer scholarship will forever remain in debt to her work.

At Michigan, our project's germination benefited from the inspired interest of Andrew Covert and proceeded with help from Kristin Hengtgen and M.-Niclas Heckner. The University of Michigan generously provided funding support—our thanks go to the Rackham Graduate School for the Spring/Summer Research Grant that enabled the initiation of the project; to the Undergraduate Research Opportunity Program for funding Kristen Hengtgen's editorial assistance; to the Office of the Vice President for Research for assisting in funding this publication; to the College of

Literature, Science, and the Arts for much-needed release time; and to the chairs of the German and Screen Arts & Cultures Departments, Scott Spector and Abé Markus Nornes, for their support.

Work on this edition was supported by a fellowship from the Alexander-von-Humboldt Foundation, which provided research and writing time in affiliation with the Free University of Berlin, where we would particularly like to thank Gertrud Koch and Hermann Kappelhoff.

Reconstructing the English language rights for Kracauer's work constituted a significant aspect of this project. Even though work remains to be done in this area for future editions, we are grateful for the patient help we received from various parties, including the now-defunct New York Association for New Americans (NYANA), Petra Hardt of the Suhrkamp Verlag, and Ingrid Belke at the Deutsches Literaturarchiv.

Mary Francis likewise provided invaluable assistance in sorting out rights, but her role as the acquiring editor of this project was far greater than that: she took an interest in our endeavors from the start and helped us see it through to the end. It has been a pleasure to work with her again. Moreover, we are delighted that this book appears in the *Weimar and Now* series, which seems tailormade for figures such as Kracauer, and for a volume of his midcentury American writings in particular, which are situated in intriguing ways precisely between "Weimar" and "Now."

Finally, we are especially grateful to Martin Jay for sharing his vast knowledge of intellectual history and his thoughts on our project, whether in conversations in Ann Arbor, Berkeley, and Berlin or in the form of the afterword he kindly agreed to write for this volume.

Introduction
Affinities

> The stranger is being discussed here, not in the sense often touched upon in the past, as the wanderer who comes today and goes tomorrow, but rather as the person who comes today and stays tomorrow.
>
> GEORG SIMMEL, "The Stranger"

On 15 April 1941, the small steamship *Nyassa* left Lisbon on its regular trans-Atlantic route. For this particular passage, however, the comparatively small ship was retrofitted with two large dormitories in cargo holds forward and aft; instead of accommodating 451 passengers at full capacity, as it had on its previous trip, it now carried a total of 816. Disembarking in New York after the ten-day voyage, passengers described the conditions aboard ship as "abominable" and reported clashes among travelers with frayed nerves.[1] Yet as they left the *Nyassa*, a sense of relief predominated: most arrived in the United States as refugees who could count themselves fortunate for having secured a ticket in the face of extortion from speculators in Portugal, thereby escaping increasingly difficult political and financial circumstances.

Among those leaving the ship on that day in April were Siegfried Kracauer, the eminent German cultural critic, and his wife, Lili, *née* Ehrenreich. The couple undoubtedly shared the feeling of relief; indeed, in future years they would mark 25 April as a "private holiday" and an occasion to remember the more pleasant aspects of the trans-Atlantic passage.[2] But even though Kracauer would later reflect in a published article on "the marvelous first meeting with life in America as we entered New York harbor,"[3] the couple had anticipated the moment of arrival with great trepidation. After a long period in French exile and many anxious months spent securing affidavits, visas, money, and boat tickets, Kracauer, on the eve of his embarkation on the *Nyassa*, wrote in a letter to his friend Theodor W. Adorno: "It is awful to arrive as we will—after eight years of an existence that does not deserve the name. I have grown older, also within myself. . . .

I will arrive a poor man, poorer than I have ever been." Entreating Adorno and other émigré friends from the Frankfurt Institute for Social Research to help him gain a foothold in America, Kracauer desperately formulated the urgency and finality of his situation: "Now comes the last station, the last chance, which I must not gamble away, lest everything be lost."[4]

Kracauer would spend the rest of his life in the United States,[5] and it is today well known that during the quarter century following his arrival on board the crowded steamship, he managed to grasp this "last chance" by publishing two of the most important books on film of the postwar era. To an American public unaware of Kracauer's prolific publications prior to 1933, his two monographs established him as a leading theorist of cinema. *From Caligari to Hitler: A Psychological History of the German Film* (Princeton University Press, 1947) modeled a form of criticism that read national cinema for its underlying sociopolitical meanings; and *Theory of Film: The Redemption of Physical Reality* (Oxford University Press, 1960) represented a sustained argument about film as a medium whose specific affinities with reality endowed it with the power to "redeem" the material world. Upon its release, Paul Rotha recognized *From Caligari to Hitler* as "a book which must at once be placed alongside the half-dozen most important works on the cinema."[6] Like *Theory of Film*, it remains a touchstone in film studies curricula even today.

Yet apart from accounts of Kracauer's work on the *Caligari* book in the recently established Museum of Modern Art (MoMA) film library, the often arduous path that led from the author's arrival in New York Harbor to these landmark publications remains virtually unknown. It was a path marked by ongoing financial worries, a string of grant applications, time-consuming consulting jobs, and various attempts to find permanent employment. It was also a path papered with a steady output of writings for journals and newspapers, including some of the elite cultural publication venues—the "little magazines"—of the time. As Kracauer himself put it, "I am writing articles, establishing contacts, and watching out for something big to come."[7]

Making a point of honing his proficiency in the language of his new home country (the Kracauers would both be naturalized in September 1946), Siegfried Kracauer began publishing almost exclusively in English only six months after his arrival in New York.[8] His brief but illuminating debut, a review of Disney's *Dumbo* for the *Nation* in November 1941, would be followed by contributions to the key cultural publications of the day, among them established journals such as the *New Republic* and *Harper's*; nascent film periodicals such as *Films in Review*, *Film Culture*, and *Cinemages*;

as well as *Partisan Review* and *Commentary*, the flagship journals of the New York intellectuals during their heyday in the 1940s and early 1950s.[9]

To date, almost none of these texts have found an English-language readership outside their original publication venues.[10] This anthology collects the essays and reviews from Kracauer's "last station" for readers to discover the dedication, wit, and erudition with which the émigré critic pursued his abiding interests in film and culture during the postwar years. Taken together, these texts model an enduringly relevant form of engaged cultural criticism, one that Kracauer had developed and refined in his native tongue during the 1920s. Whether he is discussing a recent Disney film, Jean Vigo's lyrical cinema, Hollywood's predilection for sadistic twists, or the expanding role of visual culture, Kracauer consistently locates aesthetic forms in their social contexts. Bent, in his own words, on "disclosing the social and political implications" of cinema, he treats the medium as a flashpoint for intellectual debate and cultural critique.[11]

Besides the intrinsic value of these texts, their importance is to be located in three overlapping contexts. First, the essays powerfully evoke the cultural moment during which they were written, affording insights into postwar cinema, the intellectual climate of the day, and the role of the exile critic within this culture. As Kracauer noted in a 1947 letter to a friend in France (now striking a far more confident tone than in the desperate letter to Adorno from Lisbon), "to be a refugee is also a great opportunity for those who are determined to experiment." His writings during the years of American exile testify to this spirit of experimentation from an always precarious position.[12] Written on the margins of the high-profile cohort of New York intellectuals that included Clement Greenberg, Hannah Arendt, Lionel Trilling, Dwight Macdonald, Irving Howe, and Meyer Schapiro, Kracauer's essays allow glimpses into the cultural predilections and the implicit critical protocols of that important group. To the degree that the latter also cast new light on the forms of critical theory elaborated in Frankfurt and New York by both Kracauer and the Frankfurt School, the essays that follow are emblematic of a trans-Atlantic encounter of critical traditions that scholars have only recently begun to explore.[13]

Second, these writings provide invaluable insights into the author's intellectual biography on the margins of the Frankfurt School of Critical Theory. Hitherto overlooked even by some of the most careful readers of Kracauer's works, his American writings help us to uncover continuities where others have posited an "epistemological shift" and to fill in the gaps that ostensibly separate his Weimar journalism, with its astute phenomenological method and its flashes of sociological insight, on the one hand, from the systematic, more "academic" elaboration of his *Theory of Film*, on the other.[14] Instead of a wholesale self-(re)invention of the critic in exile, the essays from the 1940s and 1950s reveal an ongoing elaboration of issues and methods that lay at the heart of Kracauer's thinking from his Weimar writings onward—even as the American postwar, post-Holocaust, and anti-Communist context mandates their modulation in the later writings.

Third, these essays, with their critical assessments of such subjects as Hollywood crime films, Italian neorealism, individual directors, and the function of particular film genres, represent an important contribution to film studies prior to its institutionalization as an academic field of study. Together with his contemporaries James Agee, Dwight Macdonald, Otis Ferguson, and Robert Warshow, Kracauer practiced a sustained, culturally relevant form of film criticism, one that in Kracauer's case had been the hallmark of his earlier Weimar writings as well. In doing so, he played his part in "inventing film studies," as a recent anthology puts it.[15] Not only because of the widespread influence of his monographs, but also by virtue of his contributions to new publication venues and other forms of disseminating film scholarship, Kracauer's work helps to illuminate the long gestation of cinema as a field of humanist inquiry.

The introductory remarks that follow are designed to situate Kracauer's American writings in these three overlapping contexts of New York's intellectual culture, Kracauer's own intellectual biography, and the rise of film studies. While we take Kracauer's arrival in New York as our starting point, thereby underlining the role of exile in each of the broader contexts we trace, we ultimately wish to shift the image of Kracauer as an "extraterritorial" critic by considering him not only as a refugee in exile, but also as an immigrant.[16] What would it mean, we ask, to consider Kracauer and his writings in terms of the citizenship he took on five years after disembarking from the *Nyassa*? How would it affect our readings of his work, from the 1941 review of *Dumbo* to his posthumously published book on historiography, if we think of Kracauer not only as an émigré critic but also as an American? What, in other words, were Kracauer's American affinities as a cultural critic?[17]

"NO LONGER A EUROPEAN OBSERVER": WRITING AS AN AMERICAN

While the arrangement of Kracauer's essays in this volume emphasizes chronology in order to provide a sense of historical and intellectual development, we have chosen to begin neither with his first report from the United States (still for a Swiss newspaper) nor with the compelling review of Disney's *Dumbo*, Kracauer's first English-language publication; rather, we have selected an important piece on French and American cinema that Kracauer published a year after arriving in the United States; containing uncharacteristically personal remarks, it charts *in nuce* the intellectual trajectory of the exile.[18] The *National Board of Review Magazine*, in which the essay "Why France Liked Our Films" (ch. 1 in this collection) appeared, supplied a brief biographical note that located the author's authority on matters of French and Hollywood cinema in his history of exile, stating that Kracauer "left Germany in 1933, and lived in France till a year ago when he escaped to America." But far more than Kracauer's French connection, it is the first-person plural pronoun that animates the article: he is speaking as a member of a group, as an American to Americans about "our" cultural export. While at first this might seem an overreading of the title (which, after all, could have been an editorial insertion), it turns out to be the punch line of the entire piece, which self-consciously works through the shift from a European perspective to an American one.

The essay opens with a question: "What would an intelligent European observer learn about American life from American films?" Kracauer announces at the outset that he will be "operating in the field of rather personal impressions." But he soon takes his subjective voice back in favor of "incontestable facts": namely, that American films have exerted an inexorable pull on the "intellectual elite in Europe," and in France in particular. In order to answer the question posed in the title, Kracauer begins by painting a picture of French cinema, characterizing it as a gaping void that American films helped to fill.

French cinema, Kracauer argues, has typically produced noncinematic films—films lacking movement, overburdened with dialogue, and out of touch with the cinema's specific ability to redeem the minutiae of everyday life. Kracauer finds that French films routinely neglect "the material details—all those objects and gestures that are so important on the screen and which only the camera is able to detect and endow with significance." Anticipating arguments he will publish in later studies on propaganda and in *Theory of Film*, he faults the French cinema for the "absolute predominance of the dialogue."[19] Especially with the advent of the "talkies," French cinema, he felt, had abandoned cinema's essential affinity for "showing hitherto unseen phenomena." If this critique reads like a preview of coming attractions in *Theory of Film*, Kracauer's comments on the characteristic disposition of "the French soul," on the "paralysis" of French society, and on the stasis of its expression in films with "nothing but atmosphere" strikingly presage his diagnosis of middle-class paralysis in Weimar cinema in *From Caligari to Hitler*. We know from Miriam Hansen's work that Kracauer had been considering the central issues of *Theory of Film* already during his French exile, where he took extensive notes on the project and engaged in conversations about it with Walter Benjamin.[20] However, "Why France Liked Our Films" not only puts the theory of realism into dialogue with the theorization of national cinema that would define *From Caligari to Hitler* (with which *Theory of Film* is often considered to be incompatible), but it also begins to sketch out a new position from which to undertake that project—after the tragedy of Benjamin's suicide, after the harrowing escape from France, and within the context of his still-uncertain existence in New York. In this regard, the brief essay reads not only as a compendium to Kracauer's thinking from the late 1930s (even the "little sales-girls" of his well-known series of essays from the *Frankfurter Zeitung* make an appearance here) through his final project on *History*, but also as a concise map to Kracauer's own positioning as an intellectual in exile.

Having reviewed the French cinema, Kracauer shifts his attention to the American scene, which he views as a positive to the French negative: where France wallowed in stasis, "Hollywood pictures appeared as the manifestation of movement and life"; where France failed to heed the details of the visible world, the action in American films "answers the demands of the film camera in that it extends over the whole material dimension and precisely includes that sector of reality which can be called camera reality."[21] Kracauer finds evidence for these claims in the western ("where else but in the Western do real horses gallop over real plains?"), in the physicality of slapstick comedy, in the "palpable" realism of Main Street in *Stella Dallas*, and even in the string of genre productions, from gangster, to boxing, to reporter and detective films. As it proceeds, Kracauer's review becomes an ode to Hollywood, a tribute so full of unadorned praise that no reader could fail to see why France would like these films: for a cinema-starved nation, these were productions too realistic, too authentic, too visually compelling to pass up.

But Kracauer does not end here; in a final twist characteristic of many of his best essays from both the Weimar era and the New York years, he once more reverses his gaze and asks what it would mean to test these (imputed) French impressions of American cinema, and the latter's triumphant realism in particular, against the reality of life in America. At this point, the personal perspective that Kracauer abandoned at the article's opening reasserts itself. In the context of a learned argument about national cinemas and recent film history, we suddenly find Kracauer reliving his own arrival in the United States a year earlier and elevating the exile's trajectory to a privileged epistemological standpoint—much as he would do later on a more philosophical plane in his final book, *History*. For there is "only one short moment," Kracauer claims, "in which the European observer can judge the validity of the image of American life he had received in European theatres: the moment of his arrival in this country . . . the marvelous first meeting with life in America." Recollecting "that decisive moment" in his own life, Kracauer notes—again in the first person plural—that "as we entered New York harbor, the strange feeling of having already seen all this began to grow upon me." The urban landscape of New York, the detectives and immigration officials who board the ship, all seem to Kracauer like old acquaintances; to the self-described "passionate movie-goer," the entire scene becomes cinematic, akin to a dream: "either he had been suddenly transplanted onto the screen or the screen itself had come into three-dimensional existence."

This oneiric perspective, which provides the refugee with an epistemological perspective from which to judge—or better, recognize—the fundamental realism of Hollywood, is fleeting, however. Kracauer ends his article by noting the way in which the immigrant's acclimatization shifts the perspective again and begins to reveal aspects of American reality that the cinema failed to capture. As an example, he notes that filmic representations of New York "neither take notice of Broadway in the morning, nor do they picture the hundreds of cross-town streets that end in the empty sky." To careful readers of Kracauer's work, this is not merely a question of adding nuance to stock footage of New York, but an early formulation of the theory of film's affinities with the fortuitous and the endless and of the medium's link to experience, which Kracauer will elaborate in *Theory of Film*.[22] To be sure, Kracauer will eventually shift his evaluation of Hollywood in favor of Italian neorealism—as the series of articles we have assembled here makes plain; but this shift, which we can trace through his essays from the 1940s all the way to the final shape of *Theory of Film*, will henceforth take place on new epistemological ground, mapped in "Why France Liked Our Films." Having begun the article as an "intelligent European observer," authorized to speak of France's film culture by virtue of the eight years he spent in exile there, and having then taken up the position of the refugee, whose flash of insight into American culture was condensed in "that decisive moment—the marvelous first meeting with life in American culture," Kracauer ends the article by adopting the first person plural of his title—by writing as an American, so to speak. Noting new details of American life that become apparent to the immigrant only after a "slow process of personal adjustment," Kracauer concludes with the acknowledgment that "it is no longer a European observer who is making these observations."

A NEW YORK INTELLECTUAL

> Having managed to get there [to America], he was in fact surprisingly successful.
>
> THEODOR W. ADORNO, "The Curious Realist: On Siegfried Kracauer"

"Why France Liked Our Films" provides a finely etched starting point for Kracauer's trajectory as an essayist and journalist during his years in America. The essay itself sets up the investigation of what it meant for Kracauer to write "no longer [as] a European observer," but as a self-identified American: an immigrant who virtually stopped writing in German after barely half a year in his new host country, who took on American citizenship at the first opportunity, and who, by the end of his life, felt distant from and at times repulsed by his home country. The importance of this position in the development of Kracauer's thinking remains inadequately understood, to the degree that we tend to place Kracauer only in the orbit of the Frankfurt School (however uneasily) and accept—if not harp on—the designations of *Obdachlosigkeit* and extraterritoriality that Kracauer occasionally claimed for his peripatetic, fragmented existence.

In arguing for "re-territorializing" Kracauer's later work within an American context, so to speak, we certainly do not dismiss the important paradigm of extraterritoriality or wish to downplay the continued plight of exile, whose relevance has been clearly demonstrated by Martin Jay, Enzo Traverso, and others;[23] nor do we espouse a straightforward assimilationist narrative that would single out the immigrants' "slow process of personal adjustment"[24] and devalue the persistent experience of difference that shaped Kracauer's life and work in the United States. But any account of this experience must be complemented, we submit, by a picture of the intellectual, social, and historical contexts in which Kracauer moved during the last twenty years of his life in his adoptive country. These contexts are not limited to the reading and screening rooms of the Museum of Modern Art (MoMA), in which readers of *The Cabinet of Dr. Caligari* in particular like to imagine Kracauer, ensconced behind towering piles of books and (by implication) out of touch with the very reality of the New York streets at daybreak that he had discovered upon his transition into American life. While MoMA did provide an important network for Kracauer's work, which we will discuss below, the principal context we have in mind is of a broader cultural and intellectual nature. For the New York in which Kracauer arrived was not merely a remarkable urban landscape where skyscrapers "produced various effects . . . to break up the monotony of the long avenues"; the city was also home to a heady community of intellectuals, most of them Jewish and many of them immigrants themselves (or at least first-generation Americans), who set the tone for some of the most important cultural debates and edited the most significant journals of the time. Unlike his fellow émigré Hannah Arendt, Kracauer never became a recognized member of that group. And yet there is much to be learned about his position, we propose, as well as about both New York and Frankfurt intellectual culture, if we consider Kracauer himself as a New York Intellectual.

The New York Intellectuals came of age during the 1930s. Mostly born and raised in New York working-class families with strong union ties, these young men started out as committed socialists who participated in the organizations, the institutions, and the debates of the American left. Whether autodidacts like Philip Rahv, accomplished young academics like Meyer Schapiro, Lionel Trilling, and Sidney Hook, or eager City College students like Irving Howe, Nathan Glazer, Daniel Bell, and Irving Kristol, they all soon combined their political allegiances with a fervent cultural commitment to literary modernism.[25] The resulting intellectual "profile," amalgamated from heritage, habitus, and a voracious appetite for learning, set the members apart from their surroundings, yielding a group that itself felt "proudly" homeless in the United States.[26] As Irving Howe would later put it, in a phrase that resonates strikingly with Kracauer's "extraterritoriality," the New York Intellectuals grew up "*willing* a new life, [driven by] our tacit wish to transform deracination from a plight into a program."[27] And yet the "sense of apartness" that Howe considered formative for the group's members was coupled, in David Denby's terms, with "an amazed and delighted discovery of the American turf"—of America's "classic texts, its real and mythic landscapes, the vitality of its cities and popular arts."[28] The story of the New York Intellectuals is in this sense itself one of Americanization, and it seems only natural that the recent exile would sense and cultivate some affinities with the group.[29]

Although his name is rarely mentioned alongside the "loose and unacknowledged tribe" (as characterized by Howe) that clustered around Philip

Rahv, William Phillips, Clement Greenberg, Dwight Macdonald, Elliot Cohen, and Howe himself, Kracauer published in the journals favored (if not founded) by the New York Intellectuals, such as the *Nation*, the *New Republic*, *Partisan Review*, and *Commentary*. Moreover, from his earliest years in the United States, Kracauer's work elicited response and generated discourse within a variety of loosely related venues, including *Politics*, *Labor Action*, *Dissent*, and the *New Leader*.[30] In ways no less significant for not always being immediately apparent, Kracauer contributed to the central debates that defined the New York Intellectuals as a group.

A number of these critics ardently admired Kracauer's writings, and Kracauer owed his entry into the United States in large part to Meyer Schapiro, an important member of the group—its "recognized scholar [and] inspiring moral force," in Howe's terms.[31] As early as 1937, Schapiro had recognized that Kracauer shared some of the sensibilities and interests that drove the New York Intellectuals—their concern with the fate of socialism, their interest in the links between economy and culture, their nervous attention to popular culture.[32] He certainly shared their bookish erudition, and we might even say that he shared their sense of style.

Like many of the New York Intellectuals, Kracauer brought to bear in his writings the skills of a journalist, albeit one steeped in literary culture and with two novels to his name. And although we would grant Adorno's lament that, perhaps as a result of writing only in English, Kracauer became comparatively "ascetic with regard to his own verbal art" in America,[33] it is difficult to imagine that the consummate stylist ever lost his love for the carefully turned phrase, delight in the witty formulation, or appreciation for the dialectical significance of form.[34]

A discerning reader as well, Kracauer no doubt appreciated the stylistic brilliance and critical acuity of the essays, reviews, and debates that filled the little magazines of the New York scene. As numerous commentators have pointed out, the New York Intellectuals were defined by the journals they edited as much as by the cultural and political theories they held. The ways in which these journals established certain stylistic and intellectual standards of discourse conveyed upon them the function of central institutions for a group that largely imagined itself as outside all institutions. To be published in *Partisan Review*, remembers one writer, "was acclamation, [it] conferred a special ideological status on the accepted."[35]

It is not our task here to reconstruct in full historical detail what constituted the "special ideological status" of the New York Intellectual of the 1940s.[36] But we may note two overarching concerns of the New Yorkers that, bound up with the weighty matter of presentation and form, intersect with Kracauer's abiding interests. For what animated the New York Intellectuals above and beyond their much-touted anti-Stalinism, and set them apart from other movements, was their combined interest in Marxism and aesthetic Modernism. After the cultural dogmatism of the American communist left during the early 1930s, which had relied on received critical paradigms to disparage modernist experimentation as "decadent," "bourgeois," and "individualistic," magazines like *Partisan Review*, *Commentary*, and *Politics* helped forge a new articulation of politics and culture, championing modernist culture with the help of Marxist explanatory models and grappling with attendant problems of popular culture and totalitarianism, avant-garde and kitsch. As Harvey Teres puts it in his searching study of the New York Intellectuals' role in the history of the left, *Partisan Review* was instrumental in "bringing the cultural avant-garde and the political vanguard into some form of productive mutual relation for the first time since the 1910s."[37] And if, in the estimation of some commentators, this flagship journal gradually abandoned that role for an anticommunist "neo-aestheticism," spin-offs and newly founded publications such as *Commentary*, *Politics*, and *Dissent* sprang into the breach.[38]

Tracing various editorial skirmishes—contestations that defined some journals, led to the splintering off of others, or inspired "dissenting" publications—gives us a sense of the political-intellectual landscape in which Kracauer moved, and in which he placed his articles during the 1940s and 50s. In returning to this vibrant New York culture, however, we would emphasize from the outset its transnational composition: leading figures such as *Partisan Review* editors William Phillips and Philip Rahv were themselves recent Russian immigrants, and the refugees arriving from Europe during the 1930s and 1940s played a central role in the shifting intellectual landscape as well.[39] We might think, for example, of Arendt, a close friend of Walter Benjamin's whose exile in Paris coincided with Kracauer's and who finally managed to secure the passage from Lisbon to New York only one month after Kracauer in 1941. Arendt, too, would learn English promptly upon her arrival, and she soon placed her increasingly influential essays not only in the German-Jewish *Aufbau*, but also in the journals of the New York Intellectuals, in whose circles she would rise to the position of an acknowledged elder.[40]

While Arendt's evolving theory of totalitarianism constitutes a crucial, if thus far unexplored, contemporary German-American reference point for Kracauer's work on film and propaganda during the 1940s,[41] another trans-Atlantic context is at least equally relevant. If the flight of German

Jews in particular led to a reconstitution of "Weimar on the Pacific," in Ehrhard Bahr's terms, the same might be said of New York. After all, before Theodor W. Adorno and Max Horkheimer penned *The Dialectic of Enlightenment* in Los Angeles, there was a Frankfurt School on the Atlantic: under Horkheimer's leadership, the Institut für Sozialforschung had become affiliated with Columbia University as early as 1934. While its members remained relatively secluded in the early years for fear of jeopardizing their tenuous exile status, Horkheimer lifted the strict policy of political isolation toward the end of 1930s. By the time that Leo Löwenthal, a member of the Frankfurt School and a friend of Kracauer's who supplied one of the requisite affidavits, met the Kracauers as they disembarked from the *Nyassa*,[42] the Frankfurt School had established a number of contacts with the New York Intellectuals, with whom they eventually even worked side by side (physically, if not intellectually) under the auspices of the American Jewish Committee. At the same time, as Thomas Wheatland outlines in his book *The Frankfurt School in Exile*, these contacts suffered from pragmatic and substantive shortcomings, ranging from Horkheimer's earlier protectionist policies and the idiosyncratic behavior of intellectuals on both sides to divergent research protocols and disagreements deriving from the Hegelian Marxism of the Frankfurters and the pragmatic socialism of the New Yorkers.[43] While some of these disagreements may have been unduly exaggerated as the "narcissism of small differences," they clearly contributed to a series of failed encounters.[44]

In retrospect and for reasons we outline below, we are tempted to see in Kracauer the missing link between the Frankfurt School and the New York Intellectuals. On the margins of both movements, Kracauer was able to forge compelling insights into the cultural phenomena of his day from a trans-Atlantic perspective that combined his deep affinities with Critical Theory (and the critical theorists he had mentored) with a commitment to grasping his American surroundings. Although this link between Frankfurt and New York was never fully articulated, the essays that we republish here offer compelling points of convergence. They permit us to rethink the relationship between the New York and the Frankfurt Intellectuals not simply in terms of missed opportunities but as an occasion for developing theoretical sightlines. These sightlines emerge clearly if we place these two influential schools of thought, usually associated with opposite sides of the Atlantic, within the perspective offered by Kracauer's American writings.[45]

As editor at the *Frankfurter Zeitung*, Kracauer had been at the epicenter of German intellectual culture before 1933. Not only did he have an outlet for his own prolific cultural reporting and his influential essays, to whose regular composition he devoted himself "with the same love as to my novel,"[46] but he also enjoyed a privileged position as reviewer and gatekeeper for the published works of others, from novelists and essayists such as Joseph Roth, Thomas Mann, and Anna Seghers, to philosophers such as Husserl and Mannheim, to his friends Theodor Adorno and Walter Benjamin. Kracauer was aware of his influence and enjoyed his position. Even if his correspondence occasionally reveals a degree of envy for the security and recognition some of his friends had managed to find within the academy, he took satisfaction in his journalistic work and happily claimed by the early 1930s that "taken together [my newspaper essays] produce a rather pretty destructive effect."[47]

For Kracauer in exile, none of this confidence remained. While he was able to continue working briefly for the *Frankfurter Zeitung* in Paris and later secured occasional work as the French correspondent for two Swiss newspapers, Kracauer's flight from Berlin after the Reichstag fire in February 1933 left him adrift, unmoored from the publishing world that had been his anchor in Germany—and which he himself had helped to anchor in turn. During the eight years in France, Kracauer was continuously beset by material worries that affected his own and his wife's health. Although he managed to complete his second novel, *Georg*, which he had begun during his years in Berlin, he was unable to secure a publisher. A "social biography" of Jacques Offenbach, meanwhile, was rewarded not only by publication but also by translations into multiple languages, but it did not bring financial stability.

From at least 1937 on, Kracauer actively sought to establish connections to America in the hope of securing affidavits and a stable income. However, negotiations with Horkheimer's Institute for Social Research failed to lead anywhere (particularly after a disastrous series of exchanges about a manuscript on propaganda that Kracauer had prepared for the Institute), and early hopes for a collaboration with the MoMA film library took almost half a decade to come to fruition.[48] With only intermittent income from various grants for book-length manuscripts, Kracauer often, if somewhat reluctantly, reverted to journalistic formats such as reviews and essays.[49]

Once he landed in New York, then, he no longer enjoyed a position as cultural arbiter, as during his years at the *Frankfurter Zeitung*. He now encountered an entirely new publishing landscape in which he had to find his bearings as occasional contributor and sometimes even as supplicant for contracted reviews. It is a testament to his expertise and tenacity that he did manage to find such work within months of his arrival. Moreover, the tribulations of exile, the recurring periods of adjustment, even the "epistemological shift" that ostensibly separated the author of the celebrated series of *Frankfurter Zeitung* articles on white-collar employees from the author of *From Caligari to Hitler*, must be measured against compelling continuities in Kracauer's thinking from the twenties through the forties.[50] Many of the pieces he managed to publish, especially during the 1940s, still reveal the same cultural and political assumptions, the same perceptiveness and intellectual acuity, that made his contributions to the *Frankfurter Zeitung* the talk of intellectual circles in the late Weimar Republic.

What, then, was the intellectual and publishing landscape that Kracauer found upon his arrival in New York? Although Kracauer continued writing briefly for the *Baseler National-Zeitung* and did contact the *New York Times* at one point to inquire about employment as a book reviewer, he held no hopes of reviving his career with a major newspaper. Rather, his eye was clearly on the "little magazines" of the day, which had been undergoing a period of intense flux and reorganization. Of particular interest here are *Partisan Review* and *Commentary*, the two longest-running journals most closely associated with the New York Intellectuals.

Partisan Review, which began as the publication arm of the Communist Party's John Reed Club, had undergone a major shift in 1936–37, when it came under the joint editorship of William Phillips and Philip Rahv, who would lead the journal for decades to come. When the journal resumed publication, after a short interlude, in December 1937, the editorial statement set the tone for a magazine that "aspire[d] to a place in the vanguard of literature" but would be "unequivocally independent" from any political party. Rejecting that "totalitarian trend" within the Communist Party in particular, the editorial nonetheless embraced "Marxism in culture" as "an instrument of analysis and evaluation." Against the genteel traditions of the old Left and its "literature of good cheer," the editors championed the "cause of revolutionary literature" for a "new and dissident generation in American letters."[51]

This shift significantly enhanced the profile of the magazine, aligning it with modernism over the traditional forms of aesthetic commitment espoused by the Communist Party that had influenced its earlier incarnation. But *Partisan Review* would remain under the sway of political developments leading up to the U.S. entry into World War II.[52] United, if not identified, by their anti-Stalinism in the wake of the 1936 Moscow trials, the members of the *Partisan Review* circle were starkly divided on the issue of whether to support the American war effort. When Rahv and Phillips came out in support of the U.S. declaration of war after Pearl

Harbor, both Dwight Macdonald and Clement Greenberg openly distanced themselves from the policy of the editors. After internal struggles over control, Macdonald left *Partisan Review* in 1943 to found *Politics*, wherein he would argue for a third-camp model as an alternative to both U.S. capitalism, on the one hand, and Fascist and Communist totalitarianism, on the other—until he surprisingly proclaimed his unequivocal alignment with the Western Bloc in a 1952 article flatly entitled "I Choose the West."[53]

While Kracauer would not publish in *Partisan Review* until 1947, it is worth noting that, as editor of *Politics*, Macdonald took a specific interest in Kracauer's ongoing work on propaganda.[54] The latter dated back to the fateful attempt at collaboration with the Institute for Social Research in the late 1930s, when Kracauer was still in Paris; but it had only recently seen publication after renewed work on the topic under the auspices of MoMA. In letters and grant applications, Kracauer would later point out the resonance his study had found even in government circles in Washington,[55] but an article by Macdonald in the May 1944 issue of *Politics*—a review of an essay by Kracauer on the Nazi newsreel that had appeared the previous year in the New School's journal *Social Research*—shows that it was warmly received among the New York Intellectuals as well. Extolling Kracauer's essay as "the best writing on films to appear in a long time," Macdonald astutely pinpointed a characteristic strength of Kracauer's work when he singled out for praise the way in which "the author combines sensitivity to film technique and historical imagination."[56]

Given this praise in Macdonald's own breakaway journal, it is doubly ironic that when Kracauer's *From Caligari to Hitler* was reviewed in *Partisan Review* only three months after he had placed an excerpt from the book in the same magazine, Macdonald—supposedly estranged from *PR*—returned to pen the review. It amounted to a scathing attack on the book. Superciliously granting the author "many fine perceptions," Macdonald took *Caligari* to task as a "'thesis-book' of the most crude and naive kind," whose "far-fetched interpretations" led the author to wrench his data into a "simplistic pattern."[57] While Macdonald anticipates some of the critiques that *Caligari* would garner over the following decades within the field of film studies (such as its overly teleological argumentation), the review disagrees most strongly with the political impetus behind Kracauer's book: its reduction of Weimar cinema to proto-fascism and its failure to define in detail the alternatives that Kracauer repeatedly intimates—democracy, humanism, and progress. These broad concepts would have needed to be tested and refined, Macdonald claims, through a comparative analysis—particularly of Hollywood films.

Macdonald's acerbic critique surely hurt Kracauer, but it should also be put into perspective. As would have been apparent to any regular reader of the "little magazines" at the time, this kind of combativeness constituted the lifeblood of the New York Intellectual debates, and Macdonald in particular was known for his "irreverent, skeptical, fun, and loudly nonconformist" attitudes.[58] This intellectual habitus also reflected and generated a relatively tight-knit "in-group," and it highlights the difficulties with which Kracauer had to contend in navigating the shifting allegiances and the intricate politics of the New York publishing establishment.

Macdonald's complaint about Kracauer's lacking attention to Hollywood, in fact, can serve to illustrate these intricacies, as it contributes to the historical irony of Macdonald's review. For, given the publishing landscape of the time, Macdonald could hardly have been unaware of Kracauer's well-received article from two years earlier, "Hollywood's Terror Films: Do They Reflect an American State of Mind?" (ch. 2). This piece, which appeared in the recently founded *Commentary* magazine (whose editorial board Clement Greenberg joined when he defected from *Partisan Review* along with Macdonald), significantly contributed to establishing Kracauer's approach to cinema, but through an engagement with contemporary American, rather than prewar German, films.

Given the importance of *Commentary* in the contemporary publishing scene generally, as well as for the encounter between the Frankfurt and New York Intellectuals, some background on its editorial politics will help to situate Kracauer's contribution. *Commentary*, published under the auspices of the American Jewish Committee (AJC), was essentially a reincarnation of the *Contemporary Jewish Record*, launched in 1938, and was aimed at reintegrating cosmopolitan Jewish intellectuals, such as those working for *Partisan Review*, with the American Jewish community. Whether or not this move brought Jewish intellectuals "back into the Jewish fold," as some have claimed, or whether the result was a rather more tenuous partnership between the intellectuals and the community at large is a matter of some debate.[59] In any case, the journal brought together "an odd mix," in Nathan Glazer's terms: members of the *Partisan Review* circle, Ivy League professors, left-wing freelance writers, and German Jewish émigrés such as Kracauer himself.[60] Upon Clement Greenberg's invitation in March 1946, he made his debut in *Commentary*'s August issue with the well-received article "Hollywood's Terror Films," which we discuss below.

In the pages of *Commentary*, Kracauer found himself in good company from his Frankfurt days. For even as the American Jewish Committee launched the new magazine, it was involved with Horkheimer's Institute for Social Research, which it had contracted for a large study on anti-Semitism. For a brief while, the Frankfurters and the New Yorkers literally worked side by side, and with a similar post-Holocaust brief from the AJC.[61] In his recent reminiscences about the early years of *Commentary*, Nathan Glazer traces his own back-door entrance into the editorial circle by way of the anti-Semitism project. At the instigation of Daniel Bell, who had previously attended seminars of the Institute for Social Research at Columbia University, Glazer made contact with Horkheimer and took up work as the latter's reader of American social science. Horkheimer's office at the AJC happened to be across the hall from the *Contemporary Jewish Record*, which was just then undergoing the transition to *Commentary* under the editorial direction of Elliot Cohen and assistants Clement Greenberg, Evelyn Shefner, and Lionel Trilling. Cohen had frequent talks with Horkheimer, who became an outspoken supporter of *Commentary* early on.[62] Glazer ended up crossing the hallway and joining the editorial team at *Commentary*, where he was placed in charge of a new social science column, "The Study of Man." In this capacity he would soon be responsible for the publication of Kracauer's "Revolt Against Rationality" (ch. 4), the author's second published piece in *Commentary*, which appeared in 1947. Like *Social Research*, then, the little magazines of the New York scene were certainly open to German Jewish émigrés: out of the immediate Horkheimer Circle, Erich Fromm, Herbert Marcuse, Leo Löwenthal, and Franz Neumann all published multiple and significant articles in *Partisan Review*, *Commentary*, and *Politics*.[63]

Commentary emerged immediately as a locus of cultural and political discourse that reverberated widely within the intellectual community. Kracauer's submission "Freedom from Fear," retiled "Hollywood's Terror Films," was included in *Commentary*'s ninth issue, appearing in August 1946, and caught the attention of intellectuals seeking material ground on which to address the relationship between cultural production, politics, and ideology. To Philip Rahv, indeed, this was "precisely the kind of writing on the films that we have been looking for," and he promptly contacted Kracauer to solicit contributions in this vein to *Partisan Review*.[64] Writing in the *Nation* later that year, James Agee, too, would associate Kracauer—along with Barbara Deming—with a particular "sort of analysis" that he regarded valuable in these two writers but pernicious in less practiced hands.[65] By the end of World War II, in other words, Kracauer had become a known quantity among the New York Intellectuals, who associated his name with a specific approach to film in particular.

What kind of "writing on the films" did Kracauer's writings model, then? "Hollywood's Terror Films" was written in a period when the author was deeply involved with the preparation of *From Caligari to Hitler*. Consequently, a number of intellectual motifs and even direct references connect the article to the book that was to appear a year later, although the article's object was not Weimar cinema but a series of Hollywood films from the war and immediate postwar years. In recent productions such as *Dark Corner, Lost Weekend,* and *Shadow of a Doubt,* Kracauer discerned an alarming sadistic tendency that called for closer analysis of both stylistic and thematic features and their social meanings. As he would in his study of prewar German films, Kracauer singled out particular aspects, such as the importance of inanimate objects, urban locations, antidemocratic plot structures, as well as the notion—which he would develop, for example, in his sustained analysis of Fritz Lang's *M*—that "present-day monsters live among us without being recognized." In an explicit reference, the representation of "chaotic street life" on Third Avenue in many of Hollywood's "terror films" took Kracauer back to the "German films of the pre-Hitler Weimar Republic" that he was analyzing at the MoMA film library at the time.[66] But most importantly, we find here already a version of Kracauer's now famous assertion in the introduction to *From Caligari to Hitler* about the relationship between film and the "psychological dispositions" of a nation. Like the book, "Hollywood's Terror Films" treats films as social symptoms, to be analyzed for what they can tell us about "popular tendencies and inclinations." Although this insight may seem worn and even tautological today, it stemmed from a novel critical approach to the cinema that Kracauer was pioneering at the time.

"Hollywood's Terror Films" clearly illustrates this approach, which combines psychoanalytic insights with cultural critique (even as it diagnoses the popular vogue of psychoanalysis as a troubling cultural symptom in its own right). Kracauer analyzes the contemporary cinema's sadistic inclinations as a lingering aftereffect of the wartime anti-Nazi film.[67] But where the latter laid claim to realist representation in portraying a sadistic enemy, sadism in the more recent films has become unmoored. With the war over, Kracauer notes the rising popularity of a "new species" of films in which images of violence appear to be free-floating as "horror for the sake of sheer entertainment." Kracauer's goal, then, is to trace this trend back to its social and political roots, which he locates in incipient postwar anxieties: the demobilization of U.S. soldiers, the nuclear threat, and the onset of the cold war. Whether or not the postwar films invoke the war directly or its afterimage—as in *The Stranger* (Orson Welles,

1946), *Somewhere in the Night* (Joseph L. Mankiewicz, 1946), and *Shock* (Alfred L. Werker, 1946)—or elicit comparable anxieties without military reference—as with *Dark Corner* (Henry Hathaway, 1946) or *Suspicion* (Alfred Hitchcock, 1941)—these films are "teeming with threatening allusions and dreadful possibilities, they evoke a world in which everyone fears anybody and no one knows when and where the inevitable will happen." Significantly, the causes for anxiety have slipped from the extraordinary to the ordinary, from the grotesque to the mysteriously attractive, and they have come home to roost: "the weird, veiled insecurity of life under the Nazis is transferred to the American scene. Sinister conspiracies incubate next door, within the world considered normal—any trusted neighbor may turn into a demon."

It is tempting to see in such statements and in Kracauer's article itself not only the spatial anxieties spawned in modernity and articulated in film noir but also the psycho-spatial dislocation of the exile who makes these observations.[68] And yet the manifest parallels between Kracauer's debut in *Commentary*, on the one hand, and his first (and ultimately most famous) book to be published in the United States, on the other, also suggest a different reading. For the similarities that Kracauer's various analyses reveal—similarities that Edward Dimendberg describes as the "isomorphism" of expressionist cinema and of what would come to be known as film noir—lay claim precisely to the generalizability of the underlying approach. Whereas critics have repeatedly accused Kracauer of essentializing notions of "the German soul" or collective "psychological dispositions" in his book on pre-fascist cinema, "Hollywood's Terror Films" shows (along with other publications such as "National Types as Hollywood Presents Them," ch. 9) that Kracauer hardly held German films to a unique standard or exempted other cinematographies from similar critique.

Nor can his reading of Hollywood fare be reduced to either the privileged or the paranoid perspective of the exile, a stance that he had striven to cast off in "Why France Liked Our Films." Instead, Kracauer was working to elaborate a method of analysis that might be applied, *mutatis mutandis*, to other national contexts as well. Kracauer's unique accomplishment, as Dimendberg points out, "is the articulation of an interactive relationship between cinema, urban space, and the psychic and cultural mood of a society, something already commenced in his Weimar writings."[69] The fact that an exasperated Agee could comment on the reification of this critical approach in the *Nation* by the end of 1946 is only one indication of Kracauer's success in "branding" his own method. Others include explicit reference to Kracauer's paradigm in the context of the influential Library of Congress Film Project during the war,[70] not to mention the later canonization of *From Caligari to Hitler* as the master text of national cinema studies.

But it was not just the method (labeled "psycho-cultural" at the time) that stuck.[71] If one considers the material corpus that Kracauer constructs in "Hollywood's Terror Films," and the stylistic and thematic features that he identifies, the article amounts to a striking—and strikingly early—identification of a cycle that would later be codified as "film noir." Kracauer's analysis is contemporaneous, in fact, with the first appearance of the term in print in France, and it predates by a decade the first serious attempt to provide an assessment of the cycle's significance by Raymond Borde and Etienne Chaumeton.[72] More importantly, as Dimendberg points out, "Kracauer's text proposes an American context for the invention of film noir."[73]

This includes, we submit, not only the postwar Hollywood context, but also the intellectual context back East. Kracauer's intervention must be considered within the discursive field in which it was solicited, written, and published, where it takes on a political function above and beyond the articulation of exilic anxiety. Thus, Kracauer's conclusion to "Hollywood's Terror Films" positions him less as an extraterritorial critic than as a grounded participant in the ongoing debate among New York Intellectuals about the politics of capitalism and Stalinist communism, of democracy and liberalism. The dilemma that these films ultimately present, Kracauer argues, is that of the individual "caught in the snarls of the free-enterprise system" yet wary of shifting his allegiance to a "planned economy" with its attendant "totalitarian potentialities." This struggle, which in Kracauer's hyperbole amounts to a "civil war . . . being fought in every soul," leads a democracy "economically out of joint . . . [to] breed nightmarish dreams of fascist pseudo-solutions" that threaten individual freedom.

Given this conclusion, it is hardly surprising that Irving Howe endorsed Kracauer's essay as an explicit critique of capitalism.[74] Summarizing Kracauer's approach in a review in *Labor Action*, Howe notes: "The films produced by Hollywood can serve as barometers of the moral and ideological climate of capitalist civilization. When that civilization is distinguished by an increasing sense of individual helplessness in a brutal meaningless world; when mass murder and terror are everyday events; when psychological disintegration is the result of social decay—then the pictures made in Hollywood will reflect, in however distorted a form, that very situation."[75]

Howe's précis not only summarizes the methodological assumptions that would underpin *From Caligari to Hitler* and gain Kracauer recognition as pioneering a new approach to the popular medium of cinema; it also serves as a reminder of the continuities between Kracauer's thinking during the 1940s and his work in the late 1920s and early 1930s, when, following the publication of his landmark study *Die Angestellten* (The Salaried Masses) in 1930, he moved decisively to the left. His film reviews and essays in the *feuilleton* of the *Frankfurter Zeitung*, moreover, had established his reputation as a cultural critic, a "physiognomist" with a gift for a particular kind of phenomenological analysis.[76] Responding to one such essay (on the fate of the piano), Walter Benjamin described Kracauer's method as "tracing the downfall of the petit-bourgeois class in a notable, 'loving' description of its [material] legacy."[77] In his glowing review of *Die Angestellten*, Benjamin further noted Kracauer's passion for "unmasking" *(entlarven)* social and cultural phenomena by penetrating them dialectically—which is another way of phrasing Kracauer's own, oft-cited commitment to attending to the surface manifestations of culture in order to deduce "the position that an epoch occupies in the historical process."[78]

In the same review, Benjamin crafted an image of Kracauer as a "rag-picker" sorting through the shards of the bourgeois era at the dawn of revolution. Kracauer clearly identified with this description of his method. In transit from late Weimar Germany via French exile to his "last station" in the United States, he may have cast off the revolutionary aspirations that Benjamin imputed to him, but the rag-picker's approach still informs the epistemology and method of his American writings, up to and including the posthumous book on history.[79] Such surface manifestations can be found not only in material objects and urban spaces (such as streets or arcades), but also, of course, in the cinema. Accordingly, Kracauer formulated programmatically in 1932 that "the film critic of note is conceivable only as a social critic. His mission is to unveil *[enthüllen]* the social images and ideologies hidden in mainstream films and through this unveiling to undermine the influence of the films wherever necessary."[80]

Readers of Kracauer's two monographs on film have often concluded that after his arrival in the United States he jettisoned this approach, with its ear for nuance and its attentiveness to the materials of culture. One contemporary reviewer of *Caligari* ventured that Kracauer had retreated to a "mixture of scholarly competence and 'Teutonic' profundity" to exact a "refugee's revenge" on the very films that had constituted his lifeline as a critic during the Weimar Republic. Even Kracauer's most well-meaning readers today have come to see *Theory of Film* as a "painful caricature of the German scholarly mind in exile."[81] But a different picture emerges if we triangulate these two monographs with Kracauer's essays from the same years. Without wishing away the often justified critiques of the film books, we would suggest that the essays attenuate the force of those critiques in that they allow us to see continuities instead of ruptures, gradual transformation instead of outright repudiation of earlier approaches, the integration of new insights rather than wholesale reversals.[82]

The same goes for Kracauer's political positions, which are inadequately grasped in terms of an exiled Marxist's self-reinvention as an anticommunist cold warrior who "made certain that all traces of his former political convictions vanished from his work."[83] Here, too, we would not deny the realignments that Kracauer underwent over the years, but we would read them again as the more gradual attenuation of a political position that had never been strident but certainly found its most forceful articulation in Kracauer's left-leaning cultural critique during the late Weimar Republic. The years of exile, certainly including those in France, surely made Kracauer more cautious politically, and his alignment with U.S. government agencies during the 1940s and 1950s speaks to an enthusiasm for certain aspects of American life and politics that he shared with many of the renegade New York Intellectuals during the cold war. His essays allow us to chart the gradations in these changes and to mark out the limits of Kracauer's epistemological as well as political shift.

Regarding his politics, these limits consist of a principled humanism that emanates from his earliest Weimar writings onward and does not deserve the constraining modifier of "cold war" that some have ascribed to his later work. Such a conclusion is borne out by the critical undertones of "Hollywood's Terror Films," as well as by Kracauer's sustained critique of the cult of psychoanalysis during the 1940s, which consistently resisted the individualization of social issues. But the humanist position finds its ultimate expression, to be sure, in his profoundly resonant and under-read posthumous work on history.

Regarding his method, the émigré Kracauer remained true to Kracauer the Weimar critic in his enduring attention to detail, to the forms and materials of culture. Looking back, Kracauer would describe this as his lifelong purpose of "rehabilitat[ing] . . . objectives and modes of being which still lack a name and hence are overlooked or misjudged."[84] Indeed, we find persistent reference across his American writings to this motif of attending to minutiae in order to reveal (and, in the language of *Theory of Film*, "redeem") their broader social and cultural meanings. Thus, we should consider the emphasis on inanimate objects, whether in "Hollywood's Terror Films," in Jean Vigo's lyrical cinema, in the comedies of silent film, or in the films he was re-viewing at MoMA, in the light of Kracauer's *feuilletons* on material culture for the *Frankfurter Zeitung*. And we can glean the formulation of Kracauer's own method of cultural critique as well as its averred goals from book and film reviews published in the United States: reviewing a 1941 book on Hollywood (ch. 29), Kracauer lauds the author Leo Rosten for his "construction within the materials themselves"—by which he means an attention to detail and analysis that eschews top-down theorizing. He might as well have been referring to his own method in *Die Angestellten, The Mass Ornament, Theory of Film,* or *History*.

These same methodological assumptions underpin most of Kracauer's critical interventions in essays published during the 1940s, right up to his 1950 critique of Preston Sturges with this programmatic statement: "Nothing should be taken more seriously than entertainment that ingratiates itself with the anonymous millions. Mass attitudes of far-reaching consequence often find an outlet in seemingly insignificant pleasures."[85] As with all of Kracauer's writings during these years, however, the Weimar resonances constitute only one vector along which they deserve to be reread; the other is, once again, the New York context, where the intellectuals' discovery of European modernism was coupled with a nervous attention to popular or "mass" culture. Although this topic was eschewed by some of the more rigidly mandarin thinkers, others—including the likes of Clement Greenberg, Dwight Macdonald, Robert Warshow, and later Leslie Fiedler and Susan Sontag—paid careful attention to everything from dime novels and horror comics to Soviet kitsch. If they arrived at markedly different evaluations of the threats and promises of mass culture, they nevertheless agreed with Kracauer and numerous other émigré intellectuals from the Frankfurt School on the importance of offering careful analysis not just of modernist, "high" culture, but of "low" cultural forms as well.[86]

MASSCULT, MIDCULT, MOVIES

Kracauer's principal contribution to the debates among New York Intellectuals was in the realm of cinema, whose role as a mass medium was hotly debated among these groups. Besides the pressing issue of Stalinism (including debates about anti-Communism, and anti-anti-Communism), few concerns animated the New York Intellectuals more during the 1940s and 1950s than the distinction between modernism and popular culture, or high and mass culture.⁸⁷ Clement Greenberg launched the opening volley in response to a *Partisan Review* piece on Soviet cinema by Dwight Macdonald. Greenberg's now (in)famous 1939 article, "Avant-Garde and Kitsch," drew the line between the avant-garde that "moves" and academicist kitsch that "stands still."⁸⁸ From here it was a short step to the indictment of mass culture as a "parasitic, cancerous growth" (Macdonald), a standardized product to pacify the masses.⁸⁹ With their pronounced affinities for the avant-garde and modernism in the arts, the New York Intellectuals worried out loud about the convergence of high and mass culture, the way that the modernist forms of the Bauhaus, for example, "trickled down, in a debased form of course, into our furniture, cafeterias, movie theatres, electric toasters, office buildings, drug stores, and railroad trains."⁹⁰ What concerned critics like Greenberg, Macdonald, and Howe, in short, was the apparent blurring of cultural boundaries, effecting a "merger" between high and low that, in Macdonald's alarmist prose, yielded "a tepid, flaccid Middlebrow Culture that threatens to engulf everything in its spreading ooze." Along with radio and pulp magazines, the cinema was singled out for its "deadening and warping effect," a "culture-pattern" that was being "stamped deep into the modern personality."⁹¹

For all their incisive rhetoric, these positions suffered from their intransigent stance, their inability to account for the material that they dismissed or to develop their theories in response to the changing historical functions of mass culture.⁹² Like the contemporaneous critique of the culture industry by Adorno and Horkheimer in their own *Zeitschrift für Sozialforschung* and in the later *Dialectic of Enlightenment*, which was referenced in a number of contributions at the time, the New York Intellectuals' theory of Mass Culture dismissed the popular—and especially the more pernicious middlebrow—as "imposed from above. It is fabricated by technicians hired by businessmen; its audiences are passive consumers, their participation limited to the choice between buying and not buying."⁹³

But here, as on other issues, the New York Intellectuals spoke not with one voice; rather, the lasting appeal of their writings resides in its agonistic character, its spirit of open—if occasionally overheated—debate.⁹⁴ Flanked by Adorno and Horkheimer in the wings, writers like Greenberg, Howe, and Macdonald generally stood on one side of this debate. But we might find Macdonald on the other side as well, in his role as an insightful and witty commentator on the movies.

Also on the editorial board of *Commentary*, wielding an equally sharp pen, was Robert Warshow, a brilliant critic who died too young to be remembered as a major contributor to the debates of the times. In retrospect, Kracauer's various interventions communicate most closely with Warshow's cultural criticism, sometimes through explicit reference,[95] and occasionally even overlapping to the point of direct competition for publication space.[96] As the posthumous anthology of his writings plainly shows, Warshow was considerably less worried about the blurred boundaries between high and low culture than was Greenberg or (at times) Macdonald. Emphasizing the "actual, immediate experience of seeing and responding to the movies as most of us see them and respond to them," Warshow advocated—and practiced—a kind of phenomenology of popular culture that shares a number of features with Kracauer's work from the Weimar years through *Theory of Film*. Writing about the power of the movies, Warshow candidly admitted that "in some way, I take all that nonsense seriously."[97]

In retrospect, and in the context of the New York Intellectuals' predilections, Warshow's attitude seems entirely fitting; moreover, it resonates deeply with Kracauer's contributions. Like Kracauer, Warshow advocated a criticism of popular culture that "finds its best opportunity in the movies, which are the most highly developed and engrossing of the popular arts, and which seem to have an almost unlimited power to absorb and transform the discordant elements of our fragmented culture."[98] If this programmatic statement evokes Kracauer's assessment of cinema's power to "redeem" physical reality in the face of modern abstraction, it also engages directly with his analysis of Hollywood in the early 1940s, and of Italian neorealism in the latter part of the decade.

In the "little magazines" of the New York Intellectuals, contributions on film jostled for very limited space.[99] But the 1950s were a decade of experimentation in film publishing. Kracauer's years in America therefore fall into a formative period between the beginnings of the U.S. study of film—which Dana Polan and Peter Decherney both date to the years prior to the founding of the film library at MoMA[100]—and the institutionalization of film studies.[101] During these years, Kracauer was manifestly at the epicenter of film study by virtue of his association with the film library, which led to the publication of *Caligari*. In this regard, he participated in a broader movement that Decherney has persuasively chronicled in terms of the collaboration between Hollywood and the "culture elite" working in museums and government agencies and within the academy.

As Decherney notes, this was "largely a New York story," in which MoMA, the Rockefeller Foundation, and Columbia University played leading roles. Well before Kracauer's arrival in the city, that story had already taken shape around the central concern of how to understand and shape the relation between cinema and national identity—in Decherney's provocative terms: how to handle cinema as a "technology of citizenship." Kracauer's work on propaganda, on the representation of national types in Hollywood films, and on the psycho-cultural history of pre-Hitler German cinema, in other words, helped define the terms of this rich discourse.

As the essays reprinted in this volume clearly suggest, Kracauer contributed to the emergence of film studies as we know it today. His writing falls into a period that saw the elaboration of standards for the study of film—including protocols for historiography, auteur study, avant-garde criticism, and, of course, the elaboration of critical models, to which Kracauer contributed decisively by virtue of his method of symptomatic reading and his realist theory of film. It is worth noting, indeed, that while other critics with whom Kracauer was in dialogue throughout the 1940s and 1950s were undoubtedly more famous at the time, they did not have the same lasting impact on the discipline as Kracauer. That said, while the critical work of his contemporaries such as Macdonald, Warshow, and Agee has meanwhile been anthologized,[102] Kracauer's contributions to the same journals in which these important critics placed their work have, for too long, remained unread. For from Kracauer's American essays there emerges a richly layered portrait of the émigré critic, indeed of postwar intellectual culture, including the protean field of cinema studies, at mid-century. Having appeared in scattered publications at irregular intervals, this body of work by an important cultural critic of the twentieth century has largely languished in the archives. Half a century on, it deserves to be revisited by an English-language readership.

PART I

A Cultural Critic in New York
Between Hollywood and Europe

This section collects Kracauer's broad-ranging contributions on cultural questions of the war and postwar era, through the 1950s. Published in a variety of venues—from general-interest magazines such as *Harper's* to more academic journals such as *Public Opinion Quarterly*, and from specialized periodicals on film and theater to the influential *Commentary*—the articles tackle an array of subjects, including current trends in Hollywood, the work of filmmakers such as Jean Vigo and Preston Sturges, the popularization of psychoanalysis, the role of Jewish culture in postwar America, and the usurpation of the humanities by quantitative methods adopted from the natural and social sciences. Throughout, Kracauer elaborates a form of cultural critique that harks back to his influential and similarly varied analyses during the Weimar era, even as he adjusts his critical vocabulary to the American political and cultural context.

The section opens with a programmatic essay on French and American cinema (ch. 1), which provides a glimpse into Kracauer's own position as a recent émigré (see our introduction to this volume). "Why France Liked Our Films" works through theoretical motifs that will continue to occupy Kracauer during the following decades, taking definitive shape in the two books for which he is now best remembered. Observations on the cinematographic and narrative "paralysis" in French cinema, for instance, prepare the ground for similar analysis of Weimar-era films in *From Caligari to Hitler* (1947); and the characterization of Hollywood as a particularly "realistic" cinema will resonate in *Theory of Film* (1960)—though by the time Kracauer's long-projected "book on film aesthetics" was published, the argument about realism had modulated significantly, due in part to the arrival of Italian neorealism, which Kracauer, much like his contemporary André Bazin, greeted with theoretical enthusiasm.

Readers familiar with Kracauer's books will recognize correspondences between his essays and the two book-length works in other instances as well. With its discussion of endlessness, "inanimate nature," and "camera reality," an article on the French filmmaker Jean Vigo (ch. 3) explores motifs that resonate later in *Theory of Film*—a connection that is all the more remarkable for the fact that Kracauer wrote this piece as early as February 1940 in France for publication in the *Baseler National-Zeitung*. (We include here the English translation as it appeared seven years later in *Hollywood Quarterly*, the forerunner to today's *Film Quarterly*.) Similarly, "The Mirror Up to Nature" (ch. 10), written for the British *Penguin Review*, adumbrates the main concern of *Theory of Film:* realism. Here, however, Kracauer treats this concept not so much in terms of an ontology of cinema, or cinema's inherent "affinities" to particular aspects of reality; rather, the argument proceeds by way of a stylistic and ideological comparison of different *approaches* to cinematic storytelling in Hollywood and Europe, where life in bombed-out cities "is more exciting than it is here." Although the critique of Hollywood's escapism may strike some as facile (and will be revised, as Kracauer refines the arguments that culminate in *Theory of Film*), the *parti pris* for realism, for an approach to film that holds the mirror up to nature remains compelling as a historically specific critical stance. In a departure from "Why France Liked Our Films," his argument culminates, as it will also in *Theory of Film*, in a celebration of Italian neorealism and of cinema's turn to "authenticity" and "experience."

Other articles, such as "Those Movies with a Message" (ch. 8), "National Types as Hollywood Presents Them" (ch. 9), and "The Decent German" (ch. 24 in part II), belong more clearly to the *Caligari* complex, with its emphasis on psychological predispositions, national identity, and a psychosocial reading of cinema. "Those Movies with a Message" analyzes eleven postwar Hollywood films that ostensibly express "liberal" or "progressive" themes, from *None but the Lonely Heart* (USA 1944, dir. Clifford Odets) to *The Best Years of Our Lives* (USA 1946, dir. William Wyler) to *Gentleman's Agreement* (USA 1947, dir. Elia Kazan). Kracauer scrutinizes the films' tropes of individual suffering and heroism, finding social and political implications that complicate, if not undermine, the films' intended messages. "Instead of showing the strength of liberalism," Kracauer concludes, these films "testify to its extreme fragility." As in "National Types as Hollywood Presents Them" and other articles of the time (e.g., "Psychiatry for Everything and Everybody," ch. 7; or "The Revolt Against Rationality," ch. 4), Kracauer's critique of Hollywood's pseudo-liberalism and its trend toward political apathy and anti-intellectualism is undergirded by his continued investment in the project of enlightenment—an investment in recovering nonalienated forms of reason, or *Vernunft*. Clearly, this is an investment Kracauer shares with his fellow émigrés from the Frankfurt School, who at the time were formulating the most penetrating critique of the enlightenment's internal contradictions.[1]

One of the key texts of these years is Kracauer's 1946 article "Hollywood's Terror Films" (ch. 2).[2] This piece, too, echoes the work the author was doing contemporaneously on *From Caligari to Hitler*—he finds the same motifs of terror and sadism that he detects in Fritz Lang's Weimar-era films, for example—but with a twist: rather than pre-Hitler Germany (or even post-Hitler Germany, as in "The Decent German"), the frame of reference here is the postwar United States. Kracauer further historicizes this context by pitting the gratuitous terror he detects in contemporary Hollywood against its productive use in the anti-Nazi films of the war years. In keeping with our goal of presenting Kracauer's work in their proper historical context, we reproduce the article here in the form in which it appeared in *Commentary*, despite Kracauer's extreme displeasure with the interventions exerted by the journal's editors. In retrospect, the author's worries strike us as overly protective of his own text (spurred, perhaps, by the nasty spat with Adorno over a piece on propaganda a few years earlier).[3] To be sure, not all emendations to the submitted manuscript were necessarily to the better, but they generally betray the mark of a stylist imposing his stamp, not that of an editor falsifying an argument, as Kracauer complained in a letter to Barbara Deming.[4]

If Kracauer began his American career in 1941 with a celebration of Hollywood in "Why France Liked Our Films," he became far more sanguine about the dream factory over the course of the decade. We can trace this disenchantment through the articles on Hollywood's phony liberalism and its sadistic leanings all the way to the 1950 critique of Preston Sturges (ch. 11), which recapitulates this decline in a consideration of one director's oeuvre. Having introduced a still-dialectical critique of Sturges in the 1949 article "The Mirror Up to Nature," Kracauer now fleshes out his criticism without the hesitation discernible a year earlier. He identifies *Sullivan's Travels* (USA 1941) as the turning point in Sturges's work, when the filmmaker retreated from the socially progressive territory marked out by his earlier films and self-consciously placed his comedic genius in the service of conformity. Registering his regret that Sturges failed to "resurrect the slapstick world of the past," as he easily could have, Kracauer detects in Sturges's later work the outlines of what Herbert Marcuse had decried, in the Frankfurt School's *Zeitschrift für Sozialforschung*, as affirmative culture.[5] From the point of view of enlightenment, Kracauer points out that the problem is not that Sturges makes audiences laugh, but that he uses satire and social critique for mere farce, thus "dulling the edges of a first-rate weapon of human liberation." As in the case of "Hollywood's Terror Films," we reprint here the version as originally published (in *Films in Review*), though in this case the divergences from the original manuscript, preserved in the Marbach archive, are substantial enough to warrant reference; we accordingly indicate divergences and restore omitted passages in the notes to the piece.

In addition to the published articles from the 1940s and 1950s, this section also contains several drafts—some, like a piece titled "On Jewish Culture" (ch. 5), advanced to the stage of page proofs for *Commentary*—and notes that remained unpublished during Kracauer's lifetime but were carefully filed in his extensive *Nachlass*. A short assessment called "Art Today" (ch. 12) mounts a critique of the reification of high culture, returning us to persistent motifs in Kracauer's thinking from the Weimar years onward—among them a sustained interest in photography ("the surest means of possessing the Parthenon columns is to use them as background to a picture of wife and daughter"), as well as the idea of *geistige Obdachlosigkeit*, rendered by Kracauer as the "ideological shelterlessness" of modern man, a motif that returns at the climax of *Theory of Film*.

Other interventions are more obviously topical, tied to observations of the contemporary academic scene, for example, as in his notes on the state of the humanities (ch. 13). Kracauer was able to hone these observations not only through extensive, first-hand experience as a reviewer for grant foundations but also, from the late 1950s onward, through numerous conversations with fellow intellectuals, especially during his annual trips to Europe. His resulting diagnosis of an "imperialism of the exact science trend," as well as his principled advocacy of "nonquantitative insight," links up with a substantive methodological reflection on "qualitative content analysis" that Kracauer published in *Public Opinion Quarterly* in 1952.[6]

Finally, we include in this section the full text of Kracauer's notes on a "talk with Teddy" that took place in Switzerland, where he and Adorno came together during the Kracauers' summer visit of August 1960. The notes are clearly intended for personal reference, and undoubtedly form the basis for Kracauer's argument against "Adorno's unfettered dialectics" in *History: The Last Things Before the Last*.[7] However, the document remains significant in its own right, not only as a record of the relationship between Adorno and Kracauer (triangulated here, no less, with Benjamin), but also as an indication of Kracauer's own position on central concepts and concerns of critical theory—including the question of utopia, ontology, dialectics, and the relation of philosophy and social critique.[8]

1 Why France Liked Our Films
(1942)

What would an intelligent European observer learn about American life from American films? I feel somewhat disquieted by the necessity of operating in the field of rather personal impressions, but fortunately the ground is solid: it is an incontestable fact that throughout the last decade the American film continued to attract the intellectual elite in Europe. True, Hollywood exported mainly grade A pictures to France—pictures that had no difficulty in competing with the bulk of the average home-made talkies. But their power of enchanting European spectators was due not so much to their comparative perfection as to certain specific traits that those spectators missed in their native productions.

What did they miss? As early as 1919 Louis Delluc, one of the pioneers of the French film, vented the dark prophecy: "I should like to believe that we shall eventually make good films. It would be very surprising, for the cinema is not in our blood.... I prophesy—we shall see in the future if I am right—that France has no more aptitude for the cinema than for music."[1]

In the meantime, such great French directors as René Clair, the late Jean Vigo, Jean Renoir, Julien Duvivier and others have achieved many a picture that belongs to the classical works of the screen. However, these are rather the exceptions, and on the whole Delluc's criticism proves right: the typical French film, and especially the French talkie of the past ten years, is far from embodying the essential possibilities inherent in that mode of expression; it reveals a mentality that would make itself manifest far better on the stage or in literature.

There is a sensible lack of action and movement in the French films. While looking at any of them, one feels that they arise from a mind not accustomed to wide spaces and to events with which the film camera is concerned. Old cultural and artistic traditions press upon this mind, so that it has lost the immediate contact with a more primitive world and prefers psychic experiences to those crude adventures and sudden changes that young, naive people enjoy. The French soul is cultivated and stationary like the charming French country, which does not inspire thoughts of long distances, overwhelming catastrophes or exciting discoveries. Characteristically, even the many films of the French Legion have rarely succeeded in materializing the enormous extension of the French Empire in Africa. Of course, such impassivity is not adequate for the medium of the cinema. It seems to me that during the pre-war period the political situation in France contributed much to transform that natural attitude into a sort of stagnation. As life slowed down, many an effective theme became too dangerous to be presented on the screen. The preference given then to films showing in a more or less literary way some crime and allowing Jean Gabin to work his spell as a good bad man can be explained by the urgent need for action. One escaped to the underworld because in the higher strata of society all was paralysed. Or the French film producers proceeded in the same manner as the French literates: they immoderately intensified the atmosphere to make it a substitute for movement. Frequently French films of those years contained nothing but atmosphere, realized through beautiful pictures which sought to conceal the deficiencies of the plot.

These films also neglected the material details—all those objects and gestures that are so important on the screen, and which only the camera is able to detect and endow with significance. Toward the end of the silent era it was precisely the French avant-garde that insisted upon showing hitherto unseen phenomena and composing them into strange pictures. But as soon as the talkies appeared, this tendency weakened more and more, and those films began to prevail which avoided trespassing the limits of our visual conventions. While the story they told was sometimes touching and of human interest, their methods of narration changed nothing of the normal image of the world. The little things remained little; the actors occupied the foreground.

This practice was strengthened by the absolute predominance of the dialogue. From time immemorial French people have been devoted to delicacy of literary language, and love nothing more than to taste a witticism, a well-calculated antithesis. Hence the French talkies tried to charm their native audiences with long conversations and explications that had been polished by Jacques Prévert or some other stylist. Such films as *Entrée des Artistes* [France 1938, dir. Marc Allégret], for instance, in which the flood of words submerged the pictures, became the delight of audiences. In consequence, the screen approached the stage and the pictures functioned as mere illustrations. Whereas the development of a true film depends upon the meaning of its pictures, in these films the dialogue alone determined the progress of the action. And since the words usually convey multifold traditional associations, even original pictures had scarcely any opportunity to pierce the dense cover of conventions that enveloped them. They simply followed the course of the words instead of directing it.

In 1937, Valerio Jahier wrote in an excellent essay on the history of motion pictures: "Let us imagine for a moment that tomorrow one would no longer be able to produce or to show films. We do not believe that French prestige would diminish then. On the other hand, we would have the impression that America suddenly has become silent. . . . For in America, cinema is in the blood."[2] This was the way in which many Europeans felt about the contrast between French and American films. And it was quite natural that to them the Hollywood pictures appeared as the manifestation of movement and life. Where else but in the Western do real horses gallop over real plains? They are representative of the swiftness of action, and, what is more important, this action, typical of American films, answers the demands of the film camera in that it extends over the whole material dimension and precisely includes that sector of reality which can be called camera reality. Even since the days of Mack Sennett, the people on the street, staircases, vehicles—all the apparently insignificant objects of everyday life—have been an essential part of the plot. This close contact with the external world enables Hollywood to show situations, events and inter-relations that are inaccessible to any other form of art. Thus little details, those usually disappearing among the mass of impressions, are given all the importance they deserve: I recall the repeatedly inserted gag with the prepared cigars and matches in *The Bowery* [USA 1933, dir. Raoul Walsh] and the "leit-motif" of the broken drinking-glasses in *One Way Passage* [USA 1932, dir. Tay Garnett]. Thus chance continuously plays its role—chance, the intervention of which indicates that the story is not skipping the various accidents of life. Illuminating in this respect is the opening sequence of *San Francisco* [USA 1936, dir. W. S. Van Dyke].[3] Amidst the street crowd on New-Year's Eve Gable and MacDonald happen to pass each other without suspecting yet that their destinies are to be joined. Thus the desire to follow material developments to their extremes leads to the inclusion of natural catastrophes and horrors, phenomena that could never be represented in art. The earthquake sequence in *San Francisco* and the hurricane in the film of that name [*The Hurricane*, USA 1937, dir. John Ford] are symptomatic.

To sum up: it is the sense of realism in the American film that attracted the European spectator surrounded by pictures of quite another attitude.

He sensed that those films in annexing new provinces of the visible world achieved one of the special missions of the cinema, and then he loved them, too, as a continual demonstration of the American conception of life. All American films seemed to reveal to him the direct and realistic way in which Americans feel, think and behave. And thanks to that basic trait which always came through, whatever Hollywood picture was shown, he learned from it—or thought he had learned—numerous facts about every-day life in America.

To be exact: it was the backgrounds in these films rather than their stories which were the main source of information. Many a picture turned out to be a blank; but even the most avidly commercial nullities frequently happened to contain some well-observed moment of life. How palpable became the Main Street of a few decades ago in the first part of *Stella Dallas* [USA 1937, dir. King Vidor]; how dense was, in *Back Street* [USA 1932, dir. John Stahl], the atmosphere of a little town's old-fashioned garden concerts. The rooming house scenes in this latter film, accompanied by the awful noise from an adjacent building under construction, were so instructive as to supersede long sociological essays on this theme. May I mention, too, those scenes from the completely average film *Mannequin* [USA 1937, dir. Frank Borzage] in which Joan Crawford, walking down a cheap staircase, switches off, from habit, the bulb, and afterwards, in the elevated train, talks and talks to her young lover. Behind such fragments of New York life the immense city itself seems to appear. Other films stressed other regions: *Our Daily Bread* [USA 1934, dir. King Vidor] turned to the land, and *Jezebel* [USA 1938, dir. William Wyler] introduced us to the customs of the South. Incidents of mere fiction, all these realistic inserts functioned nevertheless as documents. In the eyes of Europeans, even the American fiction film was set against the background of real life.

Nor is the realism confined to the backgrounds alone: it characterizes several cycles of Hollywood pictures that impressed Paris as particularly vivid portraits of American types. I think of the gangster films, so rich in discoveries; among them Raft's coin-tossing gunman[4] and the hints at the close connection between that special kind of criminal and life with posters, paper streamers and illuminated advertisements. There were a number of boxing films too, considerably augmenting the knowledge of popular pleasures in America;[5] and I remember the audiences in the theatres of the Paris Boulevard Rochechouart which, as true experts, loudly judged the pugilistic fine points in these films. And, too, a wave of such reporter films as *Hi, Nellie!* [USA 1934, dir. Mervyn LeRoy], *The Front Page* [USA

1931, dir. Lewis Milestone] and so on, in which reporters were presented as rather disturbing and quite obtrusive beings, but at the same time as courageous heroes who, at the decisive moment, solve a complicated murder or a faked bankrupt[cy] case—for Europeans this was a strange aspect of that profession. One saw them run around, shout at one another, and typewrite side by side in tremendous, noisy rooms where no one could possibly be concentrated; yet despite this chaos the newspaper never failed to appear and to prosper. The breathless confusion of the editor's offices seemed to mirror that of American business life in general.[6] Equally vigorous were the detectives who populated the screen; and in films like *[The] Citadel* [USA 1938, dir. King Vidor], the camera focussed upon the work of the medical profession. From bankers to workers, all social strata came into being—not forgetting the joys of the idle rich, tirelessly depicted for the sake of those who could not share them.

But if American films are based upon a realistic conception of the world, a comparatively few content themselves with simply echoing it. In this context, the parade of historical pictures is without interest, except for those that, in the form of elaborate Westerns, deal with the construction of the first Trans-Pacific railroad and the rush toward the West, or, like *The Bowery* and *Barbary Coast* [USA 1935, dir. Howard Hawks], describe the rough, colonial manners of the still uncivilized cities. To Europeans, apt to distinguish between poetry and truth, such illustrated primers were valuable object lessons on America's past. As for the films devoted to contemporaneous behaviour, the spectator in Paris was particularly impressed by certain Hollywood productions treating social problems with a frankness that would have been impossible in France after 1933. That *Mr. Deeds Goes to Town* [USA 1936, dir. Frank Capra] or *Dead End* [USA 1937, dir. William Wyler] dared to face such problems, was one of the reasons for their European success; they broke the rule of neutrality that weighed upon the French cinema. At the same time they furnished much enlightenment as to the political thinking and social struggle in America. As the substance of the French republican mind vanished more and more from the screen, these pictures testified to the strength of American democracy, and it did not matter so much that they were often naive, like *You and Me* [USA 1938, dir. Fritz Lang], or side-stepped the very point in question, like *You Can't Take It with You* [USA 1938, dir. Frank Capra].[7] They usually featured the optimistic attitude of Americans toward an indefinite progress and their firm belief in individual values. Burdened by complicated traditions and helpless in the face of their own actual problems European observers often condemned such views as inadequate simplifications; on the other hand, however, they could not prevent themselves from envying that simplicity and admiring the unhesitating confidence and directness with which Americans apparently try to overcome all obstacles. And were the shadows denied? Such important films as *I Am a Fugitive [from a Chain Gang]* [USA 1932, dir. Mervyn LeRoy][8] and *You Only Live Once* [USA 1937, dir. Fritz Lang] prove the contrary, and frequently the attached happy ending presented itself as an intentional fairy tale conclusion, as in *Winterset* [USA 1936, dir. Alfred Santell].

Interesting aspects were opened, too, by the treatment of erotic and psychological themes on the screen. I fancy that the influence of American films on the course of European love affairs can scarcely be overestimated. Continuously inflecting the question of how boys manage to meet girls, they determined the poise, the gestures and words of innumerable young people who, caught up in the enormous process of social change, lived in a sort of void, and yet needed models to follow as a substitute for lost conventions. Whenever Garbo made her entrance in the cheap theatres, thousands of little sales-girls left those theatres as Garbos. But the point here is rather what did these films show of American love habits? I should say that female types appeared in them with a kind of sex appeal unknown in Europe; it was the outcome of an almost mechanized surface under the cover of which one sensed, however, a nature rich in charming impulses. Europeans perhaps wondered at the obvious shyness with which the young American lover approached the subject of his intimate feelings—a behaviour that certainly could not be attributed only to the efforts of the Hays' office. Love occurs in a world regulated by unwritten laws and full of individual destinies. Insight into its structure was given through many a film that appealed to the psychological understanding. One learned from *These Three* [USA 1936, dir. William Wyler] or *Back Street* something about the might of social conventions and prejudices in America and in *Dodsworth* [USA 1936, dir. William Wyler], for instance, peered behind the scenes of marriages that seemingly were models of success and harmony. In America no less than in Europe, marriages frequently became mere routine, leaving nothing but resignation or the urge to escape. Perhaps the devastating influence of an all-consuming business life on private happiness was especially emphasized in the American film.

This superficial survey would be incomplete without a side-glance at the more or less sophisticated film comedies that were the rage in the years before the outbreak of war. Lubitsch and Capra had furnished the pattern for those gay plays in which sporty (and apparently wealthy) youth mingled with adventurers and talkative elder women, who all made love and improvised rather useless activities with the result that audacious gags were needed to disentangle the ensuing complications. *Nothing Sacred* [USA 1937, dir. William Wellman] and *Theodora Goes Wild* [USA 1936, dir. Richard Boleslawski] belonged to that kind of screen fun, featuring often Carole Lombard, Billie Burke and such young men as Cary Grant and James Stewart. Typical of American humour, they incidentally ridiculed social customs and standardized types and excelled in a witty dialogue revealing the pronounced feeling of American audiences for satire and mockery. Except for René Clair's unforgettable works, the French film comedy never reached the level of these Hollywood pictures which were, of course, stage plays rather than films. This was the more astonishing to Europeans, since the whole species was originated partly in the Paris *vaudeville*. One had to acknowledge that the Hollywood comedy flourishes less in Paris than in Hollywood.

To answer the question whether those impressions gathered in Europe stand the test in this country is not at all easy. The perspective through which American life is viewed on European screens is determined and framed by the reactions to the native European productions. If in the years before the war the French film had been marked by other characteristics, other segments of American reality would no doubt have pushed themselves forward. There is only one short moment in which the European observer can judge the validity of the image of American life he had received in European theatres: the moment of his arrival in this country. As a newcomer, he is still entirely connected with the Old World and thus can compare his fresh impressions on American soil with the pictures in his mind. These first impressions are rather superficial; but unfortunately, the more he succeeds in deepening them, the more he is unable to verify those brought over from Europe. It is not so much that they become transformed into pale reminiscences as for quite another reason: the newcomer establishes himself in America, and soon his contacts with the customs of this country are too intimate to permit dispassionate reflections about American life. The whole perspective changes. He is involved in that life, and his reactions are no longer those of a spectator but of a participant. Their views can have no common denominator. Hence, a paradox arises: as soon as the former European acquires an opinion of American reality, he loses the possibility of using it to confirm or reject his old impressions. Probably many of them cannot be maintained here; but that says nothing against their validity in Europe.

To come back to that decisive moment—the marvelous first meeting with life in America. As we entered New York harbour, the strange feeling of having already seen all this began to grow upon me.[9] Each new sight was an act of recognition. We passed such old acquaintances as the Statue of Liberty, Ellis Island and the sky-line, which, however, in the vast sky looked smaller than I had imagined it from the pictures. Then the detective-inspectors came aboard, shouting "Take it easy!" and "Go ahead!," and afterwards the dock swarmed with reporters. To the passionate movie-goer it was like a dream: either he had been suddenly transplanted onto the screen or the screen itself had come into three-dimensional existence. Nor did the dream cease in New York, where other familiar types began to emerge from the crowd: the ice-cream man, the shoe-shine boy, the Salvation Army. All the things that had filled in the background of hundreds of American films proved to be true to life. The steps before the brownstone houses were as real as the furnished rooms, the miraculous drug stores and the splendid lobbies of the apartment houses one had suspected in Europe as mere studio settings.

This was the start—a convincing proof of the realistic power with which Hollywood pictures transmit everyday American life to people abroad. Then followed the slow process of personal adjustment, and with it that change of perspective mentioned above. In due course, things came out which obviously had been overlooked in these films. In New York, for instance, films neither take notice of Broadway in the morning, nor do they picture the hundreds of cross-town streets that end in the empty sky.[10] So far as I remember, there have been no shots either that bring out the various effects produced by high houses and sky-scrapers to break up the monotony of the long avenues. Evidently the same is true of the whole style of life. But it is no longer a European observer who is making these observations.

2 Hollywood's Terror Films
Do They Reflect an American State of Mind? (1946)

Films saturated with terror and sadism have issued from Hollywood in such numbers recently as to become commonplace. The trend undoubtedly had its source in the requirements of wartime propaganda. The original task was to depict the threat of Nazism to the American public—Gestapo tortures, shining parades that alternated with silent agonies, life under the oppressive atmosphere of Nazi-conquered Europe, etc. But even in wartime, the trend went beyond exposing brutality. Along with anti-Nazi films, a number of movies appeared that cultivated the same kind of horror sheerly for the sake of entertainment. And now, with the war over, the species continues to flourish and to increase.

Thrillers are a venerable type in the films. But the current vogue is unique in its predilection for familiar, everyday surroundings as the setting in which crime and violence occur. The criminals in *Shadow of a Doubt* [USA 1943, dir. Alfred Hitchcock] and Orson Welles' *The Stranger* [USA 1946] settle down in plain small towns, places where no one would ever dream of meeting a killer in the flesh. Nightmares are seen in bright daylight, murderous traps are sprung just around the corner. Everyday life itself breeds anguish and destruction. And at the same time the villains become more prepossessing; they charm innocent girls and win the confidence of guileless bank-tellers. The Frankenstein monsters of the past made us shudder at first sight, but the contemporary monster can live among us without being recognized. Evil no longer marks and defines a person's face or manner.

Thus the weird, veiled insecurity of life under the Nazis is transferred to the American scene. Sinister conspiracies incubate next door, within the world considered normal—any trusted neighbor may turn into a demon.

Despite Hollywood's old fondness for ruthless violence and for the raw and grotesque, the cruelty it now so obsessively depicts is of a kind rarely seen before on the screen. Now it originates from compulsive, sadistic urges, is less animal—one might say that it is less spontaneous. In *Dark Corner* [USA 1946, dir. Henry Hathaway], a private detective is pursued by a gunman; he captures his pursuer and smashes his hand to make him confess the reason for his pursuit. Later the gunman sneaks into the detective's apartment and knocks him down; as he is about to leave, he turns suddenly and steps with the full weight of his body on the hand of his unconscious victim. The same lust to inflict wanton pain manifests itself in the scene in *Lost Weekend* [USA 1945, dir. Billy Wilder] in which the drunkard, after a night spent in delirium brought on by alcohol, has a hallucination in which he sees a mouse gnawing a hole in a wall and trying in vain to squeeze through it; then a bat that has been hovering about the room pounces on the animal and kills it while it is caught in the hole. As the tiny shrieks of the mouse die away a rivulet of blood slowly trickles down the wall. It is a vision that reveals for a moment the tabooed depths of our bodily existence.

Titles such as *Shadow of a Doubt* and *Suspicion* [USA 1941] (both Hitchcock movies) are typical of the emphasis many recent productions place, not so much on outright sadism, as on the permanent menace of it. Apprehension is accumulated; threatening allusions and dreadful possibilities evoke a world in which everybody is afraid of everybody else, and no one knows when or where the ultimate and inevitable horror will arrive. When it does arrive it arrives unexpectedly: erupting out of the dark from time to time in a piece of unspeakable brutality. That panic which in the anti-Nazi films was characterized as peculiar to the atmosphere of life under Hitler now saturates the whole world.

The recent and already mentioned *Dark Corner* goes the limit in terrorizing the audience. The private detective cannot imagine why he should be trailed by a gunman and gropes desperately for the identity of his enemy, only to find out in the end that what is at issue has nothing to do with him: the power behind the scenes—an unscrupulous "master mind" intent on killing his wife's lover—has staged the hunt in order to shift suspicion from himself to the detective, whom he considers a suitable scapegoat. The effect of terror, however, is only heightened by this combination of meaningless suffering and arbitrary persecution.

Hand in hand with sadism in recent movies goes the morbid. Physical handicaps are elaborated upon and mental horror is added to crude violence. The main character of *The Spiral Staircase* [USA 1945, dir. Robert Siodmak] is a mute servant girl employed in the household of a maniac who murders physically imperfect women in order to improve the human race. *Spellbound* [USA 1945, dir. Alfred Hitchcock] and *Somewhere in the Night* [USA 1946, dir. Joseph L. Mankiewicz] exploit amnesia to build up suspense.

Also much favored is the theme of psychological destruction: the pianist in *Gaslight* [USA 1944, dir. George Cukor] and the psychiatrist in *Shock*

[USA 1946, Alfred L. Werker] no longer shoot, strangle, or poison the females they want to do away with, but systematically try to drive them insane. The tide in Hollywood has turned toward sick souls and fancy psychiatrists. And many a current melodrama suggests that normal and abnormal states of mind merge into each other imperceptibly and are hard to keep separate. The young lieutenant in *Shock* returns from the war to learn that his wife has been taken to a mental clinic. Was she not always healthy and full of good sense? A naive young man, he is frightened by the thought of what nature can do, unaccountably, to an ordinary person—and his fright makes the sympathetic audience realize that none of us is immune to mental disorders.

Thus, unlike the gangster movies of the depression era, the new films deal less with social abuses than with psychological aberrations. And this time the failure of the movies to offer or suggest solutions has become particularly striking; the all-pervasive fear that threatens the psychic integrity of the average person seems accepted as inevitable and almost inscrutable. Here a comparison between the recent Italian movie *Open City* [1945, dir. Roberto Rossellini] and the bulk of our American anti-Nazi films is highly illuminating.

Open City exhibits the horrors, mental and otherwise, met by the Italian resistance in its struggle against fascism, with an uninhibited realism generally foreign to similar Hollywood productions. A Communist is tortured to death before our eyes; sophisticated cruelty, depravity, sordidness, are shown with unimaginable intensity. But at the same time the Communist martyr's determination, the priest's faith, and Pina's [Anna Magnani] natural magnanimity are shown to us in such a way that they appear as real as the terror that engulfs them. In this "morality play"—which is what Dorothy Thompson calls *Open City*—human dignity is practiced, not merely proclaimed; and even though the resistance leaders are hopelessly doomed, the vital power of their convictions wears down Nazi morale.[1]

The American anti-Nazi films do not battle evil at such close quarters—as a rule they merely circumvent it. The heroes and heroines of such movies as *Edge of Darkness* [USA 1943, dir. Lewis Milestone], *This Land Is Mine* [USA 1943, dir. Jean Renoir], *Joan of Paris* [USA 1942, dir. Robert Stevenson], and others, endure Gestapo tortures no less bravely than the Italian partisans of *Open City*, but more often than not their victories are pure cloak-and-dagger acts that leave the enemy's ideological defenses intact.[2] Hitlerism, undermined in an essential sense in *Open City*, remains virtually undefeated in Hollywood films—which seem to walk on eggs the moment they approach the positive aspects of that which they defend. Impressive surveys of Nazi might in *Prelude to War* [USA 1943, dir. Frank Capra and Anatole Litvak] and others of the army morale films are contrasted with strangely evasive scenes from life under democracy that betray indecision rather than confidence, lip-service instead of action. In almost every one of the anti-Nazi movies made in Hollywood a character comes to the fore at some moment, appropriate or otherwise, to recite as if by rote a eulogy of the democratic life and of the brave new world to come. But a creed that had a real hold on its adherents would not need to be so explicitly and superficially proclaimed; it would be an intrinsic part and culmination of the drama of the whole film.

Among the movie thrillers without a political message, *Lost Weekend* stands out for its attempt to invest horror with meaning. The drunkard here, after a bout with delirium tremens, swears off drink. But this conversion comes only at the very end of the film and is much too sketchily rendered to efface the impression of his confirmed alcoholism. Thus it seems a sham conversion.

Nor is the drunkard's hallucination exhibited in order to account for his change of heart; on the contrary, the illusion of a change serves but as a pretext for wallowing in the details of the hallucination, which are savored, illicitly, for their own sake.

But most of the current thrillers do not even pretend to motivate or excuse or rationalize the introduction of sadistic horrors. The urgency of the emotional need that is at the present moment satisfied by vicarious participation in these specific varieties of cruelty, violence, and fear becomes sufficient excuse in itself. Such being the case, the happy endings by which the movies finally escape from their psychological horrors become even more meaningless than usual. The feeling of uneasiness stirred up in the audience at the spectacle of an everyday world full of totalitarian horrors is left unrelieved.[3] The sickness of the psyche is, essentially, taken for granted, and the impression remains that nothing can be done to cure it.

All these movies manifest an unusual interest in the physical environment against which their action unrolls. Chance arrangements of inanimate objects are made conspicuous, somber backgrounds assert themselves. In *The Spiral Staircase,* the scene of the maniac's first murder is a hotel room somewhere above an old-fashioned movie house; the opening sequence dwells on the ambiguous borderline between crime and pleasure by emphasizing the startling proximity of the two décors. One of the leitmotifs of *Dark Corner* is the staircase of a dilapidated rooming house at the foot of which a ragged little girl is forever blowing her penny whistle. The little girl, an apparition rather than a real person, seems to incarnate the rooming house's despondency. A similar staircase also marks a decisive turn in *Lost Weekend:* the drunkard falls down its whole length and then enters upon the final stage of his Calvary.

The last two movies feature Third Avenue and its iron-work, its bars and its pawnshops, as the region of anarchy and distress. (Significantly enough, shots of street life were also prominent in German films of the pre-Hitler Weimar Republic period that described the tragedies of instinct-possessed beings.) There is nothing accidental about this. People emotionally out of joint inhabit a realm ruled by bodily sensations and material stimulants, a realm in which dumb objects loom monstrously high and become signal posts or stumbling blocks, enemies or allies. This obtrusiveness of inanimate objects is infallible evidence of an inherent concern with mental disintegration.

But movies not only cater to popular demands; they also reflect popular tendencies and inclinations. The conclusion therefore would be that inner disintegration, whatever its stages, has actually become a widespread phenomenon. And the images persistently repeated on the screens of our movie theaters suggest that uncontrolled sadism and apprehensiveness are involved in this disintegration. The hope of winning "freedom from fear"[4] seems to stem from a great increase in feelings of fear. But here, with an impotence similar to that already remarked upon in their anti-Nazi versions, the present Hollywood thrillers are unable to demonstrate any counter-measures that would work to restore mental stability. The horrors are never incorporated in a meaningful pattern that would neutralize them. This would indicate that real life itself fails to suggest such a pattern. Whether society be a spiritual vacuum or a battlefield of irreconcilable beliefs, it seems no longer to provide a shelter for the individual, or principles that would compel his integrity.

In *The Three Caballeros* [USA 1944], Walt Disney—whose films reveal him as particularly sensitive to contemporary undercurrents of feeling—shows us a universe torn to pieces as though it had been hit by a cluster of atomic bombs. That shattered universe is symptomatic of the way we feel about the world now around us, as Barbara Deming has suggested in "The Artlessness of Walt Disney," a recent article in the *Partisan Review*.[5] Amid the debris of such a universe dark impulses are sure to find freer play.

If such is indeed our predicament, a general desire for some sort of inner restabilization or reconstruction would seem very natural. That this desire does exist is indicated by the popularity of two other types of films at present, along with the horror thrillers. One type dramatizes psychoanalytical healing to show how mental balance can be restored from within: half-magician, half-mechanic, the psychoanalyst or psychiatrist lifts the seventh veil from before his patient's soul, ponders the scattered fragments of that soul, and in no time at all fits the jigsaw puzzle together again, with the result that the patient once more functions normally—like a repaired watch.[6]

The other type of "therapeutic" movie shows us Catholic life, and intimates that reintegration may be obtained from without, under the ministrations of the Church. Chaotic civilization is confronted with the articulate community of the faithful, and understanding priests take over the care of those who lack for mental shelter. Canon Roche in *The Green Years* [USA 1946, dir. Victor Saville] likens his vocation to that of a doctor. "The mind is father of many ills," he says to a young man whom he wants to become a clergyman. "As a champion of truth, you cure the body as well as the soul." Exponents of wishful thinking, the screen priest as well as the screen psychoanalyst rise out of a reality in which things have fallen apart and the center no longer holds.

The problems to which these current trends in Hollywood film-making lead can barely be touched upon in the space of this brief article. That the kind of horror formerly attributed only to life under Hitler, in the anti-Nazi thrillers, has now been acclimated to the American scene, is more than accidental. Aside from the genuine and constant affinity between sadism and fascism, it seems probable that the sadistic energies at large in our society at the present moment are specifically suited to provide fuel for fascism. And it is in these energies, in this emotional preparedness for fascism, that the real danger lies, more than in the agitators and rabble-rousers who, when the circumstances are right, will be able to manipulate them for tangible ends. Hatred of minorities feeds on the fears of the majority, and unless these fears subside the hatred will continue to multiply.

The particular fear we have to deal with here springs, in the final analysis, from a crucial dilemma. Caught in the snarls of the free-enterprise system, we nevertheless view with apprehension the totalitarian potentialities inherent in any sort of planned economy. Democracy, with its individual freedom, seems economically out of joint, so that it must resort to makeshifts and breed nightmarish dreams of fascist pseudo-solutions worse than the ills they are intended to cure. Shall we be able to preserve individual freedom under collectivism?

In France, the traditional sanctuary of individual liberties, this sense of having reached an impasse is especially strong. Tormented by it, the Existentialists in the beginning wooed nothingness or indifference or fatality in a last-ditch stand against the powers closing in on the individual from all sides.

The political and social struggles of our time are not concerned merely with external changes and new borders—they involve the very core of our existence. A civil war is being fought inside every soul; and the movies reflect the uncertainties of that war in the form of general inner disintegration and mental disturbance.

Fear can be exorcised only by an incessant effort to penetrate it and spell out its causes. This is the prerequisite of redemption, even though the outcome may be unpredictable. It would be a hopeful sign if films were to appear in this country that, like *Open City*, really showed the principles of human integrity at grips with a deranged world[7]—and showed them as positive forces, with a reality at least equal, if not superior to, the forces of cruelty and violence and to the fear upon which these feed. Yet it remains for life to offer these principles and confirm their efficacy.

3 Jean Vigo
(1947)

INTRODUCTORY NOTE BY VLADIMIR POZNER

I saw Jean Vigo for the last time in the summer of 1934. He looked even younger than he was—an adolescent with a pointed face, about to die from tuberculosis. Very few people knew his name then, or his work. *A propos de Nice* [France 1930, dir. Jean Vigo] had been shown in a few theaters only, *Zéro de conduite* [France 1933, dir. Jean Vigo] had been considered too "harsh" for general release, and, if I am not mistaken, *[L']Atalante* [France 1934, dir. Jean Vigo] had not yet been released. As a rule, rebels are not popular, and in the motion picture industry probably less so than anywhere else. And Vigo was a rebel, on two counts: against the screen formulas and, even more intensely, against the established order of things. He used the camera as a weapon, not as an anesthetic.

In today's France, Vigo's pictures are shown in the neighborhood theaters.

JEAN VIGO

Jean Vigo—who died before he was thirty, in the autumn of 1934—left only a few films. His first film, *A propos de Nice*, can only be mentioned here, since for years it has been inaccessible. In 1933, this satirical documentary was followed by *Zéro de conduite*, a film influenced by René Clair and the French avant-garde, depicting a students' revolt in a boarding school. The brief series ends with *Atalante* (1934), a masterpiece that brought Vigo to the forefront of French motion picture directors. Among them, perhaps only Vigo and the René Clair of the great Parisian films have been able to discover and conquer territories reserved exclusively to the film. And although Vigo lacks Clair's wonderful lightness, he surpasses him in his profound concern with truth.

His very method of composition reveals an original relation to the screen. Vigo's plots are not the classic, hermetically sealed constructions designed to produce suspense by themselves alone; rather, they are slight, very loosely knit, and not at all purposeful. The plot of *Atalante* could not be simpler: Jean, the young master of the river steamer "Atalante," has married Juliette, who soon longs for Paris, away from the monotony of cabin, water, and landscape. She deserts her husband, who, jealous of Paris and the whole world, would be lost in the city if it were not for Père Jules, his old factotum: Père Jules brings Juliette back to poor Jean. The emphasis is on the numerous little single episodes, each more pregnant with suspense than the commonplace story itself. These little episodes compose the plot without, however, depending on it for structure and meaning. The opening passage, in which Jean and Juliette in festive attire proceed like strangers, silently, side by side, through the forest across the field to the beach, far ahead of the wedding party, is a perfect piece of poetry. By stringing his episodes like pearls, Vigo endows a technical fact with aesthetic significance—the fact that the celluloid strip is virtually endless and can be interrupted at any time.

More important are the conclusions Vigo draws from the fact that the camera does not discriminate between human beings and objects, animate and inanimate nature. As if led by the meandering camera, he exhibits the material components of mental processes. In *Atalante* we experience with all our senses how strongly the fogs of the river, the avenues of trees, and the isolated farms affect the mind, and how the sailor's relationship to the city is determined by the fact that he looks at the lodgings perched on the quay from sea level. Other film directors, too, have identified objects as silent accomplices of our thoughts and feelings. But Vigo goes still further. Instead of simply revealing the role objects may play in conditioning the mind, he dwells upon situations in which their influence predominates, thus exploring camera possibilities to the full. And since increasing intellectual awareness tends to reduce the power of objects over the mind, he logically chooses people who are deeply rooted in the material world as leading characters of his two full-length films.

Immature boys are the heroes of *Zéro de conduite*. Early in this film two of them ride to school at night in a third-class railroad compartment; it is as if they were left to themselves in a wigwam that imperceptibly fuses with their dreams. We see a man's legs on one of the benches, and then, on the other bench, we see the upper half of a sleeping traveler. This halving of the sleeper, marking him as an inanimate being, increases the impression of isolation from the world, an impression already aroused by the smoke which shuts out the world behind the car window. The partition of the compartment lies somewhat obliquely in the picture, an angle which points to the fact that this entire sequence cannot be located within real space and time. Their adventurous ride stimulates the two boys to pranks. From unfathomable pockets they produce alternately a spiral with a little ball springing out of it, a flute, shriveled toy balloons blown up by the younger boy, a bunch of goose quills with which the older one adorns himself, and finally cigars a yard long. Photographed from below, they squat exaltedly as the smoke of the locomotive mingles with the smoke of the cigars, and in the haze the round balloons float to and fro in front of their pale faces. It is exactly as if the two in their magic wigwam were riding through air. With a jerk, the sleeper falls. "Il est mort!" [he's dead!] one of the boys cries, frightened. With the balloons hovering around them, they get off the train; outside we read the sign: "Non Fumeurs" [non-smoking] and immediately the wigwam is retransformed into an ordinary railroad compartment.

While the objects in *Zéro de conduite* participate in childish play or occasionally frighten the boys, they become fetishes in *Atalante*. As such, they possess Père Jules. Michel Simon's Père Jules ranks among the greatest characters ever created on the screen by any actor or director. The old man, a former sailor, takes care of the "Atalante" in company with his accordion, innumerable cats, and a feeble-minded boy. Grumbling to himself inarticulately, he walks up and down between the steering wheel and the cabin in a sort of daze—so much one with the "Atalante" that he seems carved out of its planks. All that affects him is physical actions, which he, however, does not experience consciously, but immediately translates into similar actions. Jean lifts Juliette with whom he stands back to back: witnessing this amorous scene, Père Jules begins to shadow box. Juliette tries on him the coat she is sewing: the coat induces him to imitate an African belly dancer, and since Africa to him is not far from San Sebastian, he avails himself of the same coat, as he would of a red cloth, to irritate an imaginary bull. He does not remember the events, but reproduces them following certain signals.

Instead of using the objects at his disposal, he has become their property. The magic spell they cast over him is revealed in a unique episode in which Père Jules shows Juliette all the mementos he has brought home from his voyages. The piled-up treasures which crowd his cabin are depicted in such a manner that we feel they have literally grown together over him. To evoke this impression Vigo focuses on the objects from various sides and on many levels without ever clarifying their spatial interrelationship—using nothing but the medium shots and close-ups made necessary by the narrowness of the cabin. The alarm clock, the musical box, the photograph portraying Jules as a young man between two women in glittering dresses, the tusk, and all the bric-à-brac emerging little by little, form an impenetrable wickerwork constantly interspersed with fragments of the old man himself: his arm, his tattooed back, his face. How accurately this piecemeal presentation renders his complete submission to the rarities around him can also be inferred from the fact that he preserves in alcohol the hands of a deceased comrade. The idols, on their part, display triumphantly their inherent powers. At the head of their great defile Vigo marches a doll which, when set into motion by Père Jules, conducts mechanical music from a puppet show like a bandmaster. The magical life of the doll is transmitted to the curiosities that follow in the parade.

". . . un documentaire bien romantique," Brasillach writes in his *Histoire du cinéma* about *A propos de Nice*, "mais d'une belle cruauté, où les ridicules des dames vieilles et amoureuses, des gigolos et de la bourgeoisie décadente étaient férocement stigmatisés."[1] Responding to the overwhelming appeal of material phenomena, Vigo, however, more and more withdrew from social criticism. In *Atalante* it appears, indeed, as if he actually had wanted to affirm an attitude hostile to intellectual awareness. Could it be, then, that Vigo's career had taken a retrogressive course? But in *Zéro de conduite* satire still manifested itself, and perhaps he indulged in the magic of mute objects and dark instincts only in order, some day, to pursue more thoroughly and knowingly the task of disenchantment.

4 The Revolt against Rationality
(1947)

The sizable number of recent volumes presenting in popular form analyses of race prejudice and suggestions for dispelling it indicate the wide diffusion and acceptance of both a standard analysis and a standard therapy for race prejudice. Let us look briefly at three of these books and their prescriptions.

Mr. George de Huszar, in the *Anatomy of Racial Intolerance* (New York: H. W. Wilson, 1946), has made an intelligent compilation of excerpts from magazine articles, research papers, and books, mostly written during the war and reflecting the apprehension then current of a rise in intolerance during the reconversion period. Dr. Dorothy W. Baruch, a trained psychologist, elaborates in *The Glass House of Prejudice* (New York: William Morrow, 1946) upon individual conflicts and group incidents, giving well-authenticated case histories that effectively support her arguments and suggestions. Miss Margaret Halsey (*Color Blind: A White Woman Looks at the Negro* [New York: Simon and Schuster, 1946]) confines herself to drawing on her wartime experiences in an interracial canteen.

In his eagerness for complete documentation Mr. de Huszar occasionally includes less nourishing material: specimens of arid formalism and flights into lofty regions where the assumption of an "economy of abundance" is made effortlessly. But the main body of his compilation consists, fortunately, of such substantial articles as Gordon W. Allport's analysis of bigotry in our midst; Edwin R. Embree's war survey, "Race Relations Balance Sheet"; Clyde R. Miller's presentation of the Springfield Plan; and a short piece by Horace M. Kallen that reveals the structure of democracy with a true sense of its inner workings. Here and there a less orthodox observation juts out of the rather familiar surroundings. Thus Robert Redfield infers from events in Russia that a social revolution may well do away with seemingly immovable racial prejudices.

Dorothy W. Baruch deals extensively with Mexican minority problems in California, covering ground not yet fully explored. A whole chapter is devoted to the zoot-suit riots of 1944. The book, with its emphasis on psychological readjustment, breathes a warmth that would be more effective did not Dr. Baruch repeatedly try to convince hesitant readers with rhetorical flourishes. Students of race bias will appreciate the appendix with its many references and supplementary materials.

Margaret Halsey is not a well-intentioned psychologist but a bright and sensitive woman. The way she supervised the junior hostesses in her war canteen, straightened out tangled situations and worked upon the more mildly prejudiced white servicemen while leaving the unteachable alone—all this testifies to maturity combined with tactical skill. It is true that Miss Halsey does not always avoid jumping to conclusions, but she shows that she understands Southerners and their piled-up inhibitions, and she debunks current legends about Negroes with incisive sarcasm, rightly emphasizing the role sexual jealousy and social frustration play as motives of discrimination.

All three books prove that psychiatry has made inroads in modern thinking. Many authors now dwell upon the lasting effects of early environment and explain stereotyped prejudices as the result of deep-rooted childhood impressions. The emotional consequences of economic insecurity are given no less attention; it seems to be common knowledge that such insecurities touch off certain psychological mechanisms, and it is taken for granted that the all-but-automatic release of these mechanisms accounts for the persecution of minority groups by harassed majorities. Hence educational measures are recommended—adequate child-training, schools cultivating interracial relations, group organizations for the reorientation of adults, and so on.

This whole literature is symptomatic of an almost mystic belief in the potentialities of social psychotherapy—particularly in Dr. Baruch's case. And who would deny the beneficent effects of psychotherapy? But its devotees as a rule overrate what can be achieved in this field, for they fail to acknowledge one powerful motive of racial bias in our time—a motive that despite its partly psychological origins proves inaccessible to the intervention of psychologists.

It is a motive related to a society that, like our modern one, seems unable to provide powerful cultural incentives for the total human being. Dr. Max Horkheimer, one of our foremost thinkers, attributes the actual lack of such incentives to the contemporary "deterioration of reason."[1] With the development of abstract thinking and technical proficiency, reason itself has become increasingly denaturalized. What this means can be grasped by comparing our present civilization with a past in which all reasoning involved the universe both within and outside us. Not yet emancipated from tradition and creed, reason then embraced the angelic and devilish components of nature with an acute awareness of their significance, incorporating them in a substantial, multi-faceted pattern of existence. Set against the background of such relative completeness, contemporary society appears strangely incoherent and empty.

Our society is governed by formal reason, under whose rule we have learned to control nature at the cost of sympathetic contact with its inherent urges and goals. The tissues connecting thought and matter, image and object, have withered away. Values are labels, mass culture takes the place of culture, and ideas degenerate into slogans that may affect people but fail to get under their skins. The realm of reason has become a sham reality filled with oversized vistas, unsubstantiated notions, and the bizarre shadows of things existent. Chirico's paintings reflect the *horror vacui* haunting any mind with a memory in this No Man's Land.

Abandoned by denaturalized reason, nature appears as something incomprehensible, if not hostile, something that should be eliminated rather than admitted. It not only appears this way: exactly as oppressed minorities become more and more debased, so nature disintegrates in the wake of our alienation from it. A deep gap grows between the rational and the elemental in us . . .

In his present enlightened state of mind, civilized man, not without infinite malaise, identifies the unceasing manifestations of race hatred and crude violence as relapses into that jungle region which he thought to have long since left behind. No doubt, these manifestations are relapses. But what from an enlightened point of view seems retrogression at its worst can also be considered a reaction against the emasculating effects of present-day reason.

The upsurge of primitive instincts in our society owes much to an irresistible, if unavowed, desire to re-establish the right of nature. Modern man derives a remarkable satisfaction from the shaking off of all controls. Savagery both scares and fascinates him as something that may enable him to attain a great fullness of being. Thus it should not be overlooked that the persistence of blind prejudice may still include an element of legitimate revolt. Prejudice has been called a disease, but spreading like an epidemic, it bares the disease of civilization itself.

Psychologists concerned with rehabilitating the maladjusted endorse, of necessity, rational behavior as something desirable. They restore and consolidate the rule of reason. And yet it is reason itself that, because of its denaturalized, anemic condition, calls forth the protests of neglected nature. To be sure, this does not prevent psychotherapy from removing prejudice in individual cases, but even those practitioners who knowingly co-ordinate rational aspirations and irrational drives are bound to conform to the pattern of a civilization that breeds prejudice of itself. There is something Danaïdean about their efforts in an age of mass culture.

Effective dealing with current mental disturbances depends upon a change of our general mental climate—a change in a direction pointed out by recent French writers, such as Georges Blin and Camus, who explore the tabooed regions of our bodily existence with a spiritual compassion that reveals their longing for the reconciliation of reason and nature. To express such a longing means to envisage a life in which the now prevailing abstract ideals, with their vain pretence to reality, will have yielded to incentives strong and full enough to seize upon man as a whole. Only under their auspices might we be able to put our fears to good use and come to terms with the demoniac forces of nature. This is about all that can and should be said here of matters transcending the domain of formal concepts.

5 On Jewish Culture
(1947)

Mr. Cohen defines the term "Jewish culture" in a way that seems particularly commendable to me. He naturally rejects the escapist attempt at wholesale assimilation; but he no less fervently repudiates the current wave of Jewish nationalism, which, stressing differences rather than similarities, tries to establish a new intellectual ghetto. "There is no such thing as pure Jewish culture," he says. And with that sense of the culturally relevant to which each issue of *Commentary* testifies, Mr. Cohen insists that our community leaders should neither misconceive of Jewish culture as a tool for survival nor blindly refuse hospitality to the rebel, the heretic, and the alienated.

But how delineate a culture that encompasses such heterogeneous personalities as Freud, Chagall and Proust? This is a vital question, for if the Jewish communities of America are to sponsor a cultural life, they should at least have a distinct notion of what is peculiar to it. Mr. Cohen points out that most exponents of Jewish culture have developed a passionate interest in ultimate human issues—an interest which, he adds, is not exclusively, but persistently Jewish. His answer, I think, looks in the right direction; and I only wish to elaborate a bit on it.

A common feature of many essential Jewish contributions in our era is their concern with enlightenment. Of course, Jews can be found almost everywhere and sometimes in prominent places—but what marks an endeavor or achievement as specifically Jewish is its inherent tendency to dissolve all the elements that obstruct the breakthrough and fulfillment of reason. It is their instinct of self-preservation that makes the Jews fight in this way against prejudice and any state of affairs that rigidly upholds what has no other justification than the sheer fact of existence. And yet self-interest alone, however justified, would not suffice to explain completely the inspired zeal with which Jewish scholars and artists try constantly to overcome the stubborn resistance of sheer matter and prejudiced tradition. There is something religious in this sustained effort to remove barriers and penetrate taboo zones, this effort to dissipate narrow-mindedness and cause not a single stone to withhold its meaning. In our Western world, the cause of enlightenment is the cause of the Jews. And it is as if the best of them championed it in the belief that their salvation was inseparable from the redemption of humanity as a whole.

This also accounts for the intensity that distinguishes typically Jewish accomplishments: Jews are animated so much by the desire to go the limit wherever they go, and if they seem occasionally to relax, it is only to digest the obstacle in their path. Centuries of migration, exile and eternal adjustment may have led the Jews to identify the absolute with a haven from which they could no longer be driven away.

However, every virtue breeds its own particular vice. In their eagerness for the world that ought to exist, many Jews fail to take into account the one that does exist here and now. Their unlimited trust in the redeeming power of reason is bound up with a neglect of all that grows and persists by its own right. I am thinking here of those opaque forces and substances that are as they are and cannot simply be reasoned or explained away (i.e., the Southerner's attitude toward Negroes, the German adulation of the military, the attachment to royalty shown by the English, local customs, the superstitions of farmers and peasants everywhere, loyalty to inherited procedures that are obviously insufficient, etc.). Whoever is at home somewhere experiences the impact of things like this. He is part of an environment profoundly affected by nature and mores, and even if he revolts against his environment, regional peculiarities will still grip him. Time and again Jews tend to discount the inner weight of all that this contributes to the formation of real, concrete individuals and real, concrete groups. Intent on transforming reality and realizing the absolute of reason, they frequently resort to over-rational solutions that diverge too far from bitter, contingent reality.

This does not mean that Jews invariably play the role of revolutionaries or innovators. On the contrary, more often than not they prove themselves conservatives by tenaciously clinging to their inherited way of life. Yet this way of life itself, determined, as it is, by religious notions rather than by natural and social invariants, leads straight to the absolute. In Jewish life transparence prevails over opacity. Even the most conservative Jews are therefore prone to struggle against the inertia of this world of ours.

Probably Jews see farther than people less emancipated from bias and habit; but their farsightedness is bought at a price: in aspiring to change they too rarely realize what it means to change things from within. They are wanderers. And since it is difficult for wanderers fully to grasp the beauty and ugliness of the fixed, they sometimes mistake cornerstones for mere hindrances, and spread enlightenment with a flashlight. This also explains the ambiguous character of Jewish intensity. In many cases, the quality of being intense indicates an unwillingness to wait until the time is ripe. To assail the end may mean to overrun what might better be slowly besieged. Jewish brilliance is frequently the outcome of Messianic impatience loath to adopt a middle course even in situations in which only patient, if less brilliant, tactics can be expected to alter conditions. Intensity thus threatens to degenerate into virtuosity.

All this is said only to supplement Mr. Cohen's pertinent remarks. The more deeply those in charge of promoting Jewish culture are aware of the unique merits and peculiar weaknesses of Jewish thought, the easier will they be able to foster productivity. In view of the dangerous apathy characteristic of the world of today, Jewish activism, in spite of its recklessness and impatience, becomes increasingly necessary. Mr. Cohen may have this in mind when he asks Jewish communities to accept wholeheartedly the numerous truly creative personalities who are not only "maladjusted," but constructively "maladjusting." I could think of no better advice.

6 Filming the Subconscious
(1948)

These notes on several recent experimental films are inspired by the growing response to this genre. When Cinema 16, an organization specializing in the distribution of avant-garde films of all kinds, presented its first program in New York last fall, most of its performances were sold out in advance.[1] The same interest stirs in Los Angeles, Chicago and Minneapolis. And Amos Vogel, the young director of Cinema 16, tells me of unknown amateurs whose film experiments are so promising that he plans to show them in future programs. There seems to be a new avant-garde movement in the making. In all likelihood, it owes something to the widespread discontent with the current Hollywood output.

Maya Deren, who received a Guggenheim fellowship and whose work is perhaps the most familiar of the group, has made four experimental films, of which all but one externalize psychological reality in the material of outer reality. This has been done before, in particular by Germaine Dulac in her *The Seashell and the Clergyman* ([La coquille et le clergyman, France] 1928). But Miss Deren carries on with such vitality that she instills new life into the old patterns.

Meshes of the Afternoon ([USA] 1943), which she made in collaboration with her husband, Alexander Hammid, one of our best cameramen, sets forth the state of mind of a frustrated girl. The girl returns home from a walk and finds her house deserted, with everything upside down, as if her husband or lover had run away on the spur of the moment. She falls asleep in a chair and in her subsequent dream elaborates with morbid insistence upon her experiences in the deserted house. This incident, as the dream reveals, touches off in her the sensation of being forever rejected by the world. In picturing the girl's moods, Miss Deren combines psychological insight with a film sense which enables her to draw on the expressive functions of various cinematic devices. The afternoon spectre of a black-clad woman with a mirror instead of a face intimates that the dreaming girl cannot break through the crust that separates her from others. The deliberate reiterations, only slightly varying in detail, of whole sequences and occurrences symbolize her complete stagnation. And the scene in which she, or one of her incarnations, hurries after the slowly pacing black woman and yet does not succeed in catching up with her, illustrates the girl's vain effort to overcome her inhibitions.

At Land ([USA] 1944) treats the same theme, with special emphasis on distortions of time and space provoked by frustration. A nymph-like girl, thrust ashore by the waves, feels at sea on terra firma. Whatever she pursues evades her in an endless flight of objects, persons and situations. She crawls over the table of a room in which a banquet is held, without being noticed by anyone; she sneaks into a log cabin and, frightened by a stranger in the bed, escapes through one door after another; she joins two girls on the beach who continue to play chess as if unaware of her presence; finally she runs back to the sea. To the soul lacking an exit, the world thus turns into a succession of fleeting phenomena. And so does time waver: memories and current events fuse with each other.

Miss Deren's subsequent experiment, the three-minute short *A Study in Choreography for Camera* ([USA] 1945), seems to have sprung from her increasing interest in purely formal problems. Her concern with psychological borderline cases is now superseded by her desire to establish, with the aid of the moving camera, artistic time-space relations. A dancer begins a leap in the woods and ends it in a room. In this way he circles and swirls from one setting to another, until he finally takes off to fly in slow motion toward a landscape, his ultimate goal. It is, as Miss Deren puts it, "a duet between space and a dancer."

Her last film, *Ritual in Transfigured Time* ([USA] 1945–1946), resumes the leitmotif of the frustrated girl on a more sophisticated level. This time the girl's inner life materializes in the figure of a Negro woman who embodies the desires and griefs of the soul from which she emanates. Like her predecessors, the woman attempts to escape from the prison of her self; but, unlike them, she is not doomed until she has experienced love. Artistically, this complex film indicates progress in that it aims at a synthesis of form and content, dance and psychology. The scene of a social gathering, with the Negro woman ignored by the crowd, is shot and cut in such a way that it becomes a dance involving everybody and everything. Miss Deren has arrived at the expression of meaning through rhythm; the problem is only what the meaning itself amounts to.

In *The Potted Psalm* [USA 1946], shot in San Francisco during the summer of 1946, Sidney Peterson and James Broughton mingle fragments of reality with unreal elements after the manner of Miss Deren. But here the similarity ends. Faintly reminiscent of certain surrealistic experiments of the Twenties, this film is a sequence of loosely knit associations, ranging from a man without a head to two feet rubbing their toes together and a human leg which turns into a piano leg. The program note maintains that *The*

Potted Psalm deals with "the chaotic inner complexities of our postwar society." This interpretation is rather generous, for the film-makers fail to substantiate their aspirations cinematically. The camera does not contribute much, nor is the "montage" rhythmically structured. Thus the meanings remain inchoate.

A few recent experimental films featuring non-objective patterns yield interesting results. *Glen Falls Sequence* [USA 1946] by Douglass Crockwell—an animation of pictures painted on several movable layers of glass—combines unknown shapes and vaguely familiar elements into a universe which is as impossible as it is funny. Microorganisms congregate for no imaginable purpose; mushrooms stroll through a Tanguy landscape; flourishes, never finished, cover a sort of sheet that grows out of an inkblot-like cloud; compact masses let something drop or are pregnant with minuscule crystals which emerge from sudden fissures in them; a chimney turns into a saw which tries to cut through its own smoke. Modern science defies the law of causality and considers mass a manifestation of energy. Matter is in constant flux, all substances are in principle interchangeable. Crockwell takes science at its word by transforming geometric and organic forms into one another. He is a wit who plays Providence. His abstract compositions either originate in cactuses and the like or breed themselves new creatures with a semblance of life. Now and then cultural reminiscences interfere. A death's head comes out of an urn, and a white cross is perched on what may be a mountain range, a heap of yeast or a concurrence of rolling waves.

Aided by a Guggenheim fellowship, John and James Whitney have produced a series of shorts, *Abstract Film Exercises* ([USA] 1943–1945), in which they try to establish aesthetically valid relations between form, color and sound. The forms are derived from paper cutouts; the sound effects are produced by a machine which regulates the shape of a light ray thrown directly on the sound track. Such experiments are not new, but the Whitney brothers, though not particularly inventive in rhythm and imagery, nevertheless leave all past attempts behind. Theirs is a vision of what people have come to call our atomic age. And guided by it they go to the limit in creating a cosmos filled with nothing but swirling corpuscles all aglow with reds and greens that quiver and flicker in unlimited space. Tiny balls rush to the foreground, develop into radiant suns and vanish again. Atoms thus play about aimlessly, and their games are accompanied by a music strongly reminiscent of jungle noises, as we know them from war films about Burma and Guadalcanal. It seems extremely difficult for humanity to assert itself at this juncture of cosmic and animal life.

Hans Richter's full-length color film *Dreams That Money Can Buy* [USA 1947], which received an award as "the best original contribution to the progress of cinematography" at the Venice film festival, is a mosaic of isolated episodes, each based upon the work or an idea of a contemporary artist.

The Max Ernst sequence, "Desire," inspired by six drawings of *La Semaine de Bonté*, features the voluptuous dream of a sleeping girl. Her vagabond unconscious materializes in an enraptured soliloquy through images in which fragments of conventional reality help build up a more real dream world. Shipwrecked bodies are dragged from under the girl's bed, and her bedroom itself floats through a jungle of threatening corridors and dungeons. When her lover finally joins her, the girl's solitary dream is superseded by their common dream—a succession of exuberant visions which symbolize the ecstasy of love fulfilment and its vibrant afterglow. A figure enacted by Ernst himself follows the lovers as a sort of superego, silently witnessing, and thus counterbalancing, their revel in emotional irresponsibility.

In contrast with this glowing display of passion, the Fernand Léger episode is a playful satire on mechanical love-making. Mannequins of a type common in Grand Street shop windows embark on a sentimental affair which so badly ruins the bride's beautiful wedding gown that her amorous feelings are also spoiled. Libby Holman and Josh White accompany this ill-fated flirtation with a song by John Latouche which comments ironically in ballad fashion on "The Girl with the Pre-fabricated Heart." The whole has the character of a *ballet mécanique* unfolding in the atmosphere of American folklore.

Compared to these two sequences, the Man Ray episode, drawn from his own script, is an anticlimax. Entitled "Ruth, Roses, Revolvers," it indulges in dialogue and pretends to deeper meaning. The fogs disperse only in one single passage in which fun is poked at movie audiences eager for identification with some screen character. But the fun is too obvious to be amusing. Fortunately, it is possible to identify oneself with Darius Milhaud's music.

Two other artists emerge in full splendor. The evolutions of Marcel Duchamp's moving discs are interspersed with a procession of female nudes reminiscent of his painting "Nude Descending a Staircase"—a fascinating combination of cobweb-like spirals and luxuriant bodies. Their interplay is followed by an impressive rephrasing of Alexander Calder's creations. His mobiles turn into a pageant of form and colors; and his circus figures, delightful products of an atavistic imagination, parade to a score by Paul Bowles which enhances their eerie non-existence.

In an attempt to unify these disparate elements, Richter has devised a framing story, with music by Louis Applebaum and Jack Bittner as the protagonist. Bittner's Joe, a poor young poet, determines to capitalize on his unique gift for resuscitating slumbering dreams: he settles down in a fancy office, selling to his clients whatever he molds in the material of their unconscious. There is, of course, a well-defined relationship between dreams and dreamers: the Max Ernst orgy externalizes the longings of a pale husband, while the Léger satire enables a high-strung girl to relax. In shaping these dreams, Joe proves himself an artist rather than a psychiatrist. He comforts those in distress by transforming their inmost desires into tangible works of art. The realm of art is thus presented as a refuge from the world in which we actually live.

Out of the framing story grows Richter's own episode, "Narcissus," the last of the film. It is a dream of Joe's own, rendering his inner experiences in drastic symbols. His face turns blue when he discovers his identity; and as he climbs up a ladder, intent on following his destiny, one rung after another vanishes under his feet. Thus in pictures conspicuous for their fervor, the genesis of any creator is made manifest—his insistence on self-realization, his fight against indifference and his inexorable loneliness. At the end, a bust of Zeus, suggestive of Joe's dearest memories, shatters to bits, and Joe as a person dissolves. All that remains of him are his works, bright color compositions flowing through space.

Small wonder that so ambitious a film does not fulfill all its promises. The principle, sound in itself, of featuring the "voice of the unconscious" has been exaggerated. There is also a tendency throughout the film to misuse literary metaphors as visual symbols. But these imperfections should blind no one to the film's great merits. Richter is an innovator. For the first time he transfers the essential content of modern art to the screen.

Modern art, as it appears in this film, intertwines the region of pure forms with the virgin forest of the human soul. What lies between— the vast middle sphere of conventional life—is tacitly omitted or overtly attacked. Both the Léger and Richter episodes are very explicit in defiance of our mechanical civilization. They mock at it or present the seeming normality as a distortion of the really normal. Contemporary art, the film suggests, opposes a world which smothers the expression of love and creative spontaneity—hence the sustained concern of modern artists with unconscious urges and abstract structures. Richter makes it unmistakably clear that the latter would not come into their own without the steady influx of the former. To point out their interdependence he not only superimposes the female nudes and Duchamp's rarefied movements, but lets a primitive mask and a sort of ram's horn join company with Calder's mobiles. And in the Max Ernst sequence the turmoil of sex so radically upsets the nineteenth-century interiors that they seem on the point of disintegrating—scattered elements predestined to be reborn within nonobjective textures. The inherent moods of the whole film bear out its main concepts. Melancholia, our lot as creatures, alternates with the gaiety which is inseparable from artistic fulfillment; and all the foggy sentiments characteristic of the middle sphere are suppressed mercilessly.

Richter's film is of consequence for yet another reason: it demonstrates conclusively that certain works of art have much to gain by a proper cinematic rendering. For instance, the Calder constructions yield quite unsuspected effects on the screen—effects produced by the incorporation of their shadows, artful close-ups, surprising color schemes, and not least by Paul Bowles' magnificent score. Sparkling, dangling and jingling in a universe composed of nothing but light and hue, these mobiles which we thought we knew now seethe with strange revelations. Like his Joe, Richter brings out what, all unknown to us, was latent in them.

By conjuring up the secret dream life of drawings, paintings and plastic forms, *Dreams That Money Can Buy* sets a propitious pattern for the future cooperation of art and cinema.

7 Psychiatry for Everything and Everybody

The Present Vogue—and What Is Behind It (1948)

Psychiatry and particularly psychoanalysis are now enjoying an amazing vogue in this country. In the pre-war decades, the vogue was confined to intellectuals; today it has spread until it has become a mass phenomenon. In the words of Dr. C. Charles Burlingame, a leading psychiatrist: "Hundreds of thousands of persons, satiated with a superficial knowledge of the psychological implications of life and literally preoccupied with psychiatric terminology, are beginning to interpret every trivial thought and feeling in psychological terms."

Particularly symptomatic of the fascination psychiatry exerts today are Hollywood's psychological films—a trend that began around 1944 and remains unparalleled in other countries, with the exception perhaps of England, where it has made only a hesitant beginning. These films endow psychiatry with an illusionary glamor. As pictured by Hollywood, it is not so much a science as a superior system of magic practiced by a species of miracle worker. That on occasion one of these miracle workers misuses his magic for criminal ends only enhances its awe-inspiring uncanniness. In *Spellbound* [USA 1945, dir. Alfred Hitchcock], the homicidal psychiatrist and his law-abiding colleagues engage in a struggle reminiscent of the contests between sorcerers in old fairy tales. Compared with these modern sorcerers, detectives have become rather dull-witted, as can be inferred from *The Dark Mirror* [USA 1946, dir. Robert Siodmak], in which the psychiatrist leaves the detective far behind in tracking down a smart murderess.

Thus, Sherlock Holmes has yielded to the analyst, common sense to the play of free associations, and the gun to the couch. But even the couch is no longer needed, for, unlike their counterparts in real life, most screen psychiatrists set aright the gravest mental derangements in six easy lessons. The very speed of their therapy adds to their stature as master-minds. (To be sure, in a silent film, *Secrets of a Soul*, made in 1926, the German director G. W. Pabst demonstrated that it was quite possible to impress upon spectators the slowness of psychoanalytical treatment and yet sustain dramatic suspense.) Once restored to normal, the patients usually return to the tasks of life and solve them with the greatest ease. The heroine of *Lady in the Dark* [USA 1944, dir. Mitchell Leisen] ends as a lady in the light, and the amnesia-stricken girl in *Shock* [USA 1946, dir. Alfred Werker] happily marries her lieutenant. Psychiatry, at least on the screen, appears able to solve anything.

How explain the average American's infatuation with psychological procedures? Dr. William C. Menninger recently stated that "the neurotic patient represents a majority of all the patients who seek help from physicians" (*New York Times*, April 29, 1947). And patients of this kind are found not merely among the well-to-do. Military experience has shown "that the neurotic young man, as seen in army induction centers, came from the middle class as well as from the underprivileged," Dr. Marynia F. Farnham states. People in all walks of life, then, are suffering from neuroses. And the most obvious conclusion that suggests itself is that the present-day attention to psychiatry must be accounted for by the existence of an unprecedented amount of mental maladjustment.[1]

In principle, however, most people, laymen and psychologists alike, agree in attributing the impressive spread of emotional disturbances to the heightened pressure of social factors. That we are mentally sick because the social structure is sick is the opinion most frequently heard. One might expect, therefore, that popular imagination would turn from neurotic symptoms to social causes, and emphasize not so much the importance of psychiatric cures as the necessity for environmental changes and the reform of society. Yet the spotlight remains unwaveringly focused on psychiatry.

The fact is, though most of us agree that society is at the bottom of many psychological maladjustments, we seem to act on the reverse principle that society is sick because we ourselves are sick. Dr. G. B. Chisholm, Canada's Deputy Minister of National Health and formerly Director of General Medical Services for the Canadian Army, explains wars by the frequency of neurotic ills traceable to the immaturity of the masses: "The necessity to fight wars . . . is as much a pathological psychiatric symptom as is a phobia. . . . They are alike irrational behavior patterns resulting from unsuccessful development and failure to reach emotional maturity" (*Psychiatry*, February 1946). In this country many a psychologist thinks along similar lines. For instance, Dorothy W. Baruch considers proper child training the ideal antidote to race hatred.[2]

History teaches us that this shift of emphasis from outer to inner conditions is usually provoked by the impact of drastic social change and crisis. The vogue of psychiatry in my opinion owes its existence to two attitudes forced upon us by the present pressures of American civilization. One attitude amounts to an evasion. The other results from an attempt to compensate for the lack of what I would call emotional behavior patterns.

The evasive attitude is the outcome of the all-pervasive atmosphere of menace and danger arising from the impact of such dreaded social and political developments as "the coming depression," war with Russia, and the atomic bomb. These threats fill the headlines of our newspapers and the recesses of our minds. It seems paradoxical, but the undeniable improvement of living conditions in this country has seen at the same time a steady decrease in emotional security. The naive optimism so characteristic of America, already shaken in the wake of depression, has definitely given way to widespread malaise. People are possessed by a haunting fear of what the future may have in store for them.

The fear is intensified by our awareness of how difficult it is for each of us as individuals to control or alter the course of events. Especially now that the United States has become such a dominant world power, public affairs assume giant dimensions that make it all but impossible to establish a meaningful relation between our immediate acts and the large but remote issues at stake. One act may have various incalculable effects, and one effect may be caused by several diametrically opposed acts. So the feeling grows that we are less than ever masters of our destinies. This is why many people—in particular middle-class people—have relinquished the attitude of active agents and become passive consumers who unhesitatingly buy whatever society hands down to them. This acknowledgment of social and political helplessness and the consequent adjustment to it inevitably deepen inner insecurity.

Perhaps this insecurity would be less acute were it not sustained by a spiritual crisis so profound that it affects the very roots of the American myth. Uncertainty as to the future wears away faith in attitudes and convictions held sacrosanct in the past. The present state of world affairs, along with our recent war experiences and our new international commitments, may have hastened this crisis. It is true that the average American repudiates Russian totalitarianism and looks distrustfully upon the socialist experiments in Europe; yet in a world becoming ever smaller the emergence into concrete action of hostile myths constitutes a troubling challenge to his own "American dream."

The fact is that, much as he clings to his way of life, the average American is no longer in a position to take its fundamentals as much for granted as he used to. Individual freedom has become a matter of controversy rather than a live experience; and such ultimate issues as free enterprise vs. planned economy become slogans precisely because the issues involved can no longer be decided with certainty. Values that once formed implicit parts of our myth *and therefore did not need to be mentioned* are now being dragged into the arena of discussion.

The end of our way seems lost in a mist. To be sure, we improvise day-to-day decisions, but underneath there is always a gripping uncertainty about the system of values in which they may be rooted. Emotional insecurity grows as we are deprived of the psychological shelter that supreme, unquestioned values afford us. Most of us cannot stand being mentally shelterless, and we instinctively avoid any direct approach to social and political problems for fear lest our doubts about our traditional values be resolved into a negative certainty. Instead, we use the one escape route left: we retreat from society to the individual. The Stoics under the Roman

Empire did more or less the same; and indeed all the great turning points of history have witnessed similar phenomena.

The evasive attitude is well illustrated by the hero of Arthur Koestler's novel *Arrival and Departure*.[3] A wartime refugee from a Nazi concentration camp, this young revolutionary has come to realize that he was wrong in siding with the Communists. He recants his faith in Russia without, however, coming to believe in the blessings of Western democracy. His beliefs are shaken, his mind is blank. Profoundly upset, he contracts an ailment—a lame leg. He consults a woman psychoanalyst, and she helps him identify his one-time Communist fervor as the aftermath of sinister childhood experiences. The whole process is a flight from the social to the private sphere.

This is a model case. Many people in a state of mental helplessness caused by external factors suffer intensely under their insecurity and more often than not develop neurotic symptoms like those of Koestler's hero. But in the final analysis they prefer continued neurotic suffering to the necessity of confronting their fundamental doubts. Some emotional disturbances become useful simply because they enable us to escape the sharper, but in the end more efficacious, emotional disturbance that would result from modifying our values and beliefs to fit new situations. The very same evasion that prefers to call on psychiatry to remedy its after-effects rather than face the facts, is to some extent responsible for the real difficulties that prompt the evasion. Cause and effect pursue each other in an endless circle.

It should be added that Koestler's story continues on a note that reveals an even more dangerous tendency. Having won sufficient insight into himself, the hero is relieved of his ailment. But his cure only encourages him to explain all socially accepted beliefs as projections of psychological processes. His decision to fight for England, though made to appear an act of personal decency, is a transparent device. He eludes his torturing uncertainty about values by draining the values themselves of their objective significance: values are made to seem nothing more than temporary psychological solutions. Psychological argumentation thus supersedes the concern with content—a rather popular tendency at present, but one that strips life of its meaning.

The other impulse behind the current vogue of psychiatry is, as I have intimated at the beginning, our need for, and our present lack of, behavior patterns. This need, though by no means of recent origin, has of late become particularly urgent. Growing out of the situation of a young civilization, it has been strongly determined by three factors: the primitive habits of colonial life, the sloughing off by millions of immigrants to America of their "fettering" Old World traditions, and the circumstance that the major developments of this civilization happen to have coincided with the rise of industrialism.

All three factors have left their imprint on American life. Any society provides its members with a network of rules, codes, mores, and patterns enabling them to discharge their latent instinctive energies and faculties in various commonly understandable ways. But our society is historically conditioned to neglect the emotional for the rational, to cultivate utilitarian ends more intensely than emotional aspirations. This does not mean, of course, that we are less gifted emotionally than other peoples; on the contrary, if there is such a thing as a national character, then Americans should be credited with strong and generous impulses and an uninhibited readiness to translate ideals into actions. But it does mean that our civilization or culture has developed no system of communication lines that offers really satisfactory outlets to any large part of our potentialities.

The wide dependence in this country on the radio strikingly reveals the extent to which we depend on substitutes for self-expression. Even in small private gatherings the habit of listening to the inextricable blend of opera singers, news commentators, and commercials gets the better of conversation for its own sake—that free flow of improvised thoughts and suddenly emerging sympathies which involves all its participants to the full, uncovering their boldest dreams and remotest intellectual ties. We have come to prefer any intrusion of the outer world to the intimacy of such exchange, which seems to us a dangerous self-exposure rather than a welcome means of communication. The bar-and-grill, that last refuge of people who like to be together for no purpose at all, not even for fun-making, is being increasingly invaded by juke-boxes and television screens, which further thwart the possibility of really being together.

It is as if we were frightened by the prospect of emotional adventures. Everything becomes shapeless in this menacing *terra incognita* of our personal emotions. The ceremonial of courtship still confines itself to unguarded moments in the dark—alcohol still serves to fill in the gaps; and the Sam Dodsworths with their unsatisfied longings still visit Europe in search of more substantial fulfillment. But does not Hollywood offer guidance? All that it offers is empty glamor and infantile fantasy instead of mature experience, a dazzling make-up to make up for ugliness aglow from within.

For lack of proper outlets, deep-seated desires whose satisfaction is an end in itself flare up and fade away without leaving a trace. In contrast, the slightest effort that serves business interests has at its disposal a rich variety of channels in which to fulfill itself and gain recognition. The elaborate code governing our conduct within the commercial sphere contrasts strangely with the small set of standardized directives that try in vain to cover the vast neglected areas of our emotional life. These areas resemble those blank spots on the map that represent territories not yet explored.

At the same time our industrialist society, while explicitly disavowing the seemingly purposeless, tends to exploit it for purposes of its own. Commercial considerations encroach on human pleasures and ends, perverting them into means to economic ends. And as technological reasoning and the acquisitive instinct attempt to reduce our civilization to pure calculation and exclude any kind of activity that has only its own pleasure as end, the private jungle of stillborn passions, aimless drives, and unnamed conflicts within us expands; the result is that we find it very difficult to commune with each other, since all the personal elements that go to make up real communication are kept hidden away in many different such private jungles.

For a civilization that grew up in an age of revolutionary inventions and industrial conquests, it was quite natural to seize upon psychology for the sake of its practical implications.

A twofold use has been made of psychology. First, it has served, and continues to serve, as a technique or pseudo-technique of economic and social advancement: the search for opportunities breeds "how-to-achieve-success" literature. Thus personnel selection by business organizations has come to rely on psychological testing; and at the same time intensified competition leads concerns to resort to psychological techniques to squeeze the last ounce of work out of their employees. Human-relations research in factories now applies itself to streamlining workers' mentality in the interest of higher efficiency. And since private sorrows may prevent some employee or other from giving his full, many an organization has hired psychologists whose function it is to lift production or step up sales by mending broken hearts. The relation between means and ends could not be reversed more drastically: happiness has now become a means to efficiency.

Secondly, psychology has been called upon in this country to facilitate self-expression and self-communication. It is noteworthy in this connection that psychoanalysis was adopted in America at an early date, and more readily than anywhere else. We seem to have been predisposed to it; in fact, for decades we have as a matter of course conceived of personal relations in terms of *personality* problems. This tendency pervades popular magazines and daily life. Schoolboys speak of their "inferiority complexes," lovers discuss their "frustrations," and mothers assume the attitudes of social workers. It is with the ease of an old habit that we dress personal urges in the terminology of psychological science.

That the urges for self-expression are often mixed with desires for wealth and power—"how to win friends *and* influence people"—should not prejudice one against their genuineness. People really wish and need to make friends, to shape and make manifest what they feel they have within themselves. But left in the lurch by our culture, they do not know how to formulate and express their personalities in spontaneous and accepted ways. And so, because of a shortage of socially recognized patterns for emotional exchange, they assign to psychology the task of defining their inner wants and engineering sufficient outlets.

It was only because the crises of the pre-war years did not basically affect the central nervous system of American civilization that our interest in psychology as a vehicle of self-expression remained rather subdued. However, now that we are undergoing a crisis which threatens our most cherished ideals themselves—a crisis underscored rather than contradicted by the increasingly insistent appeals made to our way of life—this interest has developed from an undercurrent into a declared and almost spectacular preoccupation. The wavering of our fundamental beliefs has still further reduced the possibility, already weak enough, of real personal communication. What few communication routes do exist for the transfer of emotional currency rest on values and common assumptions that are now imperiled by an awareness that values once held absolute might be controversial after all.

How can one express one's self when confusion as to ultimate values is added to the lack of the finer rules of conduct? Because of such difficulties many people remain, unaware, in a state of complete bewilderment. At least this is what might be inferred from the emergence of certain characters in recent Hollywood films that were rarely encountered before on the screen. I am thinking of the former flight officer in *The Best Years of Our Lives* [USA 1946, dir. William Wyler], of the murder-suspect veteran in *Crossfire* [USA 1947, dir. Edward Dmytryk], and of Henry Fonda's Joe in *The Long Night* [USA 1947, dir. Anatole Litvak]. All these ex-soldiers drift about in a visionless daze, at the mercy of every wind, benumbed even in their love-making. Perhaps they act this way under the shock of readjustment. On the other hand, if society itself were more articulate, the shock could hardly paralyze them so deeply.

The contrasts between American and French culture support these observations. France not only lost the war and endured German occupation; she now suffers from a prolonged crisis of her myth—a crisis so poignant that it divides the country into two opposite camps, with the prospect of civil war between them. Yet to all appearances this disintegration of values and beliefs has not yet succeeded in corroding the manifold traditions that control French life. There is, as no foreigner fails to notice, something Chinese about the abundance and rigidity of set conventions in France. They range from elaborate formulas for the complimentary closing in letters to suggestions for delicate love situations; from customs rhythmicizing the average existence to established literary models that qualify vague desires, anonymous moods. Many of these behavior patterns had originally practical functions, economic or otherwise; but with the passing of time they have outgrown these and, with a patina, now serve as means of emotional communication. Taken together, they form a dense texture that tends to perpetuate itself for its own sake, whether sustained by a basic national myth or not.

This texture has an objective character, strikingly illustrated, I submit, by a French colloquialism. Where we would say "I" or "we," the French more often than not use the impersonal "on"—"on s'arrange," "on va se promener," etc.—as if to indicate that private life evolves within a universal framework, a sphere of conventions to which all human beings are expected to conform. It is this participation in something objective that, despite their possession of a literature saturated with impressionistic psychological insight, immunizes the French against the encroachments upon personal life of applied psychology. They need not psychologize. Though aged and perhaps frayed, the texture of habits by which they live still protects them from sinking into the unfathomable abyss of ultra-personal subjectivity, from losing themselves in a maze of psychological relations unchecked by fixed meanings and images.

Even in this period of conflicting allegiances and intellectual despair, psychoanalysis is far from being a fashion in France (or, for that matter, anywhere else in Europe). The Existentialists, originally the vanguard of despair, now have turned activists; in an effort to compensate for the waning of the French myth, they insist that social and political decisions be made by the whole, integrated personality. Meanwhile, French interest in psychology still confines itself to investigation for its own sake, as for instance, in the poet Francis Ponge's literary attempts to X-ray the personality structure of inanimate objects and plants. In contrast to this country, France makes no real demand upon psychology as a means of expediting emotional traffic or compensating for the absence of common beliefs.

Thus the vogue of psychiatry, as I have tried to show, not only originates in extreme uncertainty, but owes much to the fact that American civilization has not yet developed the compact texture of behavior patterns woven by older cultures. If such a texture existed in this country, many would not dream of so readily identifying their personal difficulties as emotional tangles to be untied with the aid of a psychoanalyst.

This is not said by any means to belittle the merits of psychoanalytical therapy. I wish only to describe a situation in which this therapy becomes a necessity because of a scarcity of meaningful alternatives. Wide areas of our world remain a vacuum. In that vacuum psychological mechanisms inevitably turn into independent entities and inner conflicts assume an existence of their own. Psychotherapy is a technique that deals with these mechanisms and conflicts by trying to regulate them, by straightening out maladjustments and removing inhibitions. The goal is to enable the patient to cope with reality and make the best use of his energies. Modern analysts logically define their task as emotional re-education.

However, even the most successful re-education of this kind has its natural limits. It cannot alter the condition of our society, nor can it establish content and significance by itself alone. Indispensable as psychotherapy is, its cures do not fill the social void in which they evolve.

This is not generally recognized. On the contrary, there is a persistent tendency to exaggerate the functions of psychiatric practice. We expect its individual solutions to result in social solutions, and thus we burden it with responsibilities beyond its scope. The inherent danger of such an outlook, which is shared even by some misguided analysts, is that it sinks us ever deeper in sheer subjectivity.

And yet our fascination with psychiatry springs from a disquiet that in itself has elements of great hope. People seem to be increasingly aware of the vacuum around them. It is as if they could no longer bear the muddle of unchannelized, unqualified emotions, as if they finally wanted to move out of limbo into a realm in which impulses have a destination and sanctioned images articulate the infinity—evil only when unnamed—of inner processes. Behind the vogue of psychiatry lies a nostalgia for making the deeper layers of the human being really communicable—those layers that till now have been shut off from circulation and light. The will to take these hidden things in ourselves into the open air would indicate that our civilization is beginning to come of age. Should it mature through suffering and experience, its growing wealth of forms, patterns, and imagery would halt our preoccupation with psychology and automatically consume the excesses of our present dependence on it.

8 Those Movies with a Message
(1948)

Films supplement real life. They lend color to public opinion polls. They stir our awareness of the intangible, and they reflect the hidden courses of our experience. They point out situations that are often difficult to grasp directly but show, under the surface, what we think about ourselves. This is particularly true of screen motifs that seem to have been introduced unintentionally. The makers of films are vitally interested in the mass public, and such motifs—provided they occur with some regularity—can be assumed to bear on the attitudes, desires, and reactions of many, many people.

Films mirror our reality. Let us look in the mirror.

Frightened by Congressional unpleasantness, Hollywood now seems determined to concentrate on "pure entertainment," with a sprinkling of anti-Communist films thrown in to make up for past indiscretions. There will be no sequel to *The Farmer's Daughter* [USA 1940, dir. James Hogan], with its fascist-minded politicians. William Wyler has been quoted in the *New Yorker* as saying that *The Best Years of Our Lives* [USA 1946], which he directed, could not now be made in Hollywood. But meanwhile these motion pictures, together with such others as *Boomerang* [USA 1947, dir. Elia Kazan], *Crossfire* [USA 1947, dir. Edward Dmytryk], and *Gentleman's Agreement* [USA 1947, dir. Elia Kazan], have figured prominently in the Academy Awards and continue to be shown in the theaters and to draw crowds. They are thus still worth our attention today.

Products of the immediate postwar period, these movies characteristically feature ex-servicemen. The discharged GI of *Boomerang* is a suffering victim of injustice; the ex-sergeant of *The Best Years of Our Lives* tries to alleviate the lot of his fellow veterans. In the same way, both *Crossfire* and *Gentleman's Agreement* use soldiers to support their campaign against anti-Semitism. True, *The Farmer's Daughter* does not make use of GIs, but as Swedish immigrants its heroine and her relatives have much in common with returning soldiers. Veterans and aliens alike must adjust to an environment they interpret in the light of their visions.

You will remember the visions—our wartime films were full of them. Whether or not the moment was appropriate (and it often was not), some character would deliver a speech glorying in hopes for the future. "I hope . . . that all together we will try—try out of the memory of our anguish—to reassemble our broken world into a pattern so firm and so fair that another great war can never again be possible" (*The Story of GI Joe* [USA 1945, dir. William Wellman]). Or—"I want . . . peace with pride and a decent human life, with all the trimmings" (*None but the Lonely Heart* [USA 1944, dir. Clifford Odets]). This gospel of peace was invariably entwined with a eulogy of our democratic ideals and a promise to live up to them after the war. Out of the nightmare of concentration camps, Gestapo tortures, battlefields, and bombed cities arose the dream of American democracy. The words were florid, and intended to soothe the homesick.

Victory won, we descended from the clouds to the earth. Surprisingly enough, Hollywood accepted the challenge of the contrast. All of the films in question confronted the hopes of the war years with the reality of the postwar.[1] All of them went as far as Hollywood could afford to go in encouraging these same hopes. The films are slightly militant. They strike a note that sounds progressive, in a vaguely liberal way. This peculiar quality will become evident if we compare two of them: William Wyler's *The Best Years of Our Lives* and Frank Capra's *It's a Wonderful Life* [USA 1946].

II

Released at about the same time, the two films coincide in their animosity toward greedy bankers and in their compassion for those who are socially at a disadvantage. But in the Capra film everything done or said in favor of the less privileged is used only to point up the natural magnanimity of its hero, James Stewart. *It's a Wonderful Life* is primarily about individuals: on the one side the bad banker expressly marked as a black sheep, on the other the guileless and generous Stewart who, like his predecessors in earlier Capra films, is really the fairy-tale prince in thin modern disguise.

And in true fairy-tale fashion the film intimates that all social problems would be solved in no time if only such princes existed. Yet while Capra thus spirits away any abuses that might prove impenetrable to good-heartedness, Wyler in *The Best Years* comes directly to grips with them.

Wyler's characters are no less individuals than Capra's; but, unlike Capra's, they reflect the inner workings of the society to which they belong. The bankers in this film behave as typical bankers would—no better, no worse; and Fredric March as the ex-sergeant, himself no paragon of virtue, accuses them not so much of irregular villainy as of a stubborn insistence on regular practices that are apt to harm veterans. In delineating his characters, Wyler is more concerned with social mechanisms than with personal conflicts. And he never makes his audience believe, as Capra does, that human decency is alone sufficient to change the existing state of things. His film is not a fairy tale, but an attempt however limited to promote social progress.

The same holds true of the other films I have named. They expose corruption in domestic politics, middle-class complacency, racial bias, and fascist mentality with a directness unusual on the screen. So strong is the inherent tendency to tackle these problems that it even reverses the meaning of plots which try to shy away from them. *Boomerang* details the shady dealings of small-town politicians with the obvious purpose of emphasizing the integrity of its protagonist. Had this story been told in the traditional Hollywood manner, no one would feel tempted to inquire into its implications. But the documentary style in which the film is actually developed changes everything. Through numerous shots of Stamford, Connecticut, and the use of ordinary townspeople in the cast, the filmmakers convey the impression that their story is a real and contemporary event. And like any genuine documentary, *Boomerang* adds the impact of environment to the force of the mere narrative. Along with the case itself, the whole social texture from which it emerges is brought to the fore.[2] A story originally intended to feature an exceptional individual turns, by sheer dint of documentary treatment, into a vivid comment on our present *mores*.

But there is a strange inconsistency in all these "progressive" films. Upon closer inspection one cannot help noticing that they reveal the profound weakness of the very cause for which they try to enlist sympathy. No doubt they champion social progress within the dimensions of plot and dialogue, but in the less obvious dimensions they manage to suggest that liberal thought is receding rather than advancing. This impression is mainly the result of two types of characters that are common to most of Hollywood's quasi-liberal films—characters that tacitly discredit what the films themselves pretend to impart. Instead of showing the strength of liberalism, they testify to its extreme fragility.

One of these types is the weary standard-bearer of progress. The main characters of several of the films resemble each other strikingly in that they advance their beliefs with the least possible impetus. The District Attorney in *Crossfire*, who tracks down the murderer of the Jew, far from being a conquering hero, is a blasé man-about-town playing at being the liberal-minded sleuth. He himself admits that he is tired of his job. This may be an adequate pose for a screen detective intent on masking his toughness, but it is not precisely the attitude of a fighter against intolerance. The D.A. is no fighter. Even though he takes pains to persuade a Tennessee hillbilly of the dangers of anti-Semitism, he does so primarily because he wants help in capturing a murderer. It is very unlikely that this weary D.A. would ever feel tempted to spread his beliefs among the indifferent, the prejudiced, or the ignorant. He seems, rather, to be overwhelmed by a mood of resignation, as though he had discovered that the struggle for enlightenment is a Sisyphean task. Hence the all but melancholy aloofness with which he confines himself to defending the liberal position.

Nor does the ex-sergeant in *The Best Years of Our Lives* inspire any greater confidence. Out of a keen sense of social responsibility, this bank officer insists that veterans should receive loans without collateral, even though his superiors are opposed to the idea. It is true that in a toast delivered in their presence he makes no bones about their dire backwardness, but he has to get himself drunk to muster sufficient courage for this speech, and he never pushes matters beyond the point where they might imperil his position. At the end the audience is led to assume that sooner or later the bottle will serve him mainly to drown his frustrations. The older he grows the more likely he is to develop into a counterpart of the prison doctor in *Brute Force* [USA 1947, dir. Jules Dassin] (a film which grossly dramatizes a prisoners' revolt against sadistic jailers; the person of the doctor is the only link between this thriller and the series of "progressive" films). A believer in democratic methods, the doctor stands up against the disciplinarians in charge of the prison, telling them bluntly how disgusted he is with their savagery. It is the case of the ingrained democrat vs. fascist rule, yet while trying to stem the flood, the prison doctor knows that it will submerge him. He is on the verge of the grave, an old sick drunkard who, worn down by life, now speaks his mind with ill-concealed cynicism.

All these characters suggest that liberalism is on the defensive. In other films the same point is made by means of other devices. *The Farmer's Daughter* shows upright democrats defeating reactionary politicians with the greatest of ease, but the film's pronounced daydream character betrays its unconscious attempt to elude reality. A dreamlike victory of progressive elements thus in effect confirms the absence of such an event in real life. *Body and Soul* [USA 1947, dir. Robert Rossen], a boxing film stigmatizing the practice of fight-fixing, realistically admits that such abuses will continue. Although the decent champion upsets one of the New York manager's deceptive schemes, the latter continues his racket unaffected and nothing is changed.

Gentleman's Agreement, with its talkative arguments against country-club anti-Semitism, boldly touches upon a tabooed theme—and at the same time leaves it undisturbed. Besides obscuring the fight against upper-crust prejudices with a tacky love affair that increasingly gains momentum, the makers of the film—as if frightened by their own boldness—omit any action that might bear out their message. We are merely told that the journalist's fiancée eventually defies the unwritten law excluding Jews from a certain swanky settlement, and we can only guess how the Jewish boy she sponsors will manage to get along in these adverse surroundings. Instead of seeing things happen, we are left only with talk and hearsay. Liberal reasoning in *Gentleman's Agreement* results not so much in reforms as in magazine articles pretending to initiate such reforms—a mountain of dialogue bringing forth a mouse.

The other type frequently found in these movies is the potential recipient of the liberal gospel. He is invariably an ex-GI in a state of complete bewilderment. Consider, for example, the former pilot in *The Best Years of Our Lives*, the murder suspects in both *Crossfire* and *Boomerang*, and Henry Fonda's "Joe" in *The Long Night* [USA 1947, dir. Anatole Litvak], a film that I believe is loosely connected with the others. Characters of this kind have rarely been seen before on the screen. Visionless, at the mercy of any wind, benumbed even in their love-making, they drift about in a daze bordering on stupor. One is reminded of the Innocents—the characters created by Chaplin, Buster Keaton, and Harry Langdon in their slapstick comedies—who, favored by miraculous luck, always succeeded in outwitting hostile objects and evil Goliaths at the very last moment. It is as if those Innocents had been dragged out of their enchanted universe to face the world as it actually is—a world not in the least responsive to their candid dreams and hopes. The guise of the discharged soldier assures us that they are now average individuals, stunned by the shock of readjustment.

Significantly, these characters place little confidence in reason. They are not only impervious to ideas but instinctively shun them, as sources of suffering rather than means of redemption. This attitude is made most clear in Anatole Litvak's *The Long Night*, adapted from the French film *Daybreak* [*Le jour se lève;* 1939, dir. Marcel Carné]. Though a failure in many respects, the Litvak film impressively contrasts Joe, the simple-minded worker back home from the war, with a versatile night-club magician who is on rather intimate terms with Joe's girl. While Joe does not know how to express himself, the magician handles words as effortlessly as he does a pack of cards. And since he is a sadist to boot, he derives much pleasure from overpowering Joe with dialectic that throws him into ever deepening confusion. Of course, the magician's intellect is vile and corrupt, but even so it cannot deny its fundamental identity with reason proper. That the inarticulate Joe resents articulate reasoning as such follows from his conduct in the murder scene: he does not kill the magician out of jealousy—he kills him because he hates his guts. This reluctance to acknowledge reason turns into a main issue at the end of the film. After the Long Night is over, a night filled with shootings and flashbacks, Joe's girl persuades him to live up to the expectations of his many well-intentioned friends by surrendering to the police. Then, when he is walked to the police car through a crowd moved by his revolt as well as by his surrender, the shot of a Negro shaking hands with him intimates that plain people need not be taught tolerance or human dignity. The implied moral is that in the shaping of a better future good nature counts more than good thinking. Reason may deteriorate without our knowing it, but the heart is forever incorruptible.

Hollywood's "progressive" films, then, would suggest that the common man is indifferent to thought. They dwell on his intellectual apathy, occasionally playing up his generous impulses, which—they imply—more than compensate for his lack of open-mindedness. Not always did Hollywood show people in this light. When in the tavern episodes of *Ruggles of Red Gap* [USA 1935, dir. Leo McCarey] Charles Laughton recited Lincoln's Gettysburg Address, the townspeople one by one rose from their seats and gathered around him, moths irresistibly attracted to the flame. They communed in spirit, and in each of them an interpenetration of reason and emotion took place. Nothing of that kind occurs in our postwar films. As compared to those of the mid-thirties, they suggest a waning of spiritual substance.

But do not the "progressives" in these films combat prejudice and ignorance? No doubt they do. And yet their efforts seem to be ineffectual. Something emasculates them, adding to the weaknesses I have already described. All these fighters for democracy are talkers rather than doers. They are reminiscent of those commentators in the war documentaries, who indulged in flowery statements about the brave new world to come, and who could not help being very explicit in their creeds—more explicit, in fact, than the circumstances warranted. Much as the otherwise reticent D.A. in *Crossfire* avoids inflating the story he tells about his grandfather, it nonetheless affects us as propaganda—exceeding its immediate purpose. Unsubstantiated by images or actions, even the pertinent arguments give the impression of being a shade too wordy. There is a surfeit of eloquence in these films. And since this verbosity goes hand in hand with the emphasis on apathetic veterans, they are all the more suggestive of the gulf between the latter and the people who do the talking. What makes them appear so talkative is the futility of their attempt.

In sum, our postwar films present a common man reluctant to heed the voice of reason and a liberal spokesman unable to run the emotional blockade around him. I am aware, of course, that this is not intended. But there it is.

III

It is not possible, to be sure, to "prove" what these films imply.[3] But in the light of their testimony scattered everyday events gain in significance, and I am tempted to follow up one of the possibilities they hint at: that this general apathy has increased of late. The invocations now made everywhere on behalf of our way of life suggest by their very frequency that inertia is the source of them. Their stereotyped character points in the same direction; when beliefs become slogans they are not really believed. In our efforts to counterbalance Russian propaganda we show a marked lack of ingenuity, and the results show up abroad in a distrust of our "imperialist" motives. On the domestic scene, chill expediency threatens to stifle public concern with any issues beyond the merely practical. The whole climate is unfavorable to searching minds, and so the search subsides.

This apathy exists. On the surface it resembles somewhat the kind of indifference that pervades Roberto Rossellini's new film, *Paisan* [Italy 1946]. This Italian screen epic, one of the greatest films ever made, consists of six independent "real-life" episodes taking place during the Allied campaign in Italy and revealing its impact on diverse groups and individuals. All of the incidents show truly human aspirations being thwarted either by the war or by the existing order of things. *Paisan* could hardly be better contrived to show what our American movies are *not*.

I know of no film that could match this one in its grasp of the humanly essential. *Paisan* renders the fragile manifestations of human dignity with a simplicity and a directness that makes them seem as real as the hard facts of war. Human dignity is here not a matter of vague longing but an articulate experience frequently confirmed—by a Roman prostitute, an American Negro, a Neapolitan street urchin. Yet this insistence on humanity is bound up with a thorough distrust of the "messages" set forth in our own war or postwar films. To the suspicious Sicilian villagers the American Liberators look much the same as the German conquerors, and though the Italian partisans hate the Nazis, they certainly do not hate them out of a belief in democracy or in social progress.

Throughout the six episodes there is not a single pep talk, not the slightest verbal hint of a promise or a hope. Profoundly concerned with the actual existence of humaneness, the film never so much as mentions the "cause" of humanity. *Paisan*, instead of championing causes, implies that all such attempts however praiseworthy tend to smother what is uncontaminated and genuinely civilized. This is the wisdom of an old and mellow—perhaps over-mellow—people which has seen many ideas come and go, ideas invariably entailing war and misery, and is now extremely wary of them, preferring life as it is to life under such pressure.

The apathy from which we suffer has nothing in common with the Italian attitude. In their case the humane is not an abstraction but a self-sufficient reality rich in meaning. We are as remote from such an infatuation with humanity as we are from the disillusionment which spread after World War I. While the disillusioned of that period felt compelled to debunk what they considered illusions, we seem today to be gripped by a paralysis of our energies. We are passive where the others were at least "engaged"—to use the pet term of existentialism. We are not disillusioned; we are insensitive to anything ideological, even to the word itself. The apathy of this country today might be called ideological fatigue, a fatigue which in part accounts for the present vogue of psychiatry, with its emphasis on psychological relations rather than social meanings.

If it were not for our aversion to facing the latter, personal problems would not exert the fascination they now wield. It might even be said that our sudden interest in the relatively minor problems treated in our postwar films comes from our reluctance to face the major ones. The filmmakers have congratulated themselves for their courage in discussing the problem of the Jew, but they have not shown any greater interest in the problem of the Negro.

The retreat into apathy may well be an act of self-defense. Under the spell of the atom bomb, the average individual is led to believe that reason is a doubtful guide after all. This country's rise to world power exposes him to the full impact of influences that challenge his traditional values. And much as he would like to be immune to Russian Communism and European Socialism, these regimes do exist and their very existence makes him feel all the more uncomfortable as their pressure is brought home. The world has become one world indeed. In it the average individual feels completely at sea. Situations that seemed controllable in prewar days now seem confused by developments beyond his reach. Unable to orient himself, he instinctively shuts his eyes, like a man overwhelmed by dizziness on the edge of an abyss. What is the use, anyway, of trying to dissolve the impenetrable? Apathy serves him as a protective shelter.

In view of the possibility of a new recession, ideological fatigue on a mass scale is extremely dangerous. It predisposes the individual to being manipulated by anyone who, at a crucial moment, may detonate his pent-up emotions and divert them to a scapegoat. And what of the progressives, who could help us maintain our precarious balance? They competently denounce obscurantism and oppose social abuses with all the intellectual weapons at their disposal, but there is something anemic about the intellect that fashions these weapons. What is actually sailing under the flag of enlightenment is still borne on a wind of nineteenth-century optimism, with its naive belief in the appeal of reason and the virtual nonexistence of all that withstands it.

Yet evil does exist, and it cannot be drowned in bright visions. Even the most effective parade of hopes is thoroughly ineffective today—eyewash rather than white magic. A more fully orchestrated reasoning is needed to stir up hibernating minds, a reasoning that comes to grips with the dark powers that impatiently lie in wait to close in on us. Instead of lightly passing over them, we should acknowledge their existence and, so to speak, live on intimate terms with them. Blank opposition to evil is futile. Evil yields only to an embrace, to a change in the substance of what cannot otherwise be conquered.

Meanwhile the "progressive" films indicate where we stand. It is a static picture, of course, and not meant to exclude the possibility that imperceptible changes are already under way. Should Hollywood, despite its current escapism, begin to release films in which apathy gives way to insight and rhetoric to action, then the hope that reason is growing in depth would not be unfounded.

9 National Types as Hollywood Presents Them
(1949)

UNESCO has begun to inquire into the nature of tensions inimical to mutual understanding between the peoples of the world. Part of this "Tensions Project" is an analysis of "the conceptions which the people of one nation entertain of their own and of other nations."

It seems likely indeed that international understanding depends to some extent on the character of such conceptions—particularly if they assert themselves within the media of mass communication. Among these media the film is perhaps the most impressive.

If we are to study national images as presented in films, two broad areas for research immediately confront us. How do the films of any nation represent their own nation? And how do they represent others? The first of these two problems, increasingly dealt with in current writings,[1] can be dismissed here in favor of the second, which seems to me more important for UNESCO's quest. It is a new problem, not yet posed in a general way. Along with a whole family of similar problems, it has come into focus only now that world government is a possibility and world domination a threat. Only now, in fact, has the goal of mutual understanding through knowledge changed from an intellectual pleasure to a vital concern of the democracies.

The following study is by no means intended to provide a comprehensive analysis of the various screen images which the peoples of the world have formed, and continue to form, of each other. It is a pilot study and merely attempts to prepare the ground for such an investigation by examining a small sector of the total subject: the appearance of English and Russian characters in American fiction films since about 1933.[2]

In the universe of fiction films two types are of lesser importance—films about the past of the English and Russians, and screen adaptations of literary masterworks from the two countries. This is not to say that such films are rare. On the contrary, Hollywood finds Victorian England endearing and Catherine the Great amusing. Also, it often feels compelled to exchange entertainment for what it believes to be culture, and thus it eagerly exploits Shakespeare's plays and Tolstoy's novels, trying to make of them entertainment.[3] No doubt both these historical and literary films are well-established genres. And of course I do not deny that they help build up the screen images of the foreign peoples to which they refer. Yet since they deal with remote events, they are decidedly less relevant to this study than films that have a direct bearing on present-day reality.

It is these latter films on which I am concentrating here—films, that is, which involve contemporary Russian and British characters in real-life situations. There has been no lack of them since 1933. I am thinking, for instance, of *Ninotchka* [USA 1939, dir. Ernst Lubitsch], with its pleasantries at the expense of Soviet mentality, and of *Cavalcade* [USA 1933, dir. Frank Lloyd], which follows the destinies of a well-to-do English family through two generations. What concepts the American screen entertains of the English and Russians can best be elicited from such more or less realistically handled comedies and dramas.

OBJECTIVE AND SUBJECTIVE FACTORS IN NATIONAL IMAGES

In the cases of individuals and peoples alike, knowledge of each other may progress from a state of ignorance to fair understanding. It is, for instance, a far cry from what the average American knows about the Japanese to Ruth Benedict's recent disclosure of the set of motives that determine Japanese attitudes and actions. Her study, *The Chrysanthemum and the Sword*, marks progress in objectivity; it challenges us to dispose of the familiar notions and common prejudices which help fashion our standard images of that people.[4] Generally speaking, any such increase of knowledge is identical with a closer approach to the object we seek to penetrate.

This approach, however, is bound to remain asymptotic for two reasons, one of which lies in the object itself. An individual or a people is not so much a fixed entity as a living organism that develops along unforeseeable lines. Hence the difficulty of self-identification. It is true that the successive images a people creates of its own character are as a rule more reliable than those it forms of a foreign people's; but they are not complete and definite either.

The other obstacle to perfect knowledge, alone important in this context, lies in ourselves. We perceive all objects in a perspective imposed upon us by our environment as well as by certain inalienable traditions. Our concepts of a foreigner necessarily reflect native habits of thought. Much as we try to curtail this subjective factor, as we are indeed forced to do in the interest of increased objectivity, we still view the other individual from a position which is once and for all ours. It is just as impossible for us to settle down in a vacuum as it would be to fuse with him.

Any image we draw up of an individual or a people is the resultant of an objective and a subjective factor. The former cannot grow indefinitely; nor can the latter be completely eliminated. What counts is the ratio between these two factors. Whether our image of a foreign people comes close to true likeness or merely serves as a vehicle of self-expression—that is, whether it is more of a portrait or more of a projection—depends upon the degree to which our urge for objectivity gets the better of naive subjectivity.

MEDIA INFLUENCES ON OBJECTIVITY-SUBJECTIVITY RATIO

The ratio between the objective and the subjective factor varies with the medium of communication. It is evident that within the medium of the printed word objectivity may go the limit. In the radio, also, objective information plays a considerable role, even though it is hampered by various restrictions, most of them inherent in the nature of this mass medium. Yet for all its limitations the radio registers any signal increase of knowledge. I do not doubt, for instance, that the evolution of modern anthropology—resulting from the necessities of psychological warfare and this country's engagements in international affairs—has been instrumental in bringing about recent radio programs which surveyed living conditions in other countries, and in particular focused on "the character and ideals of the Russian people."[5]

And what about the film? Hollywood's fiction films are commercial products designed for mass consumption at home and, if possible, abroad. The implications of this over-all principle are obvious: Hollywood must try to captivate the masses without endangering its affiliations with vested interests. In view of high production costs it must try to avoid controversial issues lest box office receipts fall off. What the latter "must" means for the representation of foreigners is classically illustrated by the setback which the Remarque film *All Quiet on the Western Front* [USA 1930, dir. Lewis Milestone] suffered in Germany after a few Berlin performances, in December 1930. This film, with its emphasis on the anti-war mood of German soldiers in the years of trench warfare, stirred the Nazis to violent demonstrations which in turn caused the German government to suspend its further screening.[6] Similar experiences, made with vaguely anti-Fascist films in neutral countries shortly before World War II, have corroborated the sad truth that foreign peoples are as touchy as domestic groups, professional or otherwise. The film industry therefore "remains afraid of portraying characters or situations in a way which will offend its existing foreign market: why jeopardize a source of revenues?"[7]

Hollywood, then, is faced with the task of producing films that draw the masses, in particular the American masses. The problem of how it measures up to this task has long since been a subject of discussion. Many hold that Hollywood, with the support of its affiliated chains of movie houses, manages to sell films which do not give the masses what they really want. From this viewpoint it would seem that Hollywood films more often than not stultify and misdirect a public persuaded into accepting them by its own indolence and by overwhelming publicity. I do not believe that such a viewpoint is tenable. Experience has taught us that even totalitarian regimes cannot manipulate public opinion forever; and what holds true for them applies all the more to an industry which despite its monopolistic tendencies still functions within the framework of a competitive society. The film industry is forced by its profit interest to divine the nature of actually existing mass trends and to adjust its products to them. That this necessity leaves a margin for cultural initiative on the part of the industry does not alter the situation. To be sure, American audiences receive what Hollywood wants them to want; but in the long run audience desires, acute or dormant, determine the character of Hollywood films.[8]

The audiences also determine the way these films picture foreigners. The subjective factor in any such image is more or less identical with the notions American public opinion entertains of the people portrayed. It is therefore highly improbable that a nation popular with the average American will be presented unfavorably; nor should we expect currently unpopular nations to be treated with condoning benevolence. Similarly, screen campaigns for or against a nation are not likely to be launched unless they can feed on strong environmental moods in their favor.

Yet its surrender to such moods need not prevent Hollywood from volunteering information about foreign peoples. It is true that we usually want to understand other nations because of our concern with mutual understanding; but fear and distrust of a people may no less urgently compel us to inquire into the motives behind its aspirations. The desire for knowledge, an essentially independent inner drive, thrives on both antipathy and sympathy. To what extent do Hollywood films satisfy this desire? Or, more specifically: what is the ratio between the subjective and the objective factor in American screen images of foreigners? And has this ratio been stable so far, or are we justified in assuming, for instance, that the images of 1948 surpass those of 1933 in objectivity?

HOLLYWOOD'S ESTIMATE OF ITS AUDIENCE

Without anticipating answers, I wish to formulate a principle derived from the all-powerful profit motive. Hollywood's attitude toward the presentation of any given piece of information ultimately depends on its estimate of how the masses of moviegoers respond to the spread of that information through fiction films. It seems to me important in this connection that the film industry calls itself an entertainment industry—a term which, whatever it connotes, does not precisely make one think of films as carriers of knowledge (nor as works of art, for that matter). There has indeed been a widespread tendency not only to equate screen entertainment and relaxation, but to consider anything informative an undesirable admixture. This entertainment formula, championed as late as 1941 in the sophisticated Preston Sturges film *Sullivan's Travels*, rests upon the conviction that people want to relax when they go to the movies; and it further implies that the need for relaxation and the quest for knowledge oppose rather than attract each other. Of course, as always with such formulas, they characterize the mental climate without being strictly binding. Many a prewar film has defied the usual Hollywood pattern and has deepened our understanding of the world.

Only since the end of the war have ideological conventions undergone a change; and again this change must be traced to mass moods. Obviously inspired by the general desire for enlightenment in the wake of the war, spokesmen of the industry now advocate films that combine entertainment with information. "Motion pictures," says Jack L. Warner, "are entertainment—but they go far beyond that." And he coins the term "*honest* entertainment" to convey the impression of a Hollywood fighting for truth, democracy, international understanding, etc.[9] Eric Johnston, President of the Motion Picture Association, lends his authority to this view. In his statement *The Right To Know*—which is none the less pertinent for referring to fiction films and factual films alike—he contends that "the motion picture, as an instrument for the promotion of knowledge and understanding among peoples, stands on the threshold of a tremendous era of expansion."[10]

Whether the American motion picture has already trespassed this threshold remains to be seen. On the purely domestic scene it has done so—at least up to a point and temporarily. Attacking social abuses, such films as *The Best Years of Our Lives* [USA 1946, dir. William Wyler], *Boomerang* [USA 1947, dir. Elia Kazan], and *Gentleman's Agreement* [USA 1947, dir. Elia Kazan] reveal a progressive attitude which undoubtedly owes much to wartime experiences.[11] They still play to full houses, even though political pressures have meanwhile caused the industry to discontinue this trend. Will Hollywood revert to its old entertainment formula? For the time being, we must remain in suspense.

THE TIME ELEMENT

Such foreign peoples as one does see on the American screen do not appear consecutively in films about present-day life. The English were featured in a number of prewar films succeeding each other closely—among them were the above-mentioned *Cavalcade* (1933), *Of Human Bondage* [USA 1934, dir. John Cromwell], *Ruggles of Red Gap* [USA 1935, dir. Leo McCarey], *The Lives of a Bengal Lancer* [USA 1935, dir. Henry Hathaway], *Angel* [USA 1937, dir. Ernst Lubitsch], *Lost Horizon* [USA 1937, dir. Frank Capra], *A Yank at Oxford* [USA 1938, dir. Jack Conway], *The Citadel* [USA 1938, dir. King Vidor], *The Sun Never Sets* [USA 1939, Rowland Lee], *We Are Not Alone* [USA 1939, dir. Edmund Golding], *Rebecca* [USA 1940, dir. Alfred Hitchcock], *Foreign Correspondent* [USA 1940, dir. Alfred Hitchcock], and *How Green Was My Valley* [USA 1941, dir. John Ford]. No sooner did the United States enter the war than the frequency of topical films about Great Britain and her people increased, as is instanced by *Mrs. Miniver* [USA 1942, dir. William Wyler], *The Pied Piper* [USA 1942, dir. Irving Pichel], *Journey for Margaret* [USA 1942, dir. W. S. van Dyke], *The White Cliffs of Dover* [USA 1944, dir. Clarence Brown], etc.

This vogue broke off immediately after the war. To the best of my knowledge, the British postwar generation would be nonexistent in the cinematic medium were it not for *The Paradine Case* [USA 1948, dir. Alfred Hitchcock], a murder story without any bearing on current issues, and the international-minded melodrama *Berlin Express* [USA, dir. Jacques Tourneur], released as late as May 1948. Between 1945 and 1948, there was a gap spanned only by a few films that focused exclusively on the past—Lubitsch's *Cluny Brown* [USA 1946], which satirized prewar attitudes, fashionable or otherwise; *So Well Remembered* [USA 1947, Edward Dmytryk], a social-minded chronicle of small-town life between the two wars; *Ivy* [USA 1947, dir. Sam Wood]; *Moss Rose* [USA 1947, dir. Gregory Ratoff]; and *So Evil My Love* [USA 1948, dir. Lewis Allen]. The last three were mystery thrillers playing in turn-of-the-century Britain, if not earlier. Though three years may not be a long period, this sustained unconcern for the present still seems a bit strange.

During the thirties, contemporary Russians were less in view than the English, without, however, being wholly neglected. I have already mentioned *Ninotchka* (1939). Other films of the period were *Tovarich* [USA 1937, dir. Anatole Litvak] and *Comrade X* [USA 1940, dir. King Vidor]. In the war, when Stalin joined the Allies, Hollywood permitted no one to outdo it in glowing accounts of Russian heroism. *Mission to Moscow* [USA 1943, dir. Michael Curtiz], *Miss V from Moscow* [USA 1942, dir. Albert Herman], *The North Star* [USA 1943, dir. Lewis Milestone], *Three Russian Girls* [USA 1943, dir. Henry S. Kesler and Fyodor Otsep], *Song of Russia* [USA 1944, dir. Gregory Ratoff]—a veritable springtide of pro-Russian films—flooded the movie houses in 1943 and 1944.

Then, exactly as in the case of the English, the Russians disappeared for three years. They disappeared even more completely than the English, for I do not know of a single, halfway important film since Lubitsch's resurrection of Catherine the Great [*A Royal Scandal,* USA 1945] which has dealt with their literature or past. Of course, I discount the "mad Russian," who re-emerged in *The Specter of the Rose* [USA 1946, dir. Ben Hecht]; this stereotyped favorite of American audiences—usually a Russian-born artist having sought shelter in the West—is on the whole too estranged from the country of his origin to be identified as a Soviet citizen. It is true that Russians were also rare on the prewar screen, but in those days they were not featured in other media either. What makes one wonder at the absence of Soviet Russia on the postwar screen is just the fact of her omnipresence in speech and print at this time. Between 1945 and 1948, the film alone seemed unaware of a mass obsession.

That Hollywood behaved true to pattern in thus ignoring the Russians is proven by its equally conspicuous silence about the Nazis in the years preceding 1939. It is not as if Germany had played any noticeable role in American films prior to 1933. Yet precisely in the critical years 1930–1934, two grade-A films turned the spotlight on her—*All Quiet on the Western Front* and *Little Man, What Now?* [USA 1934, dir. Frank Borzage], a screen adaptation of Hans Fallada's pre-Hitler novel about unemployment in Germany. Hollywood, it appears, had become mildly interested in things German. And what came out of it? During the subsequent year Hitler was a topic everywhere but on the screen. If I am not mistaken, only two films with Germans in them appeared in this interval: *The Road Back* [USA 1937, dir. James Whale] and *Three Comrades* [USA 1938, dir. Frank Borzage]. Both were adapted from novels by Remarque, whose name meant business, and both were laid in the early Weimar Republic, which was dead and buried at the time of their release.

TIMES WHEN SILENCE SEEMS WISE

This temporary withdrawal from certain peoples at certain times can be explained only by factors affecting commercial film production. Significantly, prewar Germany as well as postwar Russia provoked impassioned controversy in the United States. Before the war the country was divided into isolationists and interventionists; immediately after the war it heatedly debated the problem of whether the United States should be tough or soft in her dealings with the Kremlin. I believe it is this split of public opinion which accounts for Hollywood's evasiveness in both cases. Hollywood, as I have pointed out earlier, is so sensitive to economic risks that it all but automatically shrinks from touching on anything controversial. Germany and Russia were tabooed as "hot stuff"; and they were hot stuff as long as everybody argued about them and a decisive settlement of this nation-wide strife was not yet in sight. They disappeared, that is, not in spite of their hold on the American mind, but because of it.

There has been no such controversy with regard to Anglo-American relations. Why, then, the scarcity of postwar-Britons in Hollywood films? Considering the impact of mass attitudes on film content, this scarcity may well result from the uneasiness with which Americans react to Labor rule in Britain. Their disquiet is understandable, for what is now going on in Britain means a challenge to American belief in free enterprise and its particular virtues. In the United States any discussion of British affairs is therefore likely to touch off an argument about the advantages and disadvantages of the American way of life. But once this kind of argument gets started you never know where it will lead. The whole matter is extremely delicate and involved, and it is for such reasons, I submit, that Hollywood producers currently neglect, perhaps without consciously intending it, the living English in favor of their less problematic ancestors.[12]

. . . AND TIMES TO SPEAK OUT

These periods of silence may suddenly come to a close, with mimosa-like shyness yielding to uninhibited outspokenness. In the prewar era, the years 1938–1939 marked a turning of the tide. At the very moment when the European crisis reached its height, the American screen first took notice of the Axis powers and their creeds. *Blockade* (1938), a Walter Wanger production, initiated this trend. It denounced the ruthless bombing of cities during the Spanish civil war, clearly sympathizing with the Loyalist cause—which, however, was left unmentioned, as was Franco, the villain in the piece. Hollywood soon overcame these hesitations. *Confessions of a Nazi Spy* [USA 1939, dir. Anatole Litvak], a realistic rendering of Nazi activities in the United States, overtly stigmatized Hitler Germany and all that it stood for. Then came the war, and anti-Nazi films, less realistic than well intentioned, grew rampant.

During those fateful years 1938–1939, other national film industries began to speak up also. The French released *Grand Illusion* [France 1938, dir. Jean Renoir], which resurrected World War I in a pacifistic spirit, and *Double Crime in the Maginot Line* [France 1937, dir. Félix Gandéra],[13] whose German characters were indistinct. Even though both these films shirked any direct mention of Nazi Germany, they effectively conjured up her giant shadow. A similar device was used by Eisenstein in his *Alexander Nevsky* [USSR 1938] shown in the United States in 1939. In picturing the defeat which thirteenth-century Russia inflicted upon the Teutonic Knights, Eisenstein—and through him Stalin—warned Hitler not to try the old game again.

Shortly after the release of *Blockade,* John C. Flinn, a *Variety* correspondent, emphasized Hollywood's vital interest in its career: "Upon its success financially revolve the plans of several of the major studios heretofore hesitant about tackling stories which treat with subjects of international economic and political controversy."[14] This expert statement sheds light on the motives that prompted the film industry into action. Despite the protests of certain Catholic groups, *Blockade* was a success financially; and though Hollywood might have felt tempted to produce anti-Nazi films even before *Blockade,* it did so only after having made fairly sure that they would be accepted on a nation-wide scale. The appearance of Nazis on the screen was connected with the evolution of public opinion in the United States. They appeared when, after the debacle in Spain and Austria's fall, the time of wavering controversy was practically over. Isolationism, to be sure, persisted; but the whole country bristled with indignation against the Nazis, and there was no longer any doubt that some day the world would have to stop Hitler and his associates. Since this conviction also prevailed in Britain, France, and elsewhere, Hollywood did not risk much in expressing sentiments so universally popular.

What happened in 1939, repeats itself in 1948: after a lull of three to four years, Russians now begin to reappear on the American screen as abruptly as did the Germans. The parallels between *The Iron Curtain* of May 1948 [dir. William Wellman] and *Confessions of a Nazi Spy* are striking. Like the latter film, this new one is a spy thriller—a pictorial account of the events that led to the discovery, in 1946, of a Russian-controlled spy ring in Canada. Both films are based on scripts by the same author, and both are narrated in documentary fashion. Should these similarities be symptomatic of analogous situations, as I believe they are, then *The Iron Curtain,* with its avowed hostility toward the Soviet regime, would indicate that American public opinion has come out of the controversial stage in favor of a tough stand on Russia.

TREATMENT OF ENGLISH CHARACTERS

For a long time Great Britain and the United States have been entertaining an alliance founded upon the community of race, language, historical experience, and political outlook. Interchange has been frequent; processes of symbiosis have been going on. To Americans the English are an "in-group" people; they belong, so to speak, to the family, while other peoples—"out-group" peoples—do not. Where such intimate bonds exist, knowledge of each other seems a matter of course. American screen images of Britons might therefore be expected to be true likenesses.

Hollywood has tried hard to justify such expectations. Many American films about the English are drawn from their own novels or stage plays; and the bulk of these films are shot on location, involving genuine mansions, lawns, and London streets. In addition, there is rarely an important English part in an American film that is not assigned to a native Britisher.

This insistence on authenticity and local color benefits films which cover a diversity of subjects: middle-class patriotism (*Cavalcade, Mrs. Miniver*); empire glorification (*The Lives of a Bengal Lancer, The Sun Never Sets*, etc.); Anglo-American relations (*Ruggles of Red Gap*); upper-class ideology (again *Ruggles of Red Gap*, then *Angel, The White Cliffs of Dover*, etc.); sports (*A Yank at Oxford*); social issues, such as the status of physicians (*The Citadel*) and of coal miners (*How Green Was My Valley*), and so on. Strictly personal conflicts prevail in *Of Human Bondage* and *Rebecca*; public school life is featured in *Goodbye, Mr. Chips* [USA 1939, dir. Sam Woods], a retrospective film.

The wealth of themes engenders a wide range of types. I dare say that, taken together, American films offer a more complete cross-section of the English than they do of any other people. From night club musicians to Kiplingese colonels and from workers to diplomats, nearly all strata of the population are presented on some occasion and somehow. Frequent among these types are well-to-do gentlemen and their manservants—a couple of figures forever illustrating the Lord-Butler relationship, which has been so delightfully patterned in *Ruggles of Red Gap*. Incidentally, in any film about foreigners the minor characters tend to be more true to type than the protagonists, because they are less deliberately constructed.

In short, the English are rendered substantially as befits the prominent place they hold in American traditions. The result is a fairly inclusive image of their national traits, an image which for all its emphasis on snobbish caste spirit permits the audience to catch glimpses of British imperturbability, doggedness, and sportsmanship. *The Lives of a Bengal Lancer*, which initiated a trend of cloak-and-dagger melodramas—films playing in an India or Africa faintly reminiscent of the Wild West—points up the frontier bravura of English Empire builders and their soldiery;[15] *The Pied Piper*, in a highly amusing sequence, shows members of a London club indulging in the native penchant for understatement while German bombers noisily drop their loads.

This many-sided approach further testifies to Hollywood's concern with the British way of life. Small wonder that several prewar films succeeded in reflecting it faithfully. A model case of objectivity is *Cavalcade*, the well-known screen version of Noel Coward's play. Before this film with its English cast went into production, its original director filmed the whole London stage performance of the play so as not to miss any of those minutiae upon which the impression of genuineness depends. Such efforts paid: *Cavalcade*, according to a report from London, "convinced the most skeptical Englishmen that the American film capital can on occasion produce a much better British picture than any English studio has yet managed to achieve."[16]

At this point the problem of the ratio between the objective and the subjective factor arises. Can the latter be neglected in the case of the English? Or, rather, does experience show that in the long run subjective influences—influences exerted by American mass attitudes—win out over that urge for objectivity of which *Cavalcade* is so impressive an instance? I wish to make it clear from the outset that all the measures Hollywood has taken in the interest of authenticity do not suffice to eliminate distortions. A script may be one hundred per cent British and yet materialize in a film imbued with Hollywood spirit. Nor do views of the Tower or a Tudor castle warrant accuracy; documentary shots, as is proven by many propaganda films and newsreels, can be juxtaposed in such a way that they falsify the very reality which they candidly capture. But are not English actors a guarantee for the truthful representation of English life? They are not, for two reasons. First, the screen appearance of any actor results not only from his own acting, but from the various cinematic devices used in building up his image on the screen, and because of their share in its establishment this image may well express other meanings than those conveyed by the actor himself. Secondly, even though an English actor is under all circumstances an Englishman, he may have to appear in a film so little suggestive of typically English behavior and thought patterns that he finds no opportunity of substantiating them. He will be neutralized within such contexts. In other words, whether or not screen portrayals of a foreign people are convincing does not solely depend upon their being enacted by native actors. What counts most is the whole film's susceptibility to the characteristics of that people.

THE SNOB

The influence of American preconceptions shows in the selection of English character traits. Hollywood films establish a hierarchy among these traits in which snobbishness, as I have indicated, figures foremost. Inseparable from class-mindedness, snobbishness pervades the servant's quarters in numerous films, confers upon screen aristocrats an air of inimitable superiority, surrounds as a palpable halo all those Englishmen who by provision of the plots defend advanced colonial outposts or mingle with Americans and Frenchmen, and makes itself felt everywhere not only in the manner of speaking but at decisive turning-points of dialogue. It is the one British characteristic which American movies never tire of acknowledging, ridiculing, condoning, or repudiating, according to the views expressed in them.

No doubt this trait actually exists. The English writer Margaret Cole, who is all against snobbishness, nevertheless admits that much in her recent Harper's article: "The British have a pretty lively sense of birth and upbringing: they like titles and honors, and they like to know people who have titles and honors . . . they are, most of them, pretty good snobs."[17] Yet this does not mean that the English are primarily snobs. Like any other people, they have a complex character structure; snobbishness therefore need not appear as their main trait. As a matter of fact, it could easily be shown that the films of different nations have conceived of Englishmen in quite different ways.[18] Take the German cinema: for all their surface similarities, the German and the American screen Britons are by no means counterparts. Such German peacetime films as dealt with the English at all paid tribute grudgingly to their way of life. Among the traits featured, however, correctness and decency (e.g. of British navy officers) were more conspicuous than snobbishness—a trait whose social implications eluded a people which had never had a society in the Western sense. And when war came the Germans expressed their pent-up resentments against the British Empire in films which made no bones about the ruthlessness of the English and about their alleged hypocrisy. The latter characteristic, passed off as an English cardinal vice by the Germans, is practically nonexistent in American films.

Any nation, it appears, sees other peoples in a perspective determined by its experience of them; and, of course, its cinema features those character traits of theirs which are an integral part of this experience. Hence the emphasis on English caste spirit in Hollywood film. To Americans this trait stands out among others because it affected them deeply under British rule. And since nations, like individuals, tend to build on their early impressions, the mass of Americans, among them swarms of Irish immigrants, took it for granted that the typical Briton is essentially a caste-proud snob. They reacted to him in two opposite ways—a further symptom of the imprint which his conduct, or, rather, their conception of it, had left on them. On the one side, they condemned British snobbishness for offending their sense of equality; on the other, they admired and imitated it. American snobbery contributes much to stabilizing the English snob on the screen; his recurrent image is both a reflection of and a protest against native cravings for nobility, Oxford, and authentic manners. This is confirmed by *Ruggles of Red Gap*, which mingles gentle gibes at the foreign idol with a solid satire of its Middle-West worshipers. Another case in point is Preston Sturges' brilliant comedy *Lady Eve* [USA 1941]. Even though this film does not include any Britons, it does show a cute American girl who reconquers her lover by posing as Lady Eve, the daughter of an English aristocrat.

The American screen image of the English is more or less standardized. True as this image is to reality, as a stereotype it has also a life of its own, a life independent of that reality. The English snob, as he appears in Hollywood films, is a figure which has in some degree drifted away from its original to join those mythological figures that people the world of American imagination. Whether angry at him or fond of him, Americans consider this kind of Briton one of theirs. He "belongs"; like Huckleberry Finn or Mickey Mouse, he is part of their universe.

This permanent preoccupation with British snobbishness is not the only subjective element in Hollywood's portrayal of the English. Other influences, equally instrumental in its composition, arise from changes on the domestic scene. In prewar days, when relations between the United States and Great Britain developed along traditional lines, there was no reason why these changes should interfere with an objective rendering of Britons. Domestic mass desires asserted themselves merely in the preference given to such film subjects as were likely to draw American audiences at a specific moment. *Cavalcade* was particularly well timed. This film, with its unflinching belief in Britain's greatness, appeared at the depths of the Depression, a comfort to all those Americans who despaired of the predicament they were in. Many wept when seeing the film, and more than one reviewer declared it to be a tribute to what is best in all national spirits. Two years later, *Ruggles of Red Gap*, a comedy about the molding of a class-conscious English butler into a free American, struck that tone of self-confidence which by then filled the air. And so it goes. It would, by the way, be tempting to inquire into the causes of the enormous popularity which films about British imperialism enjoyed for a stretch of years. That they had a definite bearing on domestic issues is evident even in their casting: the elder colonels in *The Lives of a Bengal Lancer* and *Gunga Din* fell to the charge of English actors, while the young protagonists, heroes or cowards, were played by stars genuinely American.

BRITISH CHARACTERS IN WARTIME

Once the war was on, national exigencies encroached on the tendency toward objectivity. American public opinion endorsed the war effort, and

Britain was now an Ally. For these reasons Hollywood could no longer afford to approach the English in that spirit of impartiality which is indispensable for an understanding of others. Rather, it was faced with the task of endearing everything British to the American masses. The task was not simply to represent the English, but to make them seem acceptable even to the population whose pro-British feelings were doubtful.

Significantly, most Hollywood films about Britain at war attempt to weaken the existing antipathies against English snobbishness, thus reaffirming American obsession with this trait. *Mrs. Miniver*, representative of the whole trend, shows wartime Britain undergo processes of democratization tending to transform her national character. In this film, as a reviewer judiciously points out, "even Lady Beldon, the aged, local autocrat, finally realizes that her class-conscious, if gracious, civilization has been forged into the practical democracy of an entire country united against the enemy."[19] *The Pied Piper* features an old English gentleman whose noble impulses increasingly get the better of his outward standoffishness; *The White Cliffs of Dover*, a sentimental retrospect which tries to enlist audience sympathies for British upper-class people, ends with hints of their readiness to conform to more democratic standards. It is not that such motifs had been entirely omitted in prewar films; but during the war they grew into leitmotifs, coloring all films of the period and serving as their very justification.

Produced in response to powerful domestic urges, these films, I assume, would have misrepresented English reality even if they had been shot on location. To what extent they actually distorted it can be inferred from the criticism with which they were received in Britain itself. *Mrs. Miniver*, though recognized as a laudable American tribute to English war heroism, was nevertheless blamed for "its faults and frequent air of English unreality."[20] Of *The White Cliffs of Dover* the London *Times* said that it "misses the tones and accents of the country in which the action passes."[21] And with regard to *Random Harvest* [USA 1942, dir. Mervyn LeRoy], another Hollywood wartime production, a polite reviewer remarked that "Greer Garson and Ronald Colman act away the frequent obtrusion of error in English detail and behavior."[22]

ABSENCE OF THE POSTWAR BRITAIN

The war over, one might have expected Hollywood to resume its relatively objective approach to contemporary Britons. Yet it preferred, and still prefers, to ignore their existence. Nothing proves more conclusively the overpowering effect of domestic influences in the field of screen entertainment. Now that the English in some respects really live up to the image drawn up of them in all American war films—class-mindedness is on the decline and snobbery less domineering—it would seem natural for Hollywood to acknowledge what it praised only yesterday. Instead, it resolutely turns its back on Britain, for reasons at which I have made a guess in earlier contexts. During the war, folks at home took delight in a Lady Beldon who proved herself a convinced democrat; at present, the peculiar flavor of English democracy so little pleases many Americans that the Lady Beldons are being held incommunicado until further notice.

The meaning of this temporary blackout—all the more striking in view of the influx into America of English films about postwar life in Britain—is enhanced by those Hollywood productions which introduce British characters of the past. They not only reestablish the stereotype of the English snob (*Cluny Brown*), but draw on other familiar prewar patterns as well. All of them could have been made before 1941. In thus combining disregard of the present with uninhibited rendering of the past, Hollywood follows a rule of conduct which it has already practiced before. Nor is this treatment of foreign peoples unknown to other national film industries: at a time when the German pre-Hitler cinema was completely oblivious of Soviet Russia, it elaborated profusely on the blessings of the Czarist regime. I have reason to believe that in all such cases the emergence of films about the past of a people betrays discontent with its present state of affairs. What makes these films into vehicles of indirect criticism is the fact of their appearance at a moment when any direct mention of that people is strictly avoided. They manifest apprehensions not so much through their content as their sheer existence. Only occasionally do they come into the open, picturing past events for the thinly veiled purpose of dealing with present ones. In *Alexander Nevsky*, the eyes that gleam through visors of the Teutonic Knights are unmistakably the eyes of contemporary Nazis.

In sum, the objective factor in American screen images of the English is extremely vulnerable. Much as the age-old intimacy of Anglo-American relations favors its growth, the impact of subjective influences invariably tends to stunt it. Domestic needs and mass desire have on more than one occasion caused Hollywood to portray the English inadequately or not to portray them at all, which amounts to the same thing. There is no progress of knowledge noticeable as these portrayals succeed each other—in fact, *Cavalcade*, released as early as 1933, has probably never been surpassed in objectivity. Everything, it appears, hinges on market necessities which may or may not permit Hollywood to reflect the English closely.

RUSSIAN CHARACTERS

In their *America in Midpassage,* the Beards mention the success of the first Russian Five-Year Plan among those foreign events which augmented American anxieties in the spring of 1933. "Still Russia was far off," they remark before turning to the more stirring repercussions of Hitler's rise to power, "and could be discounted as a bit oriental in its ways and values."[23]

To Americans the Russians are an "out-group" people indeed. There is a pronounced lack of traditions common to both countries, and there has never been an intermingling of their nationals as in the case of the English. The chasm separating the two countries is deepened by the antagonism between their regimes—an antagonism so laden with dynamite that it predetermines all popular notions Americans and Russians hold of each other. Unsustained by experience and inevitably biased, these notions are outright clichés. The average American has incorporated the figure of the "mad Russian" into the collection of his pet stereotypes; he knows that Russians are fond of music, ballet, and vodka. And, of course, innumerable editorials and the like have impressed upon him fixed concepts of Bolshevism as something with collective farms, secret police, and purges. Most of it is sheer hearsay, however true.

Hollywood, always inclined to capitalize on existing clichés, is not in the best of positions to breathe life into them. For obvious reasons American films about Russia are studio-made; and because of the scarcity of Russian actors in this country, their native characters are as a rule assigned to Hollywood stars or to German actors who seem to have a knack for portraying Russians. In *The Last Command* [USA 1928, dir. Josef von Sternberg], Emil Jannings was a very convincing Czarist general. I have pointed out that even films with English actors in the cast may misrepresent the English; conversely, actors in the roles of foreigners need not, under all circumstances, miss the essentials. Nevertheless, it remains true that the reliance on outside portrayals in imitation settings thwarts rather than facilitates an objective rendering of other peoples.

Such scattered Hollywood films about contemporary Russia as did appear between 1927 and 1934 frowned upon the Soviet Union with an air of grave concern. Most of them were laid in, or referred to, the early days of the Russian Revolution when everything was still fluid. Even though they did not pass over the disastrous abuses of Czarist rule—how could they?—yet they managed to make you feel gloomy about the victory of a cause so obviously barbarian. I am thinking of *Mockery* [USA 1927, dir. Benjamin Christensen], *The Tempest* [USA 1928, dir. Sam Taylor], *The Last Command,* and *British Agent* [USA 1934, dir. Michael Curtiz]. Except for Sternberg's *Last Command,* each of these films culminated in a romance between a Russian Red and his, or her, class enemy, which drove home the humanly destructive effects of Bolshevist class hatred. *Forgotten Commandments* [USA 1932, dir. Louis Gasnier and William Schorr], "a sermon on the evils of Soviet Land,"[24] accused Russia of having forsaken Christianity. Of these productions only the Sternberg film and perhaps *British Agent* had some merits. The Beards are right: "Russia was far off . . ."

She did not come nearer after her recognition by President Roosevelt late in 1933. Yet American attitudes changed. After a period of silence filled in by several films which involved Catherine the Great, Tolstoy's *Anna Karenina,* and Dostoievsky's *Crime and Punishment* (like the current films about the English past, these may have conveyed polite discontent with the stubborn survival of Russian Communism), this change showed in Hollywood's transition from serious criticism to critical comedy. *Tovarich,* I believe, was the first film to endorse the fact of political recognition by substituting light skirmishes for heavy attacks. Hostilities continued, but they adjusted themselves to the improved relations with the Soviet Union, which after all was here to stay. Lubitsch's *Ninotchka,* with Garbo in the title role, also marked a precarious rapprochement. This amusing piece of raillery, which showed Marxist-trained Russians succumbing to the frivolous attractions of the West, viewed Soviet life with the condescension of an adult who watches fledglings romp. It was a sort of shoulder-patting; why not finally grow up, the film seemed to ask. Its success bred other films in this vein: *He Stayed for Breakfast* [USA 1940, dir. Alexander Hall], "a gay spoof of the Communistic camaraderie that flourished in Paris before the war,"[25] and *Comrade X,* which, laid in Moscow, equally jeered at the conversion of rabid Communist. Released in 1940, both films not only lacked Lubitsch's finesse, but stuck a tone of poignant aggressiveness absent in his *Ninotchka.* Of *Comrade X,* Bosley Crowther says: ". . . seldom has a film . . . satirized a nation and its political system with such grim and malicious delight as does this . . . comedy."[26]

THE WARTIME RUSSIAN

The English characters in American war films about Britain still resembled their predecessors of a few years before, but no such resemblances connected the intrepid Russian woman fighter glorified by Hollywood between 1942 and 1944 with the yielding Ninotchka so popular shortly before. This was not simply a shift of emphasis, as in the case of the English, but a radical change of scene, with Stalin becoming Uncle Joe and collective farming a source of happiness. I scarcely need elaborate on characters and situations in *Mission to Moscow, The North Star,* and so on. All these films sprang from the overwhelming desire, on the part of the home front, to keep Russia in the war. The surprising thing is their unconcern for continuity: they idolized what had been condemned in times of peace, or winked at it unashamedly. It was a complete turnabout.

In thus wooing Russia for reasons of domestic self-interest, Hollywood ignored its otherwise guiding rule of leaving controversial issues untouched. Opposition against the Soviet regime was too stable a factor of American public opinion to be eliminated by the necessities of the war. Subdued as it was, it continued to smolder. This accounts for the criticism which in particular *Mission to Moscow,* with its indulgent references to the Moscow trials, met from diverse quarters. And about *The North Star,* which in its opining scenes extolled the insouciant life of Russian villagers before 1941, the *Daily News* wrote that this film is more Communistic "than the Russians themselves who have never pretended that prewar Russia was a musical-comedy paradise."[27]

... AND THE RUSSIAN OF TODAY

Now that the spell of amnesia from which Hollywood suffered in the postwar years is over, we are witnessing another turnabout. Gone are the brave Russian women fighters, the happy villagers, and the democratic allures of the rulers. In their places somber bureaucrats, counterparts of the Nazis, spread an atmosphere of oppression. This at least is the way *The Iron Curtain* pictures Soviet officials—they appear as ruthless totalitarians obeyed by devout slaves. And the only "good" Russian is a man who so firmly believes in the superior value of Western civilization that he deserts Communism and betrays his country. Similar types were also advertised in American prewar comedies; but unlike *Ninotchka, The Iron Curtain* avoids any satirical overtones that might weaken the impact of its accusations. Other current films draw no less determinedly on the anti-Communist sentiments of American audiences. In *The Fugitive* [USA 1947, dir. John Ford]—a deliberately fantastic film with exotic settings—humble priests are wantonly persecuted by all-powerful authorities which everybody is free to identify as Communists. The Russian black-market racketeer in *To The Victor* [USA 1948, dir. Delmer Daves] is no endearing figure either. And we may soon see more anti-Soviet films; two or three have already been scheduled for production. This general insistence on toughness, however, seems to be slightly mitigated by the fearful prospect of another war: *Berlin Express* and *A Foreign Affair* [USA 1948, dir. Billy Wilder], both laid in Germany, indulge in a relatively amiable approach to their Russian characters, thus intimating that we should not give up hope for an understanding after all.

DOMINANCE OF THE SUBJECTIVE FACTOR

All this illustrates Hollywood's unconcern for Russian reality. Unlike the English characters in Hollywood films, which at least give one a taste, however faint, of genuine life, American screen portrayals of Russians conform to what Americans imagine far-away Russians to be like. Even Russian-born actors are strangely colorless in plots based upon such subjective concepts; and, of course, Garbo in *Ninotchka* always remains Garbo in the guise of Ninotchka. The objective factor in these portrayals is negligible—they are not experienced, but constructed. Hence their remoteness from the originals they pretend to portray. Commenting on *The North Star*, Archer Winsten, one of the most observant New York film critics, states that its characters are "single-plane cutouts rather than those deeply modeled characterizations of the best Russian films . . ."[28] He might have added that the many Russian films shown in the United States have not in the slightest degree stimulated Hollywood to relinquish its home-bred notions of Russia.

These notions are of a political nature. All Hollywood films about Russia raise topical issues, and many of them, I presume, would have never been produced were it not for the purpose of externalizing American attitudes toward the Soviet regime. This explains why the characters in them are so poorly instrumented. As compared with English screen figures, Hollywood-made Russians are sheer abstractions. Instead of being introduced for their own sake as are the English in many cases, they merely serve to personify pros and cons in the ever-fluctuating debate on Russian Communism. It is as if they were drawn from editorials. They resemble marionettes, and you cannot help seeing the strings by which they are pulled.

And finally these marionettes lack the relative stability of English characters. The English snob has survived the war, while Ninotchka was popular only for a transient moment. Her ephemeral vogue is symptomatic of the frequent, occasionally hectic changes which Russian characters undergo in American films. They succeed each other with a disregard for psychological consistency which again testifies to their function of conveying domestic views of Russia. In 1941, when these views changed so abruptly that films in keeping with the latest developments were not yet available, Hollywood tried to adjust an existing film to the new situation. Under the heading "Whitewashing Reds," *Variety* of October 22, 1941, published the following notice: "Reflecting the changed public opinion in this country towards Russia, Metro has added an explanatory foreword on the film *Comrade X* to make clear that any spoofing of Russians in the picture was entirely intended as good clean fun." Metro simply was loath to shelve *Comrade X*, a film released only a few months before Hitler's invasion of Russia; yet this grim satire of Soviet life could not be kept in circulation unless it was made to appear as a meek banter among friends.

Russian characters in American films are projections rather than portraits. Chimerical figures, they unhesitatingly change with the political exigencies of the moment. Russia is far off.

CONCLUSIONS

The film industries of other democracies, I assume, behave in much the same way as Hollywood. Fiction films are mass entertainment everywhere, and what information they include is more or less a by-product. Any national cinema yields to the impact of subjective influences in portraying foreigners; these portrayals, that is, are strongly determined by such audience desires and political exigencies as currently prevail on the domestic scene. There are different degrees of subjectivity, though: peoples intimately connected by common experiences can be expected to form more objective screen images of each other than they do of peoples with whom they have little or nothing in common.

In other words, images of "in-group" peoples surpass those of "out-group" peoples in reliability. But even they are halfway reliable only as long as public opinion in the country of their origin does not interfere with their relatively unbiased approach. And under the pressure of alienating developments this may happen at any moment, as is instanced by Hollywood's conspicuous neglect of postwar Britons. On the whole, screen portrayals of foreigners are rarely true likenesses; more often than not they grow out of the urge for self-assertion rather than the thirst for knowledge, so that the resultant images reflect not so much the mentality of the other people as the state of mind of their own. International understanding is in its infancy.

Or, rather, does it begin to show signs of growing up? I have not yet mentioned a new international film trend which seems to justify Mr. Johnston's contention quoted above that the motion picture is on the point of becoming an "instrument for the promotion of knowledge and understanding among peoples." This trend, a spontaneous reaction to the effects of the war, originates in Europe. Representative of it are the somewhat sentimental Swiss pictures *Marie Louise* [1944, dir. Leopold Lindtberg] and *The Last Chance* [1945, dir. Leopold Lindtberg] and the two Rossellini films *Open City* [Italy 1945] and *Paisan* [Italy 1946]—wartime and postwar semi-documentaries much acclaimed by American audiences. In a similar vein is *The Search* [USA 1948. Fred Zinnemann], a Metro-sponsored film about European war orphans which has been made by the producer of *The Last Chance* and his associates in collaboration with a Hollywood director. Hollywood seems to be interested in this genre.

It is by no means a new genre. D. W. Griffith, great innovator as he was, developed some of its inherent potentialities, and his ideas were followed up by Eisenstein and Pudovkin in their classic screen epics—masterful blends of reportage and fiction, matter-of-fact statements and emotional appeals. What is new in the most recent semi-documentaries is their content: a changed outlook on the world, which, of course, entails changes of cinematic approach. All these films denounce Fascist lust for power and race hatred; and whatever they picture—Nazis torturing their enemies, scenes of heroic resistance, abandoned children, indescribable misery in bombed-out cities—is rendered with profound compassion for the tortured, the killed, the despondent. They are films with a message. They not only record the frightful encounters of persecutors and victims, masters and slaves, but glorify the bonds of love and sympathy that even now amidst lies, ruins and horrors connect people of different nations. Their goal is mutual understanding between the peoples of the world.

I do not know a single prewar film which is so deliberately international as is any of these semi-documentaries. All of them reflect, in loosely knit episodes, the vicissitudes of the war, featuring chance meetings between soldiers and civilians of diverse countries. German refugees join company with a British officer; an American G.I. makes love to an Italian girl; undernourished French children regain health in Switzerland. And most of these figures are fashioned with a minimum of subjectivity on the part of the film makers. Instead of serving as outlets for domestic needs, they seem to be elicited from reality for no purpose other than that of mirroring it. They tend to increase our knowledge of other nations out of an overwhelming nostalgia for international cooperation.

CAN HOLLYWOOD AFFORD THE INTERNATIONAL TREND?

The whole trend, provided it is one, proves that screen portrayals of foreigners need not under all circumstances degenerate into stereotypes and projections. At this point the problem arises of what can be done to improve these images. It is a vital problem in view of the influence which entertainment films exert on the masses. There is no doubt that the screen images of other peoples help to weaken or strengthen popular interest in mutual understanding.

This does not contradict the fact, emphasized throughout my study, that entertainment films on their part are strongly influenced by actually prevailing mass desires, latent tendencies of public opinion. Such desires and tendencies are more or less inarticulate, and do not materialize unless they are forced out of their pupa state: they must be identified and formulated to come into their own. Film industries everywhere, as I have mentioned earlier, are therefore faced with the task of divining audience expectations at any particular moment. Sometimes they miss their opportunities. The response which the Swiss and Italian semi-documentaries have found in the United States, for thematic rather than for aesthetic reasons, reveals a disposition in their favor on the part of American audiences which Hollywood has hitherto failed to recognize. On the other hand, Hollywood films occasionally react to well-nigh intangible emotional and social constellations with such a promptness that they seem to create desires out of nothing, especially in the dimension of taste. Characteristically, the trade has coined the term "sleeper" for films which are believed to be flops and, once released, prove themselves as hits. Film making involves constant experimenting—and many surprises.

What matters most in this context, then, is the essential ambiguity of mass dispositions. Because of their vagueness they usually admit of diverse interpretations. People are quick to reject things that they do not agree with, while they feel much less sure about the true objects of their leanings and longings. There is, accordingly, a margin left for film producers who aim at satisfying existing mass desires. Pent-up escapist needs, for instance, may be relieved in many different ways. Hence the permanent interaction between mass dispositions and film content. Each popular film conforms to certain popular wants; yet in conforming to them it inevitably does away with their inherent ambiguity. Any such film evolves these wants in a specific direction, confronts them with one among several possible meanings. Through their very definiteness films thus determine the nature of the inarticulate from which they emerge.

Once again, how can screen images of other peoples be improved? Since film producers, for all their dependence on current main trends of opinion and sentiment, retain some freedom of action, it may well be that they will find a more objective approach to foreign characters to be in their own interest. Hollywood is presently undergoing a crisis which challenges producers to probe into the minds of weary moviegoers, and documentary techniques, much-favored in Hollywood since *Boomerang,* lend themselves perfectly to objective portrayals. And has not *The Search* been a success? There is no reason why Hollywood should not explore this success and try its hand at films, semi-documentaries or not, which in however indirect a manner serve the cause of one world. U.S. audiences may even welcome a comprehensive rendering of Russian problems, or of life in Labor-governed Britain.

Or, of course, they may not. And Hollywood (any national film industry, for that matter) has some reason to believe that in the long run it knows best what spectators look out for in the movie houses. I doubt whether it will follow suggestions inconsistent with its estimate of audience reactions. Therefore a campaign for better screen portrayals of foreigners—portrayals which are portraits rather than projections—carries weight only if the motion picture industry is made to realize that the broad masses care about such portrayals. This accounts for the primary importance of mass education. Unless organizations such as UNESCO can stir up a mass desire for international understanding, prospects for the cooperation of film producers are slim. *The Last Chance* and *Paisan* came from countries where this desire was overwhelmingly strong. Can it be spread and sustained? Films help change mass attitudes on condition that these attitudes have already begun to change.

10 The Mirror Up to Nature
(1949)

There is no doubt that our films meet with increasing criticism and, even worse, disaffection. Among the possible reasons for this regrettable state of affairs one seems to me essential: Hollywood's realistic-minded films—that is, the main body of its output—are strikingly lacking in real-life experience. Perhaps it was always this way, except for a few gangster films or so. But people themselves have changed. Exposed to the impact of the post-war world, they can no longer get a thrill out of films which, under the pretence of reflecting this world, either misrepresent or elude it. As matters stand, the average spectator knows more about reality than is offered him in our movie houses. It should be the other way round.

What is wrong with Hollywood is driven home to us by a glance at various European films. They differ from our own productions precisely in that they grow out of a closer contact with life. All of them draw on first-hand experience of real persons and situations. *Brief Encounter* [GB 1945, dir. David Lean], one of the better British films, though by no means an exceptional one, perfectly illustrates the kind of experience I have in mind. It is one of those frequent extra-marital romances between middle-class people which invariably end in resignation. There is nothing to get excited about. And yet the film-makers manage to elicit from this commonplace incident a maximum of suspense. Their secret is that they are observant rather than showy. They never slur over details, as is done in so many Hollywood films.

Brief Encounter renders a brief railway junction with loving care, while, for instance, *Cass Timberlane* [USA 1947, dir. George Sidney] distorts New York society life into an unrecognisable rush of gay parties. And the heroine of the British film is not a Mrs Miniver who rarely lets you forget that, besides being Mrs Miniver, she is also a Hollywood star. This woman, instead of feeding on borrowed glamour, is, or appears to be, nothing but a housewife with a care-worn face and a timid dream behind it. She exists, we are led to believe, independently of the screen, a plain woman waiting for her lover at a railway junction that also exists. The film simply records their clandestine meetings—records them, however, with an accuracy intensified by true compassion and a sense of human values. Life is here explored on many levels. Thus, by sheer dint of inclusive observation, a seemingly banal affair is transformed into a tense experience of sporadic joy and lasting sorrow.

These examples can easily be multiplied. Whatever its shortcomings, the French screen surpasses ours in the expression of iridescent moods, amorous feelings and emotional tangles. Such films as *Children of Paradise* [France 1945, dir. Marcel Carné] and Renoir's *Une Partie de Campagne* [France 1936] afford an absorbing insight into melancholy passion and love become stale. Where the French transmit real experiences, we as a rule confine ourselves to stereotyped patterns. Even otherwise superior Hollywood films are strangely lacking when it comes to handling inner conflicts. They drown bright aspirations in phony emotions. *Gentleman's Agreement* [USA 1947, dir. Elia Kazan], for instance, combines a sophisticated crusade against anti-Semitism with a ready-made love story that rings so hollow as to belie the seriousness of the crusade.

And, finally, there are the new Italian films, with their reliance upon lay-actors and their whole documentary approach. I know of no Hollywood production—nor of a British or French film, for that matter—which could match *The Open City* [Italy 1945, dir. Roberto Rossellini], *Shoe-Shine* [Italy 1946, dir. Vittorio De Sica] and *Paisà* [Italy 1946, dir. Roberto Rossellini] in power of observation and compassion for ordinary people. These films seize upon the raw material of life, embracing it so fervently that all its humanly essential meanings are brought to the fore. You can almost touch and taste the horror, the suffering and the generosity they depict. As compared with them, Hollywood movies look particularly inexperienced. In *The Open City*, Gestapo tortures grow out of the fully substantiated interplay between the persecutors and their victims, while in most of our anti-Nazi films they merely mark the sensational climax of plots calculated to lead up to them.

Of course, life in Europe is more exacting than it is here. Bombed cities and years of Nazi terror, followed by years of starvation, have done their share to open eyes and stir the senses. It would be a miracle if films emerging from such a background fell short of authenticity. Nor should it be forgotten that some of the best among them have been improvised under incredible difficulties. Wrung from life, they bear its ineffaceable stamp.

Our films are what they are because of the circumstances of their production. Hollywood film-makers are concerned less with reality than with its dim reflection in best-sellers and Broadway hits. In tapping these doubtful sources, they are greatly hampered by the large size of our major film companies, a factor conducive to the mechanization of production methods. Improvisation yields to organisation, personal daring to the team work of specialists. The whole set-up tends to smother that adventurous spirit with which alone the screen can capture reality. Nor does the Production Code encourage such ventures. Reality thus becomes an indistinct rumour in a vacuum, crammed with formulas which further falsify this rumour.

Hollywood is not unaware of its remoteness from life. In his *Sullivan's Travels*, of 1941, Preston Sturges exposes this attitude in an attempt to justify it. The film is an autobiographical tragi-comedy, born out of qualms of conscience which do honour to Sturges. Sullivan, its protagonist, is a Hollywood film director who is so fed up with the comedies for which he is famous that he determines to devote his next film to the plight of the masses. In his compassion for their suffering he holds that our usual escapist entertainment should be superseded by films which come to grips with life as it is. But how to perceive life in a place like Hollywood? Realising that film people live in splendid isolation from their fellow-men, Sullivan visits several hobo camps in the guise of a tramp to experience what he wants to depict. He eventually lands in a Southern prison, and there learns, or thinks he learns, that he was all wrong in trying to reform Hollywood. The turning-point of the film is that scene in which he and the rest of the prisoners get a good laugh out of an old Mickey Mouse comedy—a laugh that makes them forget their hardships. Sullivan, the rebel with a mission, feels greatly elated about this lesson, which permits him to conform to Hollywood standards with a clean conscience. And back home at the studio and his swimming-pool, he gaily resumes his comedies.

This brilliant film with its cynical moral is all the more revealing, as it anticipates the course Hollywood actually took in the years subsequent to its release. After the manner of Sullivan, many a prominent film director left Hollywood for the war, acquiring a knowledge of the seamy side of life he would never have been able to acquire on Sunset Boulevard. And exactly as in the Sturges film, these excursions into blood and tears turned out to be an intermezzo of little consequence. Post-war Hollywood, whether or not adopting Sullivan's belief in the redeeming effect of laughter, continues to do what it did before the war.

And yet the analogies should not be pressed too hard. After all, there are slight differences, and they hold out a promise, however faint. Sullivan's counterparts in real life have brought back from their travels such documentaries as *The Fighting Lady* [USA 1944, dir. Edward Steichen], *San Pietro* [USA 1945, dir. John Huston] and *The Memphis Belle* [USA 1944, dir. William Wyler], which record the war without any Hollywood flourish. These films are valid statements, because they are modest, sincere and humane. And at least William Wyler, the director of *The Memphis*

Belle, has profited more than Sturges's hero from their common lesson. His *The Best Years of Our Lives* [USA 1946], though on the whole too compromising, is a far cry from his *Mrs Miniver* [USA 1942]. In particular its opening part, with the three soldiers returning home, each in his own way frightened by the task of readjustment ahead of him, testifies to an awe of facts which challenges our most sacred screen traditions. Here for once life is not cut to pattern, but laid bare, layer by layer, in a slow process.

Other films breathe a similar spirit. Differing widely in purpose, they nevertheless coincide in penetrating segments of reality that have been blurred or ignored before. A certain freshness of approach distinguishes all of them. Perhaps *Mourning Becomes Electra* [USA 1947, dir. Dudley Nichols] is not so much a film as an animated mural; but as such it is an expert depiction of grandiose compulsions and passions. *Boomerang* [USA 1947, dir. Elia Kazan], outstanding for its brisk and sympathetic observations, seems to have initiated a whole trend of films in documentary style. Unfortunately, most of them have been confined to police cases, misusing newsreel shots as trappings for otherwise conventional plots. *The Naked City* [USA 1948, dir. Jules Dassin] is symptomatic in this respect.

Yet it need not be so. This is demonstrated by *The Search* [USA 1948], in which a Hollywood director—the Austrian-born Fred Zinnemann—avails himself of documentary techniques to explore life in its fullness. The film, set against the background of displaced children camps and bombed German cities, is a fascinating blend of American and European mentality. There are still vestiges of artificial emotions and Hollywood rhetoric in it, but they all disappear among a mass of scenes which, shot on location, render real distress with real understanding.

People themselves have changed, as I have said above. Hollywood will have to change also. *The Search*, a farmed-out Hollywood film, points in the right direction. What is asked for are films that search the core of life, films founded on unadulterated experience.

11 Preston Sturges, or Laughter Betrayed

(1950)

Preston Sturges, who has been typecast as an entertainer, is undoubtedly more than this: his own credo (expounded in *Sullivan's Travels* [1941]) as well as his habit of framing his plots with significant stories reveal him as a searching, introspective mind.[1] And, besides, what if Sturges were a mere entertainer? Nothing should be taken more seriously than entertainment that ingratiates itself with the anonymous millions. Mass attitudes of far-reaching consequence often find an outlet in seemingly insignificant pleasures.

In the early '30s, when he began writing screen scenarios, Sturges did not always feel like laughing. His imagination centered around men who fight unscrupulously for power and a world in which integrity is an obstacle rather than an asset.

These preoccupations first materialized in Sturges' script of *The Power and the Glory*, a film directed by William K. Howard (1933). The plot is a variation on the "What Price Glory?" theme: a trackwalker with the instincts of a born tycoon contrives to become a railway magnate and commits suicide after having been betrayed by his own family. Sturges approached this worn-out theme from a particular angle: while fully exposing the tycoon's ruthlessness and antisocial conduct, he made considerable efforts to exculpate him. The film conveyed a moral; power, it implied, is incompatible with human loyalty, and he who conquers the world cannot but lose himself.[2]

Sturges resumed this theme in *The Great McGinty*, the first film he directed himself (drawn from a repeatedly rejected script of his own, done as early as 1933). This film presents the life story of a self-made man in flashback technique, which in this case is used to transform drama into satire. Dan McGinty, an elderly bartender in a forlorn "banana republic" dive, tells of his extraordinary past back in the States; and that past unfolds in sparkling episodes which show him making headway in a political machine. Under the wings of its highly disreputable "Boss," Dan rises from a bum in the soup line to the governor of a state, to grafting and racketeering on an ever larger scale. His upward flight would be as unlimited as his impudence, if it were not for an ingenious story twist: impelled by the woman he loves, Dan, after being sworn in as governor, decides to turn honest; and it is precisely this conversion which brings about his downfall. He joins the Boss in prison and then flees with him to the dim limbo of the banana port dive from which a half melancholy, half derisive light falls on his glorious and odious career.

This amusing attack on buccaneering in politics rests upon much the same attitude as *The Power and the Glory*.[3] The two films, moreover, coincide in their sustained concern with social criticism; up to the very end, *The Great McGinty* satirizes a society in which honesty does not pay.[4] Its unexpected success was of course not only due to the moral of this film but also, and perhaps mainly, to a cinematic treatment rich in pointed gags and with a touch of slapstick humor,[5] which readily contributes to the development of a plot that pillories social abuses; and so the laughter spread by *The Great McGinty* has a redeeming quality.[6]

Another overall feature of Sturges' imagery can be traced to his handling of the camera. He adroitly mobilizes the camera, with real film sense, whenever he wishes to point up some gag or create a comic situation; and on such occasions, his camera assumes an independence reminiscent of its role in mature silent films.[7]

The self-made man with his thirst for power (he reappeared, slightly transformed, in *The Great Moment*, a weak tragicomedy, conceived in 1939)[8] occupied one pole of the early Sturges universe. At its other pole loomed the figure of the Innocent, or whatever you want to call a naive and candid young man completely inexperienced in the ways of life. Sturges seems to have been infatuated with this antipode of his ruthless tycoons and corrupt politicians. In the two comedies following *The Great McGinty*, he featured such Innocents as lucky fellows who get everything they want.

The first of these comedies was *Christmas in July* (1940). Jimmy, its Innocent, is a gullible employee who stakes his hopes on a slogan contest offered by a coffee magnate. Naturally, Jimmy's hopes come true; but it is the finesse of the plot that he receives the $25,000 prize without really winning it. This superior trickery is achieved when several practical jokers in Jimmy's office send him a faked telegram acknowledging his victory. Overjoyed, Jimmy presents it to the coffee magnate, and since the latter is no longer on speaking terms with the contest jury, he accepts the telegram at face value and signs the check. Jimmy's gift for coining slogans thus being firmly established, he is promoted by his boss. He and his girl are in clover, and even the inevitable discovery of the fraud cannot evict them from there.

Based on a script of 1931 (when the depression was in full swing), *Christmas in July* looks like just another escapist film intent on diverting white-collar workers from their predicament. What satire the film includes is levelled against preposterous commercial slogans, mechanized furniture and overweening juries—minor shortcomings of the otherwise ideal world Sturges evokes.⁹ Yet a particularly striking testimony to the film's inherent nonconformism is its admirable denouement: In the concluding scene the jury decides to grant Jimmy the prize—a decision which implies the conformist meaning that day dreams do come true in real life; but since we already know that Jimmy's career does not depend upon the outcome of the contest, we are advised to dismiss this innuendo as soon as it arises.¹⁰ With this twist Sturges maintains the gap between his dream world and the real world precisely when he seems to bridge it.

In *The Lady Eve* (1941), the second comedy Sturges made after his *Great McGinty*, the Innocent is a young explorer who, as the son of a beer tycoon, need not be launched on a career. But money is not all that matters if you have it; and innocence ceases to be a virtue if it is tantamount to immaturity. Emotionally undeveloped, Charles undergoes a lesson in love from Jean, the world-wise and endearing member of a card-sharper trio. The plot—the successive stages of his education—proceeds with an esprit reminiscent of the best French boulevard comedies. First, Charles proposed to Jean and, having learned of her questionable profession, jilts her abruptly. Then Jean, disguised as "Lady Eve," reconquers Charles, who believes this model English aristocrat to be a twin of the card-sharper girl. She and Charles go on their nocturnal wedding trip in a Pullman car, in the course of which Jean-Eve takes hilarious revenge by confessing to her bridegroom a series of amorous adventures she had never had. Charles, shuddering, abandons her in the dead of night, and only in the finale are the two reunited.

In this picture, again business magnates are presented as funny figures, and the power they wield is minimized; again social satire is diverted from essential abuses to such inoffensive shortcomings as moral priggishness and American awe of British manners. And again this seeming complacency ultimately yields to a deeper disaffection.¹¹

In short, both comedies are in the vein of *The Great McGinty:* in making the audience laugh, they arouse its critical faculties. And this identity of attitude accounts for similarity of technique. In both comedies, significant gags predominate over fun for fun's sake.¹² On the other hand, just as in his *Great McGinty*, Sturges continues inserting pictorially arid stretches of dialogue in an otherwise brilliant imagery.

The Great McGinty and the two subsequent comedies appeared after the downfall of France, when civilized mankind lived in the fear of doom. Was laughter sufferable amidst world-wide despair? As if troubled by his role of comedy-maker in such a time, Sturges undertook to justify laughter with *Sullivan's Travels* (1941), a sort of tragicomedy written and directed immediately after *The Lady Eve*. The film is the turning point of Sturges' career.

Sullivan, a Hollywood director famous for his comedies, is so troubled by pangs of conscience that he decides to make only films which will no longer amuse the masses but, through an exposition of their intolerable plight, help promote human dignity. To experience the hardships he plans for his next film, he visits several hobo camps in the guise of a tramp. These travels, a mixture of slapstick and serious encounters, result in a catastrophe: Sullivan contracts amnesia and, under its spell, is sentenced to a long term at hard labor for having resisted the authorities. In a Southern jail, one evening he and his fellow-prisoners are allowed to look at an old Disney film. While Mickey Mouse performs, the camera dwells on the laughing faces of dejected criminals. Even though the happiness of the audience fades out with the short, it has left a lasting imprint on Sullivan. He recovers his memory and returns to Hollywood, imbued with the credo that genuine suffering can be relieved only by laughter. This is what his travels have taught him. And with a truly missionary seal he abandons his social film project for a comedy.[13]

Sullivan expressed sympathy for the suffering. Yet this does not prevent him from being interested only in picturesque tramps and jailbirds who are far less representative of our society than, for instance, the white-collar workers in *Christmas in July*. There is something evasive about Sullivan's travels; in their neglect of the inconspicuous for the spectacular, they resemble sightseeing tours through the Bowery. Besides, Sullivan cares little about the selected unfortunates he meets en route.[14] From the very outset he had avoided involvement in our workaday world. His reluctance to let himself be seriously affected by the suffering of man—by any suffering, for that matter—goes hand in hand with his belief that things are what they are and that nothing can be done about it. In calling society a "cockeyed caravan," he tacitly admits that he considers its inadequacy unchangeable.[15] His laughter suggests a conformist attitude.[16] The exoneration of tycoons in *The Power and the Glory*, and elsewhere, now appears to be a symptom of social complacency rather than a challenge to moral hypocrisy. Dan McGinty's original indifference to the poor is now pointed up by the callousness of Sullivan's butler who, in about the same words as

Dan, advises his master to leave the poor alone—an advice which Sullivan seems to reject but in effect endorses.[17] There was something Aristophanic about Sturges' beginnings, but in *Sullivan's Travels* he betrayed what was best in his laughter.

Having justified comedies as a godsend in these days of wrath, Sturges continued making them with a reassured conscience. There came *The Palm Beach Story* (1942), thematically a leftover from the period prior to *Sullivan's Travels*. This comedy about the upper crust abounds in millionaires of all shades and throws in two Innocents instead of the customary one—the impractical Tom, and John, the son of a super-magnate. Tom's loving wife, in her desire to push this stubborn ass ahead, becomes the center of an amusingly volatile intrigue which highlights the wasteful life of the rich through a blend of aggressive slapstick and condoning Lubitsch gags. In the finale, Sturges lavishes on Tom, John, and everyone concerned a fairytale happiness made palatable to the audience by just the right touch of irony.

Sturges' next two films dealt with wartime life in small towns in a manner which revealed Sturges' growing infatuation with old slapstick comedy.[18] The hero of *The Miracle of Morgan's Creek* (1944), [Norval,] played by Eddie Bracken, stutters when excited, frequently because of his adored Trudy's irresponsible behavior. Trudy had attended a gay farewell party for soldiers; it had ended, she dimly remembers, with her marrying some GI whose name she has forgotten. Unfortunately, the result is more concrete than her memory. Norval, a sweet compound of knight and simpleton, tries the impossible to save Trudy from disgrace; but of course his farcical attempts only make things worse for both of them. Gibes at hasty war marriages, hypocritical sex morals and administrative blunders contribute to producing the overall impression of a topsy-turvy society. It is also logical in such a world that a fourteen-year-old girl—one of Sturges' best comical figures—should talk and behave like a disillusioned adult. Again, the story is told in flashback fashion; but at the end, when all seems irretrievably mixed up, Sturges springs the surprise for which he has prepared the audience from the beginning: Trudy gives birth to sextuplets. And since Dan, the governor of the state, considers this miracle a unique asset to his administration, he sanctions Trudy's *faux pas* by making Norval her legitimate husband and a State Militia Colonel to boot.[19]

In *Hail the Conquering Hero* (1944), Woodrow [played by Bracken] is so ashamed of having been discharged from the array for chronic hay fever that he does not dare return to his mother, who still glories in the memory of his father, a hero of Word War I. Six marines on leave from Guadalcanal, and in search of a good time, pick up Woodrow in a bar and propose that, instead of letting his mother down, he should gratify her by posing as her hero son. They have the hesitant Innocent don a bemedaled uniform, escort him home and joyously participate in his triumphal reception by a town reveling in the local boy's alleged war exploits. Never was Sturges' satire more topical than in this hilarious concoction which, in the midst of war, not only mocked such small fry as souvenir hunters and political windbags, but assailed the sanctimoniousness of our official mother-and-hero cult. The marines' junket comes to a head when citizens, worried by the state of municipal affairs, urge Woodrow to run for mayor. Once again he yields, but this time his innate honesty conquers his shyness. At the opening electoral meeting he confesses to being a fraud—an instance of civil courage which the marines are the first to admire. The voters feel similarly, catch up with Woodrow at the station and keep him from boarding the train on which the six dashing marines depart.

Sturges' satire is here no longer what it was before he dulled its bite through systematic retreats from any advanced position. At his beginnings Sturges insisted that honesty does not pay. Now he wants us to believe that the world yields to candor.[20]

What satire *The Miracle of Morgan's Creek* offers is drowned in a plot that tends to demonstrate that our existing world, this "cockeyed caravan," is the best of all possible worlds.[21] Our society, the film implies, is constructed in such a way that in the long run any bad action serves a good purpose. But if human integrity is bound to win out—why then try to change the world?[22] Sturges, it is true, dismisses the whole marionette world with an ironic smile that is calculated to pass it all off as a superior joke. But this irony is much too superficial to be an adequate excuse for the harmony he has established between his Innocents and the powers that be.[23]

Sturges' original affinity for the old screen comedy is undeniable. Aside from the many pertinent gags in his earlier films, he proves himself a late descendant of Mack Sennett in that he has built up a sort of stock company to enact the ever-recurrent comic characters that haunt his imagination. Sturges *could* have resurrected the slapstick world of the past. The strange thing is that he seized, deliberately, upon this world just when he had turned away from its spirit. What must happen under such circumstances is predictable: his resurrection of slapstick turns out to be a mere pretense.[24] And his lack of concern for the slapstick spirit shows in the increase of meaningless gags; unmotivated buffooneries become obtrusive in all three comedies.[25]

In short, Sturges turns to the classic slapstick comedy not in spite of his conformism but because of it. Far from reviving this genre, he merely exploits its proved devices to produce as much fun as possible, regardless of the meaning they had originally conveyed.[26] Slapstick, to the later Sturges, is nothing but an arsenal of ready-made gags.[27] For whatever inner reasons, Sturges' gift for inventing funny incidents began to fail him from about the time of *Sullivan's Travels*. More readily than before, his characters tend to fall or to provoke falls; and subtle jests increasingly give way to farcical business.[28] (Complacency takes revenge on those who indulge in it: his latest comedies, *Unfaithfully Yours* [1948] and *The Beautiful Blonde from Bashful Bend* [1949], are poor in wit and slapstick out of a can.)

And what particular brand of conformism does Sturges-Sullivan administer to the public? It is a streamlined variant of the naive and uncritical conformism current among us.[29] Sturges first draws on the critical faculties of a flattered audience by having it catch a glimpse of the questionable aspects of our society; and then he gives the audience to understand that this world of ours is in effect a paradise where wrongs right themselves automatically. He conceals nothing and gilds all.[30] He uses the tools of social criticism—only to destroy its constructive power.

I do not intend to say that laughter without social significance is evil. The straight film farce, produced for its comical effect alone, is just as valid and welcome an entertainment as any other juggler's act. But the farce in the disguise of satire is dangerous. It dulls the edges of a first-rate weapon of human liberation. And it is dangerous at a time when, along with the means of mass communication, methods of psychological manipulation have been developed to an extent unknown before.[31]

12 Art Today
A Proposal (1961)

The Arts are presently in the focus of interest; and they have acquired a reputation which cannot be explained only from a wider recognition of their inherent values. Rather, the significance attributed to Art today seems to be an answer to current social needs. In worshiping the arts people obviously try to meet these needs. The cult of Art fulfills a social function.

Note, first, that we witness the emergence of a society in which more people than ever before are free, in terms of both income and time, to enjoy artistic achievements. A potential mass audience for art exhibitions and high-level artistic performances has arisen. Now these masses are all the more willing to let themselves be filled with Art if they can be coaxed into believing that their suffering under the enjoyment of it helps enhance their prestige. Hence the tendency of all culture-mongers to look particularly holy when they talk about Art, the artist, the creative process, and similar stuff. The more they glorify Art, the higher will those condemned to the role of art consumers think of themselves. Is not their being culture-minded a mark of distinction? To make the masses of art consumers believe that the art enjoyment to which they are subjected leads them to the heights of culture and therefore increases their superiority over the rest of us mortals lies of course in the interest of the various industries which mediate between Art and people. Evidently, they can sell their art products at a higher price if they pass them off as the carriers of awe-inspiring values.

Add to this that people have more leisure time on their hands, and that they would rot hopelessly were they not told how to waste their excessive spare time with a seeming purpose in mind. Art is an incomparable stopgap, not only because it endows those pretending to imbibe it with a feeling of importance but also because of its neutralizing effect on them. The prospective Art fans are unlikely to turn Communist or to indulge in neurotic shenanigans. Imagine the enormous nuisance value of people exposed to the terrible possibility of doing something on their own; absorption in Art, however simulated, is an effective antidote against their potentialities in this respect. But naturally, the stopgap must be made to appear uniquely attractive, or else people would refuse to undergo the strain of global tours, look at the sound and light spectacles, attend all the musical festivals offered them, etc. Consider, in passing, how people do seize on the art opportunities that crowd in on them. They have ingenious ways of communing with Art without ever getting in touch with it. For instance, once they have noticed that a famous art object—say, the Parthenon—is at the place where it should be, according to the guide, they immediately take a picture of it. They do not want to perceive the object; all they do want is to collect and possess it. The surest means of possessing the Parthenon columns is to use them as background to a picture of wife and daughter. This also provides irrefutable evidence that the family has been on locale. The photographs made on the trip are as many trophies heightening the traveler's prestige at home. They serve as alibis. Hunters at least eat the killed animal; it may be doubted whether the picture hunters ever do the same with the art objects and nature sights they are shooting. I mean:

do they "eat" or absorb them later on? But how could they? Unseen objects photographed resist resurrection, much as they may be looked at. In taking pictures this way people forever lose sight of the world allegedly pictured.

Finally, society's present efforts to sanctify Art and overburden it with functions it cannot possibly fulfill must be laid to a dim awareness that we are shelterless ideologically. Thus Art is assigned the task of providing a shelter for all those in need of a roof above their heads. Improbable as it is that the increasing talk about poetry should reflect an increased interest in it, it certainly gives people the pleasant illusion that there is something somewhere which can be believed in if one has the gift of believing. The idolatry of art does, for a moment, away with the fear of the vacuum.

(This motif as well as the motif that the cult of art offers a means of escape from the exigencies of mechanization and the intricate uncertainties of our total situation will still have to be worked out.)

13 About the State of the Humanities

I

The following remarks on the state of the humanities in this country summarize observations made during the last four or five years. In addition, they take into account the opinions of several European scholars with whom I discussed our intellectual situation.

To begin with, in academic circles there is a strong awareness that, because of their heavy teaching load, our young humanistic scholars have not enough time on their hands efficiently to advance their career chances. In order to get ahead in the profession they must build up a reputation by doing research of their own and publishing as much as possible. The more impressive their record in this respect, the better they usually qualify for permanent full-tenure appointments. Hence the scramble, on the part of both universities and individual young scholars, for fellowships or foundation-paid leaves of absence affording them the coveted breathing-spell. Note that the free time requested by university administrators for faculty members rarely exceeds a year or so. In the recent past MIT's School of Humanities and Social Science proceeded to establish a "Young Professors Growth Fund" designed to provide those in need of "growth" with two semesters of paid leave during their 7-year probation period. (The special conditions obtaining at this institution need not be discussed here.) Similarly, Princeton University's Council of the Humanities grants full-year and half-year fellowships enabling selected senior and junior faculty members to work on projects of their choice. It seems to be held, then, that normally a year suffices for a young scholar to produce something that will heighten his career prospects (and perhaps live up to his scholarly ambitions).

Now, this leads straight to another characteristic of the present situation—the much talked-about tendency toward specialization in practically all fields of humanistic studies. In fact, what is called "specialization" is inseparable from the consensus about time requirements and the common practice in its wake. For a younger scholar to rise from the rank and file within a short period the most natural (and easiest) way is to establish himself as an authority in some specialized area or subarea. Evidence of this may be found in the fact that an assistant or associate professor never tires of cultivating the very same specialty he already seized upon and explored in his doctoral dissertation; so he will be considered its uncontested proprietor in prominent places.

The frequent references to this state of things are invariably bound up with complaints about its dangerous implications. Most observers of the academic scene insist that, due to institutional pressures, including the relatively little time granted for scholarly pursuits, junior academic teachers are not in a position to acquire a broader cultural background. They lack the leisure to refine their sensibilities and evolve variegated interests; in other words, they must use up such leisure as they can eke out for some piece of specialized research. Specialization in the humanities has thus come to assume a negative meaning; it is identified as narrow-minded preoccupation with insignificant data, negligible details. (Undeniably, numbers of monographs in all branches of the humanities tend to bear out this verdict.)

Such opinions are fairly widespread. Last year, in a meeting I attended, Princeton's Dr. Goheen declared that at Princeton and elsewhere we seem to be doomed to breed not so much humanists as specialists. He then proceeded to discuss a project of the Princeton Council of the Humanities intended to counteract specialization and its disastrous effects on "university culture." The Council proposed to sponsor preparation and publication of studies, preferably group studies, by faculty members which would have to center on contemporary "issues of relevance"—for instance, on the fact that the sciences are becoming increasingly esoteric, or on the question as to how to reconcile the worth of the individual with the necessity of collective action. Our academic scholars, it was argued in support of the proposal, are kept so busy with teaching and specialized research that we cannot induce them to widen their horizon—to become more humanistic-minded, that is—unless we buy them the time needed for studies seemingly outside their narrow field and, moreover, endow these studies with some prestige so that they will benefit the professional careers of their authors.

II

The Princeton project is of interest inasmuch as it is symptomatic of views held not only on the campus. They may roughly be described as follows: the ongoing specialization processes lead to an ever stricter compartmentalization of knowledge and accordingly widen the gulf between researchers in different disciplines as well as between the academic world and the world at large. Knowledge in various fields turns out to be incommunicable. While even the educated is denied access to it, the specializing scholars and scientists on their part are no longer equipped actively to participate in the life of society, the life of the mind. One-sidedness is a virtue with them; the exacting nature of their microscopic investigations renders it difficult for them to develop into fully orchestrated human beings. They are, indeed, nothing more than "specialists," even if they are humanists in a technical sense.

This stereotyped image of our predicament calls forth equally stereotyped demands for a re-humanization of our technological civilization. It is not least the intellectuals who drive home the evil consequences of specialization and champion a training apt to produce better integrated personalities. The idea of human excellence underlying such claims is inseparable from the vision of a society in which the present estrangement between the scholarly and intellectual elite and the masses of the population yields to a lively exchange of communications bringing the former, so to speak, back into the fold and enabling the general public to share, somehow, in the fruits of their then allegedly more meaningful labors. Longings of this kind explain [C.P.] Snow's plea for a rapprochement between the humanities and the natural sciences—the "two cultures," as he calls them.[1] And the same longings are at the bottom of certain trends and movements currently in vogue (and perhaps too much taken for granted). I am thinking, for example, of the sustained attempts to popularize genuine insight and the results of pioneering research for the sake of adult education. Or consider the concerted efforts of all sorts of associations, agencies, and institutions to facilitate, mostly for short periods, the exchange of students, scholars, etc., and to sponsor international meetings of experts and professionals in every imaginable field of knowledge—efforts which must, at least partly, be traced to an almost mystical belief in the benefits of personal contacts for all those engaged in this global commotion and for the advance of knowledge itself. The slogan of "mutual understanding" has become a magic formula. And of course, here also belong the activities of a rapidly increasing number of organizations, commercial or not, which altogether aim at bringing the Arts to everybody's doorstep. It begins with the tots being encouraged to release their creative urges and ends with lectures in art appreciation, multiple amateur performances, and so on.

In their endeavor to check uncontrolled specialization our universities seem to be prompted by about the same apprehensions and concerns which assert themselves in the larger social environment. This can be inferred not only from the readiness with which they promote complete mobility of the academic populations—whole universities are on the move of late, like the Great Birnam Wood—but, more glaringly, from their eagerness to take over, and cultivate, the Arts (or what remains of them). Now, society undoubtedly enhances Art for a variety of reasons: popular interest in Art makes for harmless (and manipulable) leisure-time occupations, provides many new jobs, and caters to the prestige demands of a not yet fully acculturated multitude in quest of status. But as I have pointed out above, there is also a feeling underneath that annexation of the Arts on a broad scale may immunize us against the damaging aftereffects of a predominantly technological orientation. Here is where the universities join in. Art as an antidote against specialization, as a means of establishing a more balanced, more humanistic-minded culture—this is presumably the line of thought which, along with the desire for good public relations, causes the academic authorities to follow the popular movement. At any rate, nearly every university—or college, for that matter—now aspires to do something about Art in grand style. MIT's Humanities Department is all set to expand its facilities for extra-curricular work in this vast and lofty area; and Columbia dreams of an $ 8,000,000 building wholly dedicated to art education. A campus without an Art Center of its own will soon be a remote memory.

III

In sum, the ideas entertained in distinguished academic quarters about the state of the humanities are of a piece with society's conceptions of culture. This is not to say, of course, that they would do justice to the given situation. Rather, some of the practices and methods inspired by these ideas are definitely in the nature of expedients. They concern themselves with symptoms instead of trying to improve our academic system itself. So certain weaknesses inherent in it are left intact.

One of them may be identified as the habit of granting too little time to budding scholars. For example, MIT's "Young Professors Growth Fund" provides young professors in the humanities with two semesters of leave for research and writing during their first seven years at the University. While this device may facilitate the activities necessary for academic advancement, it is difficult to see how the young professors will manage to "grow" within such relatively brief intervals. True growth is a slow process. The narrow time limits set by the majority of our fellowships hardly permit a young scholar of promise really to grow—i.e., to get out of the routine for once, meander from possibility to possibility, test a new idea of his, and go astray on occasion. Such gropings and ventures are allowed more leeway in England, where two-to-three-year fellowships for qualified post-doctoral scholars seem to be the rule (so, for instance, Prof. E. R. Dodds, Oxford [a classicist whom Kracauer had visited on a recent trip to Europe]). Obviously, the thing that counts is a greater largesse in the allotment of time, not just an increase of the usual 1-year fellowships.

Another weakness of the system is, I believe, the inclination to assign to a young scholar's publication record a preponderant role among the factors which serve as criteria of his eligibility. This, along with the time restrictions imposed on them, does not precisely stimulate our junior professors to extend the scope of their research or to indulge in uncertain experiments. Need it be so? Prof. Dodds told me that British senior professors commonly assess a young man's output within the context of his whole make-up as a teacher and scholar. We watch the fellow grow, said he, and then decide upon his fitness accordingly. True, Prof. Dodds immediately added that this is a "matter of geography" inasmuch as in a small country like England everybody knows everyone, but he certainly did not wish to intimate that in a big country similar procedures are confronted with unsurmountable difficulties. As a matter of fact, when asked to evaluate the project of some young professor, many of our senior scholars dwell on his potentialities rather than his actual performances. Their subjectivity notwithstanding, such estimates complement substantially any conclusions that can be drawn from a beginner's achievements proper. If appointments were handled with less regard for the publication record, gifted aspirants might feel tempted to spend more time on their inner education—which in turn would be a gain for the humanities.

And what about the attitudes toward specialization? The fight against it, as illustrated by the Princeton project or the general craving for Art Centers, involves issues which require clarification. Let me first call to mind the frightfully primitive truth that specialization, far from being an evil, is the prerequisite of genuine insight in the humanities as well as elsewhere. It is specialized research which brings us close to the real things and their real interrelations. As Aby Warburg put it, "God is in the detail"—a dictum which no scholar would seriously question. Now, it may be assumed that those fighting specialization do not deny the need for it but simply want to help our specialists to overcome a one-sidedness which results from the academic pressures characterized just above (and in the final analysis from the shortcomings of our secondary school system). While this is a most desirable goal, the means of attaining it strike me strangely inadequate. The reason is that they rest upon a misconception about the manner in which the special and the general, micro-analysis and macro-analysis, relate to each other. Altogether the organizational arrangements made to broaden the cultural background of specialists—say, by getting them interested in the Arts or in contemporary "issues of relevance"—amount to as many attempts to add mechanically from without what can be assimilated only if it grows organically from within. Take any scholar in the humanities: Since God is in the detail, he naturally must be a specialist; but since his task is to discover Him in the detail—to interpret his material, that is—he is a good specialist only if he is more than that, i.e., a humanist. Their very subject matter, not any external stimulus, challenges, or should challenge, humanistic scholars to branch out into various fields of knowledge and experience. Some time ago Prof. Bernard Knox [at the time director of Harvard's Center for Hellenic Studies in Washington, D.C.] recommended the specialized project of a woman-archaeologist—a study of Panathenic prize amphoras—by praising her for both her competence as a specialist and the wide range of her cultural interests; indeed, he expressly mentioned that they once met each other in their common love of Rilke. It is evident that he believes, rightly so, her love of Rilke to be part and parcel of her scholarly equipment. In consequence, if a junior scholar does not feel the urge to develop, by efforts of his own, a sense of culture in connection with the work he is doing, the odds are that those organizational arrangements will be lost on him. Coming from the outside, the opportunities they offer are likely to remain sheer additions. An engineer of my acquaintance never misses a major concert in town, yet his penchant for music is so rigidly compartmentalized that it does not in the least affect his otherwise completely technical, and hence inexperienced, approach to human affairs.

IV

There would be such more to say—for instance, about the tendency, manifest in the fight against specialization, toward organizing on a large scale things which, if they can be organized at all, require a subtler treatment, one better adjusted to their peculiar modes of being; or about the excessive confidence in the alleged blessings of cultural exchanges and personal contacts ("We are overfed with communications," said Prof. Claude Lévi-Strauss to me in Paris), etc. However, the remarks submitted so far will suffice as a starting-point for discussion. Only as a postscript I wish to append to them the following, purely speculative thought: Because of the further increase of leisure time in the wake of automation—not to mention other relevant factors—"mass culture" (what an ugly word!) is bound to spread irresistibly. It involves aspirations to conformity on all fronts and organizational measures benefitting the dissemination of half-truths. We may try, or rather, we will have to try, to assist mass culture as best we can. But we must also be aware that at the present stage the chances of transforming it into a truly humanistic culture are slim. So the question arises, to what extent should we meet its demands. Does it not now that its floods are mounting lie in a strategic interest to make provisions for the undisturbed continuance of specialized studies and esoteric pursuits, no matter, for the rest, whether they serve a practical purpose or admit of popularization?

Last summer, in a conversation with me, Prof. Werner Kaegi, the Swiss historian and Jacob Burckhardt biographer, playfully compared our age with the Dark Ages, thus spinning out my suggestion that the time had come to build new monasteries that would accommodate scholars and protect them from the obtrusive noises of the world. Something of this sort seems to be already under way. The idea of institutes for advanced study is increasingly gaining ground; think of the Hellenic Center in Washington and the Institute of the University of Wisconsin. An international Academy covering many areas of the humanities may be founded near Zurich in the foreseeable future. And there are such refuges as Harvard's Florentine estate and the Rockefeller Foundation's Villa Serbelloni. It is probably not by accident that institutions of this type now spontaneously emerge in different places.

14 A Statement on the Humanistic Approach

I. The ideal of exact science—to arrive at laws and predictions by way of experiment and measurement—tends to overshadow, in the social sciences, psychology and affiliated cultural fields, the aspirations of what may be called systematic qualitative analysis or the humanistic approach. Generally speaking, the procedures of exact science are increasingly applied to phenomena which differ from the subject matter of exact science in that they are historical entities and as such carriers of unique values and qualities.

This is in a measure legitimate, for within the fields previously reserved to qualitative appraisals and humanistic insight there are many phenomena and problems which readily lend themselves to quantifications. [...]

However, the increase in objective knowledge through experiment and statistical elaboration is bought at a price. In their eagerness for quantification the strict scientists discount meanings and goals. They are concerned with means rather than ends. They are inclined to confuse the profound, if necessarily qualitative, evaluation of, say, a historical situation with a superficial "impressionist" approach to it, and they reject wholesale uncontrollable "intuition." The consequence is that their analyses frequently center round problems of a merely technical or managerial interest and that their hypotheses tend to take commonplace viewpoints, values and purposes for granted without further inquiring into them. From this angle it might be interesting to examine the assumptions behind our cultural exchange program and the methods used in checking on its results.

II. But is qualitative analysis with its ultimate reliance on intuitive perception really binding? Its validity seems particularly doubtful because of the lessened impact of the spiritual incentives that swayed the nineteenth century. It is as if we were in the middle of historical processes which make for the ever-increasing evaporation of commonly held beliefs and ideals. Ideology appears to lose its grip on the individual. In his book *Psychosocial Medicine: A Study of the Sick Society*, the Scottish psychiatrist James L. Halliday lists among the factors responsible for the decline of mental health in Britain since the end of the nineteenth century the growing reluctance, or inability, of people to let themselves be imbued with the ideas that once had a hold on their minds. According to him, the spread of what may be called "ideological fatigue" is a potential source of mental disturbances. Be this as it may, group beliefs and ideological motivations have lost much of their vital power. This is confirmed by the present vogue of psychoanalysis, with its tendency to compensate for the lack of objective obligations and convictions simply by psychologizing them ever further away.[1] Also, the phenomenon of the Western Communist intellectual indicates that Western ideology no longer retains life and fullness; his brand of fanaticism reveals not so much a belief as nostalgia for a belief.

In such a historical situation intuition lacks sanctioned sources, and what once seemed evident threatens to become a matter of sheer opinion. Accordingly, quantitative research may claim with a semblance of truth that it is the legitimate heir to the qualitative approach. This claim is sometimes upheld by the following argument: Even though exact science methods when applied to historical, highly individual entities may yield only results of minor significance, these results are at least objective and fully controllable. And in using them as a starting-point for further investigations, exact science will by and by arrive at more inclusive laws or regularities and eventually establish a body of significant knowledge which exceeds all impressionist findings in reliability and validity. However, this argument draws on an analogy which does not apply here. It is of course possible to generalize special data, provided the generalizations belong to the same area or order as the data from which they are won; but it is not possible to proceed from material of a lower dimension to material of a higher dimension without making new investigations bearing on the latter. There is no smooth transition from the American soldier as an object of quantitative analysis to the American soldier as a real-life being with a history and a certain set of values.

III. The dilemma, then, is this: on the one hand, exact science methods spread in fields where they cannot secure adequate solutions unless they take their cues from the humanistic approach. On the other hand, the humanistic approach itself suffers from historical developments which have weakened the impact of ideology—the psychological result being that modern personality, no longer under the spell of substantial ideological directives, tends to disintegrate. [...][2] The individual rarely succeeds today in unifying the various roles he is required to play in everyday life; mutual understanding in deeper psychological layers proves extremely difficult.

At first glance, this situation seems to justify the imperialism of the exact science trend. How indeed should the humanities be able to influence or even guide quantitative research at a time when they so obviously lack binding premises, when everything they advance may be traced to subjective views, and when there is no palpable agreement about the terms and methods used in their qualitative evaluations? I submit that all this neither invalidates the significance of the humanistic or qualitative approach, nor interferes with its leading role in all those areas in which human relations, human efforts and human achievements are a main concern.

IV. It can be shown that what holds true of the qualitative approach also applies to quantitative analysis in humanistic fields: the latter partakes of the uncertainties of the former. In processing his material, the quantitative analyst is time and again bound to make assumptions which cannot deny their "impressionist" origins; and even the smallest decision about some tiny unit challenges him to review the infinite contexts to which this unit belongs. In other words, our current overall situation affects the objectivity of quantitative procedures also. [. . .]

V. Even under the present circumstances qualitative inquiries are more "scientific," more trustworthy, than the champions of exact science are inclined to believe. Exactly like quantitative analysis, the humanistic approach proceeds to break down a given whole into small elements or units, thus enabling us to disentangle the fabric of its qualities and compare them with those of other, similar wholes. But unlike quantitative analysis, it is not primarily concerned with matters of quantification. Some of the elements at which it arrives may be quantifiable and therefore should by all means be coded, scored and computed; others obstruct any attempt at numerical formulation. What counts alone in qualitative analysis is the selection and rational organization of such small elements as are expressive of the essentials of the whole.

But how can we find out about these essentials without relapsing into plain subjectivism? The danger is not so great as it appears. For even though such subjective factors as the analyst's philosophical viewpoints, political convictions, etc., unavoidably influence his conception of the whole he is analyzing, they will to a large extent be neutralized in the process. Whether or not he states them overtly from the outset, they are bound to leak out anyway. And once the cards are on the table, these influences and their distorting effects can in a measure be controlled and discounted. For instance, Freud's overemphasis on sex has long since been traced to biographical factors. For the rest, access to the essentials of humanly significant entities depends upon familiarity with anything that might have contributed to their emergence, a sense of history, a flair for ideological currents, and experience of human behavior—not to forget the greatest virtue of all: circumspection in weighing and balancing against each other the various data assembled.

We submit that these abilities can be taught up to a point. It all is a matter of stressing the role of the humanities in our educational system and of training students in the successive operations that lead from the first rough scheme of qualitative analysis to its satisfactory completion. The skills involved in carrying out mental experiments or imagining possible alternatives are as teachable as are the skills of a flyer. [. . .]

VI. Conclusions:

1. The success of the humanistic approach depends largely on education and training. Increased emphasis on qualitative methods in our colleges and universities might help create an atmosphere favorable to common qualitative perceptions and evaluations.

2. What is likewise needed, is the systematic collaboration of qualitative and quantitative analysts, humanists and statisticians. An interpenetration of mathematical precision and humanistic sensibility would seem a requirement for future research.

15 Talk with Teddie
(1960)

(1) *Concept of Utopia:* I argued that he uses this concept in a purely formal way, as a borderline concept (*Grenzbegriff*) which at the end invariably emerges like a *Deus ex Machina*. In my opinion, I told him, Utopian thought makes sense only if it assumes the form of a vision or intuition with a definite content of a sort. T. was inclined to admit the justice of my argument. He says—of course, he would—that he will deal with the concept of Utopia in future, more systematic & elaborate works. His intention is then to show that the concept of utopia is a *vanishing* concept when besieged; it vanishes if you want to spell it out.

(2) *Dialectics vs. Ontology:* Teddie is presently making notes for a course on this theme. Ontology will have nothing to laugh, he says.[1] To be more precise, he rejects any ontological stipulations in favor of an infinite dialectics which penetrates all concrete things & entities, and, taking its clue from what they may reveal, works its way through them in a process which has no goal outside the movement itself and no direction that could be stated in terms other than those immanent in that movement. I told Teddie that many of his articles concocted this way make me just dizzy; that I had often the feeling that other interpretations might be as

conclusive as his or even more so; that his whole dialectics seemed inseparable from a certain arbitrariness to me; and that, in sum, my dizziness was presumably caused by the complete absence of content & direction in these series of material evaluations. I traced thus my dizziness to the fact that he seemingly deals in substances without, however, actually being attached to any substance. Hence the arbitrariness, the lack of orientation. I related this argument against his dialectics to my statement on the formality, the emptiness of his Utopian concept: indeed, if the movement he unchains gravitates toward an Utopian goal, it still remains unoriented throughout because the term "utopia," as used by him, is nothing but a conceptual stopgap.

Here Gretel [Adorno's wife, Gretel Karplus] insisted that Teddie's dialectics is like *music*. I answered: This is certainly true but is by no means an argument in favor of its philosophical validity.

Teddie's response showed that he was wounded to the quick (though he is a skilled-enough debater not to show it). My objections, said he, reveal that I still cling to obsolete, ontological, habits of thought in requesting that something fixed must be given, postulated or desired. No sooner does one fall into this common error than the consequence is a ready-made "system" starting from the vision or postulate & passing above the concrete material of things and entities instead of *through* them. And he insisted that, contrary to ontological bias, the truth, as revealed through his immanent processing of concretions, is always "hovering" (*schwebend*). As for my reproach of dizziness, arbitrariness, etc., he declares that there is after all a definite outlook in his writing which, of course, is accessible only to those absorbing his production in its entirety. He demands, in fact, that the student should understand each meaning from the contexts of what he, Teddie, has written (and will write in the future). Then, Teddie seems to believe, the student cannot but experience the substance behind it all and get the sense of direction that I am missing. [I could have answered him, but failed to do so, that, since his dialectics consists of an unending sequence of concrete moments and each moment is supposed to be interpreted in depth, the sum total of these moments is unattainable. Which means that the reader familiar with all of Teddie's writings will feel exactly as insecure & dizzy as one who has read only part of Teddie's output. The emphasis lying on the movement from moment to moment, more samples of the same, may increase the impression of the movement punctuated by "hovering" truths but are extremely unlikely to endow it with the substance it deliberately negates as sheer movement.]

Instead of bringing in this pertinent argument, which did not occur to me at the moment, I resumed my objections from an entirely different angle. I compared Teddie's dialectics with a film made up exclusively of close-ups. Such a film is of course imaginable, I said, but the close-ups of which it consists would be completely undefined and, hence, puzzling rather than revealing, were they not, every now and then, interrupted with "establishing" shots relating them to the reality with which we are confronted after all and thus defining, however tentatively, their approximate position. Otherwise expressed, the radical immanence of the dialectical process will not do; some ontological fixations are needed to imbue it with significance and direction: I spoke of *"ontologischen Würfen"* [ontological postulates] within this context and remarked that Hegel's dialectics moved toward, or implied, an ontological end. This was a bit careless of me, for Teddie, knowing that my lifelong aversion to Hegel had always prevented me from really studying him, immediately exploited the situation by saying that Hegel never committed the sin of orienting the dialectical process toward anything allegedly "objective" outside that process. But even though for Teddie Hegel is an infallible authority, it was quite obvious that my new attack came unexpected to him; all the more so since I supplemented it by the observation that a really meaningful dialectics would have to bring into play some ontological vision also. Thereupon he admitted that ontological elements might indeed be needed—but only in the form of hypostasized elements, not as eternal truths. Well, I replied, no one has spoken of eternal truths; rather, what is required is a dialectics between the endless, purely immanent movement—Teddie's procedure— and ontological stipulation outside it, a "Schau" which, itself, may, or should, not assume a definite character.

Exploring further my advantage, I cited Benjamin against Teddie. Does not Benjamin, I continued, time and again feel himself bound by visions of partial ontological truths? And does he not orient his penetrations of concrete entities toward these messianic visions which are rich in content, as indeed Utopian ideas should be in order to carry meaning? Here I had Teddie trapped. True, he tamely criticized Benjamin for not being the perfect dialectician à la Hegel and Teddie himself (who invokes the Hegel of his making as a sort of protective cover & shield), but on the other hand he could not well deny Benjamin's strengths as an autonomous thinker and try to undermine his position. I ruthlessly hit Teddie some more by drawing a graph illustrating his, Benjamin's, and my own way of thinking.[2]

Both Benjamin and I coinciding in not accepting immanent dialectics, I subtly implied that we are engaged in terms of substances. We think under a sort of ontological compunction, Utopian or not, whereas Teddie is, indeed, free-hovering and does not feel any such compunction.

At this point, I believe, Teddie was at the end of his rope. I am sure, however, he will not admit this to himself—nor will Gretel—but immediately manage to believe that all my thoughts are in reality his own, annex these thoughts, which he already considers his property, to his "system," and pass them off as the natural outgrowth of the latter. There is something paranoiac about him. You cannot upset Teddie; he grabs everything he is told, digests it and its consequences and then takes over in a spirit of superiority.

(3) *Ideology and Sociology:* The formality and possessiveness (or greed) of Teddie's mind flagrantly show in the way he relates the ideological to the sociological dimension. In all his articles or books he invariably traces the aesthetic or conceptual characteristics of some entity—a poem, a philosophical viewpoint, or the like—to the social situation from which that entity (historically) arises, but does so in a manner which unmistakingly reveals his complete unconcern for the material nature of society, past or present, and for the means of improving our social condition. His sociological concepts are much too wide to be able to characterize any social reality; they are just leftovers, never revised, from his Marxist past. This applies in particular to his term "bürgerlich" [bourgeois] which he constantly uses. Ontological thinking, ideology-formation, etc.—all this he lays to the "bürgerliche" *Warengesellschaft* [commodity society], which he makes also responsible for the "Verdinglichung" [reification] of specific values, abstractness in our approach to the world, unjustified relativism, and the loss of substance in general. I asked him to define his concept of "bürgerlich." He said it goes beyond capitalism proper, covering the "Tauschgesellschaft" [exchange society] with its exchange of goods. It goes without saying that my defense of ontology caused him to call me "bürgerlich." By the same token he, on some other occasion, declared that Aristotle's Politeia, with its emphasis on moderation, the middle way, etc., resulted from bourgeois mentality (!). What are the counterconcepts, I further asked. The feudal society, the primitive horde, and so [on], he answered. Whereupon I gave him to understand that his concept of "bürgerlich" [bourgeois] is much too wide to define the social forces which may account for this or that intellectual or artistic phenomenon. (Is not, for instance, the Renaissance contemporary with the merchant society of the Italian city states? Hauser[3] is much more circumspect and empirical than Teddie, gross as he often is.) Incidentally, when discussing the relations between ideological events and social developments, I

pointed out that it would be an urgent task for research to find out how the intellectual and social life of a given period are actually connected with each other. What are the channels, if any, that lead from a work of art to the social circumstances under which it was created? What counts now is to prove or disprove the widespread tacit assumption of the unity of any historical period. Without realizing that he proceeds from this assumption, Teddie contended that he was in complete agreement with me and had already dealt with the issue I raised in one of his essays. To repeat it, he grabs everything. In order to prove [to] him how alienated he is from all real substance, intellectual or social, he pretends to penetrate and set moving. I then told him bluntly: You curse the "bürgerliche Gesellschaft" [bourgeois society], reject Communism, frown down on the Social Democracy, etc.: what do you suggest, for God's sake, should be done in terms of social changes, other institutions? His (pitiable) answer was: I know, and say, what is bad; is this not enough? In sum, all that exists, exists only to be devoured in the dialectic process which Teddie keeps going on and on because of his lack of substance, of vision. To Teddie, dialectics is a means of maintaining his superiority over all imaginable opinions, viewpoints, trends, happenings, by dissolving, condemning or again rescuing them, as he pleases. Thus he establishes himself as the master controller of a world he has never absorbed.[4] For had he absorbed at least segments of it, his dialectics would come to a stop, somewhere. As matters stand, it reflects, viewed sociologically, a world void of beliefs and attachments. The strange thing is, that in spite of its emptiness, Teddie's output appears to be concrete and substantial. This semblance of fullness probably results from his aesthetic sensitivity. No doubt he has insight into aesthetic structure, aesthetic values; and he knows how to formulate his predominantly aesthetic experiences. This is a great asset. But all his undeniable finesse in this respect is, alas, used in such a way that it results in sheer adornments of an otherwise hollow and insubstantial dialectics. The aesthetic concretions at which he arrives do not really enter into action; they are in the nature of trimmings; they produce a glitter which conceals, to the uninitiated, the estrangement from substance of the philosophy in which they are incorporated.

During our sociological discussion I told Teddie that Soviet Russia would in the long run be faced with the same problems which bear down on Western democracy: the problem of ideological shallowness. Indeed, who guarantees that the liberal creed, which is at the bottom of Marx's doctrine, is right in assuming that once equality is achieved in all areas, true culture begins? Teddie conceded that this is problematic indeed. Yet, he added, he does not suppose that I believe culture to be possible only under constraint. Certainly not, I answered. He held that my theory may never be put to test because oppression will continue indefinitely, which means that his radicalism is too lofty to take gradual improvements etc. into account. It is easy to be so radical. Significantly he also rejects Marx to the extent that his dialectics is controlled by an ontological vision.

APPENDIX (AUG. 24, ZURICH)

It is by no means said, I said, that the liberalism—or Marx, for that matter—is right in contending that true culture begins once all constraint, economic or otherwise, is abolished. Teddie: Of course, there are problems involved. But you will not say, Friedel, that culture rests upon suppression. I replied: Certainly not. Whereupon Teddie: Well, I do not believe that your assumption will ever be put to test. Suppression of men by men is likely to continue on & on. In other words, Teddie is Marxist to the extent that he identifies the rise of the "classless society" as the end of prehistory & the beginning of history proper.

PART II

Film Reviews
A Critic at Large

In this section, we have assembled Kracauer's reviews of individual films, written between 1941 and 1961. These are occasional texts: we find Kracauer reviewing an average of one film every other year, and not even all of these reviews were published during his lifetime. While there can be no question, then, of comparing his reviewing activities with his paid employment at the *Frankfurter Zeitung*, where his reviews appeared at a rate closer to every other day, the texts assembled here do provide insights into Kracauer's critical predilections and his continuing elaboration of criteria for film and cultural criticism.

When Kracauer first arrived in the United States in 1941, film reviewing was still his *métier*: until December of that year, he would continue to submit a few pieces to Swiss newspapers, as he had from France during the previous years. We have translated these here—particularly since they all treat of American developments, beginning with Orson Welles's recently released *Citizen Kane* (USA 1941) (ch. 16), which Kracauer sees as a somewhat formalistic and technophilic exercise, even as he lauds its obvious innovations, and including the latest vehicle for Bette Davis, *Little Foxes* (USA 1941, dir. William Wyler) (ch. 20).

It only takes Kracauer half a year before he begins publishing in English. His review of Disney's *Dumbo* (ch. 17) is reminiscent of some of his best Weimar criticism—attentive to detail, with a flair for implicit theorizing along the way. Interestingly, given that Kracauer would become known as a staid "realist" in film theory, the argument here turns decisively *against* the link between film and reality, arguing for the fundamental *irreality* of animation—which, in turns, makes for its utopian, critical potential.

A few years later, we find Kracauer theorizing the question of adaptation in a review of the screen version of Hemingway's *For Whom the Bell*

Tolls (USA 1943, dir. Sam Wood) (ch. 22). Kracauer lambasts the film—and the "amateurish Hollywood experts" who adapted the novel—for the "sheer boredom" it instills in the "somnolent audience." In reviewing the film, the short piece critiques the camera work for being too static, the mise-en-scène for being too operatic, and the script for relying too heavily on dialogue and too little on action. The author's overall aim, however, is to make some remarks about adaption and cinematic specificity, or "the nature of cinematic representation," as Kracauer puts it. Consequently, we find him testing some of the arguments that he will develop in *Theory of Film* in favor of "medium specificity"—arguments, that is, that tie particular media to specific materials, approaches, and even contents in a line that extends from Lessing through most of the representative positions in classical film theory. What remains somewhat murky in Kracauer's assessment is the place of physical reality in the film: while he emphasizes here, as elsewhere, the importance of "objects," he decries the rendering of the novel's central plot device—a strategically important bridge—as "nothing more than one of the many iron bridges designed to be destroyed in the course of a war." While this formulation itself is characteristic of the irony in Kracauer's prose, it leaves a reader of the later *Theory of Film* wondering what would be wrong with such a presentation of "physical reality," let alone the film's emphasis on "purely external events." If the goal of film is to record and reveal, if not actively to "redeem," such events, why call for a more psychologically complex treatment of the bridge, its meanings for the protagonists, or its role in generating suspense for the viewer just to stay in line with Hemingway's novel? But perhaps we have here an indication of the fact that "the redemption of physical reality," in Kracauer's later formulation, *always* implies and requires more than the mere reproduction of said reality by cinematic means—that cinema's power lies just as much in its ability to alienate that reality, to charge it with psychological or affective attachments, and to imbue material existence with meaning as it does in its specific ability to render the everyday, the fortuitous, the endless, and the indeterminate. Rather than merely shoring up an ontology of the cinema, medium-specificity is here a matter of stylistic choices as well.

While such conclusions remain unarticulated in the context of Kracauer's unpublished text on the Hemingway adaptation, his review of Rossellini's *Paisan* (Italy 1946) (ch. 23), also unpublished during his lifetime, is far more straightforward and explicit in its claim: now one of the canonic works of the Italian neorealists, *Paisan* is undoubtedly *the* touchstone film for Kracauer during these years, the one that "sets a new pattern" in its documentary approach, its rendition of physical reality, and its spirit of human dignity. Kracauer returns to the film repeatedly in his published works, holding it up ever higher as an example to the lower Hollywood with its apolitical, conformist attitude.[1] To be sure, Kracauer's discussion of the film is initially heavy on content summary, but the way he presents the film's six vignettes, in terse but carefully crafted prose, conveys his great love of this film—especially the humanity and dignity of the characters, or what Kracauer, in his posthumous *History*, will celebrate as "the humane."[2] Given the incipient cold war context in which Rossellini made the film and Kracauer reviewed it, Kracauer's admiration for the characters' "marked indifference to ideas" carries a strong political undertone—all the more so since he contrasts the end of ideology in Rossellini with Eisenstein's doctrinaire approach in *Battleship Potemkin*, calling the latter's use of typecasting and symbolism heavy-handed vis-à-vis Rossellini's lighter touch ("Rossellini patiently observes where Eisenstein ardently constructs"). Importantly, however, this binary opposition receives a twist at the end, as would have been characteristic of Kracauer's reviews in the 1920s as well: having criticized the overbearing, humanity-obfuscating power of ideology, Kracauer closes with the recognition that without ideas there is no humanity, thus turning the film's quintessence around in a form of immanent critique.

While the attention of Kracauer the film critic is largely geared toward Hollywood and Italy during these years, two reviews deal with German films. Published two years after the appearance of *From Caligari to Hitler*, "The Decent German" (ch. 24)—a review of Kurt Maetzig's *Marriage in the Shadows* (Germany 1948)—extends the framework established in the monograph, further proving its usefulness for other discussions. The result is a scathing indictment of the tendency, endemic to the extended postwar situation in Germany, to distinguish between the few bad Nazis and the mass of essentially good Germans.[3] Here as elsewhere (see especially "Psychiatry for Everything and Everybody," ch. 7), Kracauer pinpoints the ideological displacement of politics by morality, the social by the individual. A rare personal note, of the kind elaborated in "Why France Liked Our Films" (ch. 1), creeps into the text in its discussion of Jewish emigration, which Kracauer faults the film for denigrating.

Kracauer's program notes on *The Eternal Jew* (Germany 1940, dir. Fritz Hippler) (ch. 25) for a screening at Amos Vogel's *Cinema 16* film society, which counted Kracauer among its members, situate Hippler's ignominious film in the context of Nazi propaganda. Kracauer considers *The Eternal Jew* something of a "desperate" attempt at justification for the horrors already under way at the time of its making, and compares it unfavorably with the newsreels he analyzed with grudging admiration in publications such as "Propaganda and the Nazi War Film" and "The Conquest of Europe on Screen."[4] In those pieces he set out to demonstrate the Nazis' adoption of what he would later describe as the "essence" of cinema, its affinity for physical reality, showing how these films—in contradistinction also to American newsreels—let the image play out that reality without overburdening it through speech. Hippler, by contrast, degrades the pictures to "sheer illustrations of the spoken text" at best.

The section concludes with notes on Shirley Clarke's *The Connection* (USA 1961) (ch. 26), which Kracauer jotted down after a private preview screening. Though perhaps of lesser significance as a piece of film criticism, the document shows Kracauer thinking through a film that is looking for its market—a renowned book author and occasional film critic involved, however marginally, in the film culture of his day.

16 An American Experiment
(1941)

Orson Welles, barely 26 years old, who in the past has attracted much attention as radio man, author, actor, and theater director, is again the talk of the town with his film *Citizen Kane*, which premiered on Broadway in May. This film is his work in every sense of the word; for not only does Welles play the protagonist of the piece, but he also directed, produced, and co-wrote the film, not to mention the fact that he drew on the actors of his Mercury Theater, all of them new names in Hollywood. The film caused a stir if only for the fact that the main character, a newspaper magnate, appears to be modeled after real life; a well-known name is mentioned, and one has heard about protests.

Far more important are the sensations that this work represents in terms of *construction* and *technique*. Rather than developing the biography of the deceased Charles Foster Kane in a chronological narrative, Welles combines different fragments of the life story in ways that make relatively high demands on the uninitiated spectator's powers of combination. A puzzle of sorts! After Kane's death, a reporter is charged with elucidating the meaning of the word "Rosebud," Kane's last utterance as he expires. The reporter interviews a few acquaintances of the deceased, whose story gradually emerges from their reminiscences—the life of a man of great dynamism, who has a fantastic career as newspaper publisher but who is so overbearing and obstinate that everything he dreams up fails. In fragments, we learn how he destroys his marriage and falls as a politician because of a mistress whom he wishes to make into a great singer despite her poor voice; how he betrays his oldest friend and ends up passing his days alone amidst his collections in a fairy-tale castle. Why did he say "Rosebud"? The beautiful punch-line of the film is that nobody knows; at the very end, as the camera glides over Kane's collections, only the spectator gets to see the word emblazoned on a sled[1] that is being burnt along with other pieces of no apparent value.

Like the construction of the story, the method by which it is presented deviates from the usual. Unlike many other directors who have ground to a halt in their routines, Welles reinvigorates lost traditions of the silent film in his approach to camera and montage; this approach is particularly felicitous in a scene that finds an effective cinematic formula for presenting the decline of Kane's marriage. Voices have rarely been calibrated with as much care in other talking pictures, nor have they been adjusted as precisely to their surroundings. The insistent use of the wide-angle lens that permits images of great depth and width while preserving the full quality of individual details is most unusual; figures in the deep background participate in the action, and the faces are all equally pronounced, as in old paintings. This leads to strange effects, including the unintended consequence that moving figures rapidly diminish or grow in size due to the distortions caused by the lens.[2]

Rich though it may be in ideas of every kind, this brilliantly acted film—Welles himself delivers an astonishing performance as Kane—certainly does not inaugurate a new era, if only because presentation noticeably outweighs the content. Neither is Kane's private life treated adequately to really captivate the viewer, nor can the admittedly marvelous motif of the quest for a keyword's meaning justify the artificiality of the film's construction. The indiscriminate proliferation of heterogeneous technical devices betrays a lack of objectively determined stylistic impulses; rather, as the treatment of music, among other things, would suggest, the desire for originality seems to have dominated—an originality that partly represents a step backward. Welles betrays a distinct dependence on the theater not only in the way he relies on dialogue, but precisely through the new use of the wide-angle lens. By employing it constantly, he represents numerous scenes and spaces in long shots. He creates images that have more in common with the stage than with film, whose function it would be, after all, to isolate a plethora of material details from the long shot and allow them to influence the action.

Regardless of such weaknesses, *Citizen Kane* is an important film, a must-see. It conjures up filmic possibilities that have been unjustly forgotten; it provides more than a few interesting impulses, and by revealing in a single stroke the *mannerism* of today's *talkies*, it has much to contribute to the loosening of outmoded conventions.

17 Dumbo
(1941)

The new model brought out this year by the Walt Disney studio is a flying baby elephant. He comes to life in the film that bears his name, *Dumbo*, a charming picture filled with marvelously conceived episodes. Despite this, Disney continues in it a development the problematic nature of which has grown more and more apparent since *Snow White* [USA 1937].

In *Plane Crazy*, Disney's first Mickey Mouse cartoon [USA 1928], a little auto is changed through the power of the cartoonist's pen alone into an airplane, which takes flight with Mickey at the controls. In *Dumbo* a similar miracle occurs: the baby elephant suddenly spreads his ears and volplanes through the air like a Pegasus or a bomber. Here, however, the miracle does not result simply from the fact that the film is a cartoon film, but originates in the psychological effect of a "magic feather" which Dumbo's friend, a little mouse, has elicited from some insolent crows. This tiny difference betrays a structural change in the Disney films. Through a long period Disney spurned the traditional notions of reality and created his own laws for the elements of our visible world: in *Plane Crazy* Mickey's girl-friend uses her petticoat as a parachute, and the skeleton in *The Skeleton Dance* [USA 1929] employs his thigh bone to play upon a xylophone made from the bones of his skeleton friends. These metamorphoses come out of the observed relations between shapes or movements; the more ruthlessly they destroy familiar connections, the more they are justified—the more they manifest the artist's power over his material. Is the cartoonist dependent on fabulous princes, wizards, and magic feathers in order to defy the laws of nature? By including such fairy-tale beings more and more Disney has unnecessarily overburdened his films.

In addition, *Dumbo* clings to camera reality and even deals with imaginary things on the same plane. There is no doubt that Disney intends here to imitate the technique of the realistic film; but it must be acknowledged, too, that this intention turns against the principles on which Disney's classic short cartoons are based. In them he sought to build a world which had as little to do with ours as Mickey with a living mouse; his creatures strolled through a cartoonist's space in a time which, like the space itself, spread or shrank to his liking. In *Dumbo* Disney treats not only imaginary objects as real, but more, he combines them with human figures and does things which could as well have been done in the studio, and thus threatens the true interest of his medium. The cartoon film tends toward the dissolution rather than the reinforcement of conventional reality, and its function is not to draw a reality which can better be photographed.

The turn to a realistic style is fostered by the full-length cartoon which requires a story. One is reminded of the old comedies; they too have suffered from their extension to feature length. Film comedy and cartoon coincide in that they do not aim at the development of plots but rather at the exposition of particular incidents. For both kinds of film the whole "story" is just a gag or a series of gags. Hence they should be brief; for only on this condition can the plot keep its quality of a thread that holds together the pearls of the gags. The nature of the incident in both comedy and cartoon influences the nature of the plot. Thus the genuine cartoon would scoff at the idea of machinery ruling mankind and, like the comedy, select as its hero the weak little creature who must assert himself against the stupid and evil powers of our world. It is to their own disadvantage that Disney's feature films do not follow this line, but submit too readily to current social conventions. Significant in this respect is the conclusion of the present film: young Dumbo, instead of flying off toward some unknown paradise, chooses wealth and security and so ends as the highly paid star of the same circus director who once flogged his mother Jumbo. Is no better solution possible? However questionable the illustration of absolute music may be, *Fantasia* [USA 1940] proved, at least, that feature cartoons are not necessarily dependent upon a "story." One could wish, too, that Disney would stop animating fairy tales into conventional everyday life and, proceeding like Chaplin, develop everyday life into fairy tales through his cartoons. As to the methods of representation, he might be able, after the example of great painters, to transform both real and imaginary objects in his art and thus bring it to a new level.

Dumbo shows that Disney has already an inclination toward such a transformation. Hopes are raised by such scenes as the erection of the circus tent—a sequence in which reality is transferred to a strange, exciting sphere. Most fortunately, too, Disney's artistic instincts frequently prevail against his artistic intentions and thrust aside the disturbing story to bring in such happy inventions as the gang of crows, the beautifully developed play of the champagne pearls, and many others quite as delightful.

18 Film Notes from Hollywood

(1941)

In view of the growing tendency toward purely informational and propagandistic films, the most recent announcement from the Hays Office warns against neglecting the predominance of the feature film designed for the purpose of entertainment. "Knowledge is not to be gained at the expense of entertaining elements," says Mr. Hays, "rather, it results from entertainment."

According to a report from Twentieth Century–Fox, the production costs of a film are now calculated in advance with almost scientific precision. Following a recently proposed scheme, the following percentages of the total costs of a film are budgeted, on average: no more than 5% for the acquisition of the "story," 5–7% for the treatment of the script, 25% for acting (including stars and extras), 10% for the director, 12.5% for the design and construction of the sets, 2% for the design and manufacture of the costumes, 0.9% for the make-up department, 2% for marketing personnel, technical consultants, etc., almost 2% for camera operators.

The influence of the war is becoming noticeable in areas adjacent to the film industry as well. Joe Delfino, the sound technician at Fox, reports that at his company's studio alone, sound effects worth at least $100,000 have been devalued by the war. "Even the sound of an airplane engine that is not even three years old is archaic today. The new types of bombs, grenades, and other explosive devices will need to be registered at great expense as sounds for future war films."

Warner Bros. has entered into a contract with the world-renowned Russian Ballet of Monte Carlo to produce a faithful filmic rendition of all of the ballet's numbers in Technicolor. For the first time in the history of film, the repertoire of a great ballet will thus appear on screen. The production is supposed to begin with *Gaîté Parisienne*.[1]

People: Jean Renoir, who has a long-term contract with Fox, will be directing the filming of *Swamp Water* [USA 1941, dir. Jean Renoir], based on the successful novel that has been published in the *Saturday Evening Post*. Charles Laughton will appear in Universal's next Deanna Durbin film, *Almost an Angel*.[2] Albert Basserman will play the doctor in charge of a sanatorium in the crime film *Fly by Night* [USA 1942, dir. Robert Siodmak].

19 A Few American Films
(1941)

To date, Hollywood has not produced many color films, but those that have recently appeared show noticeable progress. One of them, *Blood and Sand* (Twentieth Century–Fox [USA 1941, dir. Rouben Mamoulian]) revisits the theme of a Valentino film from 1922, takes place in a chromatically fertile Spain, and serves the desire for pomp and mass spectacle. Based on a novel by the Spaniard Ibáñez, it describes the life of a bullfighter, including a vamp episode and without neglecting to show how wobbly is the glory of these darlings of the masses and how much misery lurks behind the glamor. The improvements here consist mainly in the fact that the film eradicates the fuzziness of backgrounds that had marred earlier color films; and it approaches color composition with deliberate care. In slightly disorganized fashion, the MGM film *Blossoms in the Dust* [USA 1941, dir. Mervyn LeRoy] tells the touching story of an American philanthropist who manages, by several detours and by renouncing her personal happiness, to fight against the social ostracization of illegitimate children. Though the film does not benefit from the opportunity for a colorful environment, it does manage to elaborate images in which color becomes significant in its own right. One of the protagonists is Felix Bressart's old country doctor, an astonishing figure, thrilling in his humanity.—As far as the general topic of color film is concerned, it should be noted that it has not yet surpassed the stage of experimentation. Compelling effects are the exception, the rendering of faces remains a problem.

In MGM's *A Woman's Face* [USA 1941, dir. George Cukor], Joan Crawford takes revenge for the humiliations that she suffers because of her disfigured face. Together with a gang of criminals, she blackmails the rich. A surgeon, the husband of one of her victims, restores her beauty, and the soul promptly follows the transformation of the body. Hardly a device for suspense remains unused in this adaptation of a pulp fiction: the underlying design is only revealed gradually through flashbacks during a trial that provides for a dramatic atmosphere and oppressive retardations; the answer to the worried question—whether the operation on the face was successful—is postponed for as long as possible. Besides Crawford, whose art has style, two others are well cast: Albert Bassermann, unmistakably his old self, and Conny Veidt, whose outward appearance is greatly altered here.

The new RKO film *Tom, Dick, and Harry* [USA 1941, dir. Garson Kanin] met here with great and truly deserved success. With an astute sense for cinematic punch lines, it tells a lovely fairly tale from everyday life, thereby transporting the audience into the pleasurable atmosphere of fantasies. This film rests on Ginger Rogers who, in her role as a foolish little telephone operator, hooks up with three young men; afterward, she fantasizes each time how the respective man would serve as a husband, and she finds herself unable to choose any one of them. She is simply delightful, and the strong effect of her sweet babble proves that what counts in the talkies is not so much the content of what is said but the manner in which the spoken word is delivered. Pretty visual ideas compensate not only for the somewhat thin action, but also for the slight monotony of the three dreams that arise from Ginger's pillow and crudely distort an otherwise sweet reality. Right from the start, the film is witty: one sees the auditorium of a movie theater from the point of view at which one would expect the screen, and from an imaginary screen one hears the invisible heroine proclaim that she could cry for joy. Also of note: the melodic sound gag that always rings out when Ginger kisses the poorest of the three lovers.

20 William Wyler's New Bette Davis Film

(1941)

The Samuel Goldwyn production company has now released the new Bette Davis film *Little Foxes* [USA 1941], directed by William Wyler. Both for its qualities and for its flaws, the film represents an important work that met with great success in New York. Based on a stage play, the film takes place in the South and largely amounts to a character study of the mean, avaricious Regina Giddens, who sets out to win over her husband, a mortally ill banker, for the vague financial projects of her unscrupulous brothers, with whom she makes common cause; when, having seen through the conspiracy, her husband declines her wish, she attacks him verbally until he has a heart attack, and then refuses to fetch the requisite medicine from upstairs. He attempts to climb the stairs himself and falls; his death is a cold-blooded murder.

Wyler had already shown in films such as *These Three* [USA 1936] and *Dead End* [USA 1937] that he is not afraid to break with habits and conventions when he is out to pry open psychological chasms or to render problematic characters; here again, he continues along his path with a determination that deserves particular praise in view of the dominant tendency toward the standardization of film subjects.

The basic weakness of the film lies in the fact that, here as in earlier works, Wyler always makes brilliant use of film technique but fails to create from the possibilities inherent in film alone. These are all the more difficult to access since Wyler adopts a subject that was conceptualized exclusively for the theater and suggests theatrical staging; but why does he obey the directives of this material so heedlessly? Apparently because he lacks the ultimate relation to the medium of film, out of which Griffith, Stroheim, or René Clair once chose and shaped their themes. Unlike these men, who knew well that a film is only cinema when *objects*, too, actively participate in the action, Wyler fails to penetrate deeply into the adapted stage play to transform it for the purposes of film. Which is also to say that the film is courageous only in its subject matter; its treatment hews to conventional lines and sabotages the effect of the thematic conceit.—Once we have recognized Wyler's weakness, we are all the more free to admire the high degree of cultivation with which he makes human events palpable. Supported by Gregg Toland's excellent photography, he renders visible every psychological nuance. The way he describes the unease of a guest from Chicago and of several family members during a piano recital in the salon is inimitable, as is the realization of the catastrophe just before the end: Regina sits in the background, brightly lit and motionless, while her husband moves toward the stairs from the front. Then we are presented with a close-up of her face, traversed by the shadow of the staggering man, and a few moments later we see the husband crawling up the stairs behind her like a wounded animal. Since Wyler largely sticks to the conditions set by the stage, it is self-evident that he should rely heavily on the actors' performance for the purposes of characterization. From their facial and bodily gestures, he distills a maximum of significance. Under his direction, Bette Davis as Regina becomes an unforgettable character. This great and deliberate artist probably gives her most astonishing performance in the moment when her daughter threatens to leave her; it is as if she wanted to fight against her nature at this point, but the scabs of evil have already hardened to the point where she is powerless to fight it and must remain what she was. Both the husband and the daughter are well selected: Herbert Marshall's noble, kind manner and the charming innocence of Teresa Wright provide further contours to Davis's performance. Another climax of acting and directing occurs in the scene in which Regina's sister-in-law (played by Patricia Collinge) gets drunk and in her stupor blurts out her hatred for the family. Her son is the stolid, vulgar Leo, whose comic foolishness is embodied with cinematic perfection by Dan Duryea.

21 Flaherty: *The Land*
(1942)

The weak sides of this film are too obvious to dwell upon. Its plot lacks precision and fails to get hold of the very problems it attempts to attack; thus the last part dealing with the marvelous machines is of a naivety that seems to be somewhat obsolete in the face of actual life. The simplicity of representation is adequate to that of Flaherty's mind; it would have been possible, for instance, to shape the relations between commentary and pictures in a more interesting way. Perhaps Flaherty has worked too long on his film; this would be an explanation for motifs abandoned on the way and for the incoherence of the different parts.

But all these deficiencies are not weighty enough to injure the true merits of *The Land:* its deep honesty and the beauty of its pictures. Indeed, the whole is impregnated with a sincerity that cannot but impress audiences. Flaherty may be naive; in his naivety, however, he really says what he feels and avoids making hasty conclusions. And if he does not always approach the problems that he wants to expose, he proceeds, nevertheless, with an instinct so infallible as to not endanger future solutions. It is important that his own voice sounds throughout the film; this voice has the power of convincing and efficaciously bolsters the contents of the pictures. The secret of these pictures is to include *time*. They resemble fragments of a lost epic song that celebrated the immense life of the land; nothing is omitted, and each episode is full of significance. Among them that with the old peasant slowly wiping and then ringing the bell belongs to the unforgettable scenes on the screen. Such effects are deepened still by the montage. Miss van Dongen [the editor of the film] knows how to develop a situation, how to compose of a series of close-ups and long shots clear and definite spaces and to time their disclosure.

22 For Whom the Bell Tolls
(1943)

For Whom the Bell Tolls, Paramount's screen version of the famous Hemingway novel, is a film as ambitious as it is long. Made from a work of high literary standards, it puts on airs giving everyone to understand that it is a work of art as well. Nobody can overlook the amount of craft and thoroughness invested in this film. The outcome is nevertheless pitiful; for, apart from a few episodes, the film is sheer boredom throughout its three hours' length—a failure which has been certified by multiple press reviews. How did it happen that so many efforts resulted in so vain a product? The attempt at an answer gives rise to some remarks involving the problem of screen adaptations and the nature of cinematic representation.

Hemingway's novel about the Spanish Civil War lives on a minimum of external action. During the opening scenes Robert Jordan, an American dynamiter in the camp of the Loyalists, is ordered to blast a bridge in the mountains at a strategically decisive moment; in the last part he achieves this mission. The bulk of the book deals, in a more descriptive way, with Robert's life among a group of people who, hidden in the neighborhood of that bridge, wage guerilla war against the Fascists and are to help him in the fulfillment of his task. Here Robert falls in love with Maria, a Spanish girl raped by Franco soldiers and yet radiating a virgin innocence. Here he forces, through his rather unobtrusive presence, all members of that strange community to reveal their thoughts and tell life stories exposing the horrors of civil warfare.

This is about all so far as palpable events are concerned. In fact, it is not so much the externals in themselves which matter as the inner attitudes they symbolize. The blowing up of the bridge is as such of secondary importance; but it allows the artist to penetrate the mentality of guerilla soldiers who, in their struggle for freedom, are continually faced with death. All happenings in the novel center round the one problem: how are men able to carry on under such confusing and irregular conditions? To be sure, the Spanish leftists endeavor to live up to their political ideals. However, Hemingway knows that all depends upon the relationship between these ideals and the psychological reality allegedly covered by them, and therefore probes the soul of each partisan with the curiosity and precision of the born experimentalist. Some are worn-out; others have fallen back upon a harsh cynicism without entirely losing their faith.

Imbued with the love of Maria, Robert himself learns "that you must make your whole life in the two nights that are given to you; that living as we do now you must concentrate all of that which you should always have into the short time that you can have it."[1] In Robert, Hemingway's hero, social ideals and instinctive desires do not prostitute each other, but succeed in honestly coming along together. He might be the citizen of a better world. The lengthy and detached dialogue also records the experience that love unfolds nowhere more intensely than on the verge of imminent danger.

Would it be possible to transfer this delicate subject-matter to the screen? But the question is rather, what has been actually done with the novel. It is as if the film makers had started from the following reflections: Since Hemingway's book is a best-seller and, at the same time, an officially recognized work of art, its adaptation offers us the unique chance of producing an artistically elevated film without running financial risks. The only condition is not to miss any of Hemingway's fine points. Let us therefore copy the novel as exactly as possible, and, like that novel, the resultant film will be art that pays.

Indeed, the screen version renders the original with almost verbal fidelity, maintaining the succession of its episodes as well as a good deal of the dialogue. There are omissions, of course. For obvious reasons not only the intimate sleeping-bag scenes have been suppressed, but also all talks and passages disclosing the book's political implications. Thus the clarity of its mental background yields to a nebulous neutrality, narrowing the scope of the characters and blurring the whole picture. However, in spite of these compromises the film clings to its literary model more zealously than similar productions usually do. And this is its basic deficiency.

Any literary work consists of narrative elements selected and arranged so as to make them carry some intended meaning. They are impregnated with significance and connected in such a way that they mutually illuminate each other. Of course, they are what they are only within the given frame of the work. If this holds true, they cannot be removed like pieces of furniture from one medium to another—as though the same were always the same. To present approximately the same subject-matter, different media are, on the contrary, bound to use different means. A film version which confines itself to simply shifting the elements of a literary work to the screen is likely to run into a series of pictures deprived of the sense these elements originally conveyed. For such a procedure originates in the naive belief that with outward forms meanings will be automatically transferred, and therefore neglects to build up those meanings in truly cinematic terms. The pictures that finally appear are, in consequence, empty signs rather than essential symbols.

The Hemingway film is a mechanical reproduction. Symptomatically, the amateurish Hollywood experts have adopted the whole bridge affair without any changes. They literally transcribe the book in showing the bridge guarded by Fascist sentries, watched by the guerillas, and, at the end, dynamited by Robert—a finish crowned with crashing tanks, hand-to-hand fights, and corpses in both camps. This stubborn submission to the original texture is doubtless intended to make the screen version profit by the powerful suspense of the novel, where the bridge continually haunts the mind of the Loyalist group, thus assuming the gigantic proportions of a spectre. However, precisely by relying too much on the verbal references to the bridge, the film fails to realize their significance through cinematic devices. Instead of embodying the fantastic, omnipresent being of the novel, the screen bridge is nothing more than one of the many iron bridges designed to be destroyed in the course of a war. This explains why the film is so utterly tedious. It pretends to reach the level of Hemingway's story, and, as a matter of fact, develops in a dimension reserved to purely external events. The audience is entitled to feel bored by the endless talks delaying time and again the blasting business, which, moreover, cannot compete with the patterns set for military operations in such films as *Bataan* [USA 1943, dir. Tay Garnett] or *In Which We Serve* [UK 1942, dir. Noel Coward and David Lean]. To compensate for the lack of surface excitement, the film makers have tried hard to render the attack of the bridge in a dramatic manner. But the spectacular role assigned to these battle scenes tends to inflate their function. In the novel they are the natural conclusion of a story pregnant with inner action; in the film they acquire an importance unduly reducing the weight of the preceding dialogue episodes.

Eager to reproduce the novel all down the line, the film also incorporates fragments which are by no means appropriate to be drawn to the screen. During one of her first meetings with Robert, Maria demonstrates her inexperience by naively worrying about the difficult art of placing kisses. What are lovers supposed to do with the protruding noses while their mouths set out to find each other? Maria considers noses a grave disturbance . . . One may like or dislike this sweetish bit of dialogue: on the screen, Maria's attempt at surmounting the obstacle of the interfering noses is of an unbearable absurdity. In their desire to catch up with Hemingway, the film producers have overlooked that it often proves dangerous to translate the vague notions aroused by words into distinctly contoured visuals.

As a consequence of the wrong conception on which the film is founded, all cinematic possibilities are thoroughly neglected. Sam Wood, who directed many a film excelling in swift action, seems to have been awed by Hemingway's literary culture to such an extent that he sometimes behaves like a still-photographer. In general, the camera simply idles, leaving it to the characters to express their intentions. They express them in landscapes content with forming a remote background which is not at all cooperative. Snowy hills silently witness a conversation between several persons, who walk a few steps and then continue talking before other snowy hills. This kind of procedure resumes the embryonic techniques of the archaic movies, in which an immovable camera focussed upon ensemble scenes fashioned after the manner of the stage. It is not by chance that during long intervals the Hemingway film takes on the traits of an opera. Exactly as the smugglers in *Carmen*, the romantically clothed guerillas appear, disappear, and reappear according to their catchword. The whole reminds one of a theatrical performance in some provincial town—except for the good acting, of course.

Much as the actors must be praised, the fact that they alone are able temporarily to stir the somnolent audience betrays once more the basic weakness of the film. In a true film the development of the plot is not only due to the actors, but also depends upon the contributions of the objects. Things may be induced to act more effectively than any player does. By featuring the actors at the expense of the things, the Hemingway film forces them to fall into the ways of stage actors. It is as if they moved between theatrical settings, instead of forming part of a world in motion. Katina Paxinou is no doubt an outstanding figure. Gary Cooper impersonates Robert's nature without rendering his mental background. But this applies to the other characters as well. Sharing in the film's lack of significance, they all offer a merely psychological interest. Pablo, who serves Hemingway to exemplify the slow decay and yet tenacious life of revolutionary ideals in the soul of an old-timer, represents in the film the almost pathological case of a quaint and wavering drunkard.

It is not as if a film approaching the true subject-matter of Hemingway's novel were out of reach. His weird bridge can be figured on the screen; his life experience is certainly accessible to pictures. To attain such aims, one has only to supersede Hollywood's mechanical reproduction by an adaptation which unhesitatingly breaks up and reshapes the texture of the book. Thus the dialogue should not be verbally transcribed as in the Paramount product—which is a sure means to prevent the audience from grasping its implications—but handled so as to bring these implications into cinematic existence. The camera may help in advancing meanings which screen characters are unable to express through words. Here, however, the question arises whether even an adequate film version would be advisable in this special case. As an outspoken literary structure, the Hemingway novel seems to belong among those works which deeply root in their own medium; so much so that they cannot be transplanted without suffering from loss of essentials. In a strict sense Hemingway is untranslatable. Of course, to Hollywood this novel has been nothing more than a best-seller highly appreciated on behalf of its literary values. This accounts for the film as it is. It makes one yearn for a Hitchcock-thriller.

23 *Paisan*
(1948)

Roberto Rossellini's *Paisan* [Italy 1946] surpasses his *Open City* [Italy 1945] in breadth of vision and significance. *Open City* was still a drama; *Paisan* is an epic, comparable only to *[The Battleship] Potemkin* [USSR 1925, dir. Sergei Eisenstein], though profoundly different from it.

This new Italian film consists of six real-life episodes which take place during the Italian Campaign. They seem entirely unconnected, except for the fact that their succession corresponds to the advance of the Allied armies. The first episode records the adventures of an American patrol immediately after the landing in Sicily. Led by an Italian peasant girl, the Americans explore a ruined castle—a nocturnal reconnaissance which culminates in a magnificent conversation between the girl and one of the soldiers. But this bilingual idyll does not last long. A few Germans emerging from nowhere shoot the soldier and then kill the girl for having fired at them. When, alarmed by the shooting, the rest of the Americans return, they take it for granted that the girl has lured them into a trap, and her simple-hearted sacrifice passes unnoticed.

The second episode, in Naples, features a street urchin and a Military Policeman—an American Negro who is thoroughly drunk. The boy, set on stealing the Negro's shoes, guides him to a rubble heap among the ruins, where his prospective victim raves about the hero reception prepared for him in New York and his home town. But the word "home" provokes a sudden shift of moods in him. He says he will not go home; and in a state of despondency he falls asleep, an easy prey for the boy. Shortly later, the Negro captures the thief and makes him return the shoes. The boy is a war orphan living in a cave crammed with ragged women and children. Overwhelmed by pity, the Negro leaves the shoes behind in the cave. Colorful street incidents round out the brilliant thumbnail sketches of these two stray creatures. The scene in the marionette theatre in which the frantic Negro climbs the miniature stage to defend a Moor is a veritable gem sparkling with Quixotic spirit.

The subsequent Roman episode is a somewhat literary love story, with a touch of Maupassant. Six months after the fall of Rome a drunken American soldier follows a prostitute to her room. He is no drunkard but a sensitive boy appalled by the ever-increasing corruption around him. Instead of simply sleeping with the girl, he tells her about Francesca, the first girl he met on entering Rome on the day of liberation. A flashback, rich in charming details, renders their innocent flirtation and its premature end. Why did you never go back, asks the prostitute. He mutters that he could not find the house. The prostitute, trembling, describes it. He dozes off, vaguely realizing her identity. Next day, she despairingly waits for him, while he himself, on the point of leaving, tears up the slip of paper with her address. He mounts a truck, and the armies move on.

The fourth episode shows the Allies in the outskirts of Florence, preparing the last assault on the city, in which the Partisans are already at grips with the Germans and Fascists. An American nurse, eager to join her Florentine lover of prewar days, learns that he is "Lupo," the legendary Partisan leader. The whole is a pictorial report on what happens to her and an Italian friend as they slip through the front lines into the Partisan-held sector of Florence. They walk past two British officers, portrayed in all their languid fastidiousness; they pass along the corridors of the abandoned Uffizi, catching a glimpse of three German soldiers who slowly advance deep down on the street. When they finally reach a bullet-swept street corner, one of the few Partisans defending this position is fatally wounded. His comrades liquidate two Fascists on the spot. Before dying in the arms of the nurse, the wounded Partisan says that Lupo has been killed that very morning. "God," says the nurse.

In the fifth episode three American chaplains in search of shelter enter a remote Franciscan monastery in the Apennines and are accommodated there for the night. The naive unworldliness of the monks is characterized in scenes born out of respect and highlighted by an imperceptible smile. No sooner do the monks find out that one of their guests is a Protestant and the other a Jew than they involve the Catholic chaplain in a sort of religious disputation. Thesis stands against thesis: the worried monks insist that those two lost souls must be saved, while their urbane coreligionist believes them able to attain a state of grace outside the Church. This duel in pious dialectics is the more exquisite since battles are raging in the neighborhood. The end comes as a surprise. The zealous monks impose a fast on themselves for the sake of the Jew and the Protestant, and the Catholic chaplain praises their humility, instead of reaffirming his stand on tolerance. It is a strange conclusion, somewhat reminiscent of the spiritual note in Silone's novels.[1]

The last episode is a terrible nightmare unfolding in the marshes of the Po Valley, where flat land and sky fuse into a monotonous universe. A small group of Italian Partisans, British flyers, and American O.S.S. agents engage in a hopeless combat action behind the enemy lines. You do not see the Germans at first; you see only the corpse of a Partisan floating across the water. The reeds are filled with threats; unknown dangers lurk around the lonely house which in its isolation deepens the impression of monotony. Then, after an eternity of unbearable suspense, the massacre takes its course. The people in the house are killed indiscriminately, except for a little child who, outside the house, screams and screams, deserted by the dead on the ground. The Partisans, bound hand and foot, are thrown into the water. The horrified English and American prisoners see them, one by one, disappear, unable to stop the clockwork process. Another witness is left: the Partisan leader hanging behind the prisoners.

"This happened in the winter of 1944," a commentator says at the very end. "A few weeks later, spring came to Italy and the war in Europe was declared over."

All these episodes relate the experiences of ordinary people in a world which tends to thwart their noblest efforts. The dead Sicilian girl is callously slandered by those who should have honored her; Francesca, the fresh Roman girl, turns prostitute, and her decent lover sinks into emotional inertia. It is the war which dooms them. Yet it is not always the war: in the case of the Negro, his fate results from circumstances entirely unconnected with events in Italy.

What endears these people to us is their inborn dignity. They have dignity in the same way that they breathe or eat. Throughout the film, humanity appears as a quality of man's nature, as something that exists in him independently of his ideals and creeds. Rossellini's Partisans never refer to their political convictions; rather, they fight and die in a matter-of-fact way, because they are as they are. And the Negro is simply a humane creature, filled with compassion, love of music, and Quixotic reveries.

This emphasis on the reality of good nature is coupled with a marked indifference to ideas. Of course, the Nazis appear as hateful, but it seems they are hated only for their acts of savagery and their vulgar conduct. All judgments are concerned with human dignity, and what goes beyond it is completely omitted. There is in the whole film not a single verbal statement against Fascist rule, nor any message in favor of democracy, let alone a social revolution. And the surface impression, that *Paisan* advocates pacifism, must be dismissed also, for it is scarcely compatible with the experience of the Catholic chaplain, to whom the war has been a great lesson in tolerance. This deliberate disregard of all "causes," including that of humanity, can be explained only by a profound skepticism about their effects. Even the most praiseworthy cause, *Paisan* implies, is bound to entail fanaticism, corruption, and misery, thus interfering with the free flow of a good and meaningful life. Significantly, the Sicilian peasants are suspicious of American liberators and German invaders alike; and the Roman episode bears out their suspicions by highlighting the demoralization wrought upon the liberated in less than six months.

The attitude behind *Paisan* is in keeping with the film's episodic structure. In stringing together six separate episodes, Rossellini manifests his belief in the independence of human dignity from any overarching idea. If humanity materialized only under the guidance of an idea, then a single, well-composed story might suggest itself to express the latter's significance (viz. *Potemkin*). But humanity is here part and parcel of reality and therefore must be traced in various places. The six isolated episodes indicate that streaks of it are found everywhere.

Since *Paisan* confines itself to real-life experiences, its documentary style is most adequate. The style, cultivated by D.W. Griffith, Flaherty, and the Russian film directors, is genuinely cinematic, for it grows out of the urge, inherent in the camera, to explore the world of facts. Like Eisenstein or Flaherty, Rossellini goes the limit in capturing reality. He shoots on location and prefers laymen to professional actors. And instead of working from an elaborate script, with each detail thought out in advance, he lets himself be inspired by the unforeseeable situations that arise in the process of filming.

These techniques become virtues because of Rossellini's infatuation with reality and his gift for translating its every manifestation into cinematic terms. He masters horror scenes no less expertly than moments of tenderness, and the confused street crowd is as near to him as is the abandoned individual in it. His camera angles and twists of action owe their existence to sparks of intuition ignited by the closest touch with the given material. And directed by him, most people play themselves without seeming to play at all. To be sure, *Paisan* has its weak spots: parts of the Sicilian episode are shot in slapdash fashion; the Roman love story is too much of a story; the nurse and her companion in the Florentine episode are strangely flat; and the Catholic chaplain is not entirely true to type. But these occasional lapses amount to little within a film which sets a new pattern in documentary treatment. Its wonderful freshness results from Rossellini's unflinching directness in formulating his particular notion of humanity. He knows what he wants to say and says it as simply as possible.

Are examples needed? Far from capitalizing, after the manner of *The Last Chance* [USA 1945, dir. Leopold Lindtberg], on bilingual dialogue to sell the idea of international solidarity, *Paisan* presents the mingling of languages in wartime Italy without any purpose. In the opening episode, the conversation between the Sicilian girl and the American soldier in charge of her is a linguistic dabbling which, born out of the latter's boredom and loneliness, does not lead up to anything. Yet precisely by recording their pointless attempts at mutual understanding with infinite care, Rossellini manages to move and fascinate us. For in the process these two people, left speechless by their mother tongues, increasingly reveal what as a rule is buried under conventional phrases.

Each episode abounds in examples. When the drunken G.I. tells the Roman prostitute about his yearning for Francesca, he is seen lying on the couch, with his legs apart in the foreground—a shot which renders his physical disgust and moral disillusionment to perfection. Though long shots are ordinarily less communicative than close shots, Rossellini draws heavily on them in the last episode to picture the marshes. He does so on purpose, for these shots not only convey the impression of desolate monotony, but, through their very flatness, they make the ensuing massacre seem more dreadful. A model of artistic intelligence are the street scenes in the Neapolitan episode. First it is as if these loosely connected shots of performing jugglers, ragged natives, blackmarketing children, and idling G.I.'s were inserted only in the interest of local color. Shortly, however, it becomes evident that they also serve to characterize the Negro. As he reemerges from the marionette theatre, his companion, the wily boy who does not want to lose him, begins to play a harmonica; and, enticed by these heavenly sounds, the Negro follows the little Pied Piper through streets teeming with the crowds and diversions that have already been impressed upon us. So we are all the more struck by the impact of the trickling harmonica music on the Negro.

This last example well illustrates the way Rossellini organizes his material. There is a veritable gulf between his editing style and the "montage" methods used in *Potemkin* and other early Soviet films. For Rossellini deliberately turns his back on ideas, while the Russian film directors aim exclusively at driving home a message. *Paisan* deals with the human assets of ordinary people; Eisenstein's *Potemkin* shows ordinary people wedded to the cause of revolution. All editing devices in the Eisenstein film are calculated not only to render a historic uprising, but to render it in the light of Marxist doctrine. In *Potemkin,* the priest's face, besides being his face, stands for Tsarist oppression, and the sailors are made to appear as the vanguard of the proletariat. Nothing of that kind occurs in the Italian film. On the contrary, Rossellini so composes his narrative that we never feel challenged to seek symbolic meanings in it. Such instances of oppression or humanity as *Paisan* offers are strictly individual facts which do not admit of generalization. Rossellini patiently observes where Eisenstein ardently constructs. This accounts for the thrill of a few shots which represent border cases. I am thinking in particular of the documentary shot of the three German soldiers in the Florentine episode. Reminiscent, perhaps deliberately so, of similar shots in official Nazi documentaries, it is inserted in such a manner that it affects us as a true revelation of German militarism. The allusiveness of this shot is sufficiently strong to drive us beyond the bounds of immediate reality, and yet too unobtrusive to make us lose contact with it.

Paisan is all the more amazing as it defies the traditional patterns of film making in Italy. The Italian prewar screen was crowded with historical extravaganzas and beautifully photographed dramas that displayed inflated passions before decorative settings—a long progression of glossy products, led by d'Annunzio's world-famous *Cabiria,* of 1914. Taking advantage of their audience's love for theatrics, these films reflected both the glitter and the hollowness of the regime under which they flourished. . . . It is a far cry from d'Annunzio to Rossellini, from the spectacular to the real. The sudden emergence of such a film as *Paisan* indicates that many Italians actually loathe the grand-style manner of the past and all that it implied in allegiances and sham beliefs. They have come to realize the futility of Mussolini's conquests and they seem now determined to do without any messages and missions—at least for the moment.

And this moment is a precarious one for the Italians. Fascist rule has ended, the new government is weak, and the country resounds with internal strife. During this interregnum the Italians might feel completely lost, were it not for a compact cultural heritage which protects them from disintegration. Theirs is an articulate sense of art and a tested way of putting up with the tragedies common to mortals. And under the undiminishing spell of custom they knowingly enjoy the rites of love making and the gratifications of family life. No doubt, the Church has played its part in shaping and civilizing these people throughout the ages. That they are aware of it perhaps accounts for the surprise ending of the Monastery episode in *Paisan*—that scene in which the American chaplain bows to the religious ardor of the Italian monks, thus disavowing what he has said about the inclusiveness of true tolerance shortly before. His deliberate inconsistency can be considered a tribute to Italian Catholicism and its humanizing effects.

Italian everyday life, then, is rich in meaningful outlets for all imaginable needs and desires. So the Italians do not sink into a vacuum when they refuse, as they are now doing, to let themselves be possessed with ideas. Even without ideas they still have much to rely upon. And since their kind of existence, mellow and sweet as it is, has long since become second nature to them—something that seems to them as natural as the blue sky or the air they breathe—they may well believe that their repudiation of ideas relieves their lives of excess baggage. What remains, in their opinion, is humanity, pure and simple. And in their case, as *Paisan* demonstrates, humanity assumes all the traits of self-sufficient reality.

This is a mirage, though, which may appear as more than a mirage only at a very particular moment, such as the Italians are now going through. *Paisan* is delusive in that it virtually makes the triumph of humanity dependent on a world released from the strain of ideas, or "causes." We cannot feel this way. As matters stand, we know humanity would be irretrievably bogged down if it were unsustained by the ideas mankind breeds in desperate attempts to improve its lot. Whatever their consequences, they hold out a promise to us. Rossellini's film dismisses the audience without any such promise. But this does not invalidate its peculiar greatness. And precisely in these postwar years with their tangle of oblique slogans and propaganda artifices, *Paisan* comes to us as a revelation of the steady flow of humanity beneath the turmoil of sheer ideology. So, if *Paisan* does not kindle hopes, yet it reassures us of the omnipresence of their sources.

24 The Decent German
Film Portrait (1949)

Within the last few months, several German postwar films have come to us from the Soviet zone of occupation. One of these, *Marriage in the Shadows* [Germany 1947, dir. Kurt Maetzig], though not precisely a work of art, at least represents a serious attempt at self-scrutiny. It is, moreover, a film essentially German in technique and outlook; though it was made under Russian auspices, there is no significant evidence of Russian influence to be found in it. It offers, therefore, certain indications of the present state of the German mentality.

This is all the more useful because current reports from Germany, concerned with day-to-day politics rather than deeper currents, do not give a coherent picture of what is going on in the minds of the Germans.

On the one hand, they very optimistically speak of a turn to the better, with democratic thought gaining strength; on the other, they record facts which give about the reverse impression;—all too often, apparently, objective estimates are watered down by wishful thinking and moral preachment.

To be sure, the psychological meaning of a film is not always to be found on its surface. Hollywood films, for instance, have been criticized for misleading people abroad into believing that America is a paradise for gangsters, a country where money means everything and acts of unbridled violence alternate with scenes effusively sentimental. These films, it has been remarked, distort American life. No doubt they do, if they are taken at face value. Yet there is a sense in which Hollywood films—the films of all nations, for that matter—reflect a deeper reality: often they reveal less obvious motivations and behavior patterns which in one way or another do correspond to actually existing mass tendencies. In an earlier article in *Commentary* ("Hollywood's Terror Films," August 1946),[1] the writer tried to show that those screen pageants of horror and sadism which flourished immediately after the war had a distinct bearing on the mental climate of the time. Similarly, it is not difficult, at least in retrospect, to realize that there was a close relation between such a film as Capra's *Mr. Deeds Goes to Town* [USA 1936] and the era of the New Deal. Or, to take a more recent example, the Italian film *Paisan* [1946, dir. Roberto Rossellini], a blend of political inertia and stirring humanity, clearly reveals its origin in the psychological climate of a nation that has seen many ideas come and go, invariably entailing war and misery, and is now suspicious of all ideas and all politics.

Covering the period from 1933 to 1943, *Marriage in the Shadows* tells the story, said to be based on real-life events, of a popular Berlin actor and his Jewish wife, herself a prominent actress. The story begins with her enforced retreat from the stage, drags on in an atmosphere of gloom and ever-growing despair, and ends with the actor poisoning himself and his wife to spare her the horrors of imminent deportation. But this is only the nucleus of a plot which clearly aims at driving home the impact of Nazi anti-Semitism on all those liberal-minded Gentiles and Jews who in happier days unhesitatingly mingled with each other. *Marriage in the Shadows* is a chronicle of the German middle class under Hitler.

We seem to learn only what we never doubted—that decency did not die out when the Nazis took over. Wieland, the actor, refuses indignantly to divorce his Elisabeth; and neither of them would dream of deserting their Jewish friend Kurt, who chooses to emigrate after the Reichstag fire but reappears in Berlin ten years later, a fugitive from a concentration camp. Similarly, the old Jewish doctor Silbermann is not entirely wrong in relying on the loyalty of his "Aryan" patients: some of them, at least, are prepared to risk their lives to shelter him as the terror reaches its peak. Silbermann is a sort of Biblical figure, a second Nathan the Wise. What an abrupt change—slightly embarrassing for being so abrupt—from the Nazi-contrived "Jew Suess" to this paragon of mellow sweetness![2]

Nor did we ever doubt that many were less dependable. The film offers a variety of samples, ranging from meek compliance to spiteful malignity. The publisher Dr. Blohm, Elisabeth's fiancé in pre-Hitler days, is particularly interesting because he illustrates the typical self-justifications of the weak social climber. No sooner does Hitler win out than the handsome Dr. Blohm solves the conflict between love and career by exchanging his place in Elisabeth's heart for a job in the propaganda ministry and posing before her and himself as an idealist. Beneath his pretenses to culture and goodness there extends a bottomless swamp. As one of Goebbels' henchmen, he first protects Elisabeth from the Gestapo to soothe his conscience and eventually betrays her to save his skin. The swamp engulfs him.

We knew all this. Yet in confirming it, *Marriage in the Shadows* adds a touch of first-hand experience and valuable detail. The pictorial account of the anti-Jewish mob riots in 1938 reconstructs that organized fury with convincing accuracy; and many a conversation about topical issues sounds like a transcript from minutes. The film's specific merit is its honesty, which sometimes produces effects far more impressive than the glamor of Hollywood: a gay pastoral scene sandwiched between two episodes of anguish illuminates the nightmarish character of a universe in which sublime art neighbors on crude terror; and I do not recall any suicide on the screen that can match the film's concluding sequence with its drawn-out silences and its finality.

There the matter might rest, were it not for the attitudes one senses behind the film—attitudes that should alarm those concerned with German "re-education."

Steeped in purely personal moral distinctions, *Marriage in the Shadows* condemns the "bad" Germans who surrendered to Hitler, while praising the "good" ones who did not. No doubt these latter are deserving of praise; yet they talk and act in a way which, to say the least, has a strangely pathetic quality. What is wrong with them? Their whole conduct illustrates the simple truth that decency comes into its own only if it is acted out on the political scene as well as in private life. And it cannot fully be acted out unless the decent people are guided by concepts which make them grasp the significance of politics, the close interrelation of private and public morals.

It would be difficult to exaggerate the political immaturity of *Marriage in the Shadows*. By applying the yardstick of individual ethics indiscriminately to all human affairs, the film precludes any understanding of Hitler's hold on the mass mind. The Nazis—SS-men, Gestapo agents, top officials, and the like—are represented simply as conquerors who, for reasons left unexplained, have managed to seize control, attracting the weak, the mean, and the vicious. This is how they appear to Elisabeth and her friends, and the treatment of them on the screen constantly deepens the impression that they are an alien race unconnected with the rest of the people—as if the Germans, like the French, were the victims of an invasion. Need it be said that such an approach is inadequate? Before 1933 as well as later, many middle-class Germans, upset by the vast unemployment, the irreconcilable antagonism of Left and Right, and the sterility of a system which the Nazis had done so much to undermine, in all sincerity saw Hitler as a savior; the very idea of an omnipotent Führer appealed to their traditional authoritarian leanings. *Hitler came from within.* And it is absurd to pass off the bulk of his followers among the educated as simple opportunists or hypocrites.

In *Marriage in the Shadows* decency unfolds at the expense of adult political judgment. This shows most glaringly in the film-makers' tendency to deprecate Jewish emigration. To be sure, Kurt, more sensitive than the others, leaves Berlin for Vienna; and Elisabeth might have left also, had not emotion overcome her reason. But the overwhelming sympathies lie with those who bear the brunt at home. Instead of sending Elisabeth away to safety, her husband implores her to stay with him in Germany and in general looks down upon emigrants. "Maybe it won't be so bad," says Dr. Silbermann in the early days of the regime, "but should things turn worse, I would think even less of going abroad." And as if to emphasize his courage, two Jews shown in his waiting room absorbed in discussing foreign visas are characterized as pitiable, inferior creatures.

The film thus tends to cast Jewish emigrants almost in the role of deserters. But to what do they owe allegiance? And why does Elisabeth not try to argue the situation out with her husband? For all their personal integrity, the Jewish characters act out of an emotional idealism much cultivated in Germany—an idealism which holds reason in contempt and prides itself on never asking questions. In this film, its most striking result is a double suicide of no consequence; as if to emphasize the essentially unrealistic character of the suicide, it is made to parallel the final scene of a stage play that Hans and Elisabeth are shown acting when the film opens—thus supplying a framework more significant than the film-makers may have intended.

Products of a thoroughgoing effort at assimilation, the good Jews of the film resemble the good Germans in combining high sentiments with poor judgment. They take their plight for granted; the existence of other possibilities and another world—Palestine, for example—seems unknown to them.

Jews or Gentiles, these decent middle-class Germans are incapable even of an attempt to translate their decency into action. They repeatedly accuse themselves, it is true, of not having entered the arena as fighters; but these rare bits of insight turn out to be merely rhetorical protestations leading nowhere. For the rest, *Marriage in the Shadows* strictly avoids facing up to the facts. The Jewish characters die by their own hands or succeed in escaping; their fear of deportation is never borne out by a scene evoking the ultimate consequence of deportation. Nor does the film mention political activities against the Nazis. It remains unclear, for instance, whether the people who shelter Silbermann are underground fighters or not. Silbermann himself, being of a saintly nature, is politically a blank. The same holds true of Elisabeth and the others, with perhaps the one exception of Kurt, who at least is dimly aware of the impact of Hitlerism.

Politics for these people is nothing but a hateful intrusion into their emotional and cultural privacy. One episode intimates that Wieland, in the interest of his career as an actor, might readily make his peace with the Nazis were it not for his *personal* moral obligation to Elisabeth. Elisabeth herself communes with the elements at a North Sea beach while the clouds gather over Berlin, and in a despondent mood seeks comfort in Goethe's letters. She and her friends are so exclusively concerned with their private lives that they see public life as something that remains outside their reach; they are thus completely at a loss when political or social events lay claim to their common sense rather than their familiarity with Goethe. They know only that they *should* do something about the situation; but when it comes to it they are stunned into passivity.

The film fails to show any real awareness of these shortcomings. Here a side-glance at *Paisan* is rewarding. The monks in the monastery episode of *Paisan* match Silbermann in both saintliness and ignorance; but precisely because of these qualities they are portrayed with a subtle irony which quietly points up the limitations of their outlook. No such irony is used in the presentation of Silbermann, Elisabeth, and Wieland. Occasionally, it is true, these characters indulge in an optimism which is regularly discredited by the facts; yet even this emphasis on their self-deception is handled in such a way that it becomes not a criticism of their political ineptitude but only another means of arousing compassion for their tragic helplessness.

If *Marriage in the Shadows* reflects an actually existing state of mind, as I believe it does, then the unmodulated sympathy with which it surrounds its "good" characters would indicate that German middle-class mentality has not really changed. Through its one-sided emphasis on issues of personal morality, this film brings the problem of German re-education into sharp focus. For that problem does not bear on individual ethics, as many still incline to believe; rather, it bears on certain basic concepts which, common to "bad" Germans and "good" Germans alike, are responsible for their political inhibitions. What is wrong with the majority of Germans is the way they conceive of authority, of the role of reason, of the interrelation between culture and civilization. Any effective mobilization of German decency must depend on a change in habits of thought that are centuries old.

Our correspondents in Germany report an ever-increasing rehabilitation of former Nazis and a mounting wave of anti-Semitism. One fears that the decent Germans of today may again let the evil grow without penetrating and resisting it, and may again be caught in the maelstrom with nothing left intact but their precious decency. The suicide that ends this film is the ultimate response of which a purely personal morality is capable.

25 The Eternal Jew
(1956)

This is the only full-length Nazi documentary against the Jews I know of. One thing is sure: it was made after the Polish campaign (which gave the Nazis an opportunity to shoot scenes in the Jewish ghettoes). But it might as well have been compiled only at a time when the war took a bad turn for the Nazis. There is one fact which makes me assume that much. The film amounts to a wholesale condemnation of the Jews and all that is Jewish, yet achieves this goal in a very forced and artificial way. In fact, this film is much weaker in technique and power of conviction than previous Nazi documentaries, such as *Triumph of the Will* [Germany 1935, dir. Leni Riefenstahl] and *Baptism of Fire* [Germany 1940, dir. Hans Bertram]. This tends to show that it was, so to speak, a conscience-saving propaganda message issued at a moment when the Nazis prepared the death camps in Poland or had already begun to set them up. The film's intention of justifying some sinister anti-Jewish measures stands out glaringly. I have the distinct feeling that this film served to rekindle hatred against the Jews in a period when many Germans were wavering and entertaining heretic thoughts.

The weakness of the film shows in the predominance, unusual for the Nazis, of the spoken word. In their great propaganda films, the Nazis always tried to let the pictures speak, keeping the commentary subdued or only using it as a means of further increasing the impact of the imagery.[1]

This was a truly cinematic procedure, for film differs from other arts in that it reflects the visible world to a hitherto unknown extent. Everyday life, with its infinitesimal movements, its multitude of transitory action, can be disclosed nowhere but on the screen.

While the pre-Hitler Germans availed themselves of these techniques to conquer more and more provinces of the visible world, the Nazis used them with quite another intention. In emphasizing the role of the visuals, they tried to suppress the intellect and affect directly emotional life. Hence the predominance of pictures over verbal explanations in the bulk of Nazi newsreels and propaganda films. The pictures themselves are so selected that they work primarily on the instincts, on unavowed drives. Taylor has said of the Nazi propaganda tracts that they supersede rational argumentation by "pictures and symbols." Nazi speeches, too, dwell upon metaphoric turns, for the spell of the image smothers the interest in motivations and reasons. Instead of appealing to the understanding of their audiences, the Nazis attempted to weaken the faculty of understanding which might have undermined the basis of the entire system. Rather than suggesting through information, Nazi propaganda withheld information or degraded it to a further means of propagandistic suggestion. This propaganda was tantamount to psychological manipulation in grand style. Accordingly, the Nazi film propagandists were not in the least concerned with conveying reality through their candid-camera work. On the contrary. . . . But they did everything they could to drive home the fact that their films consisted of unadulterated newsreel and documentary material and to evoke the impression that, in consequence, reality itself was moving across the screen. This accounts for the disquiet and uneasiness which Nazi propaganda films arouse in unbiased minds. Before our eyes palpable reality becomes a sham—a transformation all the more upsetting as it was to exert its impact on a whole people.

In contradistinction to the earlier Nazi propaganda films, *The Eternal Jew* is a spoken lecture or, if you wish, a massive editorial which in crude anti-Semitic language assembles all the well-known and worn-out arguments against the Jews. The pictures are often degraded to sheer illustrations of the spoken text or do not relate to it at all. You see the Polish Jews in their homes and on the streets of the ghetto; while the narrator abuses them as swindlers and parasites, concerned with money only, many faces just give the lie to these accusations. Thus the image of a tired Jew, stooped over his wares, flagrantly contradicts the synchronized verbal insinuation. In other words, the commentary does not succeed in providing the stimuli needed for the hoped-for effects of the pictures.

This is particularly manifest in passages where the film makers visibly overdo their job. One is the long list of hateworthy Jews, which includes world-renowned figures like Einstein and Chaplin (a Jew, according to the Nazis). I can hardly believe that, even among the Nazis, many were willing to accept such a sweeping verdict. And this, in turn, would confirm my original assumption that the whole film was designed to justify terrible actions in preparation or already under way. There is something desperate about this late effort of the Nazis to turn the tide of public opinion in their favor.

Let me just indicate the main areas which this propaganda film covers. A large part is filled with pictures and descriptions of the Polish Jews for the purpose of impressing upon the audience the racial differences between them and the rest of the world. Some of the ghetto scenes give the impression that they were re-enacted by the Jews under pressure during the German occupation of Poland. For instance, the bodily movements of the students in the Talmud school seem grossly exaggerated; and the shots which first show Polish Jews with their beards and all, and then as clean-shaved, normally clothed Europeans, cannot have been obtained voluntarily either.

After having exhausted this theme, the film turns to a large-scale historical retrospect which deals with the migrations of the Jews in a pseudo-objective way. Then the film elaborates on the parasitic role of the Jews in Western life and culture, business and industry, stubbornly insisting that the assimilated West European Jews are but descendants of the strange and ugly-looking Polish Jews. The strongest point is made toward the end with a series of alleged documentary shots focusing on the ritual killing of animals by Jews. These pictures are horrifying indeed, but they are not any more gruesome than the images of [Georges] Franju's *Blood of the Beasts* [France 1949]. The necessity of having to eat is a bad business after all.

In spite of the fatal prevalence and omnipresence of the spoken word, however, the film still utilizes certain effective pictorial devices, rarely applied in Anglo-Saxon propaganda films. Take, for instance, the animated diagrams which picture the spread of the Jews from the Orient to Poland and from there back to Germany, etc.: the maps and figures representing the latter migration spread octopus-like, reminiscent of an army of cockroaches. No sooner has the allusive diagram been shown than the speaker compares the Jews with rats. He has already prepared us for this drastic comparison by pictures anticipating it. After a while, another diagram appears on the screen which, through a rapidly increasing maze of lines, illustrates the infiltration of the Jews in international commerce and finance all over the world. These lines resemble a spider, as they grow and interpenetrate each other.

Another cunning pictorial device is to show the Jews smiling—particularly when the worst things are being said about them. The Jewish butchers smile while animal life is ebbing away. When deceiving the tax collector or cheating in the bazaar, or doing anything that is made to appear as wicked, the Jews invariably have a smile on their face. This, of course, is to suggest to the spectator that the Jew lies eternally in ambush, always prompted by a desire of defrauding his innocent neighbor.

Also, here as elsewhere, the Nazis work by way of pictorial contrasts. In order to cater to physiognomical preferences and prejudices, they contrast close-ups of Jews with German faces. Whenever they want to show that the Jews "feed" on their host people without doing any productive work, shots of Jews trading and enjoying themselves are juxtaposed with shots of toiling German miners, peasants, and the like. And the terrible slaughter scenes are immediately followed by the apotheosis common to all Nazi documentaries: Hitler haranguing the masses; jubilant youngsters in the crowd hailing the Fuehrer; and endless columns marching toward new victories.

To sum up, behind this film you feel the concern of the German propaganda ministry over the German state of mind. Hence the excessive recourse to words, the over-argumentation, the inadequacy of the pictures. At the bottom of it all lurks despair and fatigue. One is inclined to believe that the film at least partially defeated its purpose.

26 A Few Notes on *The Connection*
(1961)

(1) The main shortcoming of this film [*The Connection* (USA 1962, dir. Shirley Clarke)] is that the milieu of the "junkies" is nowhere contrasted with the normal everyday world. The noises from street and yard are not enough to impress this world on the spectator. (I think of the children's voices, the firetruck, etc.) Everyday life through shots of people, street pictures, etc., should have been introduced at the beginning, intermittently, and certainly at the end. Why? Because only in this way there would have been a sufficient and pictorial counterweight against the jaded and stagnant band of the drug addicts. And the sights of some average, or indeed good people and of street life would by themselves alone have sufficed to press home the moral of the film, which, as matters stand now, does not really come out. For the hell is hell only if it is contrasted with transitory life on earth or a vision of paradise.

(2) Concomitant with this shortcoming is another one—that the documentary film maker who intrudes himself into the haunt of the doomed band remains a shadowy figure throughout. The idea of such a witness is good and truly cinematic; but its implementation falls flat. I assume that this figure is intended, at least partially, to represent our normal world in which drug addicts are an exception after all, not the rule. But if this was the intention it is just not put across. In order to throw him, and with him the world about us, more into relief one would have had to give him three-dimensional proportions—for instance, by an opening scene

showing how he leaves some conventional film studio in search for better pictures and for more truth. As it is now, the swamp all but overgrows him and instead of setting the corrupted company of addicts in the proper perspective, he gradually dissolves and the evil fellows get the better of him. They may be right in reproaching him with invading their haunt as a sheer non-participant, a camera-eye pure and simple, but this is not the main point to be made. The main point of the story is, rather, the revelation of the drug addicts' undoings. And this revelation does not materialize for lack of counterweights—normal life is omitted and the film maker is a lifeless person. The result is that the despair of the drug addicts is almost morally justified. One gets the impression that their attitude has deeper significance.

(3) The whole film suffers from dependence on the ways of the theatre. There is much too much superfluous talking in it; what is worse, the content of the monologues or dialogues assumes decisive functions; the action progresses through verbal communications; this being so, close shots of the ash tray and the cockroach degenerate into decorative additions rather than advancing the story. A case in point is the film maker's verbal assertion that he is tired of Hollywood and wants to revert to Eisenstein. In the theatre such an assertion might carry weight, while in a film it is just verbal ornament, without power of conviction. Also, the various movements of the actors in ever one and the same locale become boring and smell of theatrical direction. The film would have immeasurably won if half an hour had been used for characterization of the normal outside world and the film maker. One and a half hours for the drug addicts themselves would have been more than enough. Incidentally, the jazz music is badly overdone.

(4) I wonder whether it was a good idea to overemphasize the participation of Negroes in the drug traffic and drug addiction to such an extent.

PART III

Book Reviews
A Critic at Large

Besides films, Kracauer continuously reviewed books—and not only in the field of film studies. Upon his arrival in the United States, Kracauer humbly offered his services to the *New York Times* as book reviewer, but had to reject his first commission (a book on economics) as too far afield.[1] While he did end up placing the occasional review in the *Times*,[2] his book reviews, like his other writings, appeared in a broad array of venues and ranged from short notices about French and German releases in the journal *Books Abroad* to reviews for film magazines such as *New Movies*, for the *Saturday Review of Literature*, and for journals such as the *Kenyon Review*, *Commentary*, and, repeatedly, the *New Republic*.

To students of film theory, Kracauer's pair of reviews of two volumes of collected essays by Eisenstein (chs. 27 and 28)—*The Film Sense* and *Film Form*, both of which remain staples on college reading lists alongside Kracauer's own works—will be particularly intriguing. Here we find the realist film theorist venting about Eisenstein's formalism, even as he expresses admiration for the Soviet director's achievements on screen. Interestingly, Kracauer sees Eisenstein—the inveterate dialectician and advocate of "conflict" as the central principle of montage—as obsessed with harmony and betraying the essence of cinema by trying too hard to make film one among many arts, a *Gesamtkunstwerk* of Wagnerian lineage. His critique notwithstanding, Kracauer calls Eisenstein's book *The Film Sense* potentially valuable to the American war effort, a primer on how to direct film viewers' emotions. Upon the release of *Film Form* six years later, Kracauer picks up where he left off and unabashedly reviews Eisenstein's second book in cold war terms that serve to align Eisenstein with Stalinism—and Kracauer's own film theory, by extension, with democracy.

167

If the second Eisenstein review is somewhat self-serving, the same goes for Kracauer's 1942 review of Leo C. Rosten's *The Movie Colony* (ch. 29), which, in Kracauer's words, "x-ray[s] that complicated organism called Hollywood." Perhaps he was reminded of his own analyses of Ufa, Germany's dominant studios of the prewar years.[3] But more importantly, Kracauer may have been identifying with Rosten when he praised him for his method of "construction within the dimension of the materials themselves"—Kracauer's own approach precisely, as delineated in the *feuilleton* articles of the 1920s and subsequently published in book form as *Die Angestellten* in 1930.

The same methodological mirroring is evident in "Portrait in Film" (ch. 34), Kracauer's critical review of Parker Tyler's book on Chaplin. The author, he asserts, "has the stuff of which interpreters are made," but Tyler's analysis of Chaplin is marred, according to Kracauer, by the "self-indulgence of a narcissist [who] rejoices in a display of intellectual pyrotechnics" rather than respecting what Adorno would call "the preponderance of the object," and Kracauer "the construction within the dimension of the materials themselves." To really be an interpreter, to really engage in the hermeneutic enterprise, Kracauer concludes, requires the receptivity and patience of a careful observer who "learn[s] to listen to what his material may tell him."

The opposite of such materialism—which will return as the "material aesthetics" advanced in *Theory of Film*—is false idealism. The debates of the 1920s had sensitized Kracauer to the pernicious afterlife of idealist philosophy in all areas of culture, politics, and *habitus*. When he reviews a book on the German university system under the telling title "The Teutonic Mind" (ch. 31), he again mirrors himself by citing the author's powers of "bi-cultural observation," then goes on to fault the author for failing to consider "the effects of German idealism as a whole on the mentality of the middle classes." Needless to say, this assessment—in an otherwise very positive review—may have as much to do with Kracauer's own preoccupations with that mentality in *From Caligari to Hitler* as with the merits or shortcomings of the book under review.

A more complex case presents itself when Kracauer turns to French existentialism. Reviewing Jean-Paul Sartre's recent book *The Psychology of Imagination* (ch. 32), he faults the brilliant philosopher for displacing the material world into the realm of the mind, dethroning the material object in favor of the "imagined object." What Kracauer finds lacking in Sartre is a sensitivity to the limitations of imagination. Freedom for Kracauer is not an abstract category; rather, it needs to be tied to social circumstances, construed as the active freedom to *do* something. Without acknowledgment of these constraints, Kracauer argues, existentialism is bloodless, manifesting "an essential poverty of life substance."

Other reviews modulate some of these motifs—as, for instance, in Kracauer's emphasis on the relation between film and the material body, the sense organs, which we may glean from his review of a book on the use of film as a teaching tool (ch. 35) and which will return fully theorized in the important section "The Spectator" in *Theory of Film*. Conversely, a pair of reviews of Lancelot Hogben's *From Cave Painting to Comic Strip* (ch. 36) bemoans the "pictorial deluge" unleashed by modernity. Echoing his assertion in the famous 1928 essay "Photography" that "never before has a period known so little about itself," hiding meaning as it does behind the "blizzard of photographs" in illustrated magazines, Kracauer argues here that "we are submerged by pictures and at the same time prevented from really perceiving them."[4] Instead, Kracauer champions in-depth contemplation and intent looking, perceptual attitudes that are undercut by the superfluity of images in film, television, and journalism. To the attentive reader, this attitude will seem something of a step backward relative to the more dialectical evaluation reached in the essays of the 1920s, which linked the "blizzard" of photography with the utopian promise of reconciliation in the "go-for-broke game of history."[5]

Of particular note in this section, however, is "Movie Mirror," Kracauer's review of Martha Wolfenstein and Nathan Leites's *Movies: A Psychological Study* (ch. 37). This book appeared three years after *From Caligari to Hitler*, but Kracauer's review still betrays a certain anxiety of influence—or is it just the narcissism of small differences that leads him to critique, of all things, a psychological approach to film: for wasn't this precisely what the *Caligari* book, "A Psychological History of the German Film," had proposed? Kracauer begins drawing some boundaries by describing the method of *Movies* as "cultural anthropology," and he imputes to the authors an "unfamiliarity with the medium"—of which nobody who knows of Kracauer's reviewing activities during the 1920s could possibly accuse him, and yet he goes on to describe the book as if he were describing *From Caligari to Hitler*. What seems so particularly curious about this review in retrospect is that two of the objections Kracauer raises to *Movies*—specifically, the insufficient size of Wolfenstein and Leites's sample and their overemphasis on narrative at the expense of nonnarrative aspects of cinema—are precisely two objections that were leveled at *From Caligari to Hitler* in the wake of its publication. The third point of Kracauer's critique, which faults *Movies* with a lack of attention to (film) history, is less tied to the cited weaknesses of his own book. The review ends up pointing to the dangers of psychoanalysis, indicting it as a "form of escapism" and thus resuming arguments from "Psychiatry for Everything and Everybody" (ch. 7) two years prior—arguments that one is tempted, after seeing them reprised in this review, to turn back on *Caligari* as part of the author's critical engagement with his own work.

27 In Eisenstein's Workshop
(1943)

Eisenstein's name is for ever bound up with his film *Potemkin* [USSR 1925], which, through its content as well as its methods, not only impressed the world, but also influenced the development of the whole cinema. Significantly, Dr. Goebbels in the early days of the Nazi regime praised *Potemkin* as a pattern and intimated that the Nazi "revolution" should be glorified by films of a similar structure. Thus films intervene in the course of history. It must be added, however, that *Potemkin* would have been impossible without the examples the American film director D.W. Griffith set in *The Birth of a Nation* [USA 1915] and *Intolerance* [USA 1916] during the last World War. The Russians have never ceased paying homage to this great innovator.

In *The Film Sense*, Eisenstein defies the common notion that artistic inspirations and analytic faculties are of too different a nature to flourish in one mind. He aims at pointing out those methods of film composition that not only help to make the film a work of art, but also evoke an audience's desire for creative collaboration. In view of such ends he features "montage," i.e., the juxtaposition of all the aural and visual elements of which a film may consist. It is an act of self-correction (and also self-defense) that Eisenstein thus brings the art of editing to the fore. Through his own silent pictures this film director once furthered the inclination of the Soviet cinema to rely too much upon mere editing devices. Pudovkin, the author of such important films as *Mother* [USSR 1926] and *The End of St. Petersburg* [USSR 1927], did not hesitate at that time to establish a pictorial analogy between advancing revolutionary people and a river impetuously breaking up ice, or to compare the columns of a Tsarist courthouse with the jackboots of the sentry watching it—a metaphoric handling of objects that frequently violated their essential meaning. In the subsequent period that error was abandoned in favor of a no less one-sided neglect of even legitimate "montage" effects, caused by technical difficulties arising from the talkies.

Eisenstein actually strives to establish a kind of synthesis adjusting those two extreme positions. Instead of considering only "montage," he says, one has also to pay attention to the content of the shots and sound units to be juxtaposed. The shape of the film as a whole results from both the specific nature of these elements and their well-founded juxtaposition. After having developed his new concept of "montage," he turns to the problems of "audio-visual cinematography," ventilating in particular the question how, in any film, music and pictures can be combined so as to embody through their combination the film's story. A long chapter is devoted to significant correspondences between color and sound; referring to the existence of such correspondences, Eisenstein demands that the character of a film's musical and pictorial elements be in strict harmony with its main ideas. This is not all, of course; to set forth these ideas, the processions of musical themes and visual themes must be consciously connected. One may make both of them run contrapuntally throughout the film, or manage to parallel their movements. Of these two possibilities Eisenstein emphasizes but the latter one. A sequence of his last film, *Alexander Nevsky* [USSR 1938], serves as an elaborate example for the complete "congruence of the movement of the music with the movement of the visual contour."

Precisely his insisting upon congruence is symptomatic of the changes Eisenstein's thinking has undergone. In his beginnings Eisenstein left the theatre to become a film director, because he recognized that only the cinema would allow him to express the specific notions and revolutionary ideas he had in mind. The screen is better able than the stage to represent masses and collective actions. At that period he stressed all traits and techniques pertinent to the motion picture alone, and when later on the sound film emerged, he was still more interested in the contrapuntal relation of picture to sound than in their eventual consonance. This was quite plausible: things in Russia continued to be in a state of flux, and if the films desired to mirror the revolutionary movement, they had constantly to produce shock effects, requiring a contrapuntal dealing with the material involved. Now the aesthetic theories are reversed—presumably in connection with the process of stabilization that has taken place under Stalin. Far from setting off the sound film against the neighboring arts and determining its particular role, Eisenstein endeavors to prove, on the contrary, that films and works of great literature have all essential methods in common, and to these ends quotes Pushkin, Shelley, Milton, Leonardo da Vinci—as though he considered the film a kind of Cinderella and wanted her to make a social career. His aesthetic research is so anxious to place films on the same level as poems that it passes over their vital differences; hence its formal character. And since, in addition, this formalism obstinately sticks to the harmony of a film's various elements, it betrays all the more Eisenstein's present predilection for screen works that approach artistic achievements of a rather idealistic type. Is it by chance that he recently directed Wagner's *Valkyrie* at a Moscow opera house? The zeal with which he forces all aural and visual components of a film into the service of its leading ideas recalls somewhat the Wagnerian conception of the "total work of art." *Alexander Nevsky* includes, in fact, numerous scenes that could be part of a romantic opera as well.

Despite its problematic attitude, Eisenstein's book is fascinating in that it discloses with an outstanding intensity the manifold creative processes preceding the final edition of a film. No one concerned with the cinema and aesthetics in general should disregard this insight into Eisenstein's workshop. His many instructions as to how to direct the spectator's emotions may prove valuable in the production of pictures designed to support the American war effort.

28 The Russian Director
(1949)

Film Form is a sequel to *Film Sense*, the first Eisenstein anthology. The new publication—compiled by the author himself shortly before his death and, like its predecessor, edited expertly by Jay Leyda—includes several pieces never translated before; it is of particular interest because it covers the evolution of Eisenstein's thinking from 1928 to 1945. During this period his esthetic conceptions underwent profound changes, reflecting those of the political regime. Eisenstein accepted Stalinism and went far in adjusting his artistic views to the exigencies of a rigidly totalitarian system. This is evidenced by everything he wrote in later years. But the book also reveals that his life as an artist ended in plain tragedy; or, to be more cautious, his life offered the spectacle of a tragedy. For it is doubtful whether he himself would ever have admitted being involved in a conflict between outer pressure and inner calling: his ability to theorize permitted him to indulge in powerful rationalizations. Yet there is evidence that his spontaneity was not completely consumed by an all-pervading environment; that indeed his very nature rejected what his mind desperately embraced.

The drama unfolds in terms of film esthetics. Up to 1930 or so, Eisenstein, strictly in keeping with *Potemkin* [USSR 1925] and his other early screen epics, insisted that contrived stories and invented plots went against the grain of the new cinematic medium. Since films consist of a succession of shots which may picture everything from every angle, they are predestined to encompass life in its inexhaustibility. Of course, life is Russian life, as it presents itself in the twenties—revolution in process, with the masses as the hero. It is a reality in which the predominant crowd lends itself to the ubiquitous camera.

Eisenstein's infinite sense of detail led him to explore all kinds of material phenomena, and his artistic determination to organize the material prompted him to devise an ingenious method of editing: he juxtaposed seemingly unconnected shots so that their combination yielded meanings previously not implicit in them. Thus what appears on the screen is reality as a "meaningful whole"—that is, reality in the light of the Marxist doctrine, which may have appealed to Eisenstein as a socially sanctioned principle of artistic organization. But much as he is concerned with the composition of a significant whole, he does not forget that the many things which make up that whole have also a life of their own. He is fascinated by boats in the mist, streets and faces; and he delights in the idea of reconstructing on the screen the endless flow of inner monologue. The whole, instead of imposing itself on every detail, grows out of images which still preserve an independence of a sort. There is a certain openness about his early films; *Potemkin* retains a documentary quality that may well account for its survival.

After 1930, Stalinism is consolidated; the time of revolutionary mass movements and indiscriminate collectivism comes to an end. Films are now requested to feature individual heroes and to develop along the lines of definite plots. Such story films not only satisfy desires widespread in an era of stabilization, but mirror, or can easily be made to mirror, the structure of a regime which culminates in a godlike individual and plots the lives of all its subjects. In consequence, Eisenstein is blamed for neglecting the individual in mass evolutions and concentrating on special editing techniques at the expense of tightly composed stories. The latter criticism goes deep; it accuses him of emphasizing the succession of single shots instead of subordinating all of them to the binding authority of a set plot. This is a serious accusation, for such procedures must seem subversive to a regime that suppresses individual initiative for the sake of totalitarian planning.

Eisenstein surrenders. He acknowledges the timeliness of story films and individual heroes. He admits the one-sidedness of his former infatuation with sheer editing, trying to explain it by the then prevailing social conditions. He even makes an attempt to reinterpret *Potemkin* as a five-act drama, with every shot having its well-defined function within a totally prearranged unity. The whole, which formerly seemed to result from various combinations of relatively independent shots, now appears at the very beginning, determining the content and scope of each single picture frame. The art of cinematography, he says in 1932, "is in every fragment of a film being an organic part of an organically conceived whole." Totalitarianism wins out; planning supersedes the tendency, inherent in the camera, to explore unforeseeable real-life incidents.

But Eisenstein would not have been the artist he was had he been unaware of the dangers of excessive purposefulness; under its pressure the pictorial narrative can degenerate—and in many cases did degenerate—into a plain and flat illustration of the given story. Hence his insistence on an imagery which really sensualized the story. The theory he concocted in support of this demand is as sophisticated as it is unconvincing. Basically he wanted to eat his cake and have it too: films should be patterned after the model of Stalinist society and yet breathe the cinematic life of *Potemkin*. The incompatibility of these aspirations could not be demonstrated more strikingly than by his own films, *Alexander Nevsky* [USSR 1938] and *Ivan the Terrible* [USSR 1945]. Both of them, it is true, include episodes of cinematic perfection and true insight into life in the Middle Ages. But these episodes lose much of their impact because they merely serve to implement the airtight composition of operatic plots. In fact, compositional efforts encroach on every detail, choking off what independent life it might otherwise convey. Eisenstein aimed at creating "total" works of art, yet it is precisely their claim to totality that invalidates their cinematic essence. *Nevsky*, as well as *Ivan*, lacks the openness of *Potemkin*; both are grand operas rather than genuine films.

Eisenstein identifies himself unconditionally with these films. Where, then, is the tragedy? It leaks out of passages scattered through his later writings. In 1932, discussing the curriculum of the State Cinema Institute, he inserts a statement on the necessity of Marxist indoctrination in a manner that indicates he mentions it mainly for the sake of decorum. In the same essay, when he evokes the memory of his treatment of *An American Tragedy* [USA 1931, dir. Josef von Sternberg], with its new emphasis on inner monologue, the whole passage overflows with nostalgia for a cinematic rendering of life. Even though he disavowed this nostalgia a few years later, it flared up at the end of his career, in strict opposition to everything he did and preached. In 1944, he extolled D. W. Griffith's "inimitable bit characters who seem to have run straight from life onto the screen"; he praised Griffith for incorporating into his films life in its incalculable fullness. It is as if Eisenstein thus expressed, however indirectly, his own suffering under conditions which made him shut out that life; as if he glorified, through his portrayal of Griffith, a past in which he too focused on passers-by in the crowd.

But this is not the tragedy; the tragedy is that he was not even aware of its being one. Except for those occasional passages, his mind ignored what his heart demanded. Stalinism had weakened his power of resistance from within.

Pudovkin's classic writings on the motion picture have been republished also. Brilliantly prefaced by Lewis Jacobs, this anthology also includes two new contributions which deal with problems of the sound film. Pudovkin does not have a searching mind like Eisenstein, but he is a great craftsman and a great teacher. His treatises on technique and acting lead straight to the core of the matter, exposing the processes of film making with an expert's lucidity and an artist's fondness for his medium. Part of the material is still valid; the penetrating analysis of the film actor stands out unsurpassed to this day.

29 The Movie Colony
(1942)

Before considering Mr. Rosten's book [*Hollywood: The Movie Colony—The Movie Makers* (1941)] itself I should like to speak a word of praise for the understanding of its sponsors, the Carnegie Corporation of New York and the Rockefeller Foundation, who enabled the author to x-ray that complicated organism called Hollywood. Writers in Europe have rarely been given the opportunity of scrutinizing actual social problems under such favorable conditions. And Mr. Rosten seems to have been particularly well equipped to write this extensive study, for he combines the faculty of immediate observation with a far-reaching sociological background, a vivid concern for each specimen of this peculiar human fauna with an ability, if necessary, to keep at a distance, the talents of a writer with the capacity of the scholar—gifts that are seldom found together but are supremely important for a productive approach to contemporaneous social structures.

The book covers the period 1938–41, and consists of two parts, the first concerned with the social laws and regulations that determine the life of the movie colony in general, the second and more specialized section detailing the status of the producers, the directors, the actors and so on. Its pattern is what may be called construction within the dimension of the materials themselves. In other words, Mr. Rosten neither reproduces, like a journalist, mere impressions resulting from close contact with the facts and people in question, nor enshrouds his observations in generalized theory which has meshes too wide to capture the single phenomenon. His point of view is near enough to let him discriminate and characterize the multifold traits of the movie world, and at the same time it is sufficiently remote to free him from the fetters of intimacy and permit him to look at Hollywood as a whole. In addition to the methodological problem, Mr. Rosten has solved that of tact, which offered serious difficulties since he was obliged to deal with the personal qualities, hobbies, inclinations and griefs of particularly sensitive artists. But despite the discretion with which the book intentionally overlooks certain angles—emphasized, for instance, in Schulberg's novel *What Makes Sammy Run?*[1]—the author is not afraid of destroying the widespread "Hollywood Legend" and penetrating through the dense fogs produced by publicity managers and attendant gossip columnists to the very core of Hollywood's internal organization.

One underlying idea seems to me especially revealing: Mr. Rosten considers Hollywood as the "quintessence of the *nouveau riche*" and succeeds—by means of an excellent selection of examples and quotations—in paralleling it with that era of American life in which the great industrial and financial magnates worked their way up to power. "Hollywood does what is 'done,' does more of it . . .": through this formula he makes it evident that what Hollywood represents is not so much the exception as an extremely outspoken form of a social set-up which had already appeared in the United States and may still appear wherever certain presuppositions are realized. Still more important, perhaps, is his disclosure of the interrelationship between social conditions and psychological features. Also with regard to psychology Mr. Rosten finds the right perspective: he does not, like many scientists, condemn an occupation with psychological facts, nor does he stumble into the relativism connected with the overestimation of such facts. What he strives to do is to demonstrate how each characteristic trait depends upon certain fixed constants in the social sphere; the outcome is a reliable topography of Hollywood's psychic structure. Thus he explains the optimism that movie-makers exhibit as their cloak for a deep-rooted anxiety, for the subconscious conviction that luck cannot last and that catastrophe may come at any moment; and he has highly interesting things to say about Hollywood's passion for gambling, about the vague guilt complex that haunts its people. The volumes announced to follow, treating the economics of Hollywood and including analyses of its films, can be sure of the same interest as this first one.

30 A Lady of Valor
(1947)

In his biography of Adah Isaacs Menken—an American actress who in the middle of the 19th century stirred sensation everywhere between Virginia City (Nevada) and Paris—Allen Lesser tries to penetrate the secret in which this amazing Jewish woman wrapped herself. Driven by human curiosity as well as a genuine interest in stage life, he patiently elicits from old documents, newspapers, theater programs, and photographs the truth behind a legend, or at least that part of the truth which is enclosed in pertinent facts. And since he assembles these facts with literary taste and condoning irony, the result is a lively portrait of an extraordinary creature.

In 1857, Adah, then twenty-two, started her career as an amateur performer with the Crescent Dramatic Association of New Orleans. Her ambition was boundless; and once she was let loose, she soon found out that the less people knew about her the more she could impress them. In her self-dramatization, and while she did not deny her Jewish faith, she purposefully posed as a Byronic character of mysterious origin—a myth which kindled the imagination of all men-about-town. In reality, she was born Adah Bertha Theodore in a village near New Orleans. And instead of being captured by the Indians as a girl, she spent her childhood in prosaic middle-class surroundings.

The fame she won resulted from her natural gifts rather than consummate acting. When she recognized that she would not do as Lady Macbeth, she resolutely exchanged tragedy for melodrama and Protean farce, playing masculine parts, or exhibiting her bare legs and more. At the beginning of the Civil War she starred as Mazeppa in the play of this title—a Mazeppa who in the first act is stripped, lashed, and bound fast to the back of a horse which gallops away with him. It was a hit, aided by the anathemas of the Puritans. Audiences in New York, San Francisco, and London raved about this triumph of nudity and bravura, and Adah's name was on everyone's lips. In the Paris Théâtre de la Gaîté she performed in *Les Pirates de la Savane*, a French melodrama located in Mexico; but the playwrights inserted for her a run on horseback à la Mazeppa, so that the public would not miss the attraction of two continents.

And yet her fame was not entirely unmerited. Mr. Lesser points out that she contributed to the emancipation of the American theater from its European heritage. "Her success led eventually to the development of a new type of musical comedy entertainment which reached its peak in the soubrettes of the Eighties and Nineties." Imitations of her Mazeppa stunt cropped up in many parts of the world, but none of them could outshine hers. She possessed a magnetic quality; not only the undiscriminating multitude, but the old Alexandre Dumas surrendered to her charm, and so did Dickens.

Her life was a series of scandals, interrupted by four marriages which also ended in scandals. When her first husband, Alexander Isaac Menken (from a prominent Jewish family in Cincinnati), lost his money, she talked him into becoming her manager—an affair doomed to failure. Then, wrongly assuming that her rabbinical divorce was legal, she married Tom Heenan, the heavyweight boxing champion of America, who, in the belief that he was being cheated, allowed his lawyer to call her a prostitute. She pretended to commit suicide, but soon carried on with more gusto than ever before. Her subsequent husband, a literary editor, blundered in trying to reform this feminine Mazeppa, whereupon she escaped through a window after exactly one week. The fourth and final attempt at domestication did not even last that long.

Married or not, the Menken insatiably consumed what life offered her of friendships, amorous intermezzi, extravagances, and other pleasures. She mingled with the Bohemian set in New York and San Francisco, explored—dressed in male clothing—the infamous Barbary Coast, frequented gambling haunts and spiritualist sessions; and drove through

London in a brougham that sparkled with silver-plated nails and gold foliage. Her lovers ranged from shady characters to shining celebrities; one of them was the poet Swinburne, who boasted of his easy conquest with masculine pride and little taste. The newspaper gloated over these goings-on, and Adah saw to it that they had always something to gossip about. What seemed abandon on her part often sprang from an acute sense of publicity. She lavished favors on those who knew how to pull strings, and advertised herself with the ingenuity of a born huckster.

However, in spite of her sham aspirations and staged eccentricities, this amazing woman was by no means devoid of genuine dreams and emotions. Rather, she was a mixture of deceit and sincerity so imperceptibly fused that probably she herself was unable to distinguish between them. No doubt, she really loved the heavyweight champion; and while posing as a suicide, she wrote a despondent farewell letter that could not have been more convincing. Her flimsiness was also a matter of true imagination. Part of her fantasies crystalized in poems inspired by the Bible, Byron, and Walt Whitman. In fact, the Menken was something of a poet. Contributing to *The Israelite* of Cincinnati, the New York *Sunday Mercury*, and other magazines, she reveled in bold images which expressed her preoccupation with death, her despair, and the wild longings of her forever unsatisfied nature. Occasionally, she took flight to more intellectual spheres, challenging orthodox church-goers and the opponents of women's emancipation in essays that had a subversive ring. It was not all gold foliage and mere pretense. Throughout her short life—she was only thirty-three when she died—she felt attracted by literati, who in turn eagerly sought her company. The young Mark Twain asked her to criticize his sketches, and George Sand, once Chopin's muse, communed with her in impassioned discussions.

Mr. Lesser traces the meteoric career of his heroine without any real inquiry into psychological motives and social background. Who was the Menken? This question continues to intrigue the more inquisitive minds.

It is perhaps not accidental that the Menken prospered at a time when Rachel's triumphs were still alive and Sarah Bernhardt's star was beginning to rise. No one will think of comparing her with these great actresses; but she shared with them the burning desire for blazing a trail through life—an all-devouring intensity which may well have been their common Jewish heritage. Released from the ghetto one or two generations earlier, the Jews strove to assert themselves in a world of mounting industrialism which favored the expression of their long-suppressed energies. This might well account for the intensity with which they developed inner potentialities or seized upon fortuitous chances. But the world into which they emerged proved a sort of vacuum, a place outside the boundaries of fixed values and venerable traditions. As much as they tried to assimilate, they went astray in it, losing foothold, confidence, and discernment. What remained, undiminished, was their intensity, which they now mobilized in the pursuit of the futile as well as the essential. Lie and truth flowed together, and frivolous pleasures were amalgamated with profound feelings. To some extent this was the case with the Menken.

31 The Teutonic Mind
(1948)

The disgraceful speed with which the German universities surrendered to Hitler shocked a world steeped in admiration of German scholarship. And even though fifteen years have passed since then, this debacle still affects us as something utterly abrupt and incomprehensible. In the preface to his book [*The Abuse of Learning: The Failure of the German University* (1948)], Lilge promises to explain the causes of the German cultural surrender. As a critical history of the conflicting ideas that ruled German university life from about 1800 to 1933, this is an excellent work. But it falls short of its promise.

BI-CULTURAL OBSERVATION

Dr. Lilge has a special gift for unraveling the cultural and moral implications of ideas. And he has the biographical advantage of combining inside knowledge with outside experience. Educated in Germany, he came to the United States early enough to assimilate its intellectual attitudes, which enabled him to look at familiar things from an unfamiliar angle.

The book opens with a brilliant discussion of German humanism, which culminated in Wilhelm von Humboldt's liberal reforms of the educational system in Prussia. After a brief heyday at the beginning of the nineteenth century, this promising trend yielded to the impact of German idealism, triumphantly asserting itself in the philosophies of Schelling, Fichte and Hegel. Dr. Lilge points to Fichte's affinity with National Socialism, but then drops the matter without further pursuing the effects of German idealism as a whole on the mentality of the middle classes.

Fortunately, he compensates somewhat for this negligence by a penetrating analysis of the clash between the all-powerful metaphysicians and the scientists, who, newcomers in the academic world, tried to conquer the universities. After the Franco-Prussian War, everyone became infatuated with technological progress; science won out; the humanistic and idealistic conceptions of general education faded and the philosophers gave way to specialists who were absorbed in research for its own sake.

ATTACK ON REASON

The pages on the ensuing disintegration of human substance among the educated are absorbing. The void, Dr. Lilge says, was filled with nationalism. His remarks on Nietzsche's pungent criticism of the academic profession and of German culture in general are no less to the point. He endorses this criticism and yet is awake to the dangers of its underlying irrationalism, which, once formulated by Nietzsche, exerted so fatal an attraction on the rest of the Germans. The legitimate attempt to overcome sterile rationalism thus degenerated into a widespread "irrational revolt," fostered by Spengler, Heidegger and, to a lesser extent, the Stefan George clan.

In the concluding chapter, Dr. Lilge judiciously ponders Max Weber's last-ditch stand against the mounting flood of irrationalism. His praise of Max Scheler's propositions for educational reforms, made under the Weimar Republic, does not sound too convincing.

DIAGNOSIS

The problem is whether these ideological developments fully account for the collapse itself. Dr. Lilge seems to think so. It is obvious, in the author's opinion, that the collapse must be traced to the events analyzed in his historical survey. He holds, for instance, that the human void created by the rise of modern science contributed much to precipitate the catastrophe of 1933.

On the other hand, he rightly insists that the ideological battles waged in Germany occurred outside Germany as well. "Most of the problems on which German higher education foundered remain unsolved throughout the Western World. . . ." In emphasizing these analogies, Dr. Lilge is far from implying that, given similar conditions, Western cultures would surrender as German culture did. Experiences in certain of the Fascist-dominated countries during the Hitler era tend to invalidate such a premise.

OUT OF CONTEXT

This history of ideas, then, does not suffice to explain what has happened in Germany. In fact, Dr. Lilge fails to make it clear that the ideological developments which he so lucidly recounts took effect in a peculiar social climate. His sporadic references to social conditions prove only that he is basically unconcerned with the way they influence ideological factors. Here lies the weakness of his explanatory efforts. The human void to which he alludes was not destructive by itself alone; rather, it helped to bring about the collapse because it spread among middle-class people without democratic traditions, people who had never gone through a revolution. Yet he barely mentions this. He is so exclusively interested in ideas that he all but forgets to take into account the different effects they produce in different surroundings.

I need scarcely add that Dr. Lilge's book is an important contribution despite its inherent deficiency. It retraces Germany's intellectual life with an intensity that makes the ideas presented yield their full significance; and it offers a special interest to the American reader, since these ideas are still alive and strongly affect education in this country.

32 Consciousness, Free and Spontaneous
(1948)

In this volume [*The Psychology of Imagination* (1948)] Sartre again proves himself a genuine thinker. His is a prolific mind which branches out into various fields without ever relinquishing its intensity. Such a combination of latitude and power of penetration would be all but inconceivable, were it not bound up with an essential poverty of life substance.

Sartre's treatise is in the main a phenomenology of imagination. From the outset he insists that our consciousness is able spontaneously to produce mental images. Consciousness, that is, asserts itself not only in perceiving the real, but in calling forth the imaginary. There are two kinds of consciousness: the perceptual and the imaginative. This implies that mental images are not simply counterparts of real objects; nor are they reborn sensations, as the behaviorists would have it. Freely created by consciousness, the imagined object has a character of its own. It is real, yet it presents itself as non-existent; and it does not lend itself to an infinity of perceptions, as the real object does. Unlike the latter, the imagined object is poor in content.

The subsequent descriptions and interpretations serve to bear out Sartre's thesis of the spontaneity of imaginative consciousness. He first examines different kinds of "images"—signs, portraits, imitations, schematic drawings, spots on walls, hypnagogic images—in an effort to demonstrate that they are nothing but material for our consciousness, that it is our very consciousness which transforms all of them into representations of imagined, i.e. unreal, objects. Then he analyzes the ways of the mind in establishing these objects. Here again he emphasizes the spontaneity of self. The mental image, as he infers from certain results of experimental psychology, is probably a synthesis of intentional processes involving knowledge and affection—processes accompanied by muscular movements which externalize that image. And finally he inquires into the life of the products of imagination: their existence in a time which is as intangible and unreal as is the space around them. "It is a shadow of time, like the shadow of the object, with its shadow of space." Peopling the dimension of nothingness, these phantomlike units are strangely inflexible and ineffective; we cannot alter them as long as they last, nor can they by themselves alone provoke reactions on our part.

Sartre concludes with a few more general statements. Imagination, he says, evidences man's freedom. Consciousness, though embedded in the existing world, is always free to negate the world by imagining the unreal. This is no futile negation. Rather, through the use it makes of its freedom, imaginative consciousness lives up to its intrinsic task of endowing the real with meaning. Its highest achievement is the significant unreality of the work of art.

The whole is thoroughly in keeping with Sartre's overall attitude. Here as elsewhere he capitalizes on phenomenology, as developed by Husserl, Scheler, and Heidegger, to identify consciousness as a free agent. In evoking images, he time and again avers, we realize spontaneous intentions. Sartre so zealously insists on the spontaneity of consciousness that he tends to minimize, if not disregard, its undeniable limitations. When discussing dreams, for instance, he rejects Freud's doctrine of the dependence of dream content on suppressed desires. The pressure of the unconscious would indeed be incompatible with the freedom he ascribes to imagination.

This sustained attempt to disengage the mind from all bonds that might fetter it is all the more startling since it occurs in a country where widely ramified social conventions are being taken for granted. Viewed historically, French thinking differs from German philosophy precisely in that it does not cultivate the individual (or the state) at the expense of society. The reason is that the French succeeded in developing a full-fledged society, while the Germans did not. To the French, freedom is therefore not so much individual autonomy as the measured interplay between outer exigencies and inner urges. Is it still? The resonance Sartre's version of German phenomenology has found in France may well indicate that this fragile equilibrium has been disturbed of late.

Sartre's philosophy reflects social decomposition rather than individual strength. There is something sterile in his infatuation with freedom as such. Possessed by the idea that we are free to imagine or to "engage" ourselves, he rarely tells us what we should actually do with our freedom. But freedom means little unless it materializes in definite actions. It is nothing more than a point of departure. Sartre stops at the beginning. He is an archer who eternally bends the bow without ever shooting the arrow.

This explains the puzzling mixture of abundance and poverty in Sartre's writings. The impression of abundance results from his many-sidedness, his perspicacity, and his gift for observation. Yet what appears in so many guises is invariably the same preliminary problem. Sartre accumulates a multitude of brilliant details to substantiate—not the multitude of life but the necessity of engaging in it. He is poor because life itself evades him. Were he saturated with life, he would act out freedom instead of monotonously glaring at it.

33 Indologian Holiday
(1948)

This handsome volume of essays by the late Heinrich Zimmer [*The King and the Corpse: Tales of the Soul's Conquest of Evil* (1948)], a publication of the Bollingen Series, is the yield of what can be called an Indologian's holiday. Zimmer was not only a scholar versed in Sanskrit texts, but a profoundly agitated mind living in the present as well as in the past.

So he wandered to and fro between the ages, trying to decode the symbolic language of old myths in terms of contemporary experience. Here is the result of his wanderings. Expertly edited by Joseph Campbell, these essays rest upon Zimmer's belief—a belief which he shares with Jung and others—that the spiritual heritage of archaic man still survives in "the deeper unconscious layers of our soul." His meditations are a compound of psychology and mythology. They are ingratiating because they are not meant to be more than the musings of a learned dilettante.

Zimmer ambles between Orient and Occident, antiquity and the Middle Ages, leisurely recounting each story he picks up en route. The first, drawn from the Arabian Nights, is the well-known tale of the niggardly Abu Kasem and his patched-up slippers which make him the laughing-stock of the town. When he eventually attempts to dispose of them, they persistently return to their owner, causing his ruin. The miser who did not wish to part with them now is punished by their disastrous presence. The slippers, as Zimmer sees it, are an externalization of Karma—the evergrowing sum of man's actions and omissions, failures and achievements.

In this way Zimmer expounds an Irish fairy tale, a medieval German legend, four sagas from the cycle of King Arthur, the Sanskrit story of the King and the Corpse, and several Indian myths which, incidentally, have never before been translated into a European language. The stories are so arranged that they compose a sort of psychological epic. Having demonstrated the impact of Karma through Abu Kasem's slippers, Zimmer shows how we should deal with the demoniac forces that threaten to overpower us. It is the eternal conflict between the unconscious and the conscious, evil instincts and good intentions, anarchical nature and spiritual purity. In the light of Zimmer's exegesis both the Irish Conn-eda story and the German legend of John Golden-Mouth teach the reconciliation of these opposites. Conn-eda, the naive hero, must learn to be ruthless; and the bishop Golden-Mouth cannot achieve saintliness unless he lives the life of a beast.

Evil, then, demands to be accepted, for only by wrestling with it can we mature to wholeness. This is the moral of the sagas of Gawain and Owain, who trustingly follow their elemental drives and thus succeed in establishing an inner balance which benefits their highest aspirations. They become "knowers," able to see eye to eye with death; they lose their original innocence to regain it on the level of consciousness. Zimmer's psychological epic culminates in the famous Sanskrit story after which the book is named. Resuming the Karma theme, this story mirrors the relationship between an individual's conscious life and his unconscious past. The gist of it, according to Zimmer, is the feat of self-integration accomplished by the king of the story: he does not let bygones be bygones, but in a torturing scrutiny resurrects what he has left behind, exorcising *and* incorporating it.

It is true that Zimmer identifies mythical events as psychological processes, but he never follows the current practice of featuring such processes at the expense of their meanings. Many psychologists do precisely this. They are so engaged in tracing outer occurrences to inner mechanisms that they all but forget to examine the significance of what we displace, rationalize, or project. Zimmer, on the contrary, is entirely unconcerned with these mechanisms and their interplay. His objective is not so much psychology for its own sake as the psyche—inner life conceived of as a meaningful whole. To him the "soul" is the arena of forces that antagonize or attract each other in the interest of unquestionable human values. And he would not even think of isolating psychological drives to which no such values can be attached.

Zimmer seems to have been deeply disturbed by modern positivism and the blindness to values and meanings in its wake. This follows from certain passages of his book in which he elegiacally points to our remoteness from the wisdom inherent in ancient myths and tales. Science, he says, has learned to master the material forces of nature, but it has lost control "over the forces of the soul." Our psyche is undirected; we are strangely unable to determine its content and scope. Similarly, he complains of the "over-resolute morality" we display in handling individual and social problems. Such rationally streamlined behavior increasingly prevents us from communing with our instincts—those fairy horses and miraculous lions that guide the hero more safely through the danger zones of life than would all his conscious reasoning. And finally, in keeping with this trust in the animal part of our existence, Zimmer condemns any excesses of planning. He does not expressly say so. Yet his emphasis on the Indian notion of the world as a product of ever-repeated spontaneous acts clearly implies his belief in the superior blessings of continual improvisation.

Amiable as the book is, it lacks strength and precision. Zimmer is right in calling himself a dilettante. His exuberant language, visibly influenced by oriental narratives, reminds one less of these than of layers of tropical vegetation. There is a certain confusion in him which contaminates his psychological concepts and makes him undiscriminatingly endorse both genuine myths and Wagner's counterfeits. And his undialectical reveling in the old teachings reveals him to be an incorrigible romantic. But whatever its weaknesses, Zimmer's book will captivate those who, like himself, are homesick for meanings.

34 Portrait in Film
(1948)

Parker Tyler's *Chaplin: Last of the Clowns* has all the virtues and weaknesses of his earlier books. It is an inextricable blend of real depth and false glamor. Reading this book is like riding on a seesaw: at one moment you are fascinated by the author and at the next exceedingly irritated.

Tyler conceives Chaplin as a clown with an alter ego. To support his thesis, he draws heavily on biographical facts, which, in his opinion, indicate that the real Chaplin suffered from a flaw: he grew up in poverty, was small of stature and frustrated as a lover. This clown's flaw, symbolized by the clumsy shoes of the Tramp, prevented him from living up to the dream image that possessed him since childhood—an aristocrat who expects of the world leisure, power and love.

Chaplin acquired both fame and wealth, thus realizing parts of the dream self that haunted him. The screen Tramp became a "power comedian" in real life. And in the course of his career, which, however amazing, still denied him the intrinsic fulfillments he longed for, Chaplin felt more and more impelled to examine the moral significance of his Tramp with aristocratic dreams. The "power comedian" developed into an observer of the evil ambiguity within him.

Tyler does not entirely disregard the social implications of Chaplin's last full-length films, but rather views them as acts of self-scrutiny on the part of an artist who has come to realize the dangerous consequences of his dream life. In *The Great Dictator* [USA 1940], the Tramp turns out to be not only the "common man," but also Hynkel, the tyrant with the insatiable lust for power. And Monsieur Verdoux would be exactly like Chaplin—the real one *and* the Tramp—if he were not so devoid of heart.

This over-all interpretation grows out of observations which include a number of true finds. I list some at random: Tyler's comparison between *Monsieur Verdoux* [USA 1947] and *A Woman of Paris* [USA 1923]; his statements on the quality of silence and the function of speech in Chaplin's films; his analysis of the fits of amnesia that befall several characters in them; and, not the least, his brilliant conjecture that the Tramp's garb is intended to represent the image of an adult from the perspective of a child.

And yet the whole is disturbingly fictitious. Throughout this study Chaplin's alleged emotional conflicts serve to explain his films, which, in turn, serve to illuminate his psychological depths. There is a constant overplaying of the relationship between work and biography, while that between the individual and his environment is all but neglected. Tyler, that is, intertwines Chaplin's art and Chaplin's life in a manner which would be justified only if they made up a universe immune to outer contingencies. But neither Chaplin nor any other artist can be isolated from the rest of the world.

Tyler starts from a wrong assumption. He then proceeds to explore what seems to him the complete and unique Chaplin universe with a confidence in his intuition that makes him disdain more pedestrian methods. At the outset, it is true, he promises to be cautious: "The past of Charlie's life can be used for only one purpose: to fill out the patterns self-evident in the great epos which he has contributed to the history of the Clown. . . ." But in his analysis he rarely confines himself to such a prudent use of esthetic and psychological data. Rather, he gives rein to an imagination which barely touches on facts before taking off to the realm of meanings.

This suggests that Tyler's Chaplin-image is largely fantasy. A glance at Chaplin's old comedies reveals it as such. These comedies are threaded with *leitmotifs* which, had Tyler noticed them at all, should have forced him to revise his conception of Chaplin. For instance, the ambiguous figure of the policeman emerges at a very early stage, as does the David-Goliath theme, which he mentions only when it asserts itself overtly in *The Pilgrim* [USA 1923]. The Tramp is in effect less self-contained and more social-minded than he wants us to believe.

But in his eagerness to identify the artist as a narcissist, Tyler overlooks, or underrates, the many symptoms that plainly point to Chaplin's original concern with society. The result is obvious distortion. *The Kid* [USA 1921]—poor kid—is expounded in psychoanalytical terms; and the later films are made to appear as outward projections of inner problems. Are they primarily this? It should be obvious to all that they testify to Chaplin's increasing awareness of the world around him. Contrary to what Tyler says, Chaplin outgrows his ego to face the world as it is. And inevitably his Tramp is bound to disappear in a world in which there is no longer a loophole for him to slip in and out as he pleases.

Tyler's Chaplin-image has the consistency of a bubble, which is the more deplorable since he possesses a fine sense of values and an esthetic sensitivity that are extremely rare. What, then, leads him so hopelessly astray? Tyler himself, it seems, is something of a narcissist in his stubborn blindness to all those influences that shape an individual from without. And with the self-indulgence of a narcissist he also rejoices in a display of intellectual pyrotechnics in which the bits of unadulterated insight are outshone by dashing contentions and glittering allusions—allusions to contexts known to the author alone.

Tyler has the stuff of which interpreters are made. To be one, he must learn to listen to what his material may tell him.

35 Total Teaching
(1949)

There is an ever increasing demand for audio-visual aids in child and adult education. Schools, government agencies, churches, community centers, business enterprises—all of them have formed the habit of drawing on films as an effective means to further their aims. What has been achieved so far? And what might be done in the future? *Film and Education [A Symposium on the Role of the Film in the Field of Education]* provides some of the answers. It is a symposium of 37 contributions which supersedes the widely scattered literature on these topics by a one-volume survey of the immense field of the educational film. No single individual could have covered so much ground; and it is to the credit of the editor, Godfrey M. Elliot, that he has molded his disparate materials into a well-organized whole. Indispensable to sponsors and producers alike, this manual challenges them to exchange their experiences, thus discouraging a waste of energy and needless duplication of effort.

Several points made by the experts are of general interest. Most contributors agree that the current emphasis on audio-visual education must be traced to the last war, in particular to the undeniable success of the Army training films. People once engaged in making these pictures now continue along the same lines, breathing a new spirit into an old species. But the educational movie as such dates from the childhood days of the medium. Elliott himself dwells on its venerable past; and one of his collaborators insists that the first film ever produced for a government agency was made by the Department of Agriculture as early as 1908. Yet only in recent years have we begun to develop the educational film systematically in all branches of human activity. The present film program of the State

Department is released in 22 languages, with a view to making the peoples of the earth understand our way of life.

And why are movies particularly suited to implement the purposes of education and training? "The film is the best teacher," says Pudovkin, "because it teaches not only through the brain but through the whole body." The book is full of statements to corroborate this thesis. They invariably point to what may be called the psychosomatic effect of any educational film not unduly burdened with verbal comment. At least two contributors hold that such pictures surpass words in bringing about desirable attitudes; a third, speaking of industrial training films, credits the latter with directly mobilizing adequate "muscular-neural coordinations." The constant stream of images, it appears, works primarily upon the senses of the trainee, attuning them to the suggestions from the screen. He experiences what he sees not only with his intellect but throughout his entire organism. This, for instance, would explain the helpfulness of films in teaching children of low ability.

One chapter comments upon the increasing use made of entertainment films in schools, mentioning Hollywood's willingness to comply with the desires of educators within reasonable limits. The purpose is laudable, the argumentation weak. "The introduction of sound," the author says, "made it possible for the lines of Shakespeare to be heard all over America, and to acquaint the general populace with the works of Hugo, Thackeray, Dickens, and Tolstoy." Then, withdrawing to a last, seemingly unconquerable line of defense, he makes much of the fact that pictures of this kind arouse a strong appetite for the originals from which they are drawn.

I doubt that the "populace," to use the author's term, gets acquainted with Tolstoy or Dickens by looking at popular screen adaptations of their works. Such adaptations, with their necessary or unnecessary distortions, obstruct rather than further a true understanding of the masterworks themselves; so that really not much is gained when people come to them only under the impact of questionable film versions. To evoke a sense of literature is the task of schools. This does not mean that schools should refrain from showing entertainment films. On the contrary, some of them—for instance, *The Best Years of Our Lives* [USA 1946, dir. William Wyler] or *Boomerang* [USA 1947, dir. Elia Kazan]—have a high educational value because they are genuine films with a genuine message. Everything depends on the selection. *Joan of Arc* [France 1928, dir. Carl Theodor Dreyer] is quite apt to alienate the young from history, while *Stagecoach* [USA 1939, dir. John Ford] may strengthen their grasp of it.

36 Pictorial Deluge
(1950)

Ours is an age of pictorialization. Wherever we go or stay, pictures surround and besiege us. They stare at us from the pages of our tabloids and popular weeklies, pass across the screen in a nonstop procession, and, with television seeking new outlets, increasingly invade the last refuges of introspection, the bars. There is no baseball game which cannot vicariously be attended by anybody everywhere; nor is there a remote work of art that would evade mass reproduction. Thus a situation arises in which we are literally flooded with sights and spectacles—a vehement and interminable pictorial deluge.

In his recent book *From Cave Painting to Comic Strip*, the well-known English writer Lancelot Hogben makes us acutely aware of the uniqueness of this situation. What most people take for granted at present is in effect the last stage of an evolution which can be traced back to the dawn of human culture. Man as a picture-making animal, Hogben asserts, is man in quest of communication. And he bears out his thesis by emphasizing the enormous role which pictures played in the slow growth of areas of mutual understanding. His book follows closely the developments which led from prehistoric cave paintings to primitive seals and calendars, and from the creation of alphabets and numerals to the invention of the printing press and photography, these two basic tools of an era of mass communication. It is a story of tragic setbacks, uneventful intervals, and gigantic conquests rendered possible by the contributions of peoples long since forgotten or sunk into apathy. All this is not told in chronicle fashion, but with a view to relating each successive step to the material needs and conditions of the moment. In such a history of techniques the materialistic approach proves rewarding indeed. And since the author of *Mathematics for the Million* knows how to popularize intricate thought patterns, the whole is a true source of enlightenment, made even more fascinating by a wealth of beautiful illustrations.

Hogben is not just a historian but a fighter as well; and as his book draws to a close, his combative spirit visibly wins out. A fervent champion of federal world government, he urges us to use the mass media of communication in its interest. His main concern is the pictorial medium. He suggests that we should develop a sort of international pictorial language—fixed symbols which because of their universal appeal might help disseminate knowledge among the peoples of the earth and remove the barriers that separate experts and specialists from other mortals. Unless we succeed in establishing such a pictorial esperanto, he gloomily contends, western civilization will fall back into barbarism and perish, as is amply evidenced by the fate of whole peoples which failed to put their means of communication to good use.

At this point American mass culture comes into focus. Hogben indicts it for wasting invaluable energies on sheer entertainment. "If it is a platitude that America has given the world an object lesson in the popularity of the pictorial medium, it is also a truism to say that America has not as yet contributed to our common civilization any outstanding vindication of its potential value" (231). His attacks against the American output in general culminate in a criticism of our comic strips which will ingratiate itself with any American educator. In fact, there are ever more voices in our country which condemn this unquestioned delight of millions of children and adults as an excrescence on the body of our civilization. And Hogben's idea of capitalizing on the entertainment value of comic strips for educational purposes is just now materializing in a New York University course.[1]

Hogben could have gone much farther in his criticism. Contrary to what he and others want us to believe, comic strips are at best, or at worst, a minor evil easily recognizable as such. The real danger lies in the uninhibited use made of pictures for their own sake. Pictorialization has become a wanton habit with us, and this in itself constitutes a threat. For that habit results in the exhibition of a mass of pictures which seem to be shown for no other reason than to fill space. Many of them are not even particularly entertaining; and all of them make the impression of being inserted with little regard for their possible meanings. Essentially stopgaps, they either remain unnoticed like passers-by in the crowd or provoke highly confused reactions.

If looked at intently any picture will yield valuable information. But it is as if our picture makers did not wish us to look behind the scenes; as if they did everything in their power to sustain the confusion which their abundant offerings are likely to create. As a matter of fact, pictorial material is more often than not presented in a manner which effectively forestalls our attempts to grasp its significance. Take the captions in our magazines: their obtrusiveness is such as to divert our attention from the very illustrations they predigest for us. It sometimes happens that a caption attributes, say, an endearing smile to a person whose features bespeak entirely different intentions; but we usually ignore discrepancies of this kind because of the hypnotic power of the editorial suggestions. Even more striking is the negligence with which most American movies—not they alone, of course—pass over the messages their visuals might convey. Our newsreels, documentaries and feature films are overcrowded with verbal statements, thus putting the unfortunate spectator in a dilemma. If he wants to watch the pictures, subtle wisecracks and poetic love declarations are lost on him; and if he wants to follow the dialogue he inevitably misses the fine points of purely visual communications. Since verbal meanings are less evasive than pictorial ones, audiences naturally prefer the latter, relatively effortless alternative.

In sum, we are submerged by pictures and at the same time prevented from really perceiving them. Pictures, as they are presented today, are like a veil between us and the visible world. Instead of tempting us to inquire into their contents, they dull the edges of our intellect and stifle our imagination. The habit of being exposed to them blinds us to the phenomena they render. Paradoxically enough, the more reproductions we see, the less are we able or willing to practice the art of seeing, with all that it implies in spontaneous responses. We are lulled into passivity; our perceptive faculties threaten to decline. The incessant flow of visual material from the assembly belt has the soporific effect of a drug, adding to the drowsiness which our kind of mass culture tends to spread.

Hogben is all against this squandering of pictures. Yet the solution he offers is naive, to say the least. He seems to believe that a common effort in the interest of world-wide visual education will not only promote international understanding, but largely reduce the present waste and thus benefit the pictorial medium itself. This is improbable for the simple reason that pictures serve many other vital purposes than those envisaged by Hogben. They are not merely a means of communication in his sense; and even as such they may be applied in ways he never mentions. Why, then, should we assume that their increasing utilization as elements of a pictorial esperanto will suffice to channel their overpowering flow? Whatever such an esperanto may mean to us, it cannot possibly be expected to become the organizing principle of pictorialization. But Hogben is so completely possessed by his pet idea that he overestimates its wholesome influence on picture making in general as well as its educational value. His is a single-mindedness of purpose which prompts him to deprecate all seemingly useless differentiations. Significantly, he holds that we dissipate our strength by learning foreign languages and irrational spelling. He is a plain rationalist. And his dream of a uniform world culture omits the best that culture has to offer: depth.

There are problems which we should not immediately try to solve. All that counts is to pose them. Perhaps the pictorial deluge from which we suffer belongs among these problems. And perhaps its general recognition as a problem already marks the first move toward its solution.

37 Movie Mirror
(1950)

In their study of the movies [*Movies: A Psychological Study*], Martha Wolfenstein and Nathan Leites analyze many American "A" films released since September 1945 and a handful of recent British and French films. Their purpose is to establish the common story motifs of each national cinema and then apply them as clues to the subconscious processes that motivate the behavior of contemporary Americans, Britons and Frenchmen. This psychoanalytical approach to film content rests upon the assumption, plausible in itself, that films reflect or express actual fears and hopes.

The manifest themes of Hollywood's postwar movies are brought out convincingly. The authors isolate a series of standardized screen characters, defining their ever recurrent interrelations. Conspicuous among these characters are the "good-bad girl" who only seems to be promiscuous; the hero falsely accused of murder and faced with the task of clearing himself; the incompetent police; the parents invariably condemned to a background role, etc. The list also includes the two screen types of the onlooker who watches the course of events without grasping their meaning, and the professional performer who turns into a criminal—characters which, to the best of my knowledge, have not been noticed before. All this is neatly observed and wittily formulated.

The conclusions reached by the authors are, to say the least, far-reaching. Personal contacts between American male screen characters lack intimacy: this is taken as a sign that their counterparts in real life suffer from a fear of homosexuality. Young heroes are frequently persecuted by older villains: this is believed to symbolize the dormant hostility of American sons toward their fathers. And are not the sons imbued with hidden desires for their mothers? It is inevitable that the figure of the beautiful woman intent on conquering the reluctant hero should serve as a mother image.

Each character is thus assigned a latent role besides his manifest one, and the ensuing correspondences allegedly reveal what is going on behind the scenes of American life.

However, the film material selected is much too limited to justify conjectures of this kind. The authors completely neglect "B" films, which are hardly less important than the feature productions as a source of information. Further, they draw almost exclusively on the detachable film intrigue, paying no attention to other elements—camera movement, rhythm, etc.—that make up the film, although the messages a film imparts cannot possibly be inferred from its story alone. Finally, they confine themselves to postwar films, yet do not hesitate to attribute definite symbolic meanings to them. This is an unsound procedure, for, exactly like dreams, film motifs yield their significance only if traced to their origins. Since the authors never think of establishing such case histories, their contention that the beautiful woman functions as a mother substitute is just a contention; she might as easily be anything else. In addition, had they probed into the past they would have found that screen characters and plot configurations change much faster than subconscious motivation patterns are likely to change. Film content undoubtedly bears on these patterns, but it does so by way of detours which the authors fail to consider.

Their conjectures give the impression of being foregone conclusions read into the material rather than drawn from it. Where do they come from? The fact that the authors every now and then refer to Margaret Mead and Geoffrey Gorer as authorities on American culture would seem to point to possible sources of their revelations. The whole is a vaguely patterned display of psychoanalytical concepts which may or may not apply to the deeper layers of our mentality. I doubt whether such a psychological panorama is meaningful unless it is related to political, social and economic events. Unfortunately, the authors disregard the constant interplay between inner drives on the one hand, and wars, domestic pressures and the like on the other. Their psychoanalytical concepts are in effect inflated abstractions. Thus we are left in limbo.

38 *Réflexion faite*
(1952)

René Clair, who gave us *Un chapeau de paille d'Italie* [France 1928], *Sous les toits de Paris* [France 1930], and other wonderful films, assembles in this book his writings on the cinema—a series of articles, manifestoes, and speeches most of which he composed in the period from 1922 to 1935. The material is brought up-to-date by regular inserts in which the author of 1950 comments on the opinions of his former self, sometimes mitigating their intransigence and for the rest corroborating them in a majority of cases. This does credit to his critical acumen, rare in a creative artist.

Of particular interest are his observations on the use of the spoken word and his insistent attempts to define the intricate relationship between film image and film plot; significantly, he speaks admiringly of Chaplin as a story-teller. What the book lacks in theoretical insight is fully compensated for by Clair's infallible film sense. And besides, it includes a passage of great beauty: the description of a truly cinematic incident in London, when he, unawares, came across D. W. Griffith in a setting reminiscent of the dock scenes in the latter's unforgettable *Broken Blossoms* [USA 1919].

PART IV

Toward a Theory of Film

This final section assembles a series of articles that Kracauer wrote during the 1950s, when he generally tried to avoid occasional work on reviews and freelance publications such as those reprinted in the previous sections. Instead, alongside his taxing work reviewing grant applications and compiling reports for institutions such as the Bollingen Foundation, Voice of America, Columbia University's Bureau of Applied Social Research, and UNESCO, Kracauer dedicated himself to completing his "book on film aesthetics." Besides the apparently arduous writing process itself, this work included conversations and written exchanges with colleagues and friends (among them Erich Auerbach, Meyer Schapiro, Rudolf Arnheim, Robert Warshow, and Theodor Adorno), as well as the composition of shorter, self-contained parts that would later be integrated into the book as a whole. Kracauer also elaborated a 123-page "syllabus" for his book, dated 1957, which structures the vast series of notes and drafts into a rigidly organized outline for the final version.[1] An excerpt from this "syllabus" appeared in the second volume of *Film Culture*, reprinted here in the form in which it was first published (ch. 42).

Three other pieces from the beginning of the decade represent early versions of arguments that either found their way into the finished book as reworked, integral sections—such as "The Photographic Approach" from *Magazine of Art* (ch. 40), which forms the basis for the introduction, and "Stage vs. Screen Acting" from the first volume of *Films in Review* (ch. 39), which is expanded in the "Remarks on the Actor" section in chapter 6[2]—or were subsequently broken up and scattered among relevant sections and chapters, as is the case with the article on silent film comedy (ch. 41). This piece, originally published in the British journal *Sight and Sound*, sounds a number of motifs from *Theory of Film*, which are dispersed thematically into sections on the fortuitous, the chase, the found story, and the episode as particularly "cinematic" devices. In the coherently argued form presented here, the article clearly demonstrates the importance of silent film comedy for the elaboration of Kracauer's film theory.

From the work leading up to his theoretical opus we omit an article titled "Opera on Screen," which is identical to the corresponding chapter in *Theory of Film*.[3] Nor have we included any of the numerous Italian publications that Kracauer placed in *Cinema Nuovo* through his acquaintance with Guido Aristarco, its editor.[4]

Instead, we conclude the volume with the translation of a short letter to the editors of another young film journal (ch. 43). Upon receipt of the inaugural issue of *film 56*, the precursor to the venerable *Filmkritik*, Germany's leading film journal during the rise of the New Wave of the 1960s, Kracauer sent a letter to Enno Patalas lauding this promising beginning but cautioning the young critics (who, by all accounts, had read the—truncated—German translation of *From Caligari to Hitler* with great admiration and care)[5] not to overemphasize the sociological reading of film at the expense of its aesthetics.[6] In a curious balancing act, we find Kracauer responding to the first inkling of his own legacy as a film theorist by attempting to reconcile the two approaches, seemingly so different, that he himself modeled in his two books. The essays assembled in this volume, we submit, may be read as part and parcel of this balancing attempt, revealing an ongoing process with concrete historical reference points. They stand, moreover, as a counterpoint to the later reception of Kracauer's monographs, which has tended to postulate two monolithic and somewhat dogmatic works of "classical film theory."

39 Stage vs. Screen Acting
The Theoretical Differences Are Fundamental (1950)

In the primitive days when [Gabrielle] Réjane and Sarah Bernhardt acted before the camera as they acted on the stage, the result was pitiful. Why? What was wrong on the screen with the very acting that made audiences in a theatre ecstatic?

The answer is to be found in the two major ways in which stage and film acting differ.

First, in order to project the character he is portraying from the theatre stage to the theatre audience, the stage actor must *accentuate* his costume, gestures, facial expressions and inflections. But the screen actor must underplay, and eschew almost all accentuation. A story is told about a motion picture director interrupting Fredric March who had just returned to Hollywood after acting on Broadway. Mr. March sensed at once what was wrong and exclaimed: "Sorry. I did it again! I keep forgetting that this is a movie and that I mustn't act."

Second, the sets on a stage are designed, and frequently over-designed, to induce a mood. But in the motion pictures the natural world and inanimate objects become part of the cast. They do so because the camera can bestow significance on whatever background or foreground detail is momentarily effective.

To be sure, the business of *all* actors—stage or screen—is to project character. But in a theatre the distance between the audience and the actor on the stage is so great that the actor must create an illusion, an image, not a reality. He does this by means of the theatrical devices at his disposal—makeup, gestures, inflections, etc. Critics, in comparing film and stage actors, often speak of the latter's exaggerations. Instead of drawing a true-to-life portrait—which would be ineffective on the stage—the stage actor suggests to the audience what he wants it to believe. These suggestions enable the audience to visualize things not actually on the stage. The audience is helped to do this, of course, by the script, which places the stage actor in dramatic situations, forces him to do dramatic things, and to reveal in speech his motives and desires. All this is a kind of magic and its resemblance to real life is illusory. Life itself eludes the stage. Its realistic presentation is never attempted in genuine theatre.

Things are quite otherwise in the motion picture.

Close-ups almost *challenge* the spectator to find errors in an actor's depiction of a character. They *force* the actor to relinquish the gestures and inflections that are successful on the stage. Moreover, the physical appearance of the character which the actor is portraying is visible to everybody who can see the screen—and this means everybody in the movie theatre. The camera catches, and can magnify, the most ephemeral glance, the slightest shrug of the shoulder. The truth is, the film actor must act as if he were not acting at all, as if he were a person in real life who happens to be photographed. He must seem *to be* the character. In a way, and perhaps a major way, the film actor is a photographer's model.

This implies some rather subtle things. Contrary to what is usually assumed, photographic portraits are not explicit definitions of character. They are momentary records of mood, fragmentary, casual, even fortuitous. For this reason the film actor must make his gestures, poses, and expressions hint of the moments in the life of the character that are not photographed. His performance is photographic only when it impresses us as one incident out of many possible incidents in the life of the character being portrayed. Only then does the film actor render life in a truly photographic way. When movie critics sometimes blame actors for overacting, they do not necessarily mean that they act theatrically, but only that their acting is somehow too purposeful and lacks those indefinite intimations which are the truths of photographs.

This explains why the film actor is bound to his physical appearance more than the stage actor, whose face never fills the whole field of an audience's vision. The camera catches all things, all the outer movements that reveal inner psychological changes. The nuances are impossible on the stage. No actor could possibly project them to the satisfaction of an audience. The film actor's physical appearance is often in itself enough to reveal the script's most delicate intention. It is for this reason that type casting is universal in the movies.

As a matter of fact, people who have never acted are often very effective before a camera. Flaherty calls children and animals the finest of all film actors because their actions are spontaneous. Sometimes non-actors dominate a whole national cinema. The Russians cultivated non-actors in their revolutionary phase. The Italians did likewise after they were freed from Mussolini. When history is made in the streets, the streets tend to move onto the screen. In fact, profound differences aside, both *Potemkin* [USSR 1925, dir. Sergei Eisenstein] and *Paisan* [Italy 1946, dir. Roberto Rossellini] exploit environmental situations rather than individual personalities, depict real-life episodes rather than synthetic stories. These films are much in the original Lumière spirit because they emphasize the factual.

The star system is a development of type casting. It bestows commercial value upon an actor's physical appearance. The Hollywood star imposes his physical appearance on every role he creates. Whatever acting ability he may have serves to reinforce the image created by his physical appearance. Humphrey Bogart is invariably Humphrey Bogart whether he be enacting a sailor, a private eye, or a cabaret owner.

Why are some chosen for stardom instead of others? Something about the form of the star's face, his gait, his mode of speech, ingratiates itself so deeply with the masses of moviegoers that they want to see him again and again. The spell that a screen star casts upon audiences can be explained only by the assumption that his physical appearance satisfies the momentary but widespread *desires* of millions of people.

The second great difference between stage and film acting concerns the actor's position within the narrative. The theatre is exclusively human, in the sense that the action of the play is revealed by and through the actors. What they do and say makes up the play's content—is the play itself. The story line and the significance of the plot turns are all revealed by and through the characters on the stage. Even realistic settings must be adjusted to stage conditions and must be designed to enhance the illusions which the actors create. It is questionable whether stage sets are ever intended to evoke reality. They subserve stage acting. On the stage, man is the absolute measure of the universe.

The cinema is not exclusively human in this sense. The surroundings of human beings on the screen are often as important as the actors and sometimes eclipse them, as in such films as *Grapes of Wrath* [USA 1940, dir. John Ford], *The Blue Light* [Germany 1932, dir. Leni Riefenstahl], *Port of Shadows* [*Le quai des brumes*, France 1938, dir. Marcel Carné], and *The Bicycle Thief* [Italy 1948, dir. Vittorio De Sica]. There is practically no film without close-ups of inanimate objects, the facade of a row of houses, an illuminated window, a doll on the floor. Moreover, the subject matter of the cinema is not so much the purely human as it is the visible flux of infinite phenomena impinging on the human.

The film actor is not necessarily the carrier of all of the picture's meanings. Cinematic action often occurs in places that contain no human beings at all and involves them only in an accessory way. Film sequences that depict the furniture in an abandoned apartment, e.g., can be very effective, and the entrance of a human being can seem to be an interference. Who has not seen the camera pan from streetlights to the shadows on a face? Whatever meaning the face conveys derives less from character (which is obscured) than from the environmental context. Pudovkin and Kuleshov proved this. They inserted several close-ups of Mosjukhin, all of which looked noncommittal when seen by themselves, into different sequences. The result was that an uninitiated audience greatly admired Mosjukhin's ability to express grief at the sight of a dead woman, happiness at the sight of a little girl playing with a teddy bear, etc. Screen actors must, as René Barjavel said, "remain, as much as possible, below the natural." They must be restrained.

Why do films use actors at all?

They are least needed and least desirable in pictures concerned with environmental, rather than personal, problems. In such films the non-actor is preferable, even essential. He belongs in them because in them he is asked to do no more than exemplify an external situation. But whenever the interest is shifted from the environmental to the personal, as in nearly all of today's feature films, things are quite different. The non-actor loses his naturalness when he is forced to project himself continuously, and the overtaxed non-actor tends to behave like a bad actor.

Sustained characterization requires professional actors. The professional actor who knows how to use his physical appearance can appear as candid as the non-actor, and some, a very few, like the late Walter Huston and Paul Muni, can metamorphose their own nature at will, and instead of appearing on the screen as they themselves are, can become, through art, the character the author intended.

40 The Photographic Approach
(1951)

Instantaneous photography grew out of a desire older than photography itself—the wish to picture things in motion. This was a challenge to photographers and inventors. As early as the late 1850's, stereoscopic photographs appeared which evoked the illusion of capturing crowds and action. With these stereographs, instantaneous photography virtually entered the scene.

In nineteenth-century France, the arrival of photography coincided with the rise of positivist philosophy and the concurrent emphasis on science. Hence the marked concern, in the childhood days of photography, with truth to reality in a scientific sense—a concern which not only benefited the realistic trend in art and literature but facilitated the acceptance of the camera as both a recording and exploring instrument.

As a recording device, the camera was bound to fascinate minds in quest of scientific objectivity. Many held that photographs faithfully copy nature; and, eager for similar achievements, realistic and impressionist painters assumed the guise of self-effacing copyists. But it need scarcely be stressed that in actuality photographs do not copy nature but metamorphose it, by transferring three-dimensional objects to the plane and arbitrarily severing their ties with their surroundings—not to mention the fact that they usually substitute black, gray and white for the given color schemes.

In its exploration of the visible world, the camera produces images that differ from painting in two respects. Photographic records evoke not only esthetic contemplation but also an observant attitude, challenging us to discern minutiae that we tend to overlook in everyday life. In addition, photographs permit the spectator to apprehend visual shapes in a fraction of the time he would require for a similarly acute apprehension of the actual objects. There are three reasons for this: photographs, by isolating what they present, facilitate visual perception; they transform depth to one plane; and they usually also reduce the angle of vision, thus enabling the eye to comprehend with relative ease whatever is represented.

To the nineteenth century, the unsuspected revelations of photographs were something to marvel at. [Fox] Talbot, one of the founding fathers of photography, remarked as early as 1844 that, more often than not, "the operator himself discovers on examination, perhaps long afterwards, that he had depicted many things he had no notion of at the time." With the rise of instantaneous photography it became obvious that the camera is not only extremely inquisitive, but actually transcends human vision. Snapshots (in the technical sense of the word, rather than in the popular meaning of amateur photography) may isolate transitory gestures and configurations which our eye cannot possibly register. In the preface to his book *Instantaneous Photography* (1895), the English photochemist [Sir William] Abney dwelt on the "grotesqueness" of the numerous snapshots which make you believe "that figures are posed in attitudes in which they are never seen."[1]

But there is a difference between acknowledging the characteristics of a medium and actually taking advantage of them. Nineteenth-century photographers tended to submit to the visual habits and aesthetic preferences of society at large. They shrank from exploring the world photographically lest the grotesqueness of their images might be incompatible with the prevailing artistic traditions. And were they not artists, after all? Instead of defying pre-photographic fashions of seeing, therefore, these artist-photographers deliberately fell back into accepted art styles and time-honored stereotypes. Conspicuous was the case of [Antony Samuel] Adam-Salomon: a sculptor become photographer, he excelled in portraits which, because of their "Rembrandt lighting" and velvet drapery, persuaded the poet Lamartine to recant his initial opinion that photographs were nothing but a "plagiarism of nature." Lamartine now felt sure that they were art. It was the eternal conspiracy of conventional "beauty" against unwonted "truth." That the conventional sold better was all the more in its favor.

The desire for genuinely photographic ventures could not be stifled, however, by any amount of conservatism. Once instantaneous photography was firmly established, an increasing number of devotees of art-photography renounced their prejudices and scruples. This is illustrated by the dramatic conversion of P. H. Emerson, who, having for a long time emulated painting, in 1891 openly condemned as a fallacy his confusion of photography with art in the traditional sense. In spite of all temptations to the contrary, the urge to capitalize on the camera's ability to record and explore was irrepressible.

What did the photographic approach, sensitive to the potentialities and limitations of the medium, imply for the photographer, his products and the effects of the latter upon the spectator? Proust has drawn an image of the photographer which still vibrates with the nineteenth-century controversy about photography versus art. It is in that passage of *The Guermantes' Way* where the narrator enters the drawing room of his grandmother without having been announced, and finds her seated there reading:

> I was in the room, or rather I was not yet in the room since she was not aware of my presence. . . . Of myself . . . there was present only the witness, the observer with a hat and traveling coat, the stranger who does not belong to the house, the photographer who has called to take a photograph of places which one will never see again. The process that mechanically occurred in my eyes when I caught sight of my grandmother was indeed a photograph. We never see the people

who are dear to us save in the animated system, the perpetual motion
of our incessant love for them, which before allowing the images
that their faces present to reach us catches them in its vortex, flings
them back upon the idea that we have always had of them, makes
them adhere to it, coincide with it. How, since into the forehead,
the cheeks of my grandmother I had been accustomed to read all the
most delicate, the most permanent qualities of her mind; how, since
every casual glance is an act of necromancy, each face that we love
a mirror of the past, how could I have failed to overlook what in
her had become dulled and changed, seeing that in the most trivial
spectacles of our daily life our eye, charged with thought, neglects, as
would a classical tragedy, every image that does not assist the action
of the play and retains only those that may help to make its purpose
intelligible. But if, in place of our eye, it should be a purely material
object, a photographic plate, that has watched the action, then what
we shall see, in the courtyard of the Institute, for example, will be,
instead of the dignified emergence of an Academician who is going
to hail a cab, his staggering gait, his precautions to avoid tumbling
upon his back, the parabola of his fall, as though he were drunk, or
the ground frozen over. . . . And, as a sick man who for long has not
looked at his own reflection . . . recoils on catching sight in the glass,
in the midst of an arid waste of cheek, of the sloping red structure
of a nose as huge as one of the pyramids . . . I, for whom my grandmother was still myself, I who had never seen her save in my own
soul, always at the same place in the past, through the transparent
sheets of contiguous, overlapping memories, suddenly in our drawing
room which formed part of a new world, that of time, saw, sitting on
the sofa, beneath the lamp, red-faced, heavy and common, sick, lost in
thought, following the lines of a book with eyes that seemed hardly
sane, a dejected old woman whom I did not know.[2]

Proust starts from the premise that love blinds us to the changes in
appearance which the beloved undergoes in the course of time. It is logical,
therefore, that he should emphasize emotional detachment as the photographer's foremost virtue. He drives home this point by identifying the
photographer with the witness, the observer, the stranger—three types
characterized by their common unfamiliarity with the places at which
they happen to be. They may perceive anything, because nothing they
see is pregnant with memories that would captivate them and thus limit
their vision. The ideal photographer, then, is the opposite of the unseeing
lover; his eye, instead of being "charged with thought," resembles the
indiscriminating mirror or camera lens.

The one-sidedness of Proust's point of view is evident. But the whole
context indicates that he was primarily concerned with depicting a state of

mind in which we are so completely overwhelmed by involuntary memories that we can no longer register our present surroundings to the full. And his desire to contrast, for the purpose of increased clarity, this particular state of mind with the photographic attitude, may have induced him to adopt the credo of the naive realists—that what the photographer does is to hold a mirror up to nature.

Actually there is no mirror at all. Any photograph is the outcome of selective activities which go far beyond those involved in the unconscious structuring of the visual raw material. The photographer selects deliberately both his subject and the manner of presenting it. He may prefer inanimate objects to portraits, outdoor scenes to interiors; and he is relatively free to vary and combine the different factors upon which the final appearance of his product depends. Lighting, camera angle, lens, filter, emulsion and frame—all these are determined by his estimates, his esthetic judgment. Discussing the pictures Charles Marville took of doomed old Paris streets and houses under Napoleon III, Beaumont Newhall traces their "melancholy beauty" to Marville's personality, which no doubt was responsible for the knowing choice of stance, time and detail. "Documentary photography is a personal matter," he concludes. Contrary to Proust's assertion, the photographer's eye is also "charged with thought."

And yet Proust is basically right in relating the photographic approach to the psychological state of alienation. For even though the photographer rarely shows the emotional detachment Proust ascribes to him, neither does he externalize his personality but draws on it mainly for the purpose of making his account of the visible world all the more inclusive. His selectivity is empathic rather than spontaneous; he resembles not so much the expressive artist who wants to project his visions, as the imaginative reader who tries to discover the hidden significance of a given text.

There are, however, cases which at first glance do not fit into this scheme. During the last decades, many a noted photographer specialized in subjects that reflected the pictorial archetypes he found within himself. For instance, the late [László] Moholy-Nagy and Edward Weston concentrated on abstract patterns, featuring form rather than incident. The photographers in this vein seem to have overwhelmed their material instead of yielding to the impact of existence. Accordingly, their prints are often reminiscent of contemporary paintings or drawings. In this respect they somehow resemble those nineteenth-century artist-photographers who fell into line with the Pre-Raphaelites and other schools of art of their day. And like their predecessors, these modern photographers may be not only influenced by current art but so deeply imbued with its underlying concepts that they cannot help reading them into every context. Or do they rather discover them in the text? The *Zeitgeist* conditions perception, making the different media of communication approach each other.

Many photographs of this sort are ambiguous. They aim, on the one hand, at effects which might as well be obtained by the painter's brush—in fact, some of them look exactly like reproductions of works of art; on the other hand, they seem primarily concerned with certain aspects of unadulterated nature. Fascinating border cases, these photographs result from two conflicting tendencies—the desire to project inner images and the desire to record outer shapes. Obviously they are genuine photographs to the extent to which they follow the latter inclination. Their specifically photographic value lies in their realistic quality. It is noteworthy that Edward Weston, who wavered between those two tendencies, increasingly rejected the idea of photography as a means of self-projection. "The camera must be used for recording life," he remarked in his *Daybook*, "for rendering the very substance and quintessence of the thing itself. . . . I shall let no chance pass to record interesting abstractions, but I feel definite in my belief that the approach to photography is through realism." His statement would seem all the more conclusive since he himself had emphasized abstraction.

The photographic approach—that is, the effort to utilize the inherent abilities of the camera—is responsible for the particular nature of photographs. In the days of Zola and the impressionists, the properties of photographs were commonly held to be the hallmarks of art in general; but no sooner did painting and literature break away from realism than these properties assumed an exclusive character. Since they depend upon techniques peculiar to the medium, they have remained stable throughout its evolution. These properties may be defined as follows:

First, photography has an outspoken affinity for unstaged reality. Pictures which impress us as intrinsically photographic seem intended to capture nature in the raw, nature unmanipulated and as it exists independently of us. Sir John Robison, a contemporary of Daguerre, praised the first photographs for rendering "a withered leaf lying on a projecting cornice, or an accumulation of dust in a hollow moulding . . . when they exist in the original." And Talbot, in an attempt to condition public taste to the new photographic themes, invoked the precedent of many a painting immortalizing such ephemeral subjects as a "casual glance of sunshine, . . . a time-withered oak, or a moss-covered stone." It is true that in the field of portraiture, photographers frequently interfere with the given conditions to bring out what they consider the typical features of a human face. But the boundaries between staged and unstaged reality are fluid in this field; and a portraitist who provides an adequate setting or asks his model to lower the head a bit, may well be helping nature to manifest itself forcibly. What counts is his desire to do precisely this—to catch nature in the act of living without impinging on its integrity. If the "expressive artist" in him gets the better of the "imaginative reader," he will inevitably transgress the limit that separates a photograph from a painting.

Second, through this concern with unstaged reality, photography—especially instantaneous photography—tends to stress the fortuitous. Random events are the very meat of snapshots; hence the attractiveness of street crowds. By 1859, New York stereographs took a fancy to the kaleidoscopic mingling of vehicles and pedestrians, and somewhat later Victorian snapshots reveled in the same inchoate patterns. Dreams nurtured by the big cities thus materialized as pictorial records of chance meetings, strange overlappings and fabulous coincidences. Even the most typical instantaneous portrait retains an accidental character. It is plucked in passing and still quivers with crude existence.

Third, photographs tend to suggest infinity. This follows from their emphasis on fortuitous combinations which represent fragments rather than wholes. A photograph, whether portrait or action picture, is true to character only if it precludes the notion of completeness. Its frame marks a provisional limit; its content refers to other contents outside that frame, and its structure denotes something that cannot be encompassed—physical existence. Nineteenth-century writers called this something nature, or life; and they were convinced that photography would have to impress upon us its endlessness. Leaves, which they considered the favorite motive of the camera, are not only not susceptible of being "staged," but they also occur in infinite quantities. There is an analogy between the photographic approach and scientific investigation in this respect: both probe into an inexhaustible universe, whose whole forever eludes them.

Finally, photographs tend to be indeterminate in a sense of which Proust was keenly aware. In the passage quoted above, he contends that the photograph of an Academician about to hail a cab but hampered in his movements, staggering in his gait, will not convey the idea of his dignity so much as it will highlight his awkward efforts to avoid slipping. Obviously Proust has snapshots in mind. The snapshot of the Academician does not necessarily imply that its original must be thought of as being undignified; it simply fails to tell us anything specific about his general behavior or his typical attitudes. It so radically isolates his momentary pose that the function of this within the total structure of his personality remains anybody's guess. The pose relates to a context which itself is not given. The photograph thus differs from the work of art in transmitting material without defining it.

No doubt Proust exaggerates the indeterminacy of photographs just as grossly as he does their depersonalizing quality. In effect the photographer endows his pictures with structure and meaning to the extent to which he makes significant choices. His pictures record nature and at the same time reflect his attempts to decipher it. Yet, as in depicting the photographer's alienation, Proust is again essentially right; for however selective true photographs are, they cannot deny the tendency towards the unorganized and diffuse which marks them as records. If this tendency were defeated by the artist-photographer's nostalgia for meaningful design, they would cease to be photographs.

Since the days of Daguerre, people have felt that photographs are products of an approach which should not be confused with that of the artist but should be founded upon the camera's unique ability to record nature. This explains the most common reaction to photographs: they are valued as documents of unquestionable authenticity. It was their documentary quality which struck the nineteenth-century imagination. Baudelaire, who scorned both art's decline into photography and photography's pretense to art, at least admitted that photographs had the merit of rendering, and thus preserving, all those transient things which were entitled to a place in the "archives of our memory." Their early popularity as souvenirs cannot be overestimated. There is practically no family which does not boast an album crowded with generations of dear ones before varying backgrounds. With the passing of time, these souvenirs undergo a significant change in meaning. As the recollections they embody fade away, they assume increasingly documentary functions; their value as photographic records definitely overshadows their original appeal as memory aids. Leafing through the family album, the grandmother will re-experience her honeymoon, while the children will curiously study bizarre gondolas, obsolete fashions and old young faces they never saw.

And most certainly they will rejoice in discoveries, pointing to odd bagatelles which the grandmother failed to notice in her day. This too is a typical reaction to photographs. People instinctively look at them in the hope of detecting something new or unexpected—a confidence which pays tribute to the camera's exploring faculty. The American writer and physician Oliver Wendell Holmes was among the first to capitalize on this faculty in the interests of science. In the early 1860's he found that the movements of people walking, as disclosed by instantaneous photography, differed greatly from what artists had imagined them to be like, and on the grounds of his observations criticized an artificial leg then popular with amputated Civil War soldiers. Other scientists followed suit, using the camera as a means of detection. In selecting illustrations for *The Expression of the Emotions in Man and Animals*, Darwin preferred photographs to works of art, and snapshots to time exposures. Photography was thus recognized as a tool of science.

And, of course, it was always recognized as a source of beauty. Yet beauty may be experienced in different ways. Under the impact of deep-rooted aesthetic conventions many people, who undoubtedly acknowledged the documentary quality of photographs, nevertheless expected them to afford the kind of satisfaction ordinarily derived from paintings or poems—a blending of photography with the established arts. Because of the affinity between photography and the other arts, there is in fact an unending procession of artist-photographers.

But this confusion was never shared by the more sensitive—those really susceptible to the photographic approach. All of these rejected the esthetic ideal as the main issue of photography. In their opinion the medium does not primarily aspire to artistic effects; rather, it challenges us to extend our vision, and this precisely is its beauty. According to Talbot, one of the charms of photographs consists in the discoveries to which they invariably lend themselves. "In a perfect photograph," said Holmes, "there will be many beauties lurking, unobserved, as there are flowers that blush unseen in forests and meadows." Like Talbot, he considered the aesthetic value of photographs a function of their explorative powers; photographs, his statement implies, are beautiful to the extent to which they reveal things that we normally overlook. Similarly, Louis Delluc, one of the greatest figures of the French cinema after World War I, took delight—esthetic delight—in the surprising revelations of Kodak pictures. "This is what enchants me: you will admit that it is unusual suddenly to notice, on a film or a plate, that some passerby, picked up inadvertently by the camera lens, has a singular expression; that Mme. X . . . preserves the unconscious secret of classic postures in scattered fragments; and that the trees, the water, the fabrics, the beasts achieve the familiar rhythm which we know is peculiar to them, only by means of decomposed movements whose disclosure proves upsetting to us."[3] What enchanted Delluc in a photograph was the presence of the unforeseeable—that which is in flagrant contradiction to artistic premeditation.

These statements indicate the close relationship that exists between our esthetic experience of photographs and our interest in them as observers, if not scientists. Photographs evoke a response in which our sense of beauty and desire for knowledge interpenetrate; and often they seem aesthetically attractive because they satisfy that desire.[4]

41 Silent Film Comedy
(1951)

Silent film comedy, which reached its apogee in America during the 'twenties, originated in France where its essential traits were developed long before World War I. At a time when the art of story-telling was still unknown—D. W. Griffith had not yet entered upon the scene—this genre had attained near perfection. It was rooted in the traditions of the music hall, the circus, the burlesque and the fair, spectacles drawing in varying degrees on the eternal fascination which catastrophe, dangers and physical shocks exert on civilised man. From its outset film comedy piled up these kinds of thrills in ever new combinations, with the understanding, of course, that at the very last minute the characters involved would manage to escape to safety. The purpose was fun, after all. A boy tampering with a garden hose inundates the apartments of a nearby house; people on a pleasure stroll fall smack into the lake; itch powder in the fish does things to the dinner guests; a bride who gets stuck somewhere appears at the wedding party in her underwear—such gags were common in France between 1905 and 1910. Some motifs migrated to America and there became institutions. For instance, the gendarmes, standing figures of the early French farce, re-emerged as the Keystone cops and, surviving the Sennett era, continued to the last to play their double role as the pompous pursuers and the chickenhearted pursued, the former mainly for the purpose of collapsing all the more drastically. There is no short Chaplin comedy in which the Tramp would not alternately dread and outwit some bulky policeman—the mouse playing with the cat. Crumbling pillars of order, these gendarmes or cops were visibly intended to deepen the impression of a topsy-turvy world. Similarly, the nightmarish motif of being stripped of one's clothes in the presence of normally dressed people threaded slapstick from beginning to end; Harold Lloyd losing his pants was just another version of the bride in her underwear.

Film comedy evoked material life at its crudest. And since in those archaic days of the immobile camera life on the screen was synonymous with life in motion, the comedy makers did their utmost to exaggerate all natural movements. With the aid of a single camera trick they set humanity racing and revelled in games of speed. In *Onésime Horloger* [1912, dir. Jean Durand],[1] a very charming French one-reeler, Paris runs wild, the Avenue de l'Opéra turns into an agitated ant heap, and wallpaper flies onto walls that have mushroomed a second before. It was cinema; it was fun; it was as if you sat in a roller coaster driving ahead at full blast, with your stomach all upside down. The dizziness happily added to the shock effects from disasters and seeming collisions. To frame these space-devouring adventures, the chase offered itself as an invaluable pretext. Gendarmes chased a dog who eventually turned the tables on them (*La course des Sergents de Ville* [France 1907, dir. Ferdinand Zecca]);[2] pumpkins gliding from a cart were chased by the grocer, his donkey and passers-by through sewers and over roofs (*La course aux potirons* [France 1907, dir. Louis Feuillade]; English title, *The Pumpkin Race*]). For any Keystone comedy to omit the chase would have been an unpardonable crime. It was the climax of the whole, its orgiastic finale—a pandemonium, with onrushing trains telescoping into automobiles and narrow escapes down ropes that dangled above a lion's den.

As should by now be clear, these chases and states of extremity involved not only cops and robbers but pieces of furniture and highways as well. Comedy was cinematic also in that it extended its range to include the whole of physical reality that could be reached by the camera eye. The rule was that inanimate objects held important positions and developed preferences of their own. More often than not they were filled with a certain malice towards anything human. When the pumpkins rolled down or up a slope it was indeed as if they wanted to play a practical joke on their pursuers. And who would not remember Chaplin's heroic scraps with the escalator, the beach chair and the unruly Murphy bed? Among the scheming objects those devised for our comfort were in fact particularly vicious. Instead of serving man, these progressive gadgets turned out to be on the best of terms with the very elements they were supposed to harness; instead of making us independent of the whims of matter, they actually were the shock troops of unconquered nature and inflicted upon us defeat after defeat. They conspired against their masters, they gave the lie to the alleged blessings of mechanisation. Their conspiracy was so powerful that it nipped Buster Keaton's smile in the bud. How could he possibly smile in a mechanised world? His unalterable impassivity was an admission that in such a world the machines and contrivances laid down the law and that he had better adjust himself to their exigencies. Yet at the same time this impassivity, inhuman though it was, made him appear touchingly human, for it was inseparable from sadness, and you felt that, had he ever smiled while pushing the buttons or declaring his love, he would have betrayed his sadness and endorsed a state of affairs which caused him to behave like a gadget.

Of course, it was all comedy and the threats never came true. Whenever destructive natural forces, hostile objects, or human brutes seemed to win the day, the balance shifted abruptly in favour of their sympathetic victims. The pumpkins returned to the cart, the pursued escaped through a loophole and the weak reached a provisional haven. Frequently such minor triumphs were due to feats of acrobatic skill. Yet unlike most circus productions, film comedy did not highlight the performer's proficiency in braving death and surmounting impossible difficulties; rather, it minimised his accomplishments in a constant effort to present successful rescues as the outcome of sheer chance. Accidents superseded destiny; unpredictable circumstances now foreshadowed doom, now jelled into propitious constellations for no visible reason. Take Harold Lloyd on the skyscraper; what protected him from falling to death was not his prowess but a random combination of external and completely incoherent events which, without being intended to come to his help, yet dovetailed so perfectly that he could not have fallen even had he wanted to. Accidents were the very soul of slapstick. This too was intrinsically cinematic, for it conformed to the spirit of a medium predestined to capture the fortuitous aspects of physical life. Since there were so many happy endings, the spectator was led to believe that the innate malice of objects yielded to benevolence in certain cases. Harry Langdon, for instance, belonged among nature's favourites. A somnambulist fairy-tale prince, he waddled safely through a world of mortal dangers, not in the least aware that he was safe only because the elements succumbed to his babyish candour and sweet idiocy. Was it not even possible to influence chance and assuage spite? When attacked by a tough, Chaplin's Tramp in his anguish invoked the magic power of rhythm to avert the worst; he performed a few delicate dance steps and choice gestures and, with the aid of these emergency rites, hypnotized the tough into a state of incredulous wonder which paralysed him just long enough to enable the cunning Tramp to take to his heels.

Any such gag was a small unit complete in itself and any comedy was a package of gags which, in music hall fashion, were autonomous entities rather than parts of a story. As a rule, there was a story of a sort, but it had merely the function of stringing these monad-like units together. What counted was that they succeeded each other uninterruptedly, not that their succession implemented some plot. To be sure, they often happened to build up a halfway consistent intrigue, yet the intrigue was never of so exacting a nature that its significance would have encroached on that of the units composing it. Even though *The Gold Rush* [USA 1925, dir. Charles Chaplin] and *City Lights* [USA 1930, dir. Charles Chaplin] transcended the genre, they culminated in such episodes as the dance with the fork or the misdemeanour of the swallowed whistle, gag clusters which, for meaning and effect, depended so little upon the narrative in which they appeared that they could easily be isolated without being mutilated. Film comedy was an ack-ack of gags. For the rest, it indulged in absurdity, as if to make it unmistakably clear that no catastrophe was meant to be real nor any action to be of consequence. The nonsensical frolics of Sennett's bathing girls smothered the tender beginnings of comprehensible plots, and the many false moustaches on display bespoke a joyous zest for unaccountable foolishness. Absurdity stripped events of their possible meanings. And since it thus cut short the implications they might otherwise have conveyed to us, we were all the more obliged to absorb them for their own sake. It is true that comedy presented acts of violence and extreme situations only to disavow their seriousness a moment later, yet as long as they persisted they communicated nothing but themselves. They were as they were, and the shots rendering them had no function other than to make us watch spectacles too crude to be perceived with detachment in real life. It was genuine cinema, with the emphasis on the pranks of objects and the sallies of nature. This explains why from early slapstick to Chaplin's full-length films, the visuals in a measure retained the character of snapshots. They were matter of fact records rather than expressive photographs. But would not art photography have introduced all the meanings which the comedy makers instinctively wanted to avoid? Their concern was alienated physical existence.

Film comedy died with the silent film. Perhaps the Depression precipitated its death. But it did not die from the change of social conditions, however unfortunate; rather, it was killed by a change within the medium itself—the addition of dialogue. Those nightmarish tangles, games of speed and plays with inarticulate matter, which were inseparable from comedy, occurred in depths of material life which words do not penetrate; speech with all that it involves in articulate thoughts and emotions was therefore bound to obscure the very essence of the genre. Comedy ceased to be comedy when the admixture of dialogue blurred our visual experience of speechless events; when the necessity of following more or less intelligible talk lured us from the material dimension, in which everything just happened, to the dimension of discursive reasoning in which everything was, somehow, labelled and digested verbally. It was inevitable indeed that the spoken word should put an end to a genre which was allergic to it. Harpo alone survives from the silent era. Like the gods of antiquity who after their downfall lived on as puppets, bugbears and other minor ghosts, haunting centuries which no longer believed in them, Harpo is a residue of the past, an exiled comedy god condemned or permitted to act the part of a mischievous hobgoblin. Yet the world in which he appears is so crowded with dialogue that he would long since have vanished were it not for Groucho, who supports the spectre's irresponsible doings by destroying dialogue from within. As dizzying as any silent collision, Groucho's word cataclysms wreak havoc on language, and among the resultant debris Harpo continues to feel at ease.

42 The Found Story and the Episode
(1956)

A. INTRODUCTION

(a) Résumé of the two preceding chapters: Feature films follow the lines of a story or intrigue. However, there are various story types; and the question arises whether or not they are equally adequate to the medium. To answer this question it would seem best to differentiate between story types according to form and content and first to inquire into the possible impact of differences in form. Do certain story forms facilitate cinematic treatment while others are likely to obstruct it? As has been shown so far, the theatrical story—that is, a story type patterned on the theatrical play—definitely resists translation into cinematic language; and the same more or less applies to stories which take their cue from the novel. One is safe in assuming that none of the traditional literary forms is genuinely cinematic.

(b) In consequence, if there are story forms which facilitate cinematic treatment—and why could one doubt their occurrence as long as their nonexistence cannot be proved?—they must be construed independently of the established literary genres—construed in terms which make it clear that they tend to conform to the preference of the medium—for instance, its affinity for endlessness, the fortuitous, etc.

(c) Story forms are obviously cinematic to the extent that they enable the camera to explore physical reality, thereby suggesting the "flow of life." In other words, if the film-maker's formative energies associate themselves with story forms of this kind he may follow the realistic tendency inherent in photography and film and thus live up to the spirit of the medium.

(d) Two such story types are discernible: the *found story* and the *episode*, as they may be called. They overlap.

B. THE FOUND STORY

(a) Introduction

(1) Definition The name of the found story is derived from the fact that it is found in actual visible reality. When you watch long enough the surface of water you will discover certain patterns in it. Found stories are in the nature of such patterns. As has been anticipated in earlier contexts, this story type develops in the womb of documentary. Moreover, being not contrived but found, it is inseparable from films animated by documentary intentions.

(2) Characteristics The found story refers throughout to the actuality in which it lies dormant. And since it is part and parcel of the raw material on which the camera draws, it can hardly grow into a self-contained whole.

Accordingly, whatever the found story conveys will be typical of the "*world about us*" ([Paul] Rotha's term) featured by documentary.

(3) Genres Found stories differ from each other according to the degree of compactness or distinctness they attain. They may be arranged along a continuum which ranges from embryonic story patterns at the one pole to fairly well contoured stories, often packed with dramatic action, at the other. Somewhere in between lies Flaherty's "slight narrative," which represents a special case.[1] These three genres will be discussed presently.

(b) Embryonic Patterns

Take [Arne] Sucksdorff's *People in the City* [Sweden 1946], a "city symphony" picturing Stockholm street life in documentary fashion: it includes 3 found stories in a pupa state—"stories" which hardly detach themselves from the non-story texture of environmental impressions. A young man who has sought shelter from the rain in a doorway follows a young girl standing beside him after the rain has stopped. School children in a church, awed by the organ music and the sanctity of the place, try to find a marble which one of them has dropped. A young fisherman spreads his small haul on the bank and, busy with other things, discovers too late that seagulls have taken advantage of this opportunity and now fly away with his fish. These scenes or sequences with their slight emphasis on individual entanglements convey a mood which lends color to the juxtaposed documentary shots; but they do not develop into articulate stories that might interfere with the depiction of the city life submerging them. On the other hand, their nuclear character is not entirely satisfactory to the spectator; he feels he is being let down by suggestions of stories which invariably fail to materialize.

(c) Flaherty's "Slight Narrative"

The term "slight narrative" is borrowed from Rotha, who says of Flaherty: ". . . he prefers the inclusion of a slight narrative, not fictional incident or interpolated 'cameos,' but the daily routine of his native people."[2] As [John] Grierson puts it: ". . . he (Flaherty) stressed the idea of discovering the *essential human story from within.*"[3]

These definitions require specification. Flaherty himself held that "a story must come out of the life of the people, not from the actions of individuals."[4] Out of the life of a *primitive* people, he should have added in order to state to the full the formula underlying all his major films. This formula appears to be highly personal. In fact, it may be considered a rationalization of Flaherty's explorer instincts, his ingrained belief that primitive cultures are the last remainders of unadulterated—and still unspoiled—human nature and his desire to preserve their kind of life for posterity. Grierson and Rotha are certainly right in reproaching him with incurable romanticism. But however objectionable Flaherty's formula may be from a sociological point of view, it includes three elements which testify to his awareness of what might be essential to a cinematic story.

First, a story must come out of the life of a people, he says, whereby it is understood that he means primitive people. Now primitive life has the advantage of being "photogénique"; it unfolds to a large extent in the external world and it is close to bodily and natural events. Hence, if this part of Flaherty's formula is generalized it amounts to the request that the story should focus on some aspect or other of the continuum of physical existence. Here belong not only primitive people, but crowds, street life, etc.

Second, the story must not come from the actions of individuals. How strongly Flaherty felt in this respect is pointed up by the fact that he was "one of the greatest yarn-spinners of our times";[5] if he had wished so, he could have easily become a story-teller on the screen also. That he preferred the primitive scene to the drawing room, the typical to the individual, can be explained only by his conviction that too heavy a reliance on full-fledged intrigues would thwart the cinematic approach. As a film-maker he certainly felt the need for a story, but he avoided building it up for fear lest its strictures and inherent patterns of meaning might prevent the camera from rambling about.

Third, this accounts for his insistence on discovering the story in the raw material of life rather than subjugating the raw material to its demands. He was so reluctant to let story requirements interfere with camera explorations that he started shooting from a "working outline" always open to changes in the process. ". . . There is a kernel of greatness in all peoples," Flaherty said, "and it is up to the film-maker . . . to *find* the one incident, or even one movement that makes it clear."[6] Refer to Rossellini, Griffith (who did not use elaborate scripts) and the early Eisenstein (who came with a script full of analyses to Odessa but changed everything when he saw the "Odessa steps").

If told in words, Flaherty's "slight narrative" would amount to interpretative reportage, often in a poetic vein. The inevitable disadvantage of his solution is that it does not involve the audience as intensely as would a more outspoken story film. To the extent that he evades the individual, the individual does not respond spontaneously.

(d) Dramatized Actuality

The desire to *"embrace individuals"* (quoted from Rotha)[7] and thus dramatize actuality has prompted many a film-maker concerned with the *"world about us"* to transcend the borderline Flaherty has drawn. Indeed there are documentaries with stories which can no longer be called a "slight narrative." To be sure, they still are found in reality and highlight events typical of it, but at the same time they are nearly as compact and distinct as any contrived intrigue. In them compositional considerations seem to rival with documentary intentions; and they palpably try to round out the given incident—perhaps even by infusing fictional elements. Cavalcanti-Watt's *North Sea* [UK 1938] is a case in point. Here also, possibly, belong *Potemkin* [USSR 1925, dir. Sergei Eisenstein] and such Russian films about the Revolution, or parts of them, as re-enact actuality with the emphasis on typical individuals. (Would Flaherty have approved of the re-enactment? He mainly confined himself to actuality itself.) Films like these obviously lie in the border region that separates the documentary from the story film. Hence the difficulty of classifying them. If their story does not extend beyond the typical and is kept so subdued that we feel it serves intensely to familiarize us with the world about us, they may still fall under the title of documentaries. This is how Rotha defines *North Sea;* he calls it a documentary "on the verge of being a story film."[8] If, on the other hand, films in the border region feature a story which attains to such an autonomy that it threatens to obscure the non-story texture of shots rendering actuality (and thus to weaken audience interest in the latter) they should rather be labelled story films on the verge of being documentaries. One might enter *Potemkin* under the last heading. But there is no purpose in trying to achieve clear-cut distinctions in this region. For the transition between documentaries with a found story of high distinctness and the story film proper—especially the *semi-documentary*, this sub-genre of the episode film—is actually fluid.

(e) Finis Terrae

[Jean] Epstein's silent *Finis Terrae* [France 1928–29] exemplifies the difficulties that arise in the border region between documentary and feature film. Indeed, it represents a clumsy attempt to fuse into each other a documentary on Breton fishermen and a story found in the reality covered—at least found in the sense that it was drawn from the columns of a local newspaper. Epstein does not succeed in bridging the gap between the fabric of documentary shots and the narrative proper. An analysis of this interesting failure again sheds light on the cinematic merits of Flaherty's approach; since Flaherty literally found the story by exploring, with the aid of his camera, the life of the people in whose midst he lived, his documentary account and his "slight narrative" interpenetrate each other from the very outset.

C. THE EPISODE

(a) Introduction

(1) Definition The term "episode" is used here to define a story form essentially determined by the following feature: it emerges from and again

dissolves into the "flow of life," as suggested by camera explorations of physical reality. Whether or not the flow of life is identical with actuality and the story itself real or fictional has little bearing on the character of the episode. The episode is cinematic inasmuch as, by definition, its intrigue, whether a fragmentary incident or a contrived story, points up the flow of life, endorsing the latter's supremacy. (The fact that many existing episode films are adapted from *short stories* is by no means inconsistent with the cinematically neutral nature of this literary form.)

(2) Relation to the Found Story Any found story of higher distinctness— think of *Louisiana Story* [USA 1948, dir. John Flaherty] and, of course, *North Sea*—may as well be considered an episode. Yet the reverse does not hold true. An episode need not assume the character of a found story, as is illustrated by *Fièvre* [France 1921, dir. Louis Delluc], *Brief Encounter* [UK 1945, dir. David Lean], *Lonesome* [USA 1929, dir. Pál Fejös], *Dead of Night* [UK 1945, dir. Alberto Cavalcanti] and other pertinent films with a fictional flavor. Nor must it, *semi-documentary* fashion, be incorporated into actuality, whether genuine or reenacted, like the episodes of *Paisan* [Italy 1946, dir. Roberto Rossellini], *Bicycle Thief* [Italy 1948, dir. Vittorio De Sica], *Menschen am Sonntag* [Germany 1930, dir. Curt Siodmak et al.], *The Quiet One* [USA 1948, dir. Sidney Meyers], *The Little Fugitive* [USA 1953, dir. Ray Ashley], etc.; rather, the flow of life may disclaim its actuality character (silent comedy) or reflect that of a recent past (*Cavalcade*). Nor, finally, is the episode bound to render events or situations typical of the environmental life in which it is embedded. Episode films featuring extraordinary happenings and queer characters run true to type. (Examples: *Dead of Night;* the "Gigolo and Gigolette" episode with the lady high-diver in *Encore* [UK 1951, dir. Harold French et al.]; the episode of the old dancer with the youthful mask in Ophuls' Maupassant package, *Le Plaisir* [France 1952].)

(3) Compositional Varieties A film may picture one single episode (*Brief Encounter*) or string together several of them (*Paisan, Dead of Night*). In the last case the successive episodes may or may not be interconnected by an intrigue justifying their appearance at this or that place and taking a more or less pronounced course of its own. *Paisan* with its six episodes set against the common background of war—a diffuse and very cinematic frame of reference—exemplifies the second alternative, *Dead of Night* the first.

This first alternative—several episodes interlinked by a story—gives rise to the following observation concerning the character of that story. One might arrive at such an episodic story film from two sides—by bringing isolated episodes onto the common denominator of a story, as in *Dead of Night,* or by evolving a given story in such a way that it yields a succession of episodic units. An instance of the latter possibility is *Cavalcade* with its relatively independent war, beach and street episodes, not to forget the Titanic incident. In the case of this film type one thing is evident: regarding its form, the story must be loosely composed so that its episodes may retain the desirable degree of independence. (This applies perfectly to *Cavalcade* despite its theatrical origin.) Of interest with this context is Renoir's insistence on loose composition for the sake of the episodic—manifest in *La Grande Illusion* [France 1937], *The River* [France 1951], *La Règle du Jeu* [France 1939].... It is as if he wanted to disintegrate his story while evolving it, as if, in a state of absent-mindedness, he time and again permitted seemingly insignificant incidents and the like to flood the story patterns proper. (Here belongs also *Love of Jeanne Ney* [Germany 1927, dir. G. W. Pabst] as a fairly good example.) But not all intrigues lend themselves to episodic treatment. When applied to stories which call for straight narration rather than loose handling, Renoir's "absent-minded" approach, however legitimate cinematically, might well lead to confusion. In his *River* he palpably wavers between advancing his small human-interest story and displaying episodes of Indian life. Yet since the episodes do not seem to come out of the story, the whole is an awkward mixture of intentions which tend to cancel each other.

(b) Permeability

An episode is all the more true to type if it is permeable to the flow of life from which it emerges and into which it debouches again—that is, it inevitably resembles the found story in this respect. Similarly, its affinity for the cinema varies in direct ratio to the degree of its permeability for the obvious reason that any increase of the latter is tantamount to an increasing influx of the kind of reality which the camera is predestined to capture. Take *Brief Encounter:* it certainly owes much of its cinematic quality to the fact that it is punctuated by references to the material environment out of which its story grows—references which at the same time help characterize the latter as an episode. "*Brief Encounter,*" says Albert Laffay, a French writer on film, "confines itself to two or three sets, not more ... Yet these settings are 'open'; people circulate in them; one is constantly aware that they might change any moment. They send you away to other places because they reverberate with the movements of the vibrations of trains."[9] *Fièvre* incessantly reverts to the customers in the bar; *Lonesome* resounds with city life; *Menschen am Sonntag,* a remarkable semi-documentary, incorporates the amorous adventures of its two young couples into a reportage on Berlin weekend enjoyments; and what would *Überfall* [Germany 1928, dir. Ernö Metzner] be without its reiterated shots of desolate streets and dilapidated houses? One might also think here of the silent comedy, an episodic genre which not only inserts incidents but builds action from them.

(c) The Danger of Self-Containment

Consequently, the episode deteriorates if it becomes impermeable to the flow of life from which it arises. With their pores being closed, episodes in this vein threaten to gravitate toward an intrigue which has traits of the theatrical story. Many a so-called "semi-documentary" thus crosses the borderline separating the episode from the type of story which is essentially a "whole with a purpose." (This term, which covers a feature of the theatrical story, is drawn from Proust's definition of the classical tragedy as a composition which neglects "every image that does not assist the action of the play and retains only those that may help us to make its purpose intelligible.")[10] In any such case the all but hermetically sealed narrative (with patterns of meaning which tend to overshadow the references to the material environment) does no longer seem to be grounded in physical actuality but gives the impression of availing itself of documentary shots as a background to the action, a new stimulant. The closer the episode which has ceased to be one comes to a self-contained story, the more these documentary shots assume the character of "adjustments" to the medium. Compare the final episode of *Paisan* with its Roman episode: the first is in character because it is, so to speak, soaked in the terrible reality of guerilla warfare, while the second fails sufficiently to integrate into the narrative the general situation from which it is drawn. This is its real shortcoming, not the fact that it is a contrived story—a quality which need not impinge on its episodic character. True, Rossellini tries to compensate for the lack of porosity of the Roman story by concluding it with a scene in which the lover is seen waiting in the rain for a bus to take him back to the war, while the paper with the girl's address—a last reminder of the romance—floats, and dissolves, in a puddle. But this ending is not enough to make the Roman story appear as a genuine episode. The danger of self-containment is also illustrated by such "semi-documentaries" as *The Men* [USA 1950, dir. Fred Zinnemann] and *The Search* [USA 1948, dir. Fred Zinnemann]. As compared with, say, *Open City* [Italy 1945, dir. Roberto Rossellini]— a very porous episodic film with some sequences which almost look like found stories—these films reveal their true nature: They are essentially regular feature films in a more or less theatrical vein, the implication being that the documentary material used in them for references to the "world about us" never assumes any vital function; rather, it merely serves to increase interest in the story itself and enhance its suspense.

(d) A Framing Device

(1) Evidence that the episodic is felt to be in keeping with the cinematic approach may be found in occasional attempts to pass off even an avowedly theatrical film as an episode. The device is simple: the whole story is framed by scenes which try to transform it into a real-life incident. Thus *The Ideal Husband* [UK 1947, dir. Alexander Korda] opens with a scene in Hyde Park in which the film's main characters just help define the general atmosphere of high life and elegance without however distinguishing themselves as the future protagonists. Then the Wilde comedy, a pure drawing room affair, takes its course. The film concludes with the Hyde Park re-emerging so as to give the impression that the comedy itself was nothing but a sample of goings-on in the smart set. Similarly, the opening scenes of Olivier's *Henry V* [UK 1944] represent the London Globe Theatre, with the audience waiting for the curtain to rise; and the concluding shots again show the theatre after the performance is over. In this play Olivier, prompted by his film sense, attempted to make the play appear as a theatrical spectacle which took place on such and such a day in 16th-century London. It is as if he expected these framing scenes with their semblance of camera-reality to offset the uncinematic effect of the play's prearranged meanings.[11]

(2) A striking counter-example is the Italian film *Side Street Story* [1950, dir. Eduardo De Filippo] which features a group of people in a small and crowded Naples street, casually relating their destinies before, during and after the war. Episode follows episode; and no one would believe this fair semi-documentary with its loosely composed story to be adapted from a stage play were it not for the theatrical character of the framing scenes. At the beginning and end the two protagonists meet each other and philosophize about the state of the world which in their opinion remains much the same despite war and revolution. Their discussion points up the moral of the film, thus imposing meanings on it which threaten to curtail the inherent multiple meanings of the pictures themselves. Without the framing scenes the film might easily have implied that moral and yet remained an essentially cinematic communication. No sooner are they grafted upon it than it is retransformed into a "whole with a purpose."

43 Letter to the Editors of *film 56*
(1956)

I appreciated the spirit that emanates from the first article, "Panorama 1955."[1] This is a fresh start, *it sets the right tune.*[2] I believe that the social approach to film production is much needed; I only wish that you would attempt in the future more systematically to discern what is socially and politically wrong or right also in the aesthetic domain. Generally speaking, it seems to me that you overemphasize *manifest content*[3] at the expense of other considerations. But the manner of photography, of camera takes, and of editing methods contributes a lot and should be considered in the overall evaluation. In other words, I am advocating a fusion of sociological and aesthetic approaches. Berghahn's "MacArthur und die Zivilisten"[4] is a brilliant attempt at interpretation that should be read here as well—especially by those who neglect the political in favor of the psychological and the psychoanalytical—I am thinking of the Wolfenstein-Leites book on *Movies*[5] . . . und keep your tongues sharp!

Afterword

Kracauer, the Magical Nominalist

Martin Jay

Theodor Adorno's ambivalent tribute to his friend Siegfried Kracauer on the occasion of his seventy-fifth birthday in 1964, subtitled "Der wunderliche Realist," appeared in *Notes to Literature* as "The Curious Realist: On Siegfried Kracauer."[1] Other versions of the title have included "eccentric" or "whimsical realist."[2] Clearly, it has not been easy to render *wunderlich*, which the dictionary equates with "strange" or "odd," into English. It may therefore be permissible to add yet another candidate for the troublesome adjective, based on the *Wunder* or miracle in *wunderlich*: "magical." This rendering foregrounds the capacity for wonder in Kracauer's personality, that thinking with "an eye that is astonished almost to helplessness" of which Adorno wrote,[3] especially evident in his reactions to the new media of photography and film. As for Adorno's noun, *Realist*, its literal English cognate is the obvious choice, but here too a little reflection may allow us some license to suggest an alternative. For the type of "realism" that Kracauer more often than not espoused was closer to nominalism in the old medieval sense of the term than to many standard versions of realism. As a result, "Kracauer: The Magical Nominalist" may well be the most evocative way to translate Adorno's title, or at least to render Kracauer's idiosyncratic position.[4]

Why "nominalism" rather than "realism"? The term was first employed by William of Ockham, the English Franciscan, in the fourteenth century in his battle against the Scholastic faith in intelligible forms and real universals. As a number of recent commentators have emphasized—most notably Hans Blumenberg and Michael Gillespie[5]—the motivation behind the nominalist critique of the ontological reality of universals was originally theological. Stressing the absolute omnipotence of God, the nominalists were determined to abolish any constraints on His will, including the persistence of the intelligible, universal forms He may have once created. That is, by denying the inherently rational, universal, intelligible nature of the world, a world in which essences preceded the particulars that embodied them, they honored God's unlimited ability to intervene in it at any moment. Or to put it another way, miracles were less exceptions than the rule, at least potentially, for a God whose unfettered will trumped reason.

Many implications flowed from this premise, including the gradual, not always explicitly acknowledged transfer of God's unrestricted will to humankind as Western civilization became more secularized. Thus, human self-assertion and the domination of nature could be justified by denying the inherent rationality or intelligibility of the world, which was no longer a legible text to be read but rather a passive manifold of fungible objects or processes to be manipulated. If general names were imposed on a world of individual particulars rather than being inherent in universal natural forms, then the name-giver was granted special powers. The turn from ontology to epistemology, best exemplified by Kant's "Copernican revolution" in philosophy, in which the emphasis was put on the knowing subject rather than the known object, was one result. Another, even more radical outcome, was the Promethean implication drawn by later philosophers like Fichte and Marx, who stressed the role of praxis and production in making the social world, not merely knowing it. The upshot of this version of the nominalist challenge to real universals was what might be called the constructivist or conventionalist bias of a great deal of modern thought, which credits human invention—often understood as refracted through different cultures—for the "reality" in which we are immersed. Even what we recognize as "nature," the argument sometimes goes, is itself a cultural construct, or at least can never be grasped without the mediation of human categories of understanding

There is, however, an alternative version of nominalism, which steps back from this radical constructivism without retreating into an earlier faith in the rational intelligibility of a world containing real universals. It is what can be called "magical nominalism," which I want to argue tacitly informed Kracauer's worldview. Inevitably, it contains echoes of another, more familiar term: "magical realism." Although the latter has come to be identified with a recent trend in literature associated with Gabriel García Márquez, Ben Okri, and other novelists from Latin America and Africa who mix realistic with supernatural phenomena, it was already in play in Weimar Germany as a synonym for the *Neue Sachlichkeit* (New Objectivity) in painting.[6] Sharing in its resistance to the hypertrophied constitutive or expressive power of the subject, magical nominalism, as we are construing it, was less inclined to seek the occulted and uncanny nature of the world than magical realism. Whereas conventionalist nominalism accorded the bestower of generic and proper names, whether divine or human, creative priority, magical nominalism restored some of the power of the world to respond, indeed to intervene, even before the act of naming. The world that responded, however, was not composed of intelligible forms or universal essences, but rather of particular objects, discrete entities that defied reduction both to inherent universal categories and to the human imposition of nominal categories on them. To put it in the terms of the medieval theologians, its "haecceity," or thisness, was prior to its "quiddity," or whatness.

Kracauer's intellectual formation, it has often been remarked, was influenced by the mood of sobriety and moderation that characterized the *Neue Sachlichkeit* during Weimar, even as he sought to distance himself from the ideology of neutral reportage that so often characterized the movement. There is indeed little in him of that mixture of overwrought anguish and utopianism that infused the Expressionism of a slightly earlier era.[7] Ironic detachment and cool distance—what he liked to call his "extraterritorial" estrangement from the world[8]—marked his work of the middle Weimar years, work also inflected by the phenomenological critique of psychologism and its imperative, in Husserl's famous slogan, to return "zu den Sachen selbst" (to the things themselves) rather than "bei bloßen Worten stehen zu bleiben" (remaining with mere words).[9] These Kracauer celebrated in all their motley contingency rather than subsuming them under human categorizations. As Helmut Lethen put in his study of Weimar's culture of distance, *Cool Conduct*, "Kracauer stresses the camera's ability to undermine the conventions of the expressive arts, in order to make visible the natural foundation that exists unconsciously in the frozen gesture."[10] Trusting in the "primacy of the optical," Kracauer resisted not only the expression of subjective emotion, but also the hegemony of concepts and categories.[11] Although he called himself a materialist, his was rarely, if ever, of the dialectical variety. While being an acknowledged master of the *feuilleton* form, he never narcissistically foregrounded his own sensibility in the manner of many other writers in that tradition.

The same attitude carried over to his pioneering film criticism. As Sabine Hake has noted, "the kind of individualism that required the world to be a reflection of the self undermined the original project of cinema, which, according to Kracauer, involved the rediscovery of the world of objects and man's place in its changing constellation. . . . Through the equation of animate and inanimate worlds, it reinstated objects in all their power."[12]

For Kracauer, Miriam Bratu Hansen adds, "film's materialist capability not only undercuts the sovereign subject of bourgeois ideology but with it a larger anthropocentric worldview that presumes to impose meaning and control upon a world that increasingly defies traditional distinctions between the human and the nonhuman, the living and the mechanical, the unique (inner-directed) individual and the mass subject, civilization and barbarism."[13]

This is not to say, however, that Kracauer was ever an earnest positivist, placing his bets on passive observation and inductive generalization. "Naive realism has long since gone," he wrote in his posthumously published *History: The Last Things Before the Last*, "and nobody today would dream of calling the camera a mirror. Actually, there is no mirror at all."[14] When he investigated the situation of *Die Angestellten* (salaried employees) in Weimar, he had already acknowledged that "reality is a construction. Certainly life must be observed for it to appear. Yet it is by no means contained in the more or less random observational results of reportage; rather, it is to be found solely in the mosaic that is assembled from single observations on the basis of comprehension of their meaning. Reportage photographs life; such a mosaic would be its image."[15]

Although he resisted the fetish of form over content that sometimes led to the excessive use of montage, he never went to the opposite extreme of believing film was a purely mimetic medium. He understood that construction involved the creative juxtaposition of the givens already produced by the world, not the imaginative expression of the interiority of the subject doing the constructing. Mosaics, after all, are made, not found—although they don't produce the elements they assemble out of thin air. Employing the oxymoron "active passivity" in his final ruminations on the craft of the historian, Kracauer sought to find a way to limit the creation ex nihilo of the observer, while acknowledging the role he or she played in producing new constellations—to use a favorite term of his friend Walter Benjamin—of the archival materials that were imposed on him from without.[16] One likely meaning of the "redemption" of physical reality, the notoriously controversial term he applied to cinema in his 1960 *Theory of Film*, was its rescue from culture's domination of nature, the gazing subject's mastery of the object of his gaze, and the reign of homogenizing essences over discrete surface appearances.

"Redemption," of course, is a term that cannot entirely shed its religious aura, even if Kracauer was far more skeptical than some of his friends about even the weak messianic power that might somehow disrupt the deadening routines of modern life.[17] For all his stress on the sphere of the profane and resistance to utopian fantasies, he betrayed enough residual desire for some sort of potential transfiguration to alert us to his roots in a nominalism that can justly be called magical, a nominalism unwilling to rob inanimate objects of their power. What Walter Benjamin said of the experimental method of German Romanticism found its echo in Kracauer's approach to the world: "experiment consists in the evocation of self-consciousness and self-knowledge in the things observed. To observe a thing means only to arouse it to self-recognition. Whether an experiment succeeds depends on the extent to which the experimenter is capable, through the heightening of his own consciousness, through magical observation, one might say, of getting nearer to the object and of finally drawing it into himself."[18] In such a way those moments of revelatory power that Benjamin famously called "profane illuminations" might appear.

For all the changes in Kracauer's attitudes between his Weimar days and his American exile, he maintained a certain allegiance to these premises.[19] Their residues are evident throughout the essays in this volume, as the editors' introductions make clear. This is not to say, to be sure, that Kracauer brought a fully consistent worldview to all of the varied material he examined and issues he addressed throughout his American exile. Writing occasional pieces for popular consumption was not always conducive to rigorous, systematic thinking. Thus, for example, in his 1947 essay on books about race prejudice, "The Revolt Against Rationality" (ch. 4), he drew on the argument of Max Horkheimer's just published *Eclipse of Reason*, a book that bemoaned the decline of an allegedly objective reason in a way that smacked more of medieval realism with its belief in universal forms than of voluntarist nominalism. Rehearsing without comment Horkheimer's lament about the hegemony of formal and instrumental reason in the modern world, Kracauer wrote: "With the development of abstract thinking and technical proficiency, reason itself has become increasingly denaturalized. What this means can be grasped by comparing our present civilization with a past in which all reasoning involved the universe both within and outside us. Not yet emancipated from tradition and creed, reason then embraced the angelic and devilish components of nature with an acute awareness of their significance, incorporating them in a substantial, multifaceted pattern of existence." Here he sounds more like a traditional rationalist, perhaps even like the Hegelian he was wrongly accused of being by Pauline Kael in her coruscating review of *Theory of Film*, than a nominalist.[20]

But thirteen years later, in the heated polemic he conducted with Theodor Adorno in Switzerland over the latter's *Negative Dialectics* (ch.

15), Kracauer made clear his hostility to an immanent dialectics that did not acknowledge a place for an ontological moment external to its relational network. Explicitly referencing his "life-long aversion to Hegel," he identified instead with Benjamin's resistance to the closure of dialectics, whose ability to digest into its system everything with which it comes into contact he distrusted. "I subtly implied that we [Kracauer and Benjamin] are engaged in terms of substances. We think under a sort of ontological compunction, Utopian or not, whereas Teddie is, indeed, free-hovering and does not feel any such compunction." What Adorno was to lament in his ambivalent birthday tribute to Kracauer as the absence of his friend's "protest against reification,"[21] Kracauer understood as a defense against the swallowing up of entities by processes, objects by the relational context in which they are embedded.

Did this imply an "existentialist ontology," as Gertrud Koch has suggested in her insightful introduction to Kracauer?[22] If by existentialist is meant suspicion of the totalizing, rationalist pretensions of Hegelianism and a belief that existence precedes essence, the answer is clearly yes. But if existentialism means privileging the active subject able to constitute the object through its imaginative will alone, then doubts arise. As Kracauer shows in his critical review of Jean-Paul Sartre's *Psychology of Imagination* in 1948 (ch. 32), he distances himself from the overly subjectivist bias of at least the Sartrean brand of existentialism, which favors the spontaneity of the imagination over perception: "Freely created by consciousness, the imagined object has a character of its own. It is real, yet it presents itself as non-existent; and it does not lend itself to an infinity of perceptions, as the real object does. Unlike the latter, the imagined object is poor in content." If there is any magic in the object, it is prior to its being merely imagined by the subject.

Kracauer's "ontological compunction" meant he valued those objects whose richness of content exceeded any attempts to subsume them under categories or absorb them into the imaginative will of the beholder. The reviews he wrote of films during his American exile make this preference abundantly clear. At the most general level, it meant a suspicion of the role psychological projection played in, for example, Hollywood's depiction of foreigners. In his critical discussion of the way in which national stereotypes were portrayed in American cinema (ch. 9), he contended that "whether our image of a foreign people comes close to true likeness or merely serves as a vehicle of self-expression—that is, whether it is more of a portrait or more of a projection—depends upon the degree to which our urge for objectivity gets the better of naive subjectivity." It was also manifested in his praise for films like Rossellini's *Paisan* that refused to peddle ideologies, impose symbolic meanings, or parade formal innovations for their own sakes. Even the overly metaphoric use of objects in the films of Russian directors like Pudovkin or Eisenstein threatened to undercut the power of cinema to show the material world rather than subsume it under idealistic categories.

But more powerfully, the compunction was manifest in his love for the role material objects played in producing cinematic "reality." Thus, for example, in his appreciation of Jean Vigo (ch. 3), he applauds the "conclusions Vigo draws from the fact that the camera does not discriminate between human beings and objects, animate and inanimate nature. As if led by the meandering camera, he exhibits the material components of mental processes." Referring to the hero of Vigo's *Atalante*, where objects have gained a fetishistic character, he writes admiringly:

> Instead of using the objects at his disposal, he has become their property. The magic spell they cast over him is revealed in a unique episode in which Père Jules shows Juliette all the mementos he has brought home from his voyages. The piled-up treasures which crowd his cabin are depicted in such a manner that we feel they have literally grown together over him. To evoke this impression Vigo focuses on the objects from various sides and on many levels without ever clarifying their spatial interrelationship—using nothing but the medium shots and close-ups made necessary by the narrowness of the cabin. . . . The magical life of the doll is transmitted to the curiosities that follow in the parade.

Even in a generally laudatory review of Orson Welles's *Citizen Kane* (ch. 16), Kracauer could chastise what he saw as the director's failure to distinguish clearly enough between the medium specificity of film, in which the materiality of objects played a leading role, and the theater, where they did not:

> The indiscriminate proliferation of heterogeneous technical devices betrays a lack of objectively determined stylistic impulses; rather, as the treatment of music, among other things, would suggest, the desire for originality seems to have dominated—an originality that partly represents a step backwards. Welles betrays a distinct dependence on the theater not only in the way he relies on dialogue, but precisely through the new use of the wide-angle lens. By employing it constantly, he represents numerous scenes and spaces in long shots. He creates images that have more in common with the stage than with film, whose function it would be, after all, to isolate a plethora of

material details from the long shot and allow them to influence the action.

Excessive theatricality, also evident in the dominant role of dialogue to move the action in films like *The Connection* (ch. 26), means that "close shots of the ash tray and the cockroach degenerate into decorative additions rather than advancing the story."

Stressing medium specificity as rigorously as Kracauer did could create obstacles to his acceptance of innovation. For example, his faith in the special ability of cinema to reveal the magical power of discrete objects prevented him from appreciating the new advances in cartoon realism, which he resisted in his 1941 review of Walt Disney's *Dumbo* (ch. 17). Worrying that the extension of cartoons into full-length features necessitated a meaningful story, which brought with it the demand for greater "realism," he claimed the photograph's unique indexical qualities were violated by their simulation by even the most realistic cartoons: "In *Dumbo* Disney treats not only imaginary objects as real, but more, he combines them with human figures and does things which could as well have been done in the studio, and thus threatens the true interest of his medium. The cartoon film tends toward the dissolution rather than the reinforcement of conventional reality, and its function is not to draw a reality which can better be photographed." In other words, real objects can work their magic only through their indexical traces on celluloid, but not when they are produced as artificial effects of the cartoonist's art. How, one wonders, would he have responded to the miracles in digitalized animation wrought by the wizards of Pixar and other such studios in our own day, animation that is dependent not only on imagination but also on the computerized transfiguration of reality?

There is, in fact, an unintended irony in Kracauer's dedication to preserving medium specificity against the theatricalization and artificial animation of film, which I want to note in conclusion. For despite what we have been calling his nominalist sympathies, manifest in his suspicion of formalist or expressivist constructivism and preference for the contingent material object, a certain modicum of essentialism ultimately crept back into his discourse. That is, by insisting that the inherent nature of film is to redeem objects from the homogenizing gaze of the humans who subsume them under categories and imbue them with symbolic or metaphoric meaning, he inevitably resorted to a categorical universalism that imposed a priori normative limits on the medium. Adorno, who in so many ways was Kracauer's most dedicated disciple as well as his most trenchant critic, understood that nominalism, whether conventional or magical, cannot entirely avoid this outcome. As he put it in *Aesthetic Theory*, "the simple disjunction of nominalism and universalism does not hold. . . . The existence of and teleology of objective genres and types is as true as the fact that they must be attacked in order to maintain their substantial element. . . . That in nominalistically advanced artworks the universal, and sometimes the conventional, reappears results not from a sinful error but from the character of artworks as language, which progressively produces a vocabulary within the windowless monad."[23] Criticism, a fortiori, is even more a discursive enterprise, however much the critic wants to honor the "primacy of the optical." With each essay or review, after all, Kracauer himself translated visual experiences into words, words that were inevitably more than proper names referring to only one object in the world of experience. For all his reluctance to endorse Adorno's negative dialectics, Kracauer may have turned out to be one of its inadvertent exemplars, after all.

Notes

PREFACE

1. See Siegfried Kracauer, *Selected Writings on Media, Propaganda, and Political Communication*, ed. Graeme Gilloch and Jaeho Kang (New York: Columbia University Press, forthcoming).
2. Some of these texts were recently translated for inclusion in the German edition of collected works, *Werke*, from Suhrkamp.
3. Martin Jay, "Adorno and Kracauer: Notes on a Troubled Friendship," in *Permanent Exiles: Essays on the Intellectual Migration from Germany to America* (New York: Columbia University Press, 1985), 217–36.
4. Siegfried Kracauer and Theodor W. Adorno, *Der Riß der Welt geht auch durch mich: Briefwechsel 1923–1966*, ed. Wolfgang Schopf (Frankfurt a.M.: Suhrkamp, 2008); cf. Johannes v. Moltke, "Teddie and Friedel: Theodor W. Adorno, Siegfried Kracauer, and the Erotics of Friendship," *Criticism* 51, no. 4 (Fall 2010): 683–94.

INTRODUCTION

1. "Tiny Liner Brings 816 From Europe," *New York Times*, 26 April 1941.
2. Letter from Siegfried and Lili Kracauer to Eugen and Marlise Schüfftan, 22 April 1944, in *Nachrichten aus Hollywood, New York und anderswo: Der Briefwechsel Eugen und Marlise Schüfftans mit Siegfried und Lili Kracauer*, ed. Helmut G. Asper (Trier: Wissenschaftlicher Verlag Trier, 2003), 57. The cinematographer Eugen Schüfftan and his wife, Marlise, made the crossing on the same ship as the Kracauers. The Schüfftans and the Kracauers became close friends in the process, subsequently spent much time during their first six months in New York together, and exchanged numerous affectionate letters over the next two decades. On the first anniversary of their crossing, the Kracauers remembered "the marvelous time we spent together on deck and then our arrival here that marked the end of so many sufferings and the beginning of a new life for you and us." Schüfftan, however, reminded the couple of the

journey's "shady sides," even if "the light sides are paramount" in retrospect; see letters of 21 and 25 April 1945, respectively, ibid., 38–39.

3. Siegfried Kracauer, "Why France Liked Our Films" *National Board of Review Magazine* 17, no. 5 (May 1942): 15–19 (chapter 1 in this volume).

4. Letter to Theodor W. Adorno, 28 March 1941, in Theodor W. Adorno and Siegfried Kracauer, *Der Riß der Welt geht auch durch mich: Briefwechsel 1923–1966*, ed. Wolfgang Schopf (Frankfurt a.M.: Suhrkamp, 2008), 427.

5. Beginning with two trips in 1956 and 1958 and then on annual visits from 1960 until his death in 1966, Kracauer would return to Europe regularly during the summers, combining research on behalf of the Bollingen Foundation with vacation time spent primarily in Italy and the Alps.

6. Rotha is quoted in *Siegfried Kracauer: 1889–1996*, ed. Ingrid Belke und Irina Renz, Marbacher Magazin 17 (Marbach a.N.: Deutsches Literaturarchiv, 1988): 107. Both *From Caligari to Hitler* and *Theory of Film* have recently been reprinted, with new introductions by Leonardo Quaresima (2004) and Miriam Bratu Hansen (1997), respectively, by Princeton University Press.

7. Letter to Eugen Schüfftan, 18 January 1948, in *Nachrichten aus Hollywood*, 73.

8. We can measure the progress of Kracauer's facility with the English language in two letters he wrote to his friends Meyer Shapiro and Theodor Adorno, respectively. In August 1941 he still noted, in halting and self-critical sentences, that "English writing means yet hard work to me, and I only hope you will not be too sensible with respect to my funny style. . . . Accordingly to my disordered live during the last year I have no practice more in putting phrases together. What a pity! Each little step forward, formerly performed without any pain, is now the result of a tremendous effort. I have to train myself again" (letter to Meyer Shapiro, 6 August 1941, in Kracauer Nachlass, Deutsches Literaturarchiv Marbach; cited hereafter simply as DLA). Two years later he would write to Adorno in California, "I've made rather good progress with writing in English; I'm passionate about it" (letter to Theodor W. Adorno, 1 May 1943, in Adorno and Kracauer, *Der Riß der Welt geht auch durch mich*, 431). While Adorno would famously criticize Kracauer's decision virtually to abandon the German language (see "The Curious Realist: On Siegfried Kracauer," in *Notes to Literature*, ed. Rolf Tiedemann, trans. Sherry Weber Nicholsen [New York: Columbia University Press, 1992], 2:58–75), Max Horkheimer explicitly commended him for retaining his "old style, sober as well as loaded with allusions; as a matter of fact it withstands the transfer into English much better than Teddie's or my own way of expression" (quoted in Adorno and Kracauer, *Der Riß der Welt geht auch durch mich*, 433).

9. *Partisan Review*, which grew out of the John Reed Club of the American Communist Party, was founded in 1934 by William Phillips and Philip Rahv; *Commentary* followed in 1945, founded by the American Jewish Committee and initially edited by Elliot Cohen. With both of these magazines assuming substantially anticommunist editorial positions in the McCarthy years, Irving Howe launched *Dissent* as a radical alternative to what the editors

perceived as the "bleak atmosphere of conformism that pervade[d] the political and intellectual life of the United States" ("A Word to Our Readers," *Dissent* 1 [Winter 1954]: 3).

10. Kracauer's "Hollywood's Terror Films" is an exception, having been reprinted in *New German Critique*, no. 89 (Spring–Summer 2003): 105–11 (a special issue devoted to "Film and Exile"), along with an in-depth consideration of the essay's importance by Edward Dimendberg, "Down These Seen Streets a Man Must Go: Siegfried Kracauer, 'Hollywood's Terror Films,' and the Spatiality of Film Noir," pp. 113–43. The situation is somewhat different in German: a number of Kracauer's American essays were subsequently translated for inclusion in the German anthology *Kino*, ed. Karsten Witte (Frankfurt a.M.: Suhrkamp, 1974). They also appear, along with newly translated material, in the ongoing edition of Kracauer's collected works; see especially *Schriften*, vol. 6.3: *Kleine Schriften zum Film*, ed. Inka Mülder-Bach (Frankfurt a.M.: Suhrkamp, 2004).

11. Letter from Kracauer to Donald Slesinger, 12 May 1945, in DLA.

12. Letter from Kracauer to Daniel Halévy, 8 January 1947, in *Siegfried Kracauer: Neue Interpretationen*, ed. Michael Kessler and Thomas Y. Levin (Tübingen: Stauffenberg, 1990), 394–95.

13. To date, the transnational elaboration of critical theory during the 1940s has received only scant attention. We have largely anecdotal accounts of (missed) encounters between the Frankfurt exiles and the New York Intellectuals by Mark Krupnick, "Criticism as an Institution," in *Crisis of Modernity: Recent Critical Theories of Culture and Society in the United States and West Germany*, ed. Günter H. Lenz and Kurt L. Shell (Frankfurt: Center for North American Studies, Frankfurt University, 1986), 156–75; and Nathan Glazer, "*Commentary:* The Early Years," in *Commentary in American Life*, ed. Murray Friedman (Philadelphia: Temple University Press, 2006), 9–37. However, the vast literature on the New York Intellectuals pays scant attention to the Frankfurt School, let alone to Kracauer, whose name does not even appear in the indices to most of these monographs. Conversely, the literature on the Frankfurt School tends to miss the importance of the intellectual context in New York, although Martin Jay devotes insightful essays to the subject in *Permanent Exiles: Essays on the Intellectual Migration from Germany to America* (New York: Columbia University Press, 1985) and *Force Fields: Between Intellectual History and Cultural Criticism* (New York: Routledge, 1993). Again, though, Kracauer—presumably due to his marginal role in the institutional history of Critical Theory—is rarely mentioned.

That said, several recent publications have substantially opened the field up for new investigations. David Jeneman's *Adorno in America* (Minneapolis: University of Minnesota Press, 2007) takes a fresh look at archival holdings in an effort to dispel the myth that Adorno shielded himself completely from the realities of his American exile in order to work in "splendid isolation"; and Thomas Wheatman's thoroughly researched monograph *The Frankfurt School in Exile* (Minneapolis: University of Minnesota Press, 2009) includes a chapter on the interactions between the Frankfurt School and the New York Intellectuals. However, although Kracauer receives mention as a fellow-traveler of the School in Frankfurt, Wheatman does not discuss his presence in New York or his publications during these years, and Kracauer's name does not appear in the index. See also Eva Maria Ziege, *Antisemitismus und Gesellschaftstheorie: Die Frankfurter Schule im amerikanischen Exil* (Frankfurt a.M.: Suhrkamp, 2009), and Christian Fleck, *Transatlantische Bereicherungen: Zur Erfindung der empirischen Sozialforschung* (Frankfurt a.M.: Suhrkamp, 2007), both of which offer significant reappraisals of midcentury trans-Atlantic intellectual exchange, without, however, touching upon Kracauer's position within this exchange. For a first attempt to place Kracauer's work in this context, which is the object of a larger projected study, see Johannes von Moltke, "Manhattan Crossroads: *Theory of Film* between the Frankfurt School and the New York Intellectuals," in *Culture in the Anteroom: The Legacies of Siegfried Kracauer*, ed. Gerd Gemünden and Johannes von Moltke (Ann Arbor: University of Michigan Press, forthcoming).

14. On the question of continuities and shifts between the Weimar and postwar years, see Patrice Petro, "Kracauer's Epistemological Shift," *New German Critique*, no. 54 (Fall 1991): 127–38; and Miriam Hansen, "With Skin and Hair: Kracauer's Theory of Film, Marseille 1940," *Critical Inquiry* 19, no. 3 (Spring 1993): 437–69. For a reappraisal of Kracauer's American writings, see Noah Isenberg, "This Pen for Hire: Siegfried Kracauer as American Cultural Critic," in Gemünden and von Moltke (eds.), *Culture in the Anteroom*.

15. Lee Grieveson and Haidee Wasson, eds., *Inventing Film Studies* (Durham, N.C.: Duke University Press, 2008).

16. Much has been made of Kracauer's "extraterritoriality." The term is Kracauer's own, and as a motif threads through much of his work: *The Salaried Masses*, for example, centers on a passage titled "Homeless Asylum"; the subject of *Offenbach* is an extraterritorial figure; and *History* is built around the figure (and the epistemology) of the exile. In his correspondence with Adorno, Kracauer claimed the need to remain chronologically exterritorial, urging Adorno not to reveal the year of his birth in a tribute the latter had composed for Kracauer's seventy-fifty birthday. The term "exterritoriality" has been adopted by scholars attempting to make sense of Kracauer's biography—from his often noted strange physical appearance (for a summary of comments to this effect, see Jay, *Permanent Exiles*, 153) to his life in exile. Jay notes that "there is little in Kracauer's biography to suggest that the exterritoriality that marked it from an early age was ever really overcome" (ibid., 182), and Traverso even speaks of Kracauer's deterritorialized language, concluding repeatedly that "if there is a thread to his nomadic existence, it is certainly what he called his 'exterritoriality.'" Enzo Traverso, *Siegfried Kracauer: Itinéraire d'un intellectuel nomade* (Paris: La Découverte, 1994), 191.

17. The notion of "affinities" is central to the final elaboration of Kracauer's film theory, where it denotes the specific way in which photographic media gravitate toward physical reality. In addition to its theoretical meanings in

Kracauer's oeuvre, we choose this term to evoke Kracauer's own affinities, both personal and critical, with the culture in which he found himself at the close of his life.

18. For more on this article's importance in the context of Kracauer's exile, and on his intellectual self-positioning more generally, see Isenberg, "This Pen For Hire"; and Inka Mülder-Bach, "The Exile of Modernity: Kracauer's Figurations of the Stranger," in Gemünden and von Moltke (eds.), *Culture in the Anteroom*.

19. See, e.g., Siegfried Kracauer, "The Conquest of Europe on Screen: The Nazi Newsreel 1939–1940," *Social Research* 10, no. 3 (September 1943): 337–57. Although Kracauer tends to essentialize devotion to the "delicacy of literary language" as a specifically French trait in "Why France Liked Our Films" (ch. 1 this volume), he adumbrates a critique that François Truffaut would pick up over a decade later in his now-famous article "A Certain Tendency of the French Cinema" (*Movies and Methods: An Anthology*, ed. Bill Nichols [Berkeley: University of California Press, 1976], 224–37). In terms strikingly similar to Truffaut's blazing indictment of the "tradition of quality" in which directors were nothing but "metteurs-en-scène" supplying the words of the script with images, Kracauer complains that in recent French films "the flood of words submerged the pictures. . . . In consequence, the screen approached the stage and the pictures functioned as mere illustrations. Whereas the development of a true film depends upon the meaning of its pictures, in these films the dialogue alone determined the progress of the action. . . . [French films] simply followed the course of the words instead of directing it."

20. Miriam Hansen, *Cinema and Experience: Siegfried Kracauer, Walter Benjamin, and Theodor W. Adorno* (Berkeley: University of California Press, 2011), 253–79. See also Klaus Michael, "Vor dem Café: Walter Benjamin und Siegfried Kracauer in Marseille," in *"Aber ein Sturm weht vom Paradise her": Texte zu Walter Benjamin* (Leipzig: Reclam, 1992), 203–21.

21. Kracauer develops the term *camera reality* in *Theory of Film* and then references the notion extensively in his discussion of historical method in *History: The Last Things Before the Last*.

22. Indeed, his observation about the cross-streets of Manhattan reappears almost verbatim in *Theory of Film* (297), where Kracauer sounds one of Critical Theory's perennial motifs, the waning of experience: "the geometric pattern of New York streets is a well-known fact, but this fact becomes concrete only if we realize, for instance, that all the cross streets end in the nothingness of the blank sky."

23. See Jay, *Permanent Exiles*; and Traverso, *Kracauer*.

24. As in this phrase from "Why France Liked Our Films" (ch. 1) the émigrés preferred to use the term *adjustment* rather than *assimilation*—whether in a mildly approving sense, as here, or as a dire requirement, to be resisted to the best of one's abilities. The latter sense clearly predominates in Theodor Adorno's reminiscences, late in his life, in "Scientific Experiences of a European Scholar in America," in *Critical Models: Interventions and*

Catchwords, trans. Henry W. Pickford and Lydia Goehr (New York: Columbia University Press, 1999), 215– 42. Although Adorno concedes that in 1938 "adjustment" was something of a "magic word," he insists that his natural disposition and his past made him "inconceivably unsuited for adjusting in matters of intellect and spirit. As much as I recognize that intellectual individuality itself can only develop through processes of adjustment and socialization, I also consider it the obligation and the proof of individuation that it transcends adjustment" (215).

25. Peter Decherney further nuances the aesthetic politics of the New York scene in his excellent study *Hollywood and the Culture Elite: How the Movies Became American* (New York: Columbia University Press, 2005). He invokes Thomas Bender's terminology to speak of the complex relationship between a downtown political/literary crowd—comprising those most associated with *Commentary* and *Partisan Review*—and the wealthier, uptown, "civic" intellectual aesthetes most closely associated with MoMA (82). As Bender puts it, "If one group was passionate about politics and intelligent about aesthetics, the other was passionate about aesthetics and intelligent about politics" (Thomas Bender, *New York Intellect: A History of Intellectual Life in New York City, from 1750 to the Beginnings of Our Own Time* [Baltimore: Johns Hopkins University Press, 1988], 325). The civic intellectuals were historically less radical in their politics than their downtown counterparts. In the 1930s the relationship was, as Decherney puts it, a "mutually defining binary" (82). If a tentative link between these two groups existed by way of their shared Jewishness, that bridge was most often crossed by the few "downtown" individuals whose cultural and aesthetic enthusiasms extended beyond the literary: Dwight Macdonald, Harold Rosenberg, and Clement Greenberg. However, the wartime and postwar politicization of the MoMA film library, which coincided temporally with the strident anticommunism that was beginning to be practiced downtown, altered the climate considerably. The MoMA film library thus provided an intellectual and institutional meeting ground that defied the previous binary function. Provisionally, we might use this physical meeting place as a way, also, to help us visualize Kracauer's physical as well as metaphorical location in the New York intellectual geography.

26. Neil Jumonville, "Introduction," in *The New York Intellectuals Reader*, ed. Neil Jumonville (New York: Routledge, 2007), 3. See also Irving Howe's assessment of young Jewish intellectuals' double alienation in "The Lost Young Intellectual: A Marginal Man, Twice Alienated," *Commentary* 2, no. 4 (1946): 361–66.

27. Irving Howe, "New York in the Thirties: Some Fragments of Memory," *Dissent* 8, no. 3 (Summer 1961); reprinted in Jumonville (ed.), *New York Intellectuals Reader*, 29.

28. Irving Howe, "The New York Intellectuals: A Chronicle and a Critique," *Commentary* 46, no. 4 (October 1968): 29; David Denby, "Robert Warshow: Life and Works," in Robert Warshow, *The Immediate Experience: Movies, Comics, Theatre, and Other Aspects of Popular Culture*, enlarged

ed. (Cambridge, Mass.: Belknap Press, 2001), xv. Half a century on, Stanley Cavell recalls that "Robert Warshow was the principal writer constituting my strict diet of extra-curricular reading who was asking what America is, and specifically what his relation to American culture is" ("Epilogue: After Half a Century," in Warshow, *Immediate Experience*, 291).

29. Traverso (*Kracauer*, 168) formulates Kracauer's position among the New York Intellectuals paradoxically: "sans s'y identifier complètement, aussi bien à cause de son parcours culturel de Juif allemand émigré que de son extériorité aux querelles de la gauche américaine, Kracauer se situait, avec une position marginale, au sein de ce milieu."

30. Irving Howe, for example, praised Kracauer's seminal essay "Hollywood's Terror Films: Do They Reflect an American State of Mind?" (ch. 2 in this volume), in the unabashedly Marxist venue *Labor Action* (sponsored by the Young New York Socialist League), a monthly he helped edit. See Howe, "Hollywood Terror Films Mirror of Social Decay," *Labor Action*, 16 September 1946, 23. Approximately one year later, Seymour Stern published a highly critical review of the newly released *From Caligari to Hitler* ("Political History of the German Film," *New Leader* 30, no. 26 [28 June 1947]: 11) that included thinly veiled charges of communism (presumably based on Kracauer's references to the work and ideas of Harry Alan Potamkin; for more on Potamkin and film collection/criticism, see Decherney, *Hollywood and the Culture Elite*, 88–96). Robert Warshow penned an unrestrained rebuttal to Stern's review ("The German Film," *New Leader* 30, no. 32 [9 August 1947]: 14), defending Kracauer's book and its methods. Stern's charges had the potential to inflame some particularly acute anxieties, given his role in the red-baiting incidents that had rocked the MoMA film library in 1940 and led in part to the ouster of Jay Leyda. On red-baiting at MoMA, see Decherney, *Hollywood and the Culture Elite*, 138–43.

31. See Howe, 36. On the relationship between Schapiro and Kracauer, see Mark Anderson, "Siegfried Kracauer and Meyer Schapiro: A Friendship," *New German Critique*, no. 54 (Fall 1991): 19–29.

32. Schapiro had already contacted Kracauer (using Krautheimer as a reference) asking if he would write something for his journal, the *Marxist Quarterly*, in 1937. Kracauer responded (12 February 1937) with excerpts from the *Offenbach* book (DLA).

33. Adorno, "The Curious Realist," 172.

34. The importance of form, presentation, or *Darstellung* was recognized by many critics in the orbit of the Frankfurt School; it was certainly a defining aspect of Adorno's demanding style, though he arguably honed his philosophical language in part through his exchanges with Kracauer. In their correspondence, the two men debate the importance of form, for example, with regard to Kracauer's then recently published study of white-collar culture, *Die Angestellten*.

35. Karl Shapiro, quoted in Hugh Wilford, *The New York Intellectuals: From Vanguard to Institution* (Manchester: Manchester University Press,

1995), 33. Wilford's account of the New York Intellectuals' transition "from vanguard to institution" convincingly demonstrates that institutionalization was in fact part and parcel of the Intellectuals' definition as a group. In addition to the magazines, other established institutions and patrons also played a role from the very earliest days—among them the American Communist Party and affiliated organizations such as the John Reed Club (the original sponsor of *Partisan Review*) and City College, where many of the New York Intellectuals were educated in the 1930s.

36. "Who could have dreamt that in the eighties everyone would want to know what happened in those early decades?" mused William Phillips in his memoirs, *A Partisan View: Five Decades of Literary Life* (New York: Stein & Day, 1983), 12. And indeed, from the mid-1980s on there was a parade of publications on the group, initiated by Alexander Bloom, *Prodigal Sons: The New York Intellectuals and Their World* (Oxford: Oxford University Press, 1986), and Terry A. Cooney, *The Rise of the New York Intellectuals: "Partisan Review" and Its Circle* (Madison: University of Wisconsin Press, 1986), and followed by Alan Wald, *The New York Intellectuals: The Rise and Decline of the Anti-Stalinist Left from the 1930s to the 1980s* (Chapel Hill: University of North Carolina Press, 1987), and Neil Jumonville, *Critical Crossings: The New York Intellectuals in Postwar America* (Berkeley: University of California Press, 1991). Later publications built on these texts and offered new perspectives; these include Wilford's institutional investigation, *The New York Intellectuals;* and Harvey M. Teres's thought-provoking, revisionist account *Renewing the Left: Politics, Imagination, and the New York Intellectuals* (Oxford: Oxford University Press, 1996).

37. Teres, *Renewing the Left,* 21. Because the New York Intellectuals are today widely associated with the turn toward neoconservatism taken by some of the group's members, it bears repeating that the roots of the group as a whole were firmly in the culture of the left. Virtually all of the young men who would rise to prominence in the group came from Jewish immigrant workers' families with strong union allegiances and an ingrained commitment to socialist politics. For perspectives on the political, cultural, and aesthetic trajectory of the New York Intellectuals, see Serge Guilbaut, *How New York Stole the Idea of Modern Art: Abstract Expressionism, Freedom, and the Cold War,* trans. Arthur Goldhammer (Chicago: University of Chicago Press, 1983); and Francis Stoner Saunders, *The Cultural Cold War: The CIA and the World of Arts and Letters* (New York: New Press, 1999). For an anthologized set of "insider" discussions reflecting on the Intellectuals' turn to the political right, see Murray Friedman, ed., *Commentary in American Life* (Philadelphia: Temple University Press, 2005).

38. See Wheatland, *Frankfurt School in Exile,* 177.

39. On the role of émigré scholars more generally, see Lewis Coser's still useful overview *Refugee Scholars in America: Their Impact and Their Experiences* (New Haven: Yale University Press, 1984).

40. Daniel Bell lists Arendt among the Elders in his overview of the New York Jewish Intellectuals, their "gentile cousins," and their magazines in "The 'Intelligentsia' in American Society." We quote here from Joseph Dorman's adaptation of Bell's schema in *Arguing the World: The New York Intellectuals in Their Own Words* (New York: Free Press, 2000), xv. For an account of Arendt's position within the "family" of *Partisan Review* and the journal's internecine debates, see Martin Jay, "Intellectual Family Values: William Phillips, Hannah Arendt and the *Partisan Review*," *Salmagundi*, no. 143 (Summer 2004): 43–55.

41. Georg Steinmeyer's recently published dissertation, *Siegfried Kracauer als Denker des Pluralismus: Eine Annäherung im Spiegel Hannah Arendts* (Berlin: Lukas Verlag, 2008), provides some starting points for this investigation by looking at the two thinkers' notions of action, the public sphere, and history, among other topics. However, while he rightly draws on Kracauer's *History* and his Offenbach biography for comparisons with Arendt's philosophy of history and her work on Rahel Varnhagen, respectively, Steinmeyer does not pursue the historically contemporaneous development of Arendt's and Kracauer's thinking during the 1940s and 1950s. Moreover, by virtue of some rather general binaries (e.g., pluralism vs. one-dimensionality; Marxism vs. freedom from ideology) he considerably oversimplifies the comparison between these two thinkers.

42. Letter from Kracauer to Leo Löwenthal, 28 March 1941, in Leo Löwenthal and Siegfried Kracauer, *In steter Freundschaft: Briefwechsel* (Springe: zu Klampen, 2003), 121.

43. Clement Greenberg, for example, remembers a feeling of superiority that was undoubtedly mirrored on the side of the Institut members as well: "We felt in New York without being conscious of it that we were ahead of anything from abroad" (quoted in Krupnick, "Criticism as an Institution," 158).

44. See Wheatland, *Frankfurt School in Exile,* from whom I take the Freudian notion of the "narcissism of small differences."

45. See von Moltke, "Manhattan Crossroads."

46. Letter to Adorno, 22 July 1930, in Adorno and Kracauer, *Der Riß der Welt geht auch durch mich,* 232.

47. Ibid.

48. Dennis Culbert, "The Rockefeller Foundation, the Museum of Modern Art Film Library, and Siegfried Kracauer, 1941," *Historical Journal of Film, Radio, and Television* 13, no. 4 (1993): 495–511.

49. "What I don't want at any price," he wrote to his friend the cinematographer Eugen Schüfftan on 28 April 1946, "is to live again as a freelance writer, as I already got my fill of that in Paris. Please make a little propaganda for me in Hollywood" (*Nachrichten aus Hollywood,* 66). On Kracauer's freelance work, see Isenberg, "This Pen for Hire."

50. Kracauer's series of articles on white-collar employees in the late Weimar Republic were published in book form in 1933 as *Die Angestellten:*

Aus dem neuesten Deutschland. For an English version, see *The Salaried Masses: Duty and Distraction in Weimar Germany*, trans. Quintin Hoare, intro. Inka Mülder-Bach (London: Verso, 1998).

51. *Partisan Review* ceased publication between October 1936 and December 1937 due to a doubly determined shifting of political allegiances and priorities: it found itself without John Reed Club sponsorship when the club reduced its strident image in accordance with the precepts agreed upon under the newly established Popular Front (against fascism). At the same time, revelations regarding Stalin's sedition trials meant that the journal "shifted consciously away from its Russian romance." See "Editorial Statement," *Partisan Review* 4, no. 1 (December 1937), reprinted in Jumonville (ed.), *New York Intellectuals Reader*, 59–60.

52. See Cooney, *Rise of the New York Intellectuals*, 167–95.

53. Dwight Macdonald, "I Choose the West," in Jumonville (ed.), *New York Intellectuals Reader*, 63–68.

54. Following a suggestion by Meyer Schapiro, Macdonald had already solicited work from Kracauer as early as 1939, when the latter was still in Paris (letter from Dwight Macdonald, 9 February 1939 [DLA]). Kracauer promptly took up the offer, thanking Macdonald for the "invitation to collaborate on *Partisan Review*," and suggested an article on French cinema as well as one on German and Italian propaganda, though he noted that the latter was originally contracted with the Institute for Social Research (where it ended in a fiasco after Adorno's heavy-handed editing) and so directed Macdonald to Horkheimer. On the relationship with Schapiro, see Anderson, "Siegfried Kracauer and Meyer Schapiro."

55. In a letter to Donald Slesinger of 12 May 1945, Kracauer claims that his pamphlets on propaganda "were of some help for the production of our Army Morale films" (DLA).

56. Dwight Macdonald, "'The Conquest of Europe on the Screen: The Nazi Newsreel, 1939–1940,' by Siegfried Kracauer," *Politics*, May 1944. At the close of the article, Macdonald also draws attention to the "original and in some ways profound analysis" contained in Kracauer's pamphlet on Nazi propaganda, "Propaganda and the Nazi War Film," that MoMA published two years previously and that now forms the appendix to *From Caligari to Hitler.*

57. Dwight Macdonald, "Through the Lens Darkly," *Partisan Review* 14, no. 5 (1947): 526–28.

58. Jumonville (ed.), *New York Intellectuals Reader*, 64.

59. Nathan Abrams has succinctly formulated the former position in "'America Is Home': *Commentary* Magazine and the Refocusing of the Community of Memory, 1945–1960," in *"Commentary" in American Life*, ed. Murray Friedman (Philadelphia: Temple University Press, 2006), 9–37. Nathan Glazer, by contrast, stresses the distance between the AJC and young editorial assistants at *Commentary* such as Evelyn Shefner and Clement Greenberg, neither of whom "knew anything about Jewish affairs" ("*Commentary:* The Early Years," ibid., 40).

60. Glazer, "*Commentary*," 42.

61. In this respect, among others, we must revise Frank Krupnick's assertion that "the New York and Frankfurt intellectuals never joined forces, indeed hardly ever met. Only Hannah Arendt, who had not been a member of the Frankfurt group, bridged the two worlds" ("Criticism as an Institution," 158). We would also point to Kracauer as a candidate for the function that Krupnick attributes exclusively to Arendt. For evidence of the various, if not always sustained or successful, meetings between members of the two groups, see Wheatland, *Frankfurt School in Exile*.

62. In a letter to Cohen, 21 March 1946, Horkheimer wrote: "I am following the development of *Commentary* with great interest and enthusiasm. The February issue is a model of how pertinent questions of the various fields of culture can be treated on a high literary level and still make good and easy reading. The Jewish viewpoint makes itself felt as a principle which keeps the diversity of articles from tilting over into mere plurality. Also it is handled with true finesse" (quoted in Wheatland, *Frankfurt School in Exile*, 154).

63. As early as 1941, Macdonald had made contact with the Horkheimer circle. Adorno subsequently reported in a letter to Horkheimer (10 November 1941) that he had had "an uncommonly encouraging lunch with MacDonald [sic] and one of his colleagues. His circle is so taken by our stuff that they would publish every sentence." The Institut, however, retreated from the offer, insisting "that collaboration with us is impossible" (quoted ibid., 181).

64. Letter from Rahv to Kracauer, 11 September 1946 (DLA).

65. With reference to *The Killers, The Big Sleep*, and *The Dark Corner* (the latter is referenced in Kracauer's article), Agee notes that such films "were treated by a number of critics, reviewers, and editorial writers as if they were a sinister mirror of American morals, psychology, society, and art.... I realize ... that on its most careful level, as practiced by Dr. Siegfried Kracauer and Barbara Deming, this sort of analysis is of interest and value, dubious as I am about a good deal of it. But to me, the most sinister single thing that happened during the movie year [of 1946] was the emergence of just this kind of analysis—or rather, was the way in which it was indorsed [sic] by those incapable of it" (*Agee on Film* [New York: Random House, 2000], 231–32). James Naremore, in *More Than Night: Film Noir in Its Contexts* (Berkeley: University of California Press, 1998), 106, agrees with Agee's skeptical evaluation of new forms of "cultural anthropology" and "psychocultural" interpretation, which in his estimation laid "the groundwork for a glib and often tautological style of academic criticism that still flourishes today."

66. Dimendberg ("Down These Seen Streets," 119) rightly points out the very different formal (and hence social) treatment of the street in postwar Hollywood and prewar Berlin, even in films by the same director.

67. One might consider, for example, the surprisingly chilling murder of the European baker Herman Miller (played by Austro-Hungarian actor Ludwig Stössel) occurring at the outset of *All Through the Night* (Vincent

Sherman, writing credit Leo Rosten, 1941), one of several relatively graphic murders and beatings in the film, an anti-Nazi "comedy" of the wake-up-America variety, that, as it happened, was released just six days before the Pearl Harbor attack. Or we might revisit the brutal murder of the fourteen-year-old Else (Wandra Hendrix) in Hermin Shulmin's Spanish Civil War drama *Confidential Agent* (1945). Else's murder is an interesting parallel to the murder of Stevie (Desmond Tester) in Alfred Hitchcock's British film *Sabotage* of nine years previous. Yet Hitchcock's film was initially rejected by the public—British and American alike—for its unleashing of such violence on a child. What's more, relevant to Kracauer's thesis, is that the callous brutality presented in both *Confidential Agent* and *All Through the Night* takes place boldly in the face of an impotent state system that proves to be incapable of providing either protection or justice.

68. "Exile permeates the terror film as a contemporaneous social phenomenon couched in veiled references and allegories. Its circulation corresponds to a major increase in emigration into the United States" (Dimendberg, "Down These Seen Streets," 127).

69. Ibid., 128.

70. See Barbara Deming, "The Library of Congress Film Project: Exposition of a Method," *Chimera* 3, no. 2 (Winter 1945): 3–21 and no. 3 (Spring 1945): 6–26; Deming belonged to a group at the MoMA film library that had been contracted by the Library of Congress to select titles for the Film Project. As Janna Jones points out in her detailed reconstruction of the project, "The Library of Congress Film Project: Film Collecting and a United State(s) of Mind," *Moving Image* 6, no. 2 (Fall 2006): 30–51,"Deming and the staff's belief that cinema was a manifestation of an era's cultural guilt and anxiety was most likely shaped by their relationship with Siegfried Kracauer." She rightly emphasizes Kracauer's contribution to the Film Project, "for his international perspective on cinema and national discord shaped how the Film Library staff thought about and screened the films for the United States collection." In the above-cited two-part article, Deming explicitly acknowledges her "friendly debt" to Kracauer and notes that "many of the thoughts expressed here crystallized after conversations with him." Decherney, moreover, points out Kracauer's influence on Deming's book *Running Away from Myself: A Dream Portrait of America Drawn from the Films of the Forties* (New York: Grossman, 1969); see Decherney, *Hollywood and the Culture Elite*, 153, 273 n. 73. He also interprets the Film Project as an attempt to "preemptively apply Kracauer's theory" (ibid., 153), that is, "to aid and limit future Siegfried Kracauers who might attempt to reconstruct American national psychology through film" (154). See Decherney's full account, "Siegfried Kracauer and the Library of Congress Film Project," in *Hollywood and the Culture Elite*, 150–57.

71. For more on the role this approach played in Hollywood's anti-Nazi and reeducation films, see Jennifer Fay, *Theaters of Occupation: Hollywood and the Reeducation of Postwar Germany* (Minneapolis: University of Minnesota Press, 2008).

72. See Nino Frank, "The Crime Adventure Story: A New Kind of Detective Film," in *Perspectives on Film Noir*, ed. Barton Palmer (New York: G.K. Hall, 1996), 21–23 (originally published in *L'écran français* 61 [28 August 1946]); and Raymond Borde and Etienne Chaumeton, *Panorama du film noir américain, 1941–1953* (Paris: Minuit, 1955).

73. Dimendberg, "Down These Seen Streets," 124.

74. Dimendberg (ibid., 131 n. 53) notes that Kracauer's essay defies the notion that the author had turned decisively away from Marxism upon taking up residence in the United States.

75. Howe, "Hollywood Terror Films Mirror of Social Decay," 23.

76. Walter Benjamin employs the term *physiognomist* in his review of Kracauer's *Die Angestellten*, "Ein Außenseiter macht sich bemerkbar: Zu S. Kracauer, *Die Angestellten*," in *Gesammelte Schriften*, vol. 3 (Frankfurt a.M.: Suhrkamp, 1972), 219; originally published in *Die Gesellschaft* 1, no. 7 (1930): 473–77.

77. "Sie malen den Untergang der kleinbürgerlichen Klasse in einer sehr merkwürdigen 'liebevollen' Beschreibung ihrer Hinterlassenschaft" (You paint the demise of the petty bourgeoisie in a most curious, "loving" description of its legacy). Letter to Siegfried Kracauer, 20 April 1926, in Walter Benjamin, *Briefe an Siegfried Kracauer. Mit vier Briefen von Siegfried Kracauer an Walter Benjamin*, ed. Theodor W. Adorno Archiv (Marbach: Deutsche Schillergesellschaft, 1987), 17.

78. Siegfried Kracauer, "The Mass Ornament," in *The Mass Ornament: Weimar Essays*, ed. and trans. Thomas Y. Levin (Cambridge, Mass.: Harvard University Press, 1996), 75.

79. Indeed, Kracauer had apparently made plans with the journal *New Movies* for a series of articles to be published under the rubric "The Rag-Picker," though the column never materialized. See Kracauer, *Werke* 6, vol. 3 (Frankfurt a.M.: Suhrkamp, 2004), 355. On the importance of the rag-picker motif, see also Olivier Agard, *Kracauer: Le chiffonier mélancolique* (Paris: CNRS Éditions, 2010).

80. Siegfried Kracauer, "The Task of the Film Critic," in *The Weimar Republic Sourcebook*, ed. Martin Jay, Anton Kaes, and Edward Dimendberg (Berkeley: University of California Press, 1995), 635.

81. See Eric Bentley, "The Cinema: Its Art and Techniques," *New York Times*, 18 May 1947; and Hansen, "With Skin and Hair."

82. See Petro, "Kracauer's Epistemological Shift."

83. Eric Rentschler, "Rudolf Arnheim's Early Passage Between Social and Aesthetic Film Criticism," in *Arnheim for Film and Media Studies*, ed. Scott Higgins (New York: Routledge, 2011), 63.

84. Kracauer, *History: The Last Things Before the Last* (New York: Oxford University Press, 1969), 4.

85. See Siegfried Kracauer, "The Movie Colony," *Social Research* 9, no. 2 (May 1942): 282–83 (ch. 29 in this volume); "Jean Vigo," *Hollywood Quarterly* 2, no. 3 (April 1947): 261–63 (ch. 3 in this volume); and Kracauer, *History*, 5.

86. Siegfried Kracauer, "Preston Sturges, or Laughter Betrayed" (ch. 11 in this volume).

87. For an overview that anthologizes some of these different positions, see Bernard Rosenberg and David Manning White, eds., *Mass Culture: The Popular Arts in America* (New York: Free Press, 1957). The touchstone for the Frankfurt School position undoubtedly remains the "Culture Industry" chapter in Horkheimer and Adorno's *Dialectic of Enlightenment*, but see also Leo Löwenthal's contributions, e.g. "Historical Perspectives on Popular Culture," *American Journal of Sociology* 55 (1950): 323–32 (reprinted in Rosenberg and White [eds.], *Mass Culture*, 46–58).

88. See Warshow, "Father and Son—and the FBI," in *The Immediate Experience*, 133–41; Howe, "New York Intellectuals," 38–39. The nature of Jewish identity and Zionism, to be sure, were topics of intense debate in the New York Intellectual circles. The general perception of *Commentary* as a Zionist magazine obscures the anxiety that many in the group sustained regarding the formation of Israel as a Jewish state. Nathan Glazer characterizes the American Jewish Council (AJC) as being, on balance, "critical of Jewish nationalism and of any political tendency that would cast doubt on the full commitment of American Jews to the United States." He writes that "the AJC had always been a non-Zionist organization and was the most important of the Jewish groups in the United States taking this position." Glazer relates these contestations to debates regarding the groups' relative commitments to socialism. See Glazer, "*Commentary*: The Early Years," 40. For the evolution of the *Commentary* position on Zionism and the Jewish state, see Ruth R. Wisse, "The Jewishness of *Commentary*," in Friedman (ed.), "*Commentary*" *in American Life*, 56–59.

89. Clement Greenberg, "Avant-Garde and Kitsch," *Partisan Review* 6, no. 5 (1939): 34–49.

90. Dwight Macdonald, "On Lowbrow Thinking," *Politics* 1, no. 7 (August 1944): 219.

91. Dwight Macdonald, "A Theory of Mass Culture," in Rosenberg and White (eds.), *Mass Culture*, 64 (originally published in *Diogenes* 3 [1953]: 1–17).

92. Ibid., 63–64.

93. Looking back in 1968 from a radically changed cultural landscape, Irving Howe ("New York Intellectuals," 35) noted that "the theory advanced by Greenberg and Macdonald turned out to be static, it could be stated, but apparently not developed." It is worth mentioning, also, the idiosyncratic intellectual trajectory of Leslie Fiedler vis-à-vis popular and mass-culture criticism. Followers of cold war history will be familiar with Fiedler's essays of the early 1950s: his pieces on the McCarthy hearings and the Rosenberg trials—in which the author charged willful naiveté on the part of the anti-anticommunist, liberal left—touched off some of the era's most vivid debates within New York Intellectual circles. His writings of the later 1950s took on the emergent youth culture, expressing disdain for their political complacency and self-satisfaction. This time the charge was directly associated with the

threat of middlebrow political *and* cultural indeterminacy. His indictment of mass culture carried a stridency comparable to Macdonald's stance. On youth culture, see Leslie Fiedler, "The Un-Angry Young Men," *Encounter* 10, no. 1 (January 1958): 3–12; on McCarthyism, see "Hiss, Chambers, and the End of Innocence," *Commentary* 12, no. 8 (August 1951): 109–19; on the Rosenbergs, see "After-Thoughts on the Rosenbergs," *Encounter* 1, no. 1 (October 1953): 12–22. Nevertheless, among the New York Intellectuals, it was Fiedler (rather than Howe, for example) who would, by the 1970s, be held up as the counter-culture's elder ally and then as the gray eminence within the nascent field of U.S. cultural studies. See, e.g., Steven J. Kellman's introduction to his anthology edited with Irving Malin, *Leslie Fiedler in American Culture* (Cranbury, N.J.: Associated University Presses, 1999). See also Fiedler's own "On Becoming a Pop Critic," *New England Review* 5, no. 1 (Autumn 1982): 195–207. For more on the complexity of Fiedler's equivocations, see Andreas Huyssen, "The Search for Tradition," *New German Critique*, no. 22 (Winter 1981): 23–40, and "Mapping the Postmodern," *New German Critique*, no. 33 (Autumn 1984): 5–52.

94. Macdonald, "Theory of Mass Culture," 60. There was room for a certain equivocation on this subject, even in the staunchest positions on the spectrum: see Terry Teachout's recollections, by way of Norman Podhoretz, that Greenberg himself at one point labeled *Commentary* "a middlebrow magazine." Apparently Greenberg, Podhoretz, and Teachout could all ultimately concede that "where *Partisan Review* might be said to have been a magazine for 'producers' of ideas, *Commentary* was a magazine for 'consumers'." Cf. Podhoretz, *Making It* (New York: Random House, 1967); and Teachout, "*Commentary* in the Common Culture," in Friedman (ed.), *"Commentary" in American Life*, 128.

95. Howe, "The New York Intellectuals," 41: "In most of these [the New York Intellectuals'] essays, there was a sense of *tournament*, the writer as gymnast with one eye on other rings, or as skilled infighter juggling knives of dialectic. Polemics were harsh, often rude. And audiences nurtured, or spoiled, on this kind of performance, learned not to form settled judgments about a dispute until all sides had registered their blows: surprise was always a possible reward."

96. See Warshow's review of *Paisan* (reprinted in *The Immediate Experience*, 221–29), which references Kracauer's thoughts on the film; the fact that these were never published suggests that the two authors exchanged manuscripts—unless, of course, Warshow had seen Kracauer's piece as a submission for *Commentary*.

97. Letter from Philipp Rahv, editor of *Partisan Review*, 24 March 1948 (DLA): "Dear Dr. Kracauer, We do like this piece quite a bit, but it appears impossible to use it in view of the fact that another film chronicle by Warshow is scheduled for the May issue and we cannot print more than one film piece in any given issue. If, in a few weeks, you have not placed this review elsewhere, do let me know and we will take the matter up again."

98. Warshow, *Immediate Experience*, xlii.

99. Ibid., xxxviii. This stance on the movies is to be distinguished from the far more intransigent position of Irving Howe, who at the time (1948) wrote that "the majority of films do have strong psychological contact with our lives. From the tough-guy films we find so exciting because they rouse our unexpended sadism to the sophisticated comedies that play on our yearning for charm and grace, from the musical comedies that make taffy of our tensions to the socially conscious films that seek to exorcise our guilts—more movies than we know are comments on our experience and help us to 'adjust' to it, that is, to acquiesce to it" ("Notes on Mass Culture," *Politics* 5 [Spring 1948]: 121).

100. Dana Polan, *Scenes of Instruction: The Beginnings of the U.S. Study of Film* (Berkeley: University of California Press, 2007); Decherney, *Hollywood and the Culture Elite*.

101. Markers of this development would include the founding of the Society for Cinematologists (SOC) in 1959, the rise of auteurism, the growing integration of film into academic curricula during the 1960s, and the redefinition of SOC as the Society for Cinema Studies (SCS) in 1968. See Lee Grieveson and Haidee Wasson, "Introduction" to Grieveson and Wasson (eds.), *Inventing Film Studies*.

102. Dwight Macdonald, *Dwight Macdonald on Movies* (Englewood Cliffs, N.J.: Prentice Hall, 1969); Warshow, *Immediate Experience;* James Agee, *Agee on Film*.

PART I. A CULTURAL CRITIC IN NEW YORK

1. Max Horkheimer published *The Eclipse of Reason* in 1947, and *Dialectics of Enlightenment*, which Horkheimer coauthored with Theodor Adorno, appeared in the same year. Nia Perivolaropoulou has commented insightfully on the relation between Kracauer's essay "National Types as Hollywood Presents Them" and Horkheimer's book in "Les stéréotypes nationaux dans le cinéma hollywoodien vus par S. Kracauer," *Bulletin trimestriel de la fondation Auschwitz* 94 (January–March 2007): 81–90.

2. This remains one of the few pieces to have been reprinted elsewhere before its inclusion in this volume. See "Hollywood's Terror Films: Do They Reflect an American State of Mind?" *New German Critique* 89 (Spring–Summer 2003): 105–11; cf. Edward Dimendberg, "Down These Seen Streets a Man Must Go: Siegfried Kracauer, 'Hollywood's Terror Films,' and the Spatiality of Film Noir," *New German Critique* 89 (Spring–Summer 2003): 113–43.

3. See Martin Jay, "Adorno and Kracauer: Notes on a Troubled Friendship," in *Permanent Exiles: Essays on the Intellectual Migration from Germany to America* (New York: Columbia University Press, 1985), 217–36.

4. "Meanwhile, I had a nasty experience: the editor of 'Commentary' [i.e., Clement Greenberg] has completely rewritten my article on sadism: it has

become flat, explicit and vulgar in style. I was tempted to withdraw the piece, but the thought of having to try again to sell it, frightened me so much that I agreed after having made a few hasty changes. This will not happen to me a second time" (Letter to Barbara ["Bobbie"] Deming, 27 July 1946, DLA). Although we have opted here for readability rather than massive annotations, readers interested in the philological genesis of the article can compare it with Kracauer's manuscript as submitted to *Commentary*, which is reproduced in its original English version and under Kracauer's own original title, "Freedom from Fear: An Analysis of Popular Film Trends," in *Werke* 6, vol. 3 (Frankfurt a.M.: Suhrkamp, 2004), 479–85.

5. Herbert Marcuse, "Über den affirmativen Charakter der Kultur," *Zeitschrift für Sozialforschung* 6, no. 1 (1937): 54–94.

6. See "The Challenge of Qualitative Content Analysis," in *Public Opinion Quarterly* 16, no. 4 (Winter 1952–53): 631–42; reprinted in Siegfried Kracauer, *Selected Writings on Media, Propaganda and Political Communication*, ed. Graeme Gilloch and Jaeho Kang (New York: Columbia University Press, forthcoming).

7. See Kracauer, *History: The Last Things Before the Last* (New York: Oxford University Press, 1969), 201.

8. On the importance of the "talk with Teddy," see Jay, "Adorno and Kracauer: Notes on a Troubled Friendship," as well as Christina Gerhardt, "On Natural History: Concepts of History in Adorno and Kracauer," in *Culture in the Anteroom: The Legacies of Siegfried Kracauer*, ed. Gerd Gemünden and Johannes von Moltke (Ann Arbor: University of Michigan Press, forthcoming).

1. WHY FRANCE LIKED OUR FILMS

Originally published in *National Board of Review Magazine* 17, no. 5 (May 1942): 15–19. A note at the top of the article reads: "Dr. Kracauer was formerly an editor of the 'Frankfurter Zeitung,' and Berlin correspondent to 'La Revue du Cinema.' He left Germany in 1933, and lived in France till a year ago when he escaped to America. He is the author of the brilliant biography of Offenbach, 'Orpheus in Paris.'" Two years earlier, Kracauer had already published a piece entitled "Bemerkungen zum französischen Film" (Notes on French Cinema) in the Swiss *Baseler National-Zeitung*; though entirely different in scope and tenor, "Why France Liked Our Films" draws on some of the insights gathered in France and published in numerous individual reviews as well as in overviews such as "Bemerkungen." Thus, while Kracauer had reviewed the work of René Clair, Jean Vigo, Jean Renoir, and Julien Duvivier in some detail, the overview article from 1939 already sounds the critique of France's emphasis on dialogue, its "epic" films without contact with the "effect to be garnered from the small, the inconspicuous." Cf. "Bemerkungen zum französischen Film" in *Werke* 6.3, 282–86.

1. [SK] *The History of Motion Pictures* by Maurice Bardèche and Robert Brasillach, ed. and trans. Iris Barry (New York: Norton/MoMA, 1938), 134.

2. [SK] Valerio Jahier, "42 ans de cinema," in *Le rôle intellectuel du cinéma* (Paris: Société des Nations, Institut international de coopération intellectuelle, 1937), 40.

3. On *San Francisco*, see also Kracauer's article "Das Grauen im Film" (Terror in the Movies; *Werke* 6.3, 312–13), which discusses the same film as part of a series of films devoted to natural catastrophes—thus sounding the claim of *Theory of Film* that cinema is possibly a medium for coping with trauma, but also anticipating the discussion of cinema and horror in "Hollywood's Terror Films."

4. George Raft played the coin-tossing gangster Guino Rinaldo in *Scarface* (USA 1932, dir. Howard Hawks).

5. Kracauer had reviewed a number of these, conveying particular praise for King Vidor's *The Champ* (USA 1931) for its expressive power, realism, and acting. Vidor, Kracauer wrote, "discovers realities, so to speak, which are more real than any given reality." See "Neue Filme," in *Werke* 6.3, 110–11. See also Kracauer's review of *Lady and Gent* (USA 1932, dir. Stephen Roberts) in "Auf der Leinwand," *Werke* 6.3, 116–20.

6. See also Kracauer's review of *Mr. Deeds Goes to Town* under the title "Der Reporter als Filmheld" (The Reporter as Film Hero) in *Werke* 6.3, 187–88.

7. Kracauer reviewed both of these films in French exile, though only the review of the latter seems to have appeared in print. See *Werke* 6.3, 237–39, incl. n. 2, and 271–73.

8. Kracauer reviewed this film in one of his last contributions to the *Frankfurter Zeitung*, while already in exile in Paris. See *Werke* 6.3, 158–59.

9. Kracauer and his wife entered New York Harbor on board the *Nyassa* from Lisbon on 25 April 1941.

10. Kracauer will return to this motif almost verbatim in the summation of his *Theory of Film*, 297.

2. HOLLYWOOD'S TERROR FILMS

Originally published in *Commentary* 2, no. 2 (August 1946): 132–36; a slightly shortened German translation appeared later that year as "Hollywood's Greuelfilme," *Neue Zürcher Zeitung*, 1 December 1946. The text of the original manuscript, entitled "Freedom from Fear: An Analysis of Popular Film Trends," can be found in *Werke* 6.3, 479–85.

1. Dorothy Thompson (1893–1961) was a renowned American Journalist, who had reported extensively from Germany during the 1930s.

2. In the original manuscript, this sentence is preceded by "but the belief in democracy they profess never impels them to wrestle with the totalitarian gospel."

3. In the original: "Escaping from these psychological horrors into meaningless happy endings, they stir up a feeling of uneasiness, engendered by the bewildering spectacle of a world that mirrors our everyday life and yet somehow recalls Nazi savagery."

4. In a 1941 declaration that came to be known as the "Atlantic Charter," U.S. president Franklin D. Roosevelt and British prime minister Winston Churchill had formulated "certain common principles in the national policies of their respective countries on which they base their hopes for a better future for the world." Kracauer chose a phrase from the sixth of these eight principles as the title for his article, but it was changed by the editors of *Commentary*. The Atlantic Charter itself reads: "After the final destruction of the Nazi tyranny, they hope to see established a peace which will afford to all nations the means of dwelling in safety within their own boundaries, and which will afford assurance that all the men in all the lands may live out their lives in freedom from fear and want" (Douglas Brinkley and David A. Facey-Crowther, eds., *The Atlantic Charter* [New York: St. Martins Press, 1994], xvii).

5. Barbara Deming, "The Artlessness of Walt Disney," *Partisan Review* 12, no. 2 (Spring 1945): 226–31.

6. Kracauer would expand on this subject in a subsequent piece for *Commentary*, entitled "Psychiatry for Everything and Everybody: The Present Vogue—and What Is Behind It," included in this volume.

7. The original manuscript ends here; the concluding lines after the dash appear to have been inserted by Clement Greenberg in his role as editor at *Commentary*.

3. JEAN VIGO

Published in *Hollywood Quarterly* 2, no. 3 (April 1947): 261–63, translated by William Melnitz. The original article appeared as "Wiedersehen mit alten Filmen. VII. Jean Vigo" in *Baseler National-Zeitung*, 1 February 1940; see *Werke* 6.3, 299–303. The 1947 version was preceded by a biographical note:

1. "Jean Vigo, who died all too early, made a documentary film about Nice, romantic but full of magnificent cruelty, in which the absurdities of amorous elderly ladies, of gigolos and of the decadent bourgeoisie were fiercely stigmatized" (Maurice Bardèche and Robert Brasillach, *The History of Motion Pictures*, ed. and trans. Iris Barry [New York: Norton/MoMA, 1938], 240).

4. THE REVOLT AGAINST RATIONALITY

Published in *Commentary* 3, no. 6 (June 1947): 586–87.

1. See Max Horkheimer, *The Eclipse of Reason* (New York: Oxford University Press, 1947).

5. ON JEWISH CULTURE

This text represents a rejoinder to Elliot Cohen's article "Jewish Culture in America: Some Speculations by an Editor" published in the May 1947 issue of *Commentary*. Cohen's piece had already been preceded by a discussion, dating back to November 1946, of Jewish culture in the United States as a function of "exile or home" (see Israel Knox, "Is America Exile or Home? We Must Begin to Build for Performance," *Commentary* 2, no. 11 [1946]: 401–8; as well as the responses by Moses Lasky and Herbert Ehrmann in *Commentary* 3, no. 3 [March 1947]: 250–55). In October 1947, Cecil Roth presented a British perspective in a piece titled "Jewish Culture: Renaissance or Ice Age? A Scholar Discusses the Creative Outlook" (*Commentary* 4, no. 10 [October 1947]: 329–33). The editors introduced Roth's article with a note promising a "symposium on the problem of creating Jewish culture in America, taking its departure from Elliot E. Cohen's article in the May *Commentary*"; contributors were to include Hannah Arendt, Benjamin Ginzburg, Jacob B. Agus, Siegfried Kracauer, and Solomon Grayzel. On 9 August, Kracauer confirmed in a letter to Cohen that "I shall be glad to write a comment on your article, 'Jewish Culture in America.' The problem you pose is interesting indeed." The present piece represents that response, reproduced here from the proofs *Commentary* sent to Kracauer for approval on 21 October 1947. However, for reasons unknown, Kracauer's article ultimately remained unpublished; responses published in the November issue of *Commentary* came from David Baumgardt, Hannah Arendt, Jacob B. Agus, Benjamin Ginzburg, and Erwin R. Goodenough. Unpublished ms. in DLA, dated 14 February 1961.

6. FILMING THE SUBCONSCIOUS

Originally published in *Theatre Arts* 32, no. 2 (February 1948): 37–44.

1. *Cinema 16* was created by Amos Vogel and his wife, Marcia; Kracauer was a regular at their screenings.

7. PSYCHIATRY FOR EVERYTHING AND EVERYBODY

Originally published in *Commentary* 5, no. 3 (March 1948): 222–28, with the following editorial note:

> For a few years now we have been deep in a flood of Hollywood films and fictional and non-fictional best-sellers built around psychiatry and psychoanalysis; and there have been few days when the press has not featured a pronouncement by some governmental, welfare, educational, or military authority on similar themes. All these testify, if not to the fact that all Americans are mentally sick, to the presumption that most literate people in this country seem to think they are. How account for this psychiatric vogue? Siegfried Kracauer, who here attempts to explain the larger significance of this current mass preoccupation, has a distinguished record as a social psychologist. From 1920 to 1933 he was on the staff of the *Frankfurter Zeitung* and directed that paper's literary supplement. He came to this country in 1941. Dr. Kracauer is the author of the much-discussed *From Caligari to Hitler: A Psychological History of the German Film*, published

last year by Princeton University Press, and his article "Hollywood's Terror Films" appeared in this magazine in August 1946.

1. [SK] Is the current ratio of neuroses higher than in the past? This question is difficult to answer, for what we have meanwhile learned to define as a neurosis may, prior to Charcot and Freud, have been diagnosed as a case of witchcraft, traced to organic diseases, or considered a moral deficiency.

2. [SK] Dorothy S. Baruch, *The Glass House of Prejudice* (New York: William Morrow, 1946). At one point she says: "The ideal thing, obviously, would be if hostility could be recognized right in the family where it usually generates. If children could grow up learning to face themselves in their moments of anger, and bring the anger out directly, they would not have to repress it so that it would move out of their conscious minds, and, in consequence, out of control." [See also "The Revolt against Rationality," Kracauer's review of Baruch's book, in this volume.—Eds.]

3. Arthur Koestler, *Arrival and Departure* (New York: Macmillan, 1943).

8. THOSE MOVIES WITH A MESSAGE

Appeared in *Harper's Magazine* 196 (June 1948): 567–72. The original typescript, which differs slightly from the published version, was titled "The Message of Hollywood's 'Progressive' Films" and is reproduced in *Werke* 6.3, 486–96.

1. ". . . of our way of life" in the original ms.

2. Omitted sentence from original ms.: "*Boomerang* resembles the *March of Time* films in structure of design."

3. The typescript begins this paragraph with the sentence "Hollywood's thinly veiled revelations are the more poignant as they go against the grain of the films in which they occur."

9. NATIONAL TYPES AS HOLLYWOOD PRESENTS THEM

Published in *Public Opinion Quarterly* 13 (1949): 53–72. An editorial headnote reads:

> Hollywood, and any national film industry for that matter, is both a leader and follower of public opinion. In portraying foreign characters it reflects what it believes to be the popular attitudes of the time, but it also turns these often vague attitudes into concrete images. This process is dramatically highlighted by the treatment which American films have given British and Russian characters from about 1933 to the present. Our images of foreign peoples result from a ratio between objective and subjective factors, and Hollywood can make a considerable contribution to international understanding by increasing the objective factor in its treatment of foreign characters to the extent that current public opinion will allow.

This study is one of a number of pilot studies undertaken in connection with the UNESCO project for studying international tensions.

The article resulted from a commission by Hadley Cantril, professor of social psychology at Princeton and director of the Office of Public Opinion Research. When Kracauer, in search of paid work, learned that Cantril had been selected to head a UNESCO "Inquiry into the Tensions Affecting International Understanding," he wrote to Cantril to offer his services. Responding favorably to Kracauer's suggestion, Hadley was unable, however, to finance the full study proposed by Kracauer and instead commissioned a "pilot study," as Kracauer himself points out in the article. The present text thus represents only one aspect of the larger project Kracauer had conceived, but which he was unable to realize for lack of funding. Soon after its appearance as a UNESCO brochure and in *Public Opinion Quarterly*, the text was reprinted, slightly abridged, as "How U.S. Films Portray Foreign Types: A Psychological View of British and Russians on Our Screen," in *Films in Review* 1, no. 2 (March 1950): 21–22 and 45–47; translations in French and Danish followed within a year: "Les types nationaux vus par Hollywood," in *Revue internationale de filmologie* 2, no. 6 (1950): 115–33; and *Udlaendinge i amerikanske film* (Copenhagen: Det Danske Filmmuseum, 1951). For an in-depth discussion of the article, its methodological importance for Kracauer and Critical Theory, and the outlines of the broader study Kracauer initially proposed to Hadley, see Nia Perivolaropoulou, "Les stéréotypes nationaux dans le cinéma hollywoodien vus par S. Kracauer," in *Bulletin trimestriel de la fondation Auschwitz* 94 (January–March 2007): 81–90.

1. The principal contribution at the time was, of course, Kracauer's own recently published *From Caligari to Hitler*; however, other projects—some of them inspired directly by Kracauer's methods—adopted similar approaches, notably Martha Wolfenstein and Nathan Leites's *Movies: A Psychological Study* (Glencoe: Free Press, 1950), which Kracauer would review for the same journal, *Public Opinion Quarterly*, in which the above article appeared (reprinted in this volume); and Barbara Deming's work for the Library of Congress Film Project, outlined in Deming, "The Library of Congress Film Project: Exposition of a Method," *Library of Congress: Quarterly Journal of Current Acquisitions* 2, no. 1 (November 1944), reprinted in an expanded two-part version in *Chimera* 3, no. 2 (Winter 1945): 3–21 and no. 3 (Spring 1945): 6–26.

2. [SK] Films of fact—documentaries and newsreels—will not be considered here, even though they frequently picture foreigners and events abroad. To exclude them is not to belittle their significance as a means of conveying information, but is simply acknowledgment of the fact that they all but disappear in the mass of fiction films. Except perhaps for their transitory wartime vogue, films of fact still belong among the sideshows, at least in the United States.

3. [SK] Professor Robert H. Ball, of Queens College, is presently preparing a survey of the innumerable American and European screen versions of

Shakespearean plays. In it he plans to comment on the national differences between these versions as well as on the changes they have undergone in each country with the passing of time.

4. Ruth Benedict, *The Chrysanthemum and the Sword: Patterns of Japanese Culture* (Boston: Houghton Mifflin, 1946).

5. [SK] "You and the Russians: A Series of Five Programs Presented on the Columbia Broadcasting System . . . ," a pamphlet issued by CBS. The programs were broadcast in November 1947.

6. [SK] Siegfried Kracauer, *From Caligari to Hitler: A Psychological History of the German Film* (Princeton: Princeton University Press, 1947), 206.

7. [SK] Leonard W. Doob, *Public Opinion and Propaganda* (New York: Henry Holt, 1948), 507.

8. [SK] For the whole argument, see Kracauer, *From Caligari to Hitler*, 5–6.

9. [SK] Jack L. Warner, "What Hollywood Isn't," publicity sheet issued by *Hollywood Citizen News and Advertiser*, 1946.

10. [SK] *Motion Picture Letter* (issued by the Public Information Committee of the Motion Picture Industry) 5, no. 6 (June 1946).

11. [SK] See Kracauer, "Those Movies with a Message," *Harper's*, June 1948, 567–72.

12. [SK] More immediate reasons for Hollywood's conduct may be found in the "cold war" between American and British film industries and also in the gloomy aspect of life in Britain, hardly attractive to a screen infatuated with glamor. But what weight these reasons carry accrues to them from the atmospheric pressures on the political scene.

13. Kracauer misdates this film to 1939.

14. [SK] John C. Flinn, "Film Industry Watching 'Blockade' as B.O. Cue on Provocative Themes," *Variety*, 22 June 1938.

15. [SK] Other films in this vein: *The Charge of the Light Brigade* [USA 1936, dir. Michael Curtiz], *Gunga Din* [USA 1939, dir. George Stevens], *The Sun Never Sets*, etc.

16. [SK] Ernest Marshall, "Screen Notes from London Town: 'Cavalcade' and 'Good Companions' Rivals in West End—Ten Featured Players and Costly Sets in Film of Priestly Story," *New York Times*, 9 April 1933.

17. [SK] Margaret Cole, "How Democratic Is Britain?" *Harper's*, July 1948, 106.

18. [SK] It even seems that the images which one and the same nation forms of a foreign people in different media of mass communication are far from concurring with each other. In American radio comedies, as Mr. Oscar Katz of Columbia Broadcasting System has informed me, the English are typecast as dull-witted fellows unable to understand a joke.

19. [SK] "Mrs. Miniver's War," *Newsweek*, 15 June 1942.

20. [SK] Evelyn Russel, "The Quarter's Films," *Sight and Sound* 11 (Winter 1942): 69.

21. [SK] Quoted from Lewis Gannett, "British Critics' Storm Lashes 'White Cliffs,'" *New York Herald Tribune*, 20 August 1944.

22. [SK] Evelyn Russel, "The Quarter's Films," *Sight and Sound* 12 (Summer 1943): 17.

23. [SK] Charles A. Beard and Mary R. Beard, *America in Midpassage*, vol. 3: *The Rise of American Civilization* (New York: Macmillan, 1941), 201.

24. [SK] "It Isn't the Screen; It's the Story," *New York World Telegram*, 4 June 1932.

25. [SK] Quoted from Kate Cameron's review of this film in the *New York Daily News*, 31 August 1940.

26. [SK] Quoted from Bosley Crowther's review of this film in the *New York Times*, 26 December 1940.

27. [SK] Quoted from Kate Cameron's review of this film in the *New York Daily News*, 5 November 1940.

28. [SK] Quoted from Archer Winsten's review of this film in the *New York Post*, 5 November 1943.

10. THE MIRROR UP TO NATURE

Originally published in *Penguin Film Review* 9 (1949): 95–99.

11. PRESTON STURGES OR LAUGHTER BETRAYED

Originally published in *Films in Review* 1, no. 1 (February 1950): 11–13 and 43–47. The text was apparently commissioned in early 1946 and was to appear in the journal *Measure*, according to a note on the original typescript. It is unclear why this publication failed to materialize. For the publication in the first issue of the new journal *Films in Review*, Kracauer added references to Sturges's most recent films, *Unfaithfully Yours* and *Beautiful Blonde from Bashful Bend*, but otherwise the printed version was variously abridged from the original typescript. We reproduce the text here as it appeared in *Films in Review*, but restore substantive cuts from the typescript (signaled "TS") by including the omitted text as notes. For a complete version of the English typescript and further information on the publication history of the article, see *Werke* 6.3, 511.

1. The following lines precede this sentence in TS: "Preston Sturges, whose meteoric career as a director-writer is within everyone's memory, has aroused nation-wide laughter through films which, from *The Great McGinty* (1939/40) to *Hail the Conquering Hero* (1943/44), brilliantly blend satire and comedy. Distinguished by wit, inventiveness and vehemence of action, they offer, I think, a unique opportunity to catch a glimpse of what people laugh at today and what their laughter means. I am quite aware that such an analysis of a few gay films may be accused of taking entertainment too seriously."

2. TS: "These efforts even determined the form of the film. To evoke a sympathy which the audience might not otherwise feel, the story is narrated, flashback fashion, by the dead railway magnate's secretary, who has known him since childhood and firmly believes in his basic mobility. The whole

plot, constantly changing sides, reveals a wavering in Sturges' evaluation of tycoons and their like. But despite its inherent ambiguity, the film culminates in a verdict on society: power, the tycoon's suicide implies, is incompatible with human loyalty, and he who conquers the world cannot but lose himself."

3. TS: "Exactly as the railway magnate, Dan McGinty, is both stigmatized and exonerated: now he appears as a brazen rogue, now as an essentially decent fellow who should not be condemned on surface evidence. (Incidentally, this somewhat inconsistent emphasis on the human qualifications of a parasite may result from Sturges' desire to challenge moral hypocrisy wherever he encounters it.)"

4. TS: "This film was what the trade calls a 'sleeper': notwithstanding little advance publicity, it made big box-office records. Thus, Sturges proved (or could have proved) to Hollywood that a screen hit need not be conformist or wind up a happy ending."

5. TS: "For instance, whenever Dan and the Boss meet, they become involved in a scuffle—a running gag splendidly characterizing the relation between two racketeers forever welded together."

6. TS: "It enlightens. But besides the bulk of pertinent gags there remains an amount of pictorial jokes which make no definite sense. And this unaccountable fun seems to spring from the inner wavering manifest in the narrative's ambiguity."

7. TS: "But every now and then, these truly cinematic sequences give way to episodes with no pictorial life of their own. Then the whole emphasis shifts from the visual to fine points of dialogue—and as if stunned by verbal impact, an all but motionless camera indulges in tableaux vivants. It is a bewildering spectacle: the most imaginative use of camera devices constantly alternating with relapses into stage technique. These spells of visual inertia will be discussed later."

8. Kracauer is mistaken on the date; the film was conceived and produced in 1942–44.

9. TS:

> In it, employees are a lucky lot, Jews fully accepted neighbors, and tycoons no longer bogies. In fact, the coffee magnate is just a harmless grumbler forever frustrated by the small incident of everyday life's routines. The moral: no one should grudge tycoons their millions.
>
> Yet *Christmas in July* is not as conformist as it seems. Its complacency is unsettled, if not outbalanced, by an uneasiness manifest in Sturges' endeavour to denounce the film's fairytale character by deliberately overplaying it. For instance, the supervisor in Jimmy's office radiates the incredible benevolence of those cops who in the dream sequence of Chaplin's *Kid* [1921] were metamorphosed into angels. And bitter reality breaks repeatedly through the wrappings of wishful thinking: Jimmy, in a talk with his girl, despairs of a future under the eternal pressure of poverty, and the girl tries to move their boss by talking of the many who might make good if they were only given a chance.

10. TS: "In consequence, the final verdict in Jimmy's favor serves merely to ridicule the procedures of juries."

11. TS: "When Charles at the end of his flight from Jean meets her once more, he accepts her unreservedly as the girl she is. The Innocent has learned his lesson; grown adult, he challenges society in the interest of what he considers genuine human values."

12. TS: "The slapstick incidents during the beer magnate's breakfast in *The Lady Eve* characterize him as a frustrated tycoon; and that Charles falls down six times throughout his intricate love affair is a contribution to Freud's Psychopathology of Everyday Life."

13. TS:

> The question is: what kind of laughter does Sullivan advocate? At the end of the film he summarizes its moral: laughter "is better than nothing in this cockeyed caravan." On the surface, Sullivan's definition seems in keeping with Chaplin's defense of himself against the many critics who had accused his *Great Dictator* [1939/40] of making fun of a tragedy: "Laughter is the tonic, the relief, the surcease from pain. It is healthy, the healthiest thing in the world—and it is health-giving" ("Mr. Chaplin Answers His Critics," *New York Times*, October 27, 1940). The intention behind this exuberant statement, which more or less applies to all Chaplin films, is made nowhere as clear as in *The Great Dictator* itself. When the film draws to its close, laughter is superseded by the famous speech in which Chaplin, under the transparent mask of his barber, exhorts the soldiers to fight for a world of reason, liberty and universal brotherhood. (This overt plea for democracy has been indicted as a sentimental propaganda speech, transgressing the borderline between art and reality. But great art, consumed by desire to attain the unattainable, sometimes goes beyond its set limits; and what counts in the speech is the intensity of its emotion rather than its explicit wording. Perhaps no silent Chaplin film was as silent as this passage with its overflow of rhetoric.) It is as if Chaplin had felt that laughter might not be enough to press home the impending danger of tyranny and had therefore resorted to the ultimate expedient of a direct appeal. This appeal does not disavow Chaplin's use of laughter; on the contrary, it reveals its implications to the full. His laughter is health-giving because of its sympathy for man's attempt to make the world a healthier place for himself.

14. TS: "When the happily laughing prisoners come in focus, it does not matter to him whether their happiness will shortly yield to despondency again or really alter their inner condition. And back home, Sullivan pleads the cause of laughter without so much as mentioning the cause of human dignity which had originally lured him away from his comedies."

15. TS: "Since he takes man's existing condition for granted, his laughter is confined to momentarily soothing those in distress. Chaplin's laughter encourages people in their striving for a better life; Sullivan's makes them forget their predicament. It is a soporific."

16. TS: "That Sturges identifies himself with his Sullivan follows from the introductory caption, which dedicates this film to the memory of those who made us laugh: the motley mountebanks, the clowns, the buffoons, in all times and in all nations, whose efforts have lightened our burden a little. *Sullivan's Travels* is an autobiographical statement—one of the few ever made on our screen. With gratifying frankness it tells the audience that Sturges has come to terms with society. In the light of this statement certain features and details of his previous films acquire a new meaning or assert themselves more vividly than before."

17. TS: "Yet in spite of all this, those earlier films with their bright laughter were a good antidote against obscurantism. Sturges' peace with the powers that be grew out of a complex mind which might have just as well led him in another direction."

18. TS: "Both starred Eddie Bracken, whose Innocents were something between Harry Langdon and Buster Keaton; and both exposed him to situations as funny and muddled as the ordeals with which those classic screen characters kept coping in by-gone happier days."

19. TS: "A sword dangles down from the stuttering father's side—a witty comment on what he had experienced at the sight of his *embarras de richesse*."

20. In the published version, the preceding paragraph replaces the following longer explanation from the original typescript:

> The three comedies that followed *Sullivan's Travels* could have been devised by Sullivan himself—by Sullivan who finally desired nothing but to make laughter lighten our burden a little. Their common characteristics are particularly conspicuous in *Hail the Conquering Hero*, even though this film includes such an amount of social satire that it seems the unswerving equal to Sturges' nonconformist earlier films. And yet, Sturges' satire is here no longer what is was before *Sullivan's Travels*. Sturges dulls its bite through systematical retreats from any advanced position. True, he jeers at the current worship of (matrimonial) motherhood; but Woodrow's mother is nevertheless a womanly paragon to do credit to the *Saturday Evening Post*. True, Sturges attacks the homefront for wantonly idolizing heroes; but the six marines in charge of his attack nevertheless solemnly salute the photograph of Woodrow's father, who was one. His satire thus consumes itself; his bullets are blanks. That this is precisely Sturges' intention can be shown by a comparison of *Hail the Conquering Hero* and *Christmas in July*. In *Christmas*, Sturges ingeniously manages to launch Jimmy, its Innocent, on a career without suggesting that reality bears out our daydreams: Jimmy's success is not founded upon the jury's ultimate decision in his favor, and throughout the

film there remains a gap between real life and wishful thinking. This gap, kept open in every Sturges film prior to *Sullivan's Travels*, is definitely bridged in *Hail the Conquering Hero*. Here reality obliges our most extravagant hopes; Woodrow seems done for, after having confessed his guilt, yet he conquers the town. Nor does he even have to conquer it—the town surrenders. At his beginning Sturges insisted that honesty does not pay. Now he wants us to believe that the world yields to candor. To be sure, the plot evolves in a fairytale atmosphere; and is it not natural for fairytales to indulge? But Sturges himself had forestalled such justification: in the fairytale of *Christmas in July*, he has proven that he knows how to obstruct playfully any mood of appeasement. When he started appeasing, he did it on purpose—and not because of insufficient armament.

21. TS: "There is virtue everywhere; unsought favors are showered upon the stuttering Norval; his benefactor is the same McGinty who once illustrated that power breeds evil. Dan McGinty may now be just as corrupt as he was before, but he has turned from a ferment of social malaise into a source of blessings."

22. TS: "This is also the moral of *The Palm Beach Story*, with its assortment of well-to-do parasites. In the very satirizing of their way of life Sturges reveals them as the instruments of a providence sponsoring the guileless and the pure in heart. He introduces a foolish old business magnate who indulges in acts of unselfish generosity; tycoons, whom Sturges had previously indicted for ruthlessness, are now advertised as models of kindliness."

23. TS:

In this turn to conformism, Sturges adopted slapstick wholesale. This is puzzling and demands an explanation. Unlike Sturges' films since *Sullivan's Travels*, the classic slapstick comedies never belittled the dangers to which their heroes were invariably exposed. Buster Keaton was forever victimized by mechanization; Harry Langdon lived under the omnipresent threat of emotional inertia; and Chaplin seemed eternally on the verge of being defeated by the Goliaths of our world. All of them showed little fellows in a struggle for survival or a better life; and since they were favored by luck, they used to win the battle in the very last moment. But it is by no means accidental that these comedies had the character of episodes resumed over and over again: triumphs of their heroes were provisional escapes rather than definite victories, and the happy ending was merely an armistice with no guarantees for the future. Of course, the whole species sides with the little pigs against the big bad wolf. This inherent nonconformism, particularly manifest in *The Great Dictator*, where for once the wolf was called by its real name, colored all genuine slapstick gags. They were not just fun; they evoked sympathetic understanding for the hero's plight by exhibiting his dependence upon the whims of luck and risky expedients.

24. TS: "This is evidenced by the very key episode in *Sullivan's Travels* through which Sturges announces his purpose of reverting to the Mack Sennett tradition. When he shows the prisoners under the spell of one of those Disney cartoons in which Mickey Mouse was still a worthy mate of the early Chaplin, he entirely disregards the specific nature of slapstick laughter. Without so much as mentioning its encouraging effect upon the less fortunate, he simply emphasizes the fact that the prisoners laugh—and then plays up the salutary role of laughter as such."

25. TS: "In *The Lady Eve*, which preceded this film, Charles tumbled to the ground time and again—only Charles, and he in strict keeping with his inhibitions; in the swimming-pool sequence of *Sullivan's Travels*, all characters, whether or not inhibited, get drenched."

26. TS: "What once sharpened the wits of the onlooker, now serves to lull him into acceptance of Sturges' serene ideas about the world as it is."

27. TS: "His slapstick manner since *Sullivan's Travels* might be traceable to certain psychological mechanisms touched off in anyone who, consciously or unconsciously, deserts a cause. It is as if Sturges were driven by a desire to make himself believe that he did not betray his laughter."

28. TS:

And now it is possible to account for Sturges' strange reluctance to move the camera during passages of vivid dialogue. Such passages occur in every Sturges film since *The Great McGinty*. They are not technical shortcomings. Sturges had shown his ability to progress the action through pictures alone: his realistic shots in *Sullivan's Travels* are as eloquent as many of his visual gags. Nor can Sturges possibly have intended to stress the verbal argument by draining the synchronized visual part of its significance. He is too experienced a film maker not to know that pictorially unsupported dialogue is dead weight rather than a positive contribution. The one explanation left is, therefore, that he inserts these wordy passages because he does not want to follow up the witticisms and heretic opinions in which he delights as a man of the spirit. It would be easy for him to elaborate with adequate interpretative shots; but he prefers to have his characters rattle their dangerous lines off in a pictorial vacuum, so that they evaporate without leaving a trace behind—fireworks instantly dissolved into darkness. Sturges' dialogue technique amounts to an instinctive escape from the implications of his thoughts. He obviously does not dare to face his inner tendency toward conformism, which was responsible for the ambiguity in his earlier films and has determined the character of the later ones. The same fear of self-exposition which since *Sullivan's Travels* made him capitalize on slapstick caused him, from the outset, to immobilize his camera whenever its actions threatened to become indeed revealing.

29. TS: "Sturges should not be mistaken for one of his Innocents. Having decided to throw in his lot with the 'cockeyed caravan' of the world as it is, he does not relinquish his onetime social criticism. He retains it to the full. But the function he now assigns to social satire is that of a spice adding flavor to the pretty common dish. Pungent sallies become cues for complacent gags, readily exposed abuses turn into pleasing stimulants."

30. TS: "He shows the black and metamorphoses it into white. Thus the spectators are led to believe that they can be enlightened and subordinate their knowledge to opportunism. Sturges, to the extent of his success, makes conformism invulnerable."

31. The TS concludes: "Ours is an age of giant organizations whose psychological imperialism produces prefabricated souls. In such an age, the Sturges laughter has a sinister ring because its refined conformism facilitates the dissolution of spontaneity, of self. In such an age, the cardinal virtue is nonconformism."

12. ART TODAY

Unpublished ms. in DLA, dated 14 February 1961.

13. ABOUT THE STATE OF THE HUMANITIES

Unpublished typescript in DLA, presumably from the mid-1960s; likely a discussion paper for the Bollingen Foundation. Kracauer had met with the Irish classical scholar E. R. Dodds, the French anthropologist Claude Lévi-Strauss, and the Swiss historian Werner Kaegi on his European tour in 1965.

1. C. P. Snow, *The Two Cultures and the Scientific Revolution* (New York: Cambridge University Press, 1959).

14. A STATEMENT ON THE HUMANISTIC APPROACH

Unpublished "Draft" ms. in DLA, dated 2 April 1951.

1. See "Psychiatry for Everything and Everybody," in this volume.
2. The ms. includes a parenthetical reference here: "See my proposals for 'a study of personality developments in the U.S.' and 'an inquiry into typical differences in content between different media of mass communication.'"

15. TALK WITH TEDDIE

Notes on a conversation with Theodor W. Adorno at the Hotel Sonnenheim in Bergün (Switzerland) dated 12 August 1960. Ms. in DLA.

1. "Die Ontologie wird nichts zu lachen haben," meaning that onotology will be put on the defensive.
2. The ms. includes a three-part drawing here that visualizes the relationship between an "ontological area" and thought for "Teddie" (Adorno), Benjamin, and Kracauer, respectively. The drawing is reproduced in Siegfried

Kracauer and Theodor W. Adorno, *Briefwechsel: Der Riß der Welt geht auch durch mich* (Frankfurt: Suhrkamp Verlag, 2009), 736.

3. The reference is presumably to the Hungarian-German art historian Arnold Hauser (1892–1978), author of *The Social History of Art* (New York: Knopf, 1951).

4. Crossed out in ms.: "experienced."

PART II. FILM REVIEWS

1. *Paisan* also functions as a touchstone of sorts in the dialogue between Kracauer and Robert Warshow; the two authors' respective analyses of the film are mutually enriching. For Warshow's review, which originally appeared in *Partisan Review* in July 1948, see Warshow, *The Immediate Experience: Movies, Comics, Theatre, and Other Aspects of Popular Culture*, enlarged ed. (Cambridge, Mass.: Belknap Press, 2001), 221–29.

2. See Kracauer, *History: The Last Things Before the Last* (New York: Oxford University Press, 1969), 9.

3. This topic has meanwhile received sustained, scholarly attention across disciplines, from history to film studies, political science to literature. The list of publications is too large to go into here, but Robert G. Moeller's *War Stories: The Search for a Usable Past in the Federal Republic of Germany* (Berkeley: University of California Press, 2003) remains an excellent place to start. The significance of Kracauer's contribution to this line of thinking lies, of course, in its early formulation—comparable, say, to the essays of his fellow émigré Hannah Arendt from the same time.

4. "Propaganda and the Nazi War Film" appeared as an appendix to *From Caligari to Hitler;* "The Conquest of Europe on the Screen: The Nazi Newsreel" reworked aspects of the former essay and was published in *Social Research* 10, no. 3 (September 1943): 337–57. The argument is extended to the American context in a review of American newsreels coauthored with Joseph Lyford: "A Duck Crosses Main Street," *New Republic,* 13 December 1948, 13–15. These texts will be available in Siegfried Kracauer, *Selected Writings on Media, Propaganda and Political Communication* ed. Graeme Gilloch and Jaeho Kang (New York: Columbia University Press, forthcoming).

16. AN AMERICAN EXPERIMENT

Published in German as "Ein amerikanisches Experiment," *Neue Zürcher Zeitung,* 15 July 1941. This was the first review Kracauer submitted from New York. It is translated here by Johannes von Moltke from Siegfried Kracauer, *Werke* 6.3: *Kleine Schriften zum Film 1932–1961* (Frankfurt a.M.: Suhrkamp, 2004).

1. Instead of a sled, Kracauer had mistakenly identified a children's bed.

2. The original reads "Objekt," or object, but Kracauer undoubtedly intended "Objektiv," or lens, here.

17. DUMBO

Originally published in *The Nation* 19 (8 November 1941): 463. This was Kracauer's first publication in English.

18. FILM NOTES FROM HOLLYWOOD

Published in German as "Filmnotizen aus Hollywood," *Neue Zürcher Zeitung*, 30 November 1941. It is translated here by Johannes von Moltke from Siegfried Kracauer, *Werke* 6.3: *Kleine Schriften zum Film 1932–1961* (Frankfurt a.M.: Suhrkamp, 2004).
    1. See *The Gay Parisian* (USA 1941, dir. Jean Negulesco).
    2. The film was released as *It Started with Eve* (USA 1941, dir. Henry Koster).

19. A FEW AMERICAN FILMS

Published in German as "Ein paar amerikanische Filme," *Neue Zürcher Zeitung*, 7 December 1941. It is translated here by Johannes von Moltke from Siegfried Kracauer, *Werke* 6.3: *Kleine Schriften zum Film 1932–1961* (Frankfurt a.M.: Suhrkamp, 2004).

20. WILLIAM WYLER'S NEW BETTE DAVIS FILM

Published in German as "William Wylers neuer Bette Davis-Film," *Neue Zürcher Zeitung*, 14 December 1941. It is translated here by Johannes von Moltke from Siegfried Kracauer, *Werke* 6.3: *Kleine Schriften zum Film 1932–1961* (Frankfurt a.M.: Suhrkamp, 2004).

21. FLAHERTY: *THE LAND*

The Land (USA 1942, dir. Robert Flaherty). Unpublished typescript, DLA, dated 16 April 1942.

22. FOR WHOM THE BELL TOLLS

For Whom the Bell Tolls (USA 1943, dir. Sam Wood). Undated typescript, DLA.
    1. Ernest Hemingway, *For Whom the Bell Tolls* (New York: Scribner, 1940), 169.

23. PAISAN

Unpublished typescript, DLA, dated 7 March 1948.
    1. Ignazio Silone (1900–1978), Italian author and politician.

24. THE DECENT GERMAN

Originally published in *Commentary* 7 (1949): 74–77. An accompanying note reads: "'On the Horizon,' devoted to comment on cultural and social events and trends, presents this month an analysis by Siegfried Kracauer of a postwar German film, *Marriage in the Shadows*, which reveals disturbing facts about the present state of the German mind. . . . Dr. Kracauer is the author of *From Caligari to Hitler*, a psychological history of the German cinema."

1. See ch. 2 in this volume.
2. Kracauer is referring here to Veit Harlan's infamous *Jud Süß* (Germany 1940).

25. THE ETERNAL JEW

These are program notes on Fritz Hippler's infamous film *Der ewige Jude* (The Eternal Jew; Germany 1940), compiled by Siegfried Kracauer for a special screening at New York's "Cinema 16" film society. Amos Vogel, the society's founder and executive secretary, had prepared an "English adaptation" of the film, narrated by Robert Carter. Vogel also introduced the film, which was shown by a special arrangement with the Netherlands Film Archive, at its screening on 4 November 1958. We reprint these notes from Scott Macdonald, *Cinema 16: Documents toward a History of the Film Society*, Wide Angle Books (Philadelphia: Temple University Press, 2002), 351–54. A note at the top of the document reads:

> This program note is compiled from a recording of remarks made by Dr. Siegfried Kracauer after a screening of the film as well as from his studies of the Nazi propaganda film, "The Conquest of Europe on the Screen" (*Social Research*, September 1943) and "Propaganda and the Nazi War Film" in his book *From Caligari to Hitler* (Princeton University Press, 1947). Dr. Kracauer, well known in this country as the author of the just-mentioned book and a social scientist, was an editor of *Frankfurter Zeitung* in 1920–1933. He was the recipient of two Rockefeller grants and a Guggenheim Fellowship for his research on the history and philosophy of the German cinema. Presently he is completing a book on the aesthetics of film which will be published by the Oxford University Press.

1. Cf. Kracauer's above-mentioned contributions, "The Conquest of Europe on Screen" and "Propaganda and the Nazi War Film."

26. A FEW NOTES ON *THE CONNECTION*

Unpublished typescript, DLA, dated 5 May 1961. The notes "were apparently not designed to be published. The film, which Kracauer saw on May 4, 1961, in a non-public screening at the Preview Theater on Broadway, was also shown at Cannes during the same month, at the invitation of the French screenwriters' association. It was the first U.S. film to be awarded this honor" (Kracauer, *Werke* 6.3: *Kleine Schriften zum Film 1932–1961*, ed. Inka Mülder-Bach with Mirjam Wenzel and Sabine Biebl [Frankfurt a.M.: Suhrkamp, 2004], 473 n. 2).

PART III. BOOK REVIEWS

1. Letter to Robert Van Gelder of the *New York Times*, 28 June 1943 (DLA).
2. In the 4 January 1948 issue of the *New York Times Book Review*, Kracauer reviewed Marshall Mason Knappen's *And Call It Peace* under the title "Re-education Program for the Reich." We do not include that review in this volume, however, because Kracauer essentially gives a summary of the book rather than a critique with an authorial "signature."
3. See, e.g., "Calico World: The UFA City in Neubabelsberg" (1926), in Kracauer, *The Mass Ornament: Weimar Essays*, ed. and trans. Thomas Y. Levin (Cambridge, Mass.: Harvard University Press, 1996), 281–88.
4. Siegfried Kracauer, "Photography" (1928), ibid., 47–63; here: 58.
5. See Miriam Hansen, "Kracauer's Photography Essay: Dot Matrix—General (An-)Archive—Film," in *Culture in the Anteroom: The Legacies of Siegfried Kracauer*, ed. Gerd Gemünden and Johannes von Moltke (Ann Arbor: University of Michigan Press, forthcoming).

27. IN EISENSTEIN'S WORKSHOP

Review of Sergei M. Eisenstein's *The Film Sense*, ed. and trans. Jay Leyda (New York: Harcourt, Brace, 1942), in *Kenyon Review* 5, no. 1 (Winter 1943): 151–53.

28. THE RUSSIAN DIRECTOR

Review of Sergei Eisenstein, *Film Form: Essays in Film Theory*, ed. and trans. Jay Leyda (New York: Harcourt, Brace, 1949), and V.I. Pudovkin, *Film Technique and Film Acting*, trans. Ivor Montagu, intro. Lewis Jacobs (New York: Bonanza Books, 1949), in *New Republic*, 26 September 1949, 22–23.

29. THE MOVIE COLONY

Review of Leo C. Rosten's *Hollywood: The Movie Colony—The Movie Makers* (New York: Harcourt, Brace, 1941), in *Social Research* 9, no. 2 (May 1942): 15–19.

1. Budd Schulberg, *What Makes Sammy Run?* (Garden City: Sun Dial Press, 1943).

30. A LADY OF VALOR

Review of Allen Lesser's *Enchanting Rebel: The Secret of Adah Isaacs Menken* (New York: Beechhurst Press, 1947), in *Commentary* 4, no. 4 (October 1947): 394–95.

31. THE TEUTONIC MIND

Review of Frederic Lilge's *The Abuse of Learning: The Failure of the German University* (New York: Macmillan, 1948), in *New Republic*, 23 February 1948, 23–24.

32. CONSCIOUSNESS, FREE AND SPONTANEOUS

Review of Jean-Paul Sartre's *The Psychology of Imagination* (New York: Philosophical Library, 1948), in *Saturday Review of Literature* 31, no. 26 (26 June 1948): 22–23.

33. INDOLOGIAN HOLIDAY

Review of Heinrich Zimmer's *The King and the Corpse: Tales of the Soul's Conquest of Evil*, ed. Joseph Campbell, Bollingen Series (New York: Pantheon Books, 1948), in *Saturday Review of Literature* 31, no. 30 (24 July 1948): 15–16.

34. PORTRAIT IN FILM

Review of Parker Tyler's *Chaplin: Last of the Clowns* (New York: Vanguard, 1948), in *New Republic*, 26 July 1948, 24–26.

35. TOTAL TEACHING

Review of *Film and Education: A Symposium on the Role of the Film in the Field of Education*, ed. Godfrey M. Elliott (New York: Philosophical Library, 1948), in *New Republic*, 6 June 1949, 23.

36. PICTORIAL DELUGE

Review of Lancelot Hogben's *From Cave Painting to Comic Strip: A Kaleidoscope of Human Communication* (New York: Chanticleer Press, 1949), in *trans/formation* 1, no. 1 (1950): 52–53.

    1. [SK] See "Course in Comics Seeks Social Good," *New York Times*, 16 November 1949.

37. MOVIE MIRROR

Review of Martha Wolfenstein and Nathan Leites, *Movies: A Psychological Study* (Glencoe, Ill.: Free Press, 1950), in *New Republic*, 31 July 1950, 19–20.

38. RÉFLEXION FAITE

Review of René Clair, *Réflexion faite: Notes pour servir à l'histoire de l'art cinématographique de 1920 à 1930* (Paris: Gallimard, 1951), in *Books Abroad* 26, no. 1 (Winter 1952): 48–49.

PART IV. TOWARD A THEORY OF FILM

1. For the "production history" of *Theory of Film*, see Miriam Hansen, "Introduction," in Siegfried Kracauer, *Theory of Film: The Redemption of Physical Reality* (Princeton: Princeton University Press, 1997), vii–xlv; and Inka Mülder-Bach with Sabine Biebl, "Nachbemerkung und editorische Notiz," in Siegfried Kracauer, *Werke* 3: *Theorie des Films*, 847–74.
2. Kracauer, *Theory of Film*, 93–101.
3. *Film Culture* 1, no. 2 (March–April 1955): 19–21; cf. *Theory of Film*, 153–56.
4. For a full list of these articles, which also indicates the corresponding sections of *Theory of Film*, see Mülder-Bach and Biebl, "Nachbemerkung," 869–70.
5. On the reception of Kracauer's work in Germany, see Eric Rentschler, "Kracauer, Spectatorship, and the Seventies," in *Culture in the Anteroom: The Legacies of Siegfried Kracauer*, ed. Gerd Gemünden and Johannes von Moltke (Ann Arbor: University of Michigan Press, forthcoming).
6. For more on the significance of this brief missive, see Johannes von Moltke, "2 February 1956: In Letter to Enno Patalas Siegfried Kracauer Advocates a Socio-Aesthetic Approach to Film," in *New History of German Cinema*, ed. Jennifer Kapczynski and Michael Richardson (Rochester, N.Y.: Camden House, forthcoming).

39. STAGE VS. SCREEN ACTING

Originally published in *Films in Review* 1, no. 9 (December 1950). An accompanying note reads: "This article is based on a chapter of a book Dr. Kracauer is preparing for the Oxford University Press." Kracauer had previously published related material in two articles for the *Baseler National-Zeitung* during his French exile, in May 1940. See *Werke* 6.3, 317–23.

40. THE PHOTOGRAPHIC APPROACH

Originally published in *Magazine of Art* 44, no. 3 (March 1951): 107–13. The text forms the basis for chapter 1 of Kracauer's *Theory of Film*, pp. 13–23: "Photography."

1. William de Wiveleslie Abney, *Instantaneous Photography* (New York: E. & H.T. Anthony, 1896).
2. Marcel Proust, *Guermantes' Way*, Part I (New York: Modern Library, 1925), 186–88.
3. *Photogénie* 1920, 5.
4. The article concluded with the following note: "The historical references throughout have largely been drawn from Beaumont Newhall's article 'Photography and the Development Kinetic Visualization' (*Journal of the Warburg and Courtauld Institutes*, London, 1944, VII, pp. 40–45) and his *History of Photography* (New York, Museum of Modern Art, 1949)."

41. SILENT FILM COMEDY

Originally published in *Sight and Sound* 21, no. 1 (August/September 1951): 31–32.

1. Kracauer misdated the film to 1908.
2. Kracauer guessed, "ca. 1910?" for this film's date.

42. THE FOUND STORY AND THE EPISODE

Originally published in *Film Culture* 2, no. 1 (1956): 1–5. The author bio reads: "Dr. Kracauer is preparing a book on the aesthetics of film which will be published by the Oxford University Press. During the recent past he has drafted a comprehensive syllabus of his book, including all relevant concepts, arguments, analyses. The following pages are drawn from this syllabus."

1. Robert Flaherty (1884–1951) was an American director of nonfiction films. Kracauer was involved with the "Flaherty Film Seminars" during the 1950s.
2. Paul Rotha, *Documentary Film* (New York: Norton, 1939), 106.
3. John Grierson, "Robert Flaherty: An Appreciation," *New York Times*, 29 July 1951; emphasis in original.
4. Quoted in Arthur Rosenheimer Jr., "They Make Documentaries: Number One—Robert J. Flaherty," *Film News* 7, no. 6 (April 1946): 9.
5. Grierson, "Robert Flaherty."
6. Quoted in Rosenheimer, "They Make Documentaries," 10.
7. Rotha, *Documentary Film*, 147.
8. Ibid., 195.
9. Albert Laffay, "Les grands thèmes de l'écran," *Revue du cinéma* 2, no. 12 (April 1948): 8.

10. Marcel Proust, *Remembrance of Things Past*, vol. 1 (New York: Random House, 1932), 815.

11. Here Kracauer cites Erwin Panofsky, "Style and Medium in the Motion Pictures," in *Three Essays on Style*, ed. Irving Lavin (Cambridge, Mass.: MIT Press, 1997), 91–123.

43. LETTER TO THE EDITORS OF *FILM 56*

Originally published in German in *film 56* 2 (March 1956). It is translated here by Johannes von Moltke from Siegfried Kracauer, *Werke* 6.3: *Kleine Schriften zum Film 1932–1961* (Frankfurt a.M.: Suhrkamp, 2004).

1. See Enno Patalas, Theodor Kotulla, and Ulrich Gregor, "Panorama 1955," *film* 56 1 (January 1956): 2–9.
2. English in the original.
3. English in the original.
4. Wilfried Berghahn, "MacArthur und die Zivilisten: Nationale Leitbilder im amerikanischen Film und ihre politische Bedeutung," *film* 56 1 (January 1956): 28–34.
5. Martha Wolfenstein and Nathan Leites, *Movies: A Psychological Study* (Glencoe, Ill.: Free Press, 1950). Cf. Kracauer's review "Movie Mirror" in this volume.

AFTERWORD

1. Theodor W. Adorno, "The Curious Realist: On Siegfried Kracauer," in *Notes to Literature*, vol. 2, ed. Rolf Tiedemann, trans. Sherry Weber Nicholsen (New York: Columbia University Press, 1992). The original was a talk for the Hessische Rundfunk that was published in *Neue Deutsche Hefte*, no. 101 (September–October 1964): 58–75.
2. The first is found in David Frisby, *Fragments of Modernity: Theories of Modernity in the Work of Simmel, Kracauer, and Benjamin* (Cambridge, Mass.: MIT Press, 1986), 125; the second is my own in *Permanent Exiles: Essays on the Intellectual Migration from Germany to America* (New York: Columbia University Press, 1985), 225.
3. Adorno, "The Curious Realist," 61.
4. For a more general account of the concept, which applies it to photography, see Martin Jay, "Magical Nominalism: Photography and the Reenchantment of the World," in *The Pictorial Turn*, ed. Neal Curtis (New York: Routledge, 2010), 69–87.
5. Hans Blumenberg, *The Legitimacy of the Modern Age*, trans. Robert Wallace (Cambridge, Mass.: MIT Press, 1985); Michael Allen Gillespie, *The Theological Origins of Modernity* (Chicago: University of Chicago Press, 2008).
6. Franz Roh, *Nach-Expressionismus, magischer Realismus: Probleme der neuesten europäischen Malerei* (Leipzig: Klinkhardt & Biermann, 1925).

7. In 1918, Kracauer wrote an unpublished piece entitled "Über den Expressionismus: Wesen und Sinn einer Zeitbewegung. Abhandlung" (subsequently published in *Werke: Frühe Schriften aus den Nachlass*, vol. 9.2, ed. Inka Mülder-Bach [Frankfurt a.M.: Suhrkamp, 2004]) in which he called the movement a vitalist response with religious overtones to the technological rationality of modern life. But his interest in the movement was not sustained as he developed an interest in the sphere of the profane rather than sacred.

8. For an account of this metaphor, which he explicitly used throughout his career, see Martin Jay, "The Extraterritorial Life of Siegfried Kracauer," in *Permanent Exiles: Essays on the Intellectual Migration to Germany* (New York: Columbia University Press, 1985).

9. Edmund Husserl, *Logische Untersuchungen*, vol. 19.1 of *Husserliana* (The Hague: Martinus Nijhoff, 1975), 10.

10. Helmut Lethen, *Cool Conduct: The Culture of Distance in Weimar*, trans. Don Reneau (Berkeley: University of California Press, 2002), 88

11. For a discussion of the "primacy of the optical" in Kracauer, see Gertrud Koch, "Athenes blanker Schild: Siegfried Kracauers Reflexe und die Vernichtung," in *Die Einstellung ist die Einstellung: Visuelle Konstruktionen des Judentums* (Frankfurt a.M.: Suhrkamp, 1992), 133–37. The term was first used by Adorno in "The Curious Realist."

12. Sabine Hake, *The Cinema's Third Machine: Writing on Film in Germany, 1907–1933* (Lincoln: Nebraska University Press, 1993), 254–59.

13. Miriam Bratu Hansen, "Introduction," in Siegfried Kracauer, *Theory of Film: The Redemption of Physical Reality* (Princeton: Princeton University Press, 1997), xvii.

14. Kracauer, *History: The Last Things Before the Last* (Oxford: Oxford University Press, 1969), 52.

15. Kracauer, *The Salaried Masses: Duty and Distraction in Weimar Germany*, trans. Quinton Hoare, intro. Inka Mülder-Bach (London: Verso, 1998), 32. In *Cool Conduct*, Lethen compares this position to Brecht's critique of mimetic realism and argues that Kracauer adopted it at the end of Weimar as a critique of his earlier "pathos of perceptual acuity" (148).

16. Kracauer, *History*, 85.

17. For a discussion of the theological subtext of his desire to redeem creation, see Gertrud Koch, *Siegfried Kracauer: An Introduction*, trans. Jeremy Gaines (Princeton: Princeton University Press, 2000), 105.

18. Walter Benjamin, "The Concept of Criticism in German Romanticism" (1920), in *Selected Writings*, vol. 1: 1913–1926, ed. Marcus Bullock and Michael W. Jennings (Cambridge, Mass.: Belknap Press of Harvard University Press, 1996), 148.

19. For an insightful appreciation of the continuities and discontinuities of Kracauer's position on many issues, see Hansen's introduction to *Theory of Film*.

20. Pauline Kael, "Is There a Cure for Film Criticism? Or, Some Unhappy Thoughts on Siegfried Kracauer's *Theory of Film: The Redemption*

of Physical Reality," in *I Lost it at the Movies* (Boston: Little, Brown, 1965), 245–46. During the Weimar period, Kracauer had, in fact, occasionally gestured in the direction of defending a more substantive rationalization. Thus, for example, in "The Mass Ornament" he wrote that "the rationale of the capitalist system is not reason itself but obscured reason" (*New German Critique* 5 [Spring 1975]: 72). For a comparison of Horkheimer and Kracauer, see my essay "Mass Culture and Aesthetic Redemption: The Debate Between Max Horkheimer and Siegfried Kracauer," in Martin Jay, *Fin-de-siècle Socialism and Other Essays* (New York: Routledge, 1988).

21. Adorno, "The Curious Realist," 75. He then added with more sympathy that "to a consciousness that suspects it has been abandoned by human beings, objects are superior. In them thought makes reparations for what human beings have done to the living. The state of innocence would be the condition of needy objects, shabby, despised objects alienated from their purposes. For Kracauer they alone embody something that would be other than the universal functional complex, and his idea of philosophy would be to lure their indiscernible life from them."

22. Koch, *Kracauer*, 103. Adorno also noted a certain affinity with "Kierkegaard and existential philosophy, which he came close to in monographs like the unpublished one on the detective novel" ("The Curious Realist," 65).

23. Theodor W. Adorno, *Aesthetic Theory*, ed. Gretel Adorno and Rolf Tiedemann, trans. Robert Hullot-Kentor (Minneapolis: University of Minnesota Press, 1997), 201–7.

Index

Abney, William, 205
Abrams, Nathan, 246n59
Abstract Film Exercises (Whitney brothers), 59–60
academia: German, 181–83; humanities in, 117–23
Academy Awards, 72
acting, in film, 92, 138, 144–45, 201–4. *See also* stage acting
Adam-Salomon, Antony Samuel, 206
Adorno, Theodor W., 12, 24, 168, 234–35, 241–42n24, 247n63, 252n1; essay on Kracauer by, 227, 232, 276nn21–22; and relations with Kracauer, x, 1–2, 3, 10, 13, 29, 30–31, 127–32, 199, 227, 231–32, 234–35, 238n8, 243n34, 246n54, 266–67nn1–2
aesthetics: Adorno's concept of, 131; of New York Intellectuals, 11, 242n25
Agee, James, 4, 17, 19, 26, 247n65
Agus, Jacob B., 256
Alexander Nevsky (Eisenstein), 89, 96, 172, 173, 175, 176
Allégret, Marc, 34
Allen, Lewis, 87
Allport, Gordon W., 51
All Quiet on the Western Front (Milestone), 84, 88
All Through the Night (Sherman), 247–48n67
Almost an Angel. See *It Started with Eve*
American Jewish Committee (AJC), 12, 16–17, 238n9, 246n59, 250n88
An American Tragedy (Von Sternberg), 176

Angel (Lubitsch), 86, 91
Die Angestellten (Kracauer), 21, 23, 168, 230, 240n16, 243n34, 249n76
animated films, 133, 139–40, 234
anti-Communist films, 72, 90, 99–100
anti-Nazi films, 18, 29, 41, 42, 43–44, 45, 46, 89, 90, 106, 158–61, 248n67
anti-Semitism: East German film's portrayal of, 158–61; in Nazi documentary, 135–36, 162–65; "progressive" films' campaign against, 73, 75, 76, 106
anti-Stalinism, 11, 14
apathy, political, 29, 79–80
A propos de Nice (Vigo), 47, 48, 50, 255n1
Arendt, Hannah, 3, 9, 11, 245nn40–41, 247n61, 256, 267n3
Aristarco, Guido, 200
Aristotle, 130
Arnheim, Rudolf, 199
art, modern, 61, 115–17
Ashley, Ray, 222
[L']Atalante (Vigo), 47, 48–50, 233
At Land (Deren), 58
Atlantic Charter, 255n4
atom bomb, 45, 64, 80
Auerbach, Erich, 199
Aufbau (periodical), 11
avant-garde films, 34, 57–62

Back Street (Stahl), 36
Bahr, Ehrhard, 12
Ball, Robert H., 258n3
Baptism of Fire (Bertram), 162
Barbary Coast (Hawks), 37

277

Barjavel, René, 204
Baruch, Dorothy W., 51, 64, 257n2
Baseler National-Zeitung (newspaper), 14, 28
Bassermann, Albert, 142
Bataan (Garnett), 148
[The Battleship] Potemkin (Eisenstein), 135, 150, 155, 171, 174, 175, 203, 221
Baudelaire, Charles, 211
Baumgardt, David, 256
Bazin, André, 27
Beard, Charles and Mary, 97, 98
The Beautiful Blonde from Bashful Bend (Sturges), 115, 260
Bell, Daniel, 9, 17, 245n40
Bender, Thomas, 242n25
Benedict, Ruth, 82
Benjamin, Walter, 6, 11, 13, 21, 31, 129, 230, 231, 232, 249nn76–77, 266n2
Berghahn, Wilfried, 226
Berlin Express (Tourner), 87, 100
Bernhardt, Sarah, 180, 201
Bertram, Hans, 162
The Best Years of Our Lives (Wyler), 28, 69, 72, 73, 74, 75, 76, 86, 108, 191
The Bicycle Thief (De Sica), 203, 222
The Big Sleep (Hawks), 247n65
The Birth of a Nation (Griffith), 171
Blin, Georges, 54
Blockade (Wanger), 89–90
Blood and Sand (Mamoulian), 142
Blood of the Beasts (Franju), 164
The Blue Light (Riefenstahl), 203
Blumenberg, Hans, 227
Body and Soul (Rossen), 76
Bogart, Humphrey, 203
Boleslawski, Richard, 39
Bollingen Foundation, 199, 238, 266
Bollingen Series, 185
Bolshevism, 97, 98
Boomerang (Kazan), 72, 74, 76, 104, 108, 191
Borde, Raymond, 20
Borzage, Frank, 36, 88
bourgeois society, 130–31
The Bowery (Walsh), 35, 37
Bowles, Paul, 61, 62
boxing films, 6, 36, 76, 254n5
Bracken, Eddie, 113
Brasillach, Robert, 50
Bressart, Felix, 142
Brief Encounter (Lean), 105, 222, 223

British Agent (Curtiz), 98
Broken Blossoms (Griffith), 197
Broughton, James, 58
Brown, Clarence, 86
Brute Force (Dassin), 75
Burckhardt, Jacob, 123
Burke, Billie, 39
Burlingame, C. Charles, 62–63

Cabiria (Pastrone), 155
Calder, Alexander, 60–61, 62
camera reality, 6, 28, 35, 139, 225, 241n21
Campbell, Joseph, 186
Camus, Albert, 54
Cantril, Hadley, 258
capitalism, 15, 20, 130, 276n20
Capra, Frank, 37, 39, 44, 73–74, 86, 157
Carné, Marcel, 77, 106, 203
Carnegie Corporation, 176
Cass Timberlane (Sidney), 105
Catherine the Great, 87, 98
Catholicism, 46, 90, 151–52, 156
Cavalcade (Lloyd), 82, 86, 91–92, 94, 96, 222, 223
Cavalcanti, Alberto, 221, 222
Cavell, Stanley, 243n28
Chagall, Marc, 54
The Champ (Vidor), 254n5
chance, represented in film, 35, 44
Un chapeau de paille d'Italie (Clair), 197
Chaplin, Charlie, 76, 140, 163, 197, 213, 214, 215, 216, 261n9, 262n13, 264n23; Tyler's biography of, 168, 188–90
Chaumeton, Etienne, 20
Children of Paradise (Carné), 106
Chirico, Giorgio de, 53
Chisholm, G. B., 64
Christensen, Benjamin, 98
Christmas in July (Sturges), 110–12, 261–62nn9–10, 263–64n20
Churchill, Winston, 255n4
Cinema 16 (film society), 57, 135, 256n1, 269
Cinemages (periodical), 2
The Citadel (Vidor), 37, 86, 91
Citizen Kane (Welles), 133, 137–38, 233
City Lights (Chaplin), 216
Clair, René, 33, 39, 48, 144, 197, 253
Clarke, Shirley, 136, 165
class, social: and American films about England, 91, 92–94, 95; and American films about Russia, 98

close-ups, in film, 50, 62, 144, 145, 164, 202, 203, 204, 233
Cluny Brown (Lubitsch), 87, 96
Cohen, Elliot, 10, 17, 54, 56, 238n9, 255–56
cold war, 22, 135, 167
Cole, Margaret, 93
Collinge, Patricia, 145
Colman, Ronald, 95
color, in film, 141, 142
Columbia University, 12, 17, 25, 120, 199
comedy, film, 38–39, 76, 94, 98, 99, 140; and silent film, 213–17; and Sturges's work, 29–30, 112–15, 260n1. *See also* satire; slapstick
comedy, radio, 259n18
Commentary (periodical), 3, 10, 11, 16–17, 19, 24, 27, 29, 30, 54, 157, 238n9, 246n59, 247n62, 250n88, 251n94, 252–53n4, 254, 255–56
commercialism, social impact of, 68
commodity society, 130
Communism, 10, 14, 15, 43, 66, 80, 98, 125, 131, 238n9. *See also* Bolshevism; Stalinism
Comrade X (Vidor), 87, 98, 101
Confessions of a Nazi Spy (Litvak), 89, 90
Confidential Agent (Shulmin), 248n67
conformism, social, 135, 239n9; in Sturges's films, 29, 111, 112, 114, 115, 261nn4,9, 264n23, 266nn30–31
The Connection (Shirley Clarke), 136, 165–66, 269–70
constructivism, 228, 230, 234
consumerism, 65
Contemporary Jewish Record (periodical), 16, 17
Conway, Jack, 86
Cooper, Gary, 149
La course aux potirons (Feuillade), 214
La course des Sergents de Ville (Zecca), 214
Coward, Noel, 91, 148
Crawford, Joan, 36, 142
Crockwell, Douglass, 59
Cromwell, John, 86
Crossfire (Dmytryk), 69, 72, 73, 75, 76, 78
Crowther, Bosley, 98
Cukor, George, 42, 142
culture, concept of, 131–32
Curtiz, Michael, 87, 98

Daguerre, Louis, 209
d'Annunzio, Gabriele, 155
Dark Corner (Hathaway), 18, 19, 41–42, 44–45, 247n65
The Dark Mirror (Siodmak), 63
Darwin, Charles, 212
Dassin, Jules, 75, 108
Daves, Delmer, 100
Davis, Bette, 133, 143–45
Daybreak (Carné), 77
Dead End (Wyler), 37, 144
Dead of Night (Cavalcanti), 222, 223
Decherney, Peter, 25, 26, 242n25, 248n70
De Filippo, Eduardo, 225
Delfino, Joe, 141
Delluc, Louis, 33, 212
Deming, Barbara, 17, 29, 45, 247n65, 248n70
democracy, as filmic theme, 20, 37, 44, 46, 76, 78, 95, 96, 262n13
Denby, David, 9
Depression, Great, 43, 64, 94, 111
Deren, Maya, 57–58
De Sica, Vittorio, 106, 203, 222
Dialectic of Enlightenment (Horkheimer and Adorno), 12, 24, 250n87
dialectics, 21, 31, 127–29, 131, 232
dialogue, in film: and Clarke's work, 166, 234; and comedy, 216–17; content vs. delivery in, 143; in French films, 5, 34–35, 241n19; and literature adapted to film, 147, 148, 149; in Rossellini's work, 154; in Sturges's work, 111, 265n28
Dickens, Charles, 191
Dimendberg, Edward, 19, 20, 239n10, 247n66
Disney, Walt, 2, 5, 45, 133, 234, 265n24
Dissent (periodical), 10, 11, 238n9
Dmytryk, Edward, 69, 72, 87
documentaries and documentary style, 74, 92, 102, 103, 104, 106, 107, 108, 153–54, 155, 219, 258n2. *See also* semi-documentary, in film
Dodds, E. R., 121, 266
Dodsworth (Wyler), 38
Dostoyevsky, Fyodor, 98
Double Crime in the Maginot Line (Gandéra), 89
Dreams That Money Can Buy (Richter), 60–62
Dreyer, Carl Theodor, 191
drug abuse, film representing, 165–66

Duchamp, Marcel, 60–61, 62
Dulac, Germaine, 57
Dumbo (Disney), 2, 4, 5, 133, 139–40, 234
Durand, Jean, 214
Durbin, Deanna, 141
Duryea, Dan, 145
Duvivier, Julien, 33, 253

Edge of Darkness (Milestone), 43
editing, film, 145, 155, 174, 175, 226
educational film, 190–91
Ehrmann, Herbert, 256
Einstein, Albert, 163
Eisenstein, Sergei, 89, 102, 135, 150, 155, 166, 167–68, 171–76, 203, 220, 221, 233
Elliot, Godfrey M., 190
Embree, Edwin R., 51
Emerson, P. H., 206
Encore (French et al.), 222
The End of St. Petersburg (Pudovkin), 171
England. *See* Great Britain
English language, Kracauer's use of, x, 2, 5, 10, 133, 238n8
enlightenment, 29, 30, 55, 80
Entrée des Artistes (Allégret), 34
episode, in film narrative, 218, 221–25
Epstein, Jean, 221
Ernst, Max, 60, 61, 62
escapism, 28, 54, 81, 103, 111
The Eternal Jew (Hippler), 135–36, 162–65, 269
evil: confrontation of reason and, 80; represented in myth, 186
existentialism, 47, 70, 79, 168–69, 183–85, 232, 276n22
experimental films, 57–62
expressionism, 229, 275n7
extraterritoriality, 4, 8, 9, 20, 229, 240n16

fairy tales, 38, 63, 73–74, 139–40, 186, 261n9, 264n20
Fallada, Hans, 88
Fantasia (Disney), 140
The Farmer's Daughter (Hogan), 72, 73, 76
Farnham, Marynia F., 63
fascism: and postwar Italy, 155; and "progressive" films, 74; and terror films, 46

Fejös, Pál, 222
Ferguson, Otis, 4
Feuillade, Louis, 214
Fichte, Johann Gottlieb, 181, 228
Fiedler, Leslie, 23, 250–51n93
Fièvre (Delluc), 222, 223–24
The Fighting Lady (Steichen), 107
film 56 (periodical), 200, 226
Film Culture (periodical), ix, 2, 199
Film Form (Eisenstein), 167, 173–78
film library, MoMA, 2, 13, 18, 25, 242n25, 243n30, 248n70
film noir, 19, 20, 247n65
The Film Sense (Eisenstein), 167, 171–73
Films in Review (periodical), 2
film studies, emergence of, 25–26, 252n101
Finis Terrae (Epstein), 221
Flaherty, Robert, 145, 153, 202, 218, 219–20, 221, 222, 273n1
Flaherty Film Seminars, 273n1
Flinn, John C., 89
Fly by Night (Siodmak), 141
Fonda, Henry, 69, 76
Ford, John, 35, 86, 99, 191, 203
A Foreign Affair (Wilder), 100
Foreign Correspondent (Hitchcock), 86
Forgotten Commandments (Gasnier and Schorr), 98
For Whom the Bell Tolls (film version, dir. Sam Wood), 133–34, 146–50
found story, in film, 218–21, 222
framing device, in film, 225
France: cultural vs. psychological relations in, 70–71; existentialism in, 47, 70, 168–69, 185; films produced in, 5–6, 33–35, 39, 47–50, 89, 106, 213, 214, 241n19; Kracauer's exile in, 6, 11, 13, 22, 254n8; literature in, 54, 71; reception of American films in, 5, 27, 33–40
Franco, Francisco, 89
Franco-Prussian War, 182
Franju, Georges, 164
Frankfurter Zeitung (newspaper), 6, 12–14, 21, 23, 133, 253, 256, 269
Frankfurt School, 3, 8, 12, 16–17, 23, 29, 30, 239–40n13, 243n34, 247n61, 250n87
freedom, Sartre's concept of, 168–69, 184–85
French, Harold, 222
Freud, Sigmund, 54, 126, 184–85, 257n1

From Caligari to Hitler (Kracauer), ix, 2, 8, 14, 15, 18, 20, 21, 27, 28, 29, 168, 169–70, 200, 243n30, 256–57, 258n1
Fromm, Erich, 17
The Front Page (Milestone), 36–37
The Fugitive (Ford), 99–100

Gabin, Jean, 34
Gable, Clark, 35
Gandéra, Félix, 89
gangster films, 6, 36, 105
Garbo, Greta, 38, 98, 100
García Márquez, Gabriel, 228
Garnett, Tay, 35, 148
Garson, Greer, 95
Gaslight (Cukor), 42
Gasnier, Louis, 98
The Gay Parisian (Negulesco), 141, 268n1
Gentleman's Agreement (Kazan), 28, 72, 73, 76, 86, 106
George, Stefan, 182
Germany: academia in, 181–83; films produced in, 29, 93, 96, 135, 157–65; and Germans represented in American films, 88, 89, 90, 108; and Germans represented in French films, 89; middle class in, 158, 159, 160, 161, 182, 183; philosophy in, 168, 181–82, 184–85; reception of American films in, 84; Weimar Republic in, 45, 88, 182. *See also* Nazis and Nazi period
Gettysburg Address, 77
Gillespie, Michael, 227
Gilloch, Graehme, ix
Ginzburg, Benjamin, 256
Glazer, Nathan, 9, 16, 17, 246n59, 250n88
Glen Falls Sequence (Crockwell), 59
God, nominalist concept of, 227–28
Goebbels, Joseph, 171
Goethe, Johann Wolfgang von, 161
Golding, Edmund, 86
The Gold Rush (Chaplin), 216
Goodbye, Mr. Chips (Woos), 91
Goodenough, Erwin R., 256
Gorer, Geoffrey, 196
Grand Illusion (Renoir), 89, 223
Grant, Cary, 39
The Grapes of Wrath (Ford), 203
Grayzel, Solomon, 256

Great Britain: American affinity with, 90; and Britons represented in American films, 81–82, 86–87, 88–89, 90–97, 98, 100, 257, 259n12; and Britons represented in American radio comedies, 259n18; films produced in, 96, 105, 225; Labor government in, 88, 104; reception of American films in, 95; represented in German films, 93; scholarship in, 121; social class in, 91, 92–94, 95
The Great Dictator (Chaplin), 188, 262n13, 264n23
The Great McGinty (Sturges), 109–12, 260–61nn1–7, 264n21, 265n28
The Great Moment (Sturges), 110
Greenberg, Clement, 3, 10, 15, 16, 17, 23, 24, 242n25, 245n43, 246n59, 250n93, 251n94, 252n4, 255n7
The Green Years (Saville), 46
Grierson, John, 219
Griffith, D.W., 102, 144, 153, 171, 178, 197, 213, 220
Gunga Din (Stevens), 94

Hail the Conquering Hero (Sturges), 113–14, 260n1, 263nn18,20
Hake, Sabine, 229
Hall, Alexander, 98
Halliday, James L., 124
Halsey, Margaret, 51, 52
Hammid, Alexander, 57
Hansen, Miriam, 6, 230
happy endings, in film, 38, 44, 215, 254n3
Harper's (periodical), 2, 27
Harvard University, 122, 123
Hathaway, Henry, 19, 41, 86
Hauser, Arnold, 130, 267n3
Hawks, Howard, 37, 254n4
Hays Code, 38, 107
Hays Office, 141
Hecht, Ben, 87
Hegel, G.W.F., 12, 129, 181, 231, 232
Heidegger, Martin, 182, 184
Hemingway, Ernest, 133, 134, 146–47, 149–50
Hendrix, Wandra, 248n67
Henry V (film by Olivier), 225
Herman, Albert, 87
He Stayed for Breakfast (Hall), 98
Hi, Nellie! (LeRoy), 36

Hippler, Fritz, 135, 136, 269
history, concept of, 124, 125, 126, 131, 132
History: Last Things Before the Last (Kracauer), ix, 6, 7, 23, 230, 240n16, 241n21
Hitchcock, Alfred, 19, 41, 42, 63, 86, 87, 150, 248n67
Hitler, Adolf, 88, 89, 90, 97, 158, 159, 160, 165, 181
Hogan, James, 72
Hogben, Lancelot, 169, 192–95
Hollywood, sociological study of, 168, 176–78
Hollywood films: and anti-Communism, 72, 90, 99–100; and anti-Fascism, 84, 106; Britons represented in, 81–82, 86–87, 88–89, 90–97, 98, 100, 257, 259n12; French reception of, 35–39; and gangster films, 36, 105; German reception of, 84; Germans represented in, 88, 89, 90, 108; industrial mode of producing, 106–7, 141; and international film trend, 102–4; and Kracauer's post-emigration essays, 6–7; and market factors in representation of foreigners, 83–86; and political factors in representation of foreigners, 88–90, 96, 97–98, 99–101; and production costs, 141; profit motive in production of, 84, 85; and "progressive" films, 28–29, 72–78, 86; and psychological films, 63, 69; and realism, 6, 36–37, 105–8, 157; Russians represented in, 81–82, 87–88, 90, 97–101, 102, 104, 257; and terror films, 16, 29, 41–46
Holman, Libby, 60
Holmes, Oliver Wendell, 211–12
Hook, Sidney, 9
Horkheimer, Max, 12, 13, 17, 24, 52, 231, 238n8, 247nn62–63, 252n1
Howard, William K., 109
Howe, Irving, 3, 9, 10, 20–21, 24, 238n9, 243n30, 250–51n93, 251n95, 252n99
How Green Was My Valley (Ford), 86, 91
Hugo, Victor, 191
humanism, espoused by Kracauer, 22
humanistic approach, in social science, 124–27
humanities, as academic discipline, 30, 117–23

Humboldt, Wilhelm von, 181
The Hurricane (Ford), 35
Husserl, Edmund, 13, 184, 229
Huston, John, 107
Huston, Walter, 204
Huszar, George de, 51

I Am a Fugitive [from a Chain Gang] (LeRoy), 38
The Ideal Husband (Korda), 225
idealism, German, 168, 181–82
ideology: end of, 135; psychological aspects of, 124–25; sociopolitical aspects of, 130, 131, 182, 183
imagination, Sartre's phenomenology of, 168, 183–85, 232
impressionism, 209
individualism, 65
Institute for Social Research, 12, 13, 15, 17, 246n54
Intolerance (Griffith), 171
In Which We Serve (Coward and Lean), 148
The Iron Curtain (Wellman), 90, 99
irrationalism, 182
Italy, films produced in, 106, 156, 203; and Rossellini's work, 43, 78–79, 102, 106, 150–56, 157–58, 203
It's a Wonderful Life (Capra), 73–74
It Started with Eve (Koster), 268n2
Ivan the Terrible (Eisenstein), 175
Ivy (Wood), 87

Jacobs, Lewis, 176
Jahier, Valerio, 35
Japan, American representations of, 82
Jay, Martin, x, 8, 239n13, 240n16
Jeneman, David, 239n13
Jews and Judaism: culture of, 54–56, 180, 255–56; and emigration from Nazi Germany, 11–12, 17, 135, 159–60; and Frankfurt School, 12, 16–17; and Nazi occupation of Poland, 162, 163–64; and New York Intellectuals, 9, 16, 17, 244n37, 250n88. *See also* anti-Semitism
Jezebel (Wyler), 36
Joan of Arc (Dreyer), 191
Joan of Paris (Stevenson), 43
John Reed Club, 14, 238n9, 244n35, 246n51
Johnston, Eric, 86

Jones, Janna, 248n70
journalists, represented in film, 36–37
Journey for Margaret (Van Dyke), 86
Jung, Carl Gustav, 186

Kaegi, Werner, 123, 266
Kael, Pauline, 231
Kallen, Horace M., 51
Kang, Jaeho, ix
Kanin, Garson, 143
Kant, Immanuel, 228
Katz, Oscar, 259n18
Kazan, Elia, 28, 72, 86, 106, 108, 191
Keaton, Buster, 76, 214–15, 264n23
Kenyon Review (periodical), 167
Kesler, Henry S., 87
The Kid (Chaplin), 189, 261n9
Kierkegaard, Søren, 276n22
The Killers (Siodmak), 247n65
Knappen, Marshall Mason, 270n2
Knox, Bernard, 122
Koch, Gertrude, 232
Koestler, Arthur, 66
Korda, Alexander, 225
Koster, Henry, 268n1
Kracauer, Lili Ehrenreich, 1, 13, 237n2
Kracauer, Siegfried: death of, 238n5; and emigration from Europe, 1–2, 4, 6, 13, 40, 237–38n2, 254n9; English language used by, x, 2, 5, 10, 133, 238n8; and exile in France, 6, 11, 13, 22, 254n8; Guggenheim fellowship received by, 269; and involvement with Flaherty Film Seminars, 273n1; and journalistic activity in Europe, 3, 12–13, 21, 23, 28, 133; as New York City resident, 4, 6, 7, 9–10, 40, 241n22, 242n25; as novelist, 13; political views of, 21, 22; and post-emigration visits to Europe, 238n5; and relations with Adorno, x, 1–2, 3, 10, 13, 29, 30–31, 127–32, 199, 227, 231–32, 234–35, 238n8, 243n34, 246n54, 266–67nn1–2; and relations with Benjamin, 6, 13, 21, 31, 249n77; and relations with Frankfurt School, 3, 8, 16–17, 29; and relations with New York Intellectuals, 9–12, 15, 16, 17, 22, 23, 25, 243n29; Rockefeller grants received by, 269; as U.S. citizen, 2, 8; in Weimar period, 3, 4, 6, 14, 19, 21, 22, 23, 27, 30, 133, 229, 230, 231, 276n20

Kracauer, Siegfried, nonfiction books by. See *Die Angestellten*; *From Caligari to Hitler*; *History: Last Things Before the Last*; *The Mass Ornament*; *Orpheus in Paris: Offenbach and the Paris of His Time*; *Theory of Film*
Kristol, Irving, 9
Krupnick, Frank, 247n61
Kuleshov, Lev, 204

Labor Action (periodical), 10, 20, 243n30
Lady and Gent (Roberts), 254n5
The Lady Eve (Sturges), 94, 111–12, 262nn11–12, 265n25
Lady in the Dark (Leisen), 63
Laffay, Albert, 223
Lamartine, Alphonse de, 206
The Land (Flaherty), 145
Lang, Fritz, 18, 37, 38
Langdon, Harry, 76, 215, 264n23
Lasky, Moses, 256
The Last Chance (Lindtberg), 102, 104, 154
The Last Command (Von Sternberg), 97, 98
Latouche, John, 60
Laughton, Charles, 77, 141
Lean, David, 105, 148, 222
Lee, Rowland, 86
Léger, Fernand, 60, 61
Leisen, Mitchell, 63
Leites, Nathan, 169, 195, 226
Leonardo da Vinci, 173
LeRoy, Mervyn, 36, 38, 95
Lesser, Allen, 178–81
Lethen, Helmut, 229
Lévi-Strauss, Claude, 123, 266
Leyda, Jay, 173, 243n30
liberalism: and cultural development, 131–32; and Kracauer's film criticism, 20; represented in films, 28–29, 73–76, 78
Library of Congress Film Project, 20, 248n70
Lilge, Frederic, 181–83
Lincoln, Abraham, 77
Lindtberg, Leopold, 102, 154
Little Foxes (Wyler), 133, 143–45
The Little Fugitive (Ashley), 222
Little Man, What Now? (Borzage), 88
Litvak, Anatole, 44, 69, 76, 77, 87, 89

The Lives of a Bengal Lancer (Hathaway), 86, 91, 94
Lloyd, Frank, 82
Lloyd, Harold, 214, 215
Lombard, Carole, 39
Lonesome (Fejös), 222
The Long Night (Litvak), 69, 76–77
long shots, in film, 138, 145, 154, 233, 234
Lost Horizon (Capra), 86
Lost Weekend (Wilder), 18, 42, 44, 45
Louisiana Story (Flaherty), 222
Love of Jeanne Ney (Pabst), 223
Löwenthal, Leo, 12, 17
Lubitsch, Ernst, 39, 82, 86, 87, 98
Lumière brothers, 203

M (Lang), 18
Macdonald, Dwight, 3, 10, 15–16, 23, 24, 26, 242n25, 246nn54,56, 247n63, 250–51n93
MacDonald, Jeanette, 35
Maetzig, Kurt, 135, 157
magical nominalism, 228–29, 231
Magnani, Anna, 43
Mamoulian, Rouben, 142
Mankiewicz, Joseph L., 19, 42
Mann, Thomas, 13
Mannequin (Borzage), 36
Mannheim, Karl, 13
March, Fredric, 74, 201
Marcuse, Herbert, 17, 30
Marie Louise (Lindtberg), 102
Marriage in the Shadows (Maetzig), 135, 157–61, 269
Marshall, Herbert, 144
Marville, Charles, 208
Marx, Karl, 132, 228
Marx brothers, 217
Marxism, 11, 12, 14, 22, 131–32, 155, 174, 175, 243n30
Massachusetts Institute of Technology (MIT), 117, 120, 121
mass communication, 81, 192
mass culture, 23, 24, 53, 54, 123, 193, 250–51n93
The Mass Ornament (Kracauer), 23, 276n20
Maupassant, Guy de, 222
McCarey, Leo, 77, 86
Mead, Margaret, 196
medium shots, in film, 50, 233

The Memphis Belle (Wyler), 107–8
The Men (Zinnemann), 224
Menken, Adah Isaacs, 178–81
Menninger, William C., 63
Menschen am Sonntag (Siodmak et al.), 222, 224
Meshes of the Afternoon (Deren), 57
methodology, Kracauer's critical, 18–23, 26, 229–31
Metzner, Ernö, 224
Mexican immigrants, 51
Meyers, Sidney, 222
Mickey Mouse, 94, 107, 112, 139, 265n24
middle class, 65, 74; in Germany, 158, 159, 160, 161, 182, 183
Milestone, Lewis, 37, 43, 84, 87
Milhaud, Darius, 60
Miller, Clyde R., 51
Milton, John, 173
The Miracle of Morgan's Creek (Sturges), 113, 114, 263nn18–19, 264n21
Mission to Moscow (Curtiz), 87, 99
Miss V from Moscow (Herman), 87
Mockery (Christensen), 98
modern art, 61, 115–17
modernism, 11, 23, 24
Moeller, Robert G., 267n3
Moholy-Nagy, László, 208
Monsieur Verdoux (Chaplin), 188
montage, in film, 59, 138, 145, 155, 167, 171, 172, 230
Moss Rose (Ratoff), 87
Mother (Pudovkin), 171
Mourning Becomes Electra (Nichols), 108
Mr. Deeds Goes to Town (Capra), 37, 157
Mrs. Miniver (Wyler), 86, 91, 95, 105, 108
Muni, Paul, 204
Museum of Modern Art (MoMA), New York, 2, 8–9, 13, 15, 18, 23, 25, 242n25, 243n30, 248n70
Mussolini, Benito, 155, 203
mythology, 186–87

The Naked City (Dassin), 108
narrative, film, 169, 213, 217–25
The Nation (periodical), 2, 10, 17, 19
National Board of Review Magazine, 5

national types: and American behavior patterns, 67; objective vs. subjective construction of, 82–83; and UNESCO study, 81, 258
national types, represented in Hollywood films: and Britons, 81–82, 86–87, 88–89, 90–97, 98, 100, 257, 259n12; and Germans, 88, 89, 90; and market relations, 83–86; objective vs. subjective construction of, 85, 92, 96–97, 100, 101–2, 104, 232, 257; political factors determining, 88–90, 96, 97–98, 99–101; prevalence of, 86–90, 96; and Russians, 81–82, 87–88, 90, 97–101, 102, 104, 257
natural disasters, represented in film, 35, 254n3
Nazis and Nazi period: academia under, 181–83; and anti-Nazi films, 18, 29, 41, 42, 43–44, 45, 46, 89, 90, 106, 158–61, 248n67; films produced under, 155, 162–65, 269; and reception of American films, 84; represented in American films, 88, 89, 90, 254n3; represented in postwar German film, 158–61; represented in Russian films, 96
Negulesco, Jean, 268n1
neorealism, Italian, 4, 7, 25, 27, 28
Neue Sachlichkeit, 228, 229
Neue Zürcher Zeitung (newspaper), x
Neumann, Franz, 17
New Deal, 157
Newhall, Beaumont, 208, 273n4
New Leader (periodical), 10
New Republic (periodical), 2, 10, 167
New Wave film, 200
New York Intellectuals, 9–12, 14–17, 20, 22–25, 239–40n13, 242n25, 243n29, 244nn35,37, 247n61, 250–51n93, 250n88, 251n95
New York Times, 14, 167
Nichols, Dudley, 108
Nietzsche, Friedrich, 182
Ninotchka (Lubitsch), 82, 87, 98, 99, 100
nominalism, 227–29, 231, 234–35
nonconformism, 111, 263n20, 264n23, 266n31
None but the Lonely Heart (Odets), 28, 73
North Sea (Cavalcanti-Watt), 221, 222
The North Star (Milestone), 87, 99
Nothing Sacred (Wellman), 39

objectivity: and Hegelian dialectics, 129; and perception of national types, 82–83, 85, 92, 96, 104, 232; and photography, 205; and social science, 124, 125, 126
Odets, Clifford, 28, 73
Offenbach, Jacques, 13, 253
Of Human Bondage (Cromwell), 86, 91
Okri, Ben, 228
Olivier, Laurence, 225
Onésime Horloger (Durand), 214
One Way Passage (Garnett), 35
ontology, 127–29, 130, 132, 232, 266n1
Open City (Rossellini), 43, 47, 102, 106, 150, 224
Ophuls, Max, 222
optimism, 80, 161, 178
Orpheus in Paris: Offenbach and the Paris of His Time (Kracauer), 13, 240n16, 243n32, 245n41, 253
Otsep, Fyodor, 87
Our Daily Bread (Vidor), 36
Oxford University, 121

Pabst, G. W., 63, 223
Paisan (Rossellini), x, 78–79, 102, 104, 106, 134–35, 157–58, 161, 204, 222, 224, 233, 251n96, 267n1
The Palm Beach Story (Sturges), 113, 264n22
The Paradine Case (Hitchcock), 87
Une Partie de Campagne (Renoir), 106
Partisan Review (periodical), 2, 10, 11, 14–17, 45, 238n9, 244n35, 245n40, 246nn51,54, 251nn94,97
Patalas, Enno, 200
Paxinou, Katina, 149
People in the City (Sucksdorff), 219
Peterson, Sidney, 58
phenomenology, Sartre's, 183–85
Phillips, William, 10, 11, 14, 238n9, 244n36
philosophy, German, 168, 181–82, 184–85; and Kracauer's talk with Adorno, x, 31, 127–32, 231–32. *See also* existentialism; ontology; phenomenology
photography, 169, 202, 204–13
Pichel, Irving, 86
pictorial medium, 169, 192–94
The Pied Piper (Pichel), 86, 91, 95

The Pilgrim (Chaplin), 189
Le Plaisir (Ophuls), 222
Plane Crazy (Disney), 139
Podhoretz, Norman, 251n94
Polan, Dana, 25
Poland, Jews in, 162, 163–64
political relations: and Eisenstein's accommodation to Stalinism, 173–78; and filmic representation of foreigners, 88–90, 96, 97–98, 99–101; Kracauer's views on, 21, 22; and New York Intellectuals, 11–12, 14, 15, 16, 20, 22, 23, 244nn35,37, 250–51n93; and reception of Kracauer's film criticism, 20–22
political relations, represented in film: and Eisenstein's work, 155; and French reception of American films, 37; and postwar German film, 159–61; and "progressive" films, 72–81, 86; and Rossellini's work, 155; and terror films, 20, 46–47
Politics (periodical), 10, 11, 15, 17
Ponge, Francis, 71
Port of Shadows (Carné), 203
portraits, photographic, 206
positivism, 187, 205, 230
Potamkin, Harry Alan, 243n30
Potemkin. See *[The Battleship] Potemkin*
The Potted Psalm (Peterson and Broughton), 58–59
The Power and the Glory (Howard), 109, 110, 112
Pozner, Vladimir, 47–48
Prelude to War (Capra and Litvak), 44
Prévert, Jacques, 34
Princeton University, 118, 122
"progressive" films, 28–29, 72–81, 86
propaganda, 41, 78, 92; Kracauer's writings on, ix, 5, 11, 13, 15, 26, 29, 135–36, 246nn54–56; Nazi, 135–36, 162–65, 171, 269
Proust, Marcel, 54, 206–8, 210–11, 224
psychiatry, vogue of, 62–63, 64, 66, 71, 256
psychoanalysis: and film criticism, 18–19, 169–70, 195–96; and incidence of neuroses, 63–64, 257n1; represented in film, 46, 63; vogue of, 18, 62, 71, 125

psychological relations: and behavior patterns, 64, 66–68, 70, 71; and business practices, 68; and denaturalized reason, 53–54; and evasive attitude, 64–66; and Hollywood filmmakers, 177–78; and Howe's film criticism, 252n99; and ideology, 124–25; and Kracauer's critical methodology, 18–20, 169; and literature, 66, 71; and mythology, 186–87; popular interest in, 62–63, 71–72; and psychological films, 63; and race, 51–54, 64; and self-expression, 68–69; sociopolitical aspects of, 64–71; and terror films, 18–19, 42–44, 45–46, 157; and war veterans portrayed in films, 69–70
Public Opinion Quarterly, 27, 30
Pudovkin, V.I., 102, 171, 178, 191, 204, 233
The Pumpkin Race (Feuillade), 214
Pushkin, Aleksandr, 173

qualitative vs. quantitative method, 30, 124–27
The Quiet One (Meyers), 222

race relations, 51–54, 64, 77, 79–80
radio: and comedy programs, 259n18; and foreign relations, 83; social impact of, 67
Raft, George, 36, 254n4
Rahv, Philip, 9, 10, 11, 14, 17, 238n9, 251n97
Random Harvest (LeRoy), 95
rationality. See reason
Ratoff, Gregory, 87
Ray, Man, 60
realism: and animated film, 140, 234; in European films, 43, 102, 105–8; as focus of Kracauer's film criticism, 28, 133, 134, 227, 233; in Hollywood films, 36–37, 105–8, 157; and photography, 208; and postwar semi-documentary films, 102–3, 106; and Rossellini's work, 43, 106, 134, 153. See also neorealism, Italian
reason: and confrontation with evil, 80; denaturalized, 52–54, 231; and German culture, 182; and Jewish culture, 55–56; and nominalist theology, 228; and "progressive" films, 29, 77, 78
Rebecca (Hitchcock), 86, 91

Redfield, Robert, 51
Réflexion faite (Clair), 197
Réjane, Gabrielle, 201
Remarque, Erich Maria, 84, 88
Renoir, Jean, 33, 43, 89, 106, 141, 223, 253
reporters, represented in film, 36–37
Richter, Hans, 60–62
Riefenstahl, Leni, 162, 203
Rilke, Rainer Maria, 122
Ritual in Transfigured Time (Deren), 58
The River (Renoir), 223
The Road Back (Whale), 88
Roberts, Stephen, 254n5
Robison, John, 209
Rockefeller Foundation, 25, 123, 176
Rogers, Ginger, 143
Roman Empire, 65–66
Romanticism, German, 231
Roosevelt, Franklin D., 98, 255n4
Rosenberg, Harold, 242n25
Rossellini, Roberto, x, 43, 78–79, 102, 106, 134–35, 150–56, 157, 203, 220, 222, 224, 233
Rossen, Robert, 76
Rosten, Leo C., 23, 168, 176–78, 248n67
Roth, Cecil, 256
Roth, Joseph, 13
Rotha, Paul, 2, 218, 219, 220, 221
A Royal Scandal (Lubitsch), 87
Ruggles of Red Gap (McCarey), 77, 86, 91, 93–94
Rules of the Game (Renoir), 223
Russia: Bolshevism in, 97, 98; films produced in, 24, 89, 96, 100, 102, 153, 155, 171–78, 203, 221, 233; revolution in, 51, 97, 174, 221; and Russians represented in American films, 81–82, 87–88, 90, 97–101, 102, 104, 257; and Russians represented in German films, 96; U.S. relations with, 64, 65, 80, 97, 98. *See also* Soviet Union
Russian Ballet of Monte Carlo, 141

Sabotage (Hitchcock), 248n67
sadism, represented in film, 18, 29, 41–42, 44, 45, 46, 157, 252n99
The Salaried Masses (Kracauer). See *Die Angestellten* (Kracauer)
Sand, George, 180
San Francisco (Van Dyke), 35, 254n3
San Pietro (Huston), 107
Santell, Alfred, 38

Sartre, Jean-Paul, 168–69, 183–85, 232
satire, 30, 39, 60, 61; and films about national types, 87, 94, 98, 101; and Lubitsch's work, 87; and Sturges's work, 109, 110, 111, 114, 115, 260n1, 263n20, 266n29; and Vigo's work, 48, 50
Saville, Victor, 46
Scarface (Hawks), 254n4
Schapiro, Meyer, 3, 9, 10, 199, 238n8, 243n32, 246n54
Scheler, Max, 182, 184
Schelling, F. W. J. von, 181
Schorr, William, 98
Schüfftan, Eugen, 237n2, 245n49
Schulberg, Budd, 177
science: critique of, 30, 182, 187; and German culture, 182; and photography, 205, 210, 212; qualitative vs. quantitative method in, 124–27; represented in film, 59–60
The Search (Zinnemann), 102, 104, 108, 224
The Seashell and the Clergyman (Dulac), 57
Secrets of a Soul (Pabst), 63
Seghers, Anna, 13
semi-documentary, in film, 220–21, 222, 224, 225
Sennett, Mack, 35, 114, 213, 216, 265n24
sexual relations: and psychoanalytic method, 126; represented in film, 38, 60–62
Shadow of a Doubt (Hitchcock), 18, 41, 42
Shakespeare, William, 82, 191, 225, 259n3
Shefner, Evelyn, 17, 246n59
Shelley, Percy Bysshe, 173
Sherman, Vincent, 247–48n67
Shock (Werker), 19, 42–43, 63
Shoe-Shine (De Sica), 106
Shulmin, Hermin, 248n67
Side Street Story (De Filippo), 225
Sidney, George, 105
silent film, 23, 34, 63, 110, 138, 171, 188, 199, 200, 213–17, 221, 222, 224, 262n13
Simmel, Georg, 1
Simon, Michel, 49
Siodmak, Curt, 222
Siodmak, Robert, 42, 63, 141
The Skeleton Dance (Disney), 139

288 / Index

slapstick, 6, 30, 76, 213, 215, 264n23; and Sturges's work, 110, 112, 113, 114–15, 264n23, 265nn24,28
"sleeper" films, 103, 261n4
slight narrative, Flaherty's concept of, 218, 219–20, 221
snob, British, represented in film, 92–94, 95, 96
Snow, C. P., 119
social relations: and ideology, 130, 131, 182, 183; and Kracauer's critical methodology, 20–23; and modern art, 115–17
social relations, represented in film: and American films about England, 91, 92–94, 95; and British reception of American films, 95; and French reception of American films, 37, 39
Social Research (periodical), 15, 17
social science: debate between Adorno and Kracauer on, 130–32; humanistic approach in, 124–27; and study of Hollywood, 168, 176–78
So Evil My Love (Allen), 87
Somewhere in the Night (Mankiewicz), 19, 42
Song of Russia (Ratoff), 87
Sontag, Susan, 23
sound effects, in film, 141
Sous les toits de Paris (Clair), 197
Soviet Union: films produced in, 24, 89, 96, 100, 102, 153, 155, 171–78, 203, 221, 233; and ideological shallowness, 131; represented in American films, 82, 87, 90, 96–101
So Well Remembered (Dmytryk), 87
Spain: civil war in, 89, 146, 248n67; represented in American film, 89, 142, 146–50
specialization, academic, 20, 118–19, 122, 123, 182
The Specter of the Rose (Hecht), 87
Spellbound (Hitchcock), 42, 63
Spengler, Oswald, 182
The Spiral Staircase (Siodmak), 42, 44
stage acting, 201, 203
Stagecoach (Ford), 191
Stahl, John, 36
Stalin, Josef, 87, 89, 99, 246n51
Stalinism, 20, 23, 167, 173, 174, 175, 176
stardom, in film, 203

Steichen, Edward, 107
Steinmeyer, Georg, 245n41
Stella Dallas (Vidor), 6, 36
stereographs, 204–5, 210
Stern, Seymour, 243n30
Stevenson, Robert, 43
Stewart, James, 39, 73
Stoicism, 65–66
story, in film, 169, 213, 217–25
The Story of GI Joe (Wellman), 73
Stössel, Ludwig, 247n67
The Stranger (Welles), 18, 41
Stroheim, Erich von, 144
A Study in Choreography for the Camera (Deren), 58
Sturges, Preston, 23, 27, 29–30, 85, 94, 107, 108, 109–15, 260–66
subjectivity: and perception of national types, 82–83, 85, 92, 100, 101–2, 232; and social science, 125, 126
Sucksdorff, Arne, 219
Sullivan's Travels (Sturges), 29, 85, 107, 109, 112–13, 115, 262–63nn14–17, 263–64n20, 265nn24–25,27–28
The Sun Never Sets (Lee), 86
surrealism, 58, 60–62
Suspicion (Hitchcock), 19, 42
Swamp Water (Renoir), 141
Swinburne, Algernon Charles, 180
Switzerland, films produced in, 102

Talbot, Fox, 205, 209, 212
Tanguy, Yves, 59
Taylor, Sam, 98
Teachout, Terry, 251n94
Technicolor, 141
technique, film: and Eisenstein's work, 155, 167, 171–72, 174, 175; and film actors, 203–4; and Nazi propaganda, 162, 164; and Rossellini's work, 153, 155; and silent film comedy, 214; and Vigo's work, 50; and Welles's work, 138; and Wyler's work, 144
The Tempest (Taylor), 98
terror films: compared to anti-Nazi films, 18, 29, 41, 42, 43–44, 45, 46; everyday life represented in, 41; natural disasters represented in, 254n3; political aspects of, 20, 46–47; psychological aspects of, 18–19, 42–44, 45–46, 157; sadism represented in, 18, 41–42, 44, 45, 46, 157; settings of, 41, 44–45

Tester, Desmond, 248n67
Thackeray, William Makepeace, 191
theater, acting in, 201, 203
Theodora Goes Wild (Boleslawski), 39
Theory of Film (Kracauer), 2, 5–6, 7, 21–22, 23, 25, 27–28, 30, 134, 168, 169, 230, 231, 241nn21–22, 253n3; syllabus of, 199, ix, 217–25
These Three (Wyler), 38, 144
This Land Is Mine (Renoir), 43
Thompson, Dorothy, 43, 254n1
The Three Caballeros (Disney), 45
Three Comrades (Borzage), 88
Three Russian Girls (Kesler and Otsep), 87
Toland, Gregg, 144
Tolstoy, Leo, 82, 98
Tolstoy, Lev, 191
Tom, Dick, and Harry (Kanin), 143
totalitarianism, 11, 14, 15, 20, 44, 46, 65, 84, 99, 173, 175, 254n2
To the Victor (Daves), 100
Tourner, Jacques, 87
Tovarich (Litvak), 87, 98
Traverso, Enzo, 8, 240n16, 243n29
Trilling, Lionel, 3, 9, 17
Triumph of the Will (Riefenstahl), 162
Truffaut, François, 241n19
Twain, Mark, 180
Twentieth-Century Fox, 141
Tyler, Parker, 168, 188–90

Überfall (Metzner), 224
unconscious: and avant-garde film, 61; Freud's concept of, 185; and myth, 186
UNESCO, 81, 104, 199, 258
Unfaithfully Yours (Sturges), 115, 260
utopia, concept of, 127, 128, 129, 133

Valentino, Rudolph, 142
Van Dyke, W. S., 35, 86
Variety (periodical), 101
vaudeville, 39
Veidt, Conrad, 142
veterans. *See* war veterans
Vidor, King, 36, 37, 86, 87, 254n5
Vigo, Jean, 23, 27, 28, 33, 47–50, 233, 253, 255n1
Vogel, Amos, 57, 135, 256n1, 269
Von Sternberg, Josef, 97, 176

Wagner, Richard, 167, 173
Walsh, Raoul, 35
Wanger, Walter, 89
war, represented in film, 148, 150–52, 224
Warburg, Aby, 122
Warner, Jack L., 85–86
Warner Brothers, 141
Warshow, Robert, 4, 23, 24–25, 26, 199, 243nn28,30, 251nn96–97, 267n1
war veterans, portrayed in films, 69–70, 72–73, 76, 77, 78, 108
Watt, Harry, 221
We Are Not Alone (Golding), 86
Weber, Max, 182
Weimar Republic, 15, 18, 45, 88, 182, 228; Kracauer's activity in, 3, 4, 6, 14, 19, 21, 22, 23, 27, 30, 133, 229, 230, 231, 276n20
Welles, Orson, 18, 41, 133, 137–38, 233
Wellman, William, 39, 73, 90
Werker, Alfred L., 19, 43, 63
Westerns, film genre of, 6, 35, 37
Weston, Edward, 208, 209
Whale, James, 88
What Makes Sammy Run? (Schulberg), 177
Wheatland, Thomas, 12, 239–40n13
White, Josh, 60
The White Cliffs of Dover (Brown), 86, 91, 95
Whitney, John and James, 59
Wilder, Billy, 42, 100
Wilford, Hugh, 243–44n35
William of Ockham, 227
Winsten, Archer, 100
Winterset (Santell), 38
Wolfenstein, Martha, 169, 195, 226
A Woman of Paris (Chaplin), 188
A Woman's Face (Cukor), 142
Wood, Sam, 87, 91, 134, 149
World War I, 79, 89, 212, 213
World War II, 14–15, 17, 84; and American films about England, 94–95; and American films about Russia, 98–99; and Rossellini's *Paisan*, 150–52
Wright, Teresa, 145
Wyler, William, 28, 36, 37, 38, 69, 72, 73, 74, 86, 107–8, 133, 143–45, 191

A Yank at Oxford (Conway), 86, 91
You and Me (Lang), 37
You Can't Take It with You (Capra), 37
You Only Live Once (Lang), 38

Zecca, Ferdinand, 214
Zéro de conduite (Vigo), 47, 48, 49, 50
Zimmer, Heinrich, 185–87
Zinnemann, Fred, 102, 108, 224
Zionism, 250n88
Zola, Émile, 209

Text: 10/13 Aldus
Display: Aldus
Compositor: Toppan Best-set Premedia Limited
Indexer: Andrew Joron

www.ingramcontent.com/pod-product-compliance
Lightning Source LLC
Chambersburg PA
CBHW030525230426
43665CB00010B/774